DESIGN
DIMENSIONS

CYNTHIA MARIS DANTZIC

DESIGN DIMENSIONS

AN INTRODUCTION TO THE VISUAL SURFACE

PRENTICE-HALL
Englewood Cliffs, New Jersey

North and South American Edition first
published in 1990 by
Prentice-Hall, Inc,
Englewood Cliffs,
NJ 07632

Copyright © 1990 Prentice-Hall, Inc.

ISBN 0-13-199985-0

This book was designed and produced
by John Calmann & King Ltd, London

Designer: Richard Foenander
Typeset by Keyspools Ltd
Printed in Hong Kong

Front cover detail and back cover:
Piet Mondrian, *Victory Boogie Woogie*,
1943–44. Oil on canvas, $49\frac{5}{8} \times 49\frac{5}{8}$ ins
(126×126 cm). Collection: Mr. and
Mrs. S. I. Newhouse Jr.

Frontispiece:
Ludwig Wilding, *Kinetic Structure*,
1963. Painted wood and glass,
$34\frac{1}{4} \times 26\frac{1}{4}$ ins (87×67 cm). Photograph by Ingeborg Wilding-König.
Courtesy; Archiv Wilding.

Acknowledgements

My thanks go to everyone whose encouragement and assistance has helped this book
spring to life and take shape.

Through extraordinary good fortune I
have often found myself in the company of
classmates, teachers, fellow artists, colleagues,
students, friends and family, who are distinguished by exceptional enthusiasm, ability,
loyalty and patience, and who are committed
to excellence, passionate in their convictions
and warm-hearted in their generosity. Association with these people has enabled me to
supplement my own resources with theirs to
produce a book of far greater richness than I
would have been able to achieve alone.

I would like to thank, in particular: Patricia
Tobin, for arranging boxes of 3×5 cards into
the nucleus of a 15-chapter book; Frances
Shaw, for translating my creative typing into
carefully processed words; and, finally, Robert
Lucas, for giving my photographic needs such
personal care at his Gene Barry lab.

Among the former classmates, teachers
and their families, fellow artists, colleagues,
students and friends whose participation has
been invaluable, I would like to thank the
following for the sharing of ideas, books, art
works, time and energies: Louise Odes Neaderland, Naomi Bossom, Marcia King Speier and
Robert Speier, Robert Slutzky, Irwin Rubin,
Charles Francis Tauss, Lois Swirnoff, Richard
Anuszkiewicz, Lucian Krukowski, Lita de
Rivera, Lois Dinnerstein, Harvey Dinnerstein,
Martin Ries, Virginia Hoyt Cantarella, Joseph-
ine Burns and Jerry Burns, Evelyn Yee, Vivian
Tsao, Hélène Manzo and Nancy Gleason.

My former students at The Baldwin School,
The Bentley School, The Berkeley Institute,
The Montessori School of Brooklyn, South
Shore High School and Long Island University
have also earned a special word of thanks. So
too have my current students at both the
Brooklyn and C. W. Post Campuses of Long
Island University, particularly those who took
part in the amazing Spring 1989 Color Workshop, studies from which appear in several
chapters. I would also like to thank the many
students of Robert Slutzky, Irwin Rubin, Lois
Swirnoff and John Hejduk, whose works were
considered and in some cases selected for
inclusion.

My thanks too to Research Time Awards
Committee of Long Island University for grant-
ing me precious hours of time released from my
teaching duties, for several years, in order to
complete this book. I thank also the Josef
Albers Foundation, its director Nicholas Fox
Weber, and Anni Albers, for their generous
assistance and the BACA for a grant to further
the progress of "Flip", the animated short
being put on film by Sheila Schwid Milder,
using flip pads drawn by me and my students.

My special thanks go to the patient and
cooperative members of the photographic staff
and the rights and reproductions staff of
museums, galleries and collections throughout the United States and abroad, in particular,
Mac Chambers, of the Grace Borgenicht
Gallery.

At Prentice-Hall, I would like to thank:
Bruce Collins, who first suggested the idea for
this volume; my editor, Bud Therien, who
provided support, encouragement and freedom in just the right proportion; his assistants,
Jean Wachter, who facilitated the project in its
early days, and Barbara Barysh, who has
carried it through to this day. In London, I
would like to thank Carolyn Yates, a rare mix
of energy, professionalism and charm at John
Calmann & King Ltd, and Rosemary Bradley
and Melanie White who inherited this complex
and detailed project in its later stages.

I particularly wish to thank the following
artists whose works I had chosen for inclusion,
but which had to be omitted due to lack of
space: Anita Rehbock, George Forss, Arthur
Coppedge, Stan Hadden, Gabriele Roos, Gail E.
Haley, Marion Greenstone, Monika Bittman,
Lucy Sikes, Sewell Sillman, and Joan and Alan
Root, photographers for Survival Anglia.

My thanks and my love go to my mother,
Sylvia Gross, for correcting my English all
those years; Jerry, for every kind of support,
confidence and love, and particularly for your
distinguished, fat-free cuisine which has kept
me energized and trim; and Grayson, for the
privilege of using the title, "mother", and for
suggesting a splendid title for this book: "2-D
or not 2-D …"

Professor of Art, Long Island University,
Brooklyn, New York, May, 1989

The author and Publishers would like to thank
the following reviewers for their valuable
advice on this book: Majorie Bevlin, a founding
chairman of Fine Arts at Otero Community
College, Colorado; Jim Howze, Department of
Art, Texas Technical University; Jerry A. Kal-
back, Associate Professor, School of Art, Kent
State University; Charles E. Borman, Depart-
ment of Art, California State University;
Pamela Lowrie, Department of Art, College of
Du Page; Robert Morton, Department of Art,
Plymouth State College; Phillip Vanderweg,
Art Department, Western Michigan Univer-
sity; Cynthia Kukla, Department of Art, North-
ern Kentucky University; Patrick James Shuck,
Art Department, St Louis Community College
at Meramec; Don Cowan, Department of Art,
El Paso Community College; Sylvia R. Green-
field, School of Art and Design, Southern
Illinois University.

Contents

(Bold numbers enclosed in square brackets, appearing within the text, refer to Exercise numbers.)

INTRODUCTION

Without human beings there is design in the world, but not art. Design, or arrangement, ordered relationship of parts, is seen on a human scale in the simplest seashell, butterfly or spider's web; on a microscopic scale in snow-crystals (**Fig. 0.1**), microorganisms, atomic particles (**Fig. 0.2**), and on a celestial scale in planetary paths and galactic events (**Fig. 0.3**). But unless people value, understand and enjoy the universal structure surrounding us, these things cannot be said to have beauty, harmony or meaning, qualities we ascribe to objects, often in very different ways. Objects created or selected for their aesthetic qualities—harmonious relationships, beauty, expressive content, or simply their undeniable power to attract the attention—can be called art objects, although not everyone will agree to the lofty designation "art" for any particular example.

Among the activities yielding experiences or products called "art" are human movement, as DANCE; creation or arrangement of sounds, as MUSIC; discursive written description, dialogue and commentary, as PROSE; metric or expressive structuring of words to distill essential meaning, as POETRY; presentation of realistic or symbolic human interaction, as DRAMA; designing of shelters and structures for human use, as ARCHITECTURE; arranging or constructing three-dimensional material in space, as SCULPTURE; and finally the concern of this book: two-dimensional arrangement, selection or creation of markings and materials on a surface within a specified or suggested boundary, including painting, drawing, design and graphics, often called simply, ART.

Several of these arts—poetry, prose, drama—use words, written or spoken. Visual arts may also include their depiction, incorporating verbal meanings within a work, but such use of language is at best optional (**Fig. 0.4**). By definition visual arts must be seen; they cannot be told in words (**Fig. 1.4**). If Picasso had wanted to *tell* us about Guernica (p. 205), he might have written a play or epic poem. He preferred to *show* us choosing the "universal language," the unspoken language of painting. Renoir acknowledged the non-verbal, uniquely personal aspects of art when he included among his criteria, "it must be indescribable . . . and inimitable."

If meanings conveyed by art and design cannot be told in words, certainly no book can provide the direct experience of seeing and studying actual works. Even so basic a quality as "red" can only be seen or remembered to be understood. Visualize in your mind's eye the reddest object you know, something really *red*: a tomato, fire engine, lipstick, apple peel, drop of blood, American flag stripe or a tube of Cadmium Red Medium may come to mind. All these reds, stored in memory, must have been seen directly at some time. Is it possible to communicate a specific red to anyone else? No matter how precisely you choose words, the redness cannot be told; there is no way to verify what the listener sees in his or her own mind. If it is true that a poem paints a picture in the mind, then each listener receives a different work of art.

Asked to provide a verbal equivalent for red to a person who has never seen it, someone born without sight, we might say red is a warm color. The listener might reply, "Ah, red is like flame or fire." But this translation to a tactile, non-verbal sensation does not enable us to know what the listener imagines aside from temperature.

On the other hand, a person who has lost the power of sight still retains the memory of visual experience, often dreaming in color. Such an artist, like the American painter Delmonico, may enjoy creating two-dimensional works to be seen by others (**Fig. 0.5**). Only those who have never seen are truly unable to visualize and are totally without the concept as well as the power of sight. In experiencing objects in the round (sculpture, utensils or textured surfaces such as burlap and sandpaper) the ability to see is less critical. Many born-blind artists create fully realized three-dimensional works, through touch-responsive, space-sensory, non-visual means.

The concern of this book is two-dimensional design, which exists or looks as though

Fig. 0.1 (*top left*) Snow Crystals. Courtesy: Department of Library Services, American Museum of Natural History.

Fig. 0.2 (*top right*) Atomic diffraction pattern at tip of platinum needle.

Fig. 0.3 A typical galaxy. Courtesy: Department of Library Services, American Museum of Natural History.

it exists on a relatively flat surface and must be seen to be experienced. Works physically uneven in surface, textured, or actually solid but conceived as two-dimensional are discussed. The criterion is always the *visual* identity, not the *physical* reality of a work. This volume introduces many basic, traditional elements of the two-dimensional world, with a wide range of their uses, relationships and applications to provide you with a rich background. This can serve as a resource in the creation of your own work and in the appreciation or understanding of the works of others.

New ways of looking at familiar ideas are introduced; novel, provocative suggestions offered. With the aid of memory, curiosity and a willingness to test and evaluate even those statements presented as fact, you must make them live or be of value in unique, personal ways.

Illustrations include pictorial representation of works by well-known and lesser-known artists, and by students. Keep in mind that a greatly reduced, untextured, ink and screen-printed photograph of an actual work, which may possess surface feel, a variety of materials, varying reflectivity, unreproducible colors, an integral relationship to its environment, deep and unprintable blacks and tones of gray and shimmering whites, cannot be presented on the printed page with a reliable degree of approximation to the original. This is true even when slides are used to show paintings, drawings, prints, collages or photographs. There is no substitute for seeing original work, preferably in the setting selected by the artist, but a book or slide can point the way and serve as a guide to later gallery or museum visits.

To assist you in duplicating the precise colors used in the charts and basic color studies in this book, a listing of specific paints is given. You may re-create the often subtle visual effects of these studies exactly, as only unmixed color direct from the tube or jar has been used (p. 184).

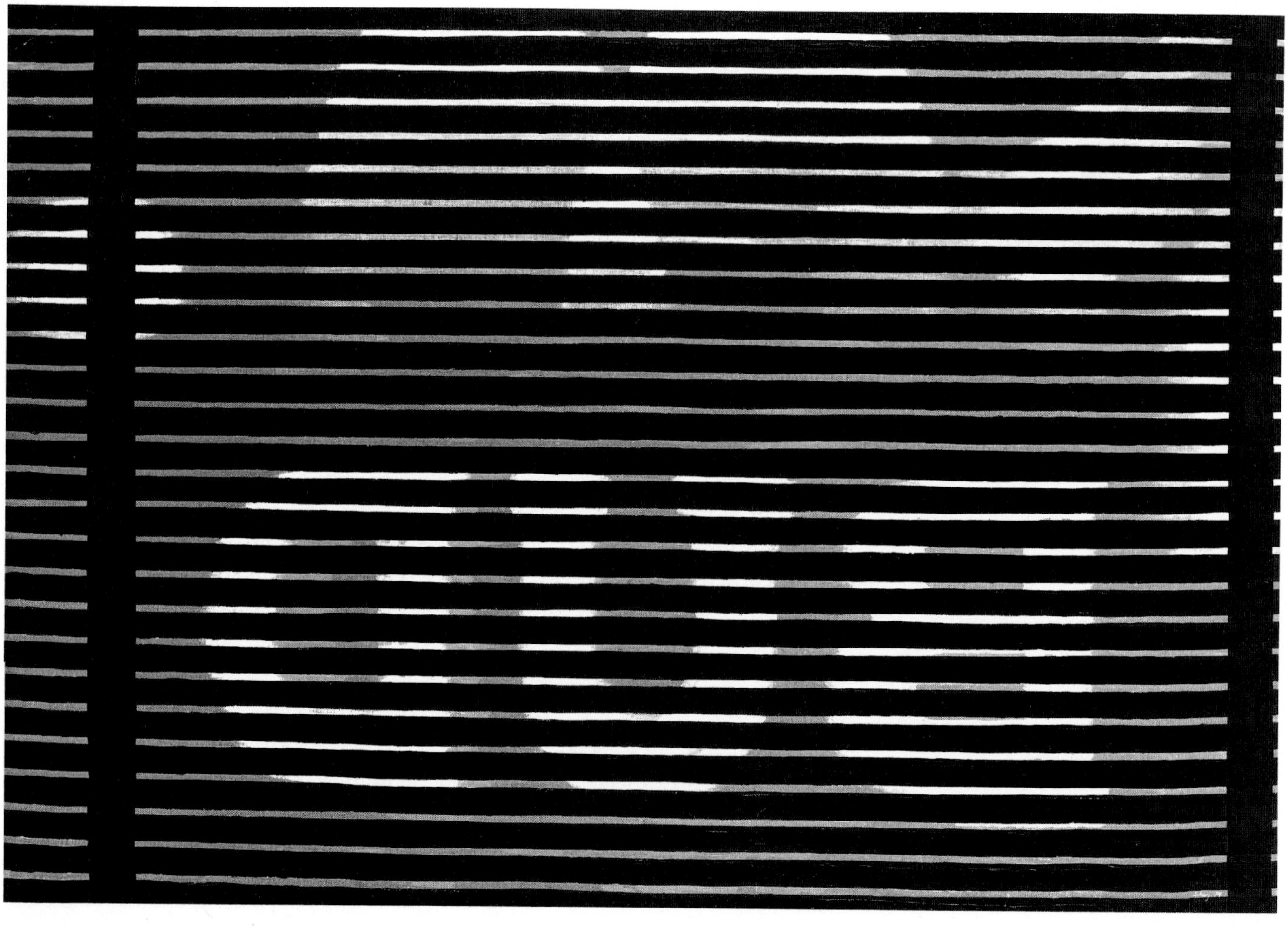

Fig. 0.4 Shunji Sakuyama. *Night 1984.* Oil on canvas, 50 × 34 ins (127 × 86 cm). Courtesy of the artist.

Fig. 0.5 **C. Crist Delmonico**, Morristown, NJ, *Two Sisters*, © 1981 C.C.D.IV. Mixed media, pencil and pastel, 21 × 29 ins (53 × 73.5 cm).

The prehistory and history of art and design includes objects and markings created and selected by human beings as early as 30,000 BC on the walls of caves in France and Spain and as recently as today in studios and classrooms around the world. It includes works made for many reasons and uses, some of whose creators would not have thought themselves artists, nor would they always have known what it is we today include in the broad, changing definition of art. Some works we call art originally served clearly utilitarian functions, some were made to satisfy ceremonial, spiritual or other personal requirements, and some were completed to the specifications of patrons or clients. Of the countless objects made or selected for such a variety of purposes, completely different examples might have been shown in this book. Certain works, because of their special history or significance, their generally agreed-upon power, emotive appeal, purity of means or other unique quality, will appear in this and almost every study of design.

A special feature of the treatment in this book is the large number of examples you will not have seen elsewhere, including kinds of objects not generally called art objects, works often considered in different classifications than those selected here and works by non-professionals and students. The intention is to provide as broad a base as possible to be used in asking questions, applying criteria, creating your own solutions to problems stated or in redefining the questions themselves. Instead of being told that a modular, hand-stitched, pieced quilt (**Fig. 0.6**) is a work of art, a fabric painting, a color study or a "mere" work of craft (and therefore a "lesser" achievement), you will find such categorizations, if needed at all, are left to each reader. What you believe and

Fig. 0.6 Thousand Triangles, stitched cotton quilt, c. 1870. Unknown Pennsylvanian artist, $80\frac{1}{2} \times 78$ ins (205×198 cm). Collection of Jonathan Holstein and Gail van der Hoof.

come to value are choices only you can make, regardless of the fervor of any author or teacher.

From an involvement with several thousand students for the past thirty years, I have learned that no two individuals respond alike to any lesson or introduction of technique. Respect for the uniqueness of each individual demands that the special place each reader occupies in this world be acknowledged and that each be considered an active participant in the fulfillment of the goals addressed here. Recommendations for better illustration of a point or extension of the discussion of any topic are welcome. Where possible, reader participation will affect changes in future editions.

Perhaps you are convinced that, since art and design are non-verbal, no book can hope to provide a substitute for hands-on studio experience, and, since the history of art and design is so rich with works of high quality, most illustrations used here can be replaced with others. Also, since memory and imagination are the sources of most art and design, any book must be limited in aiding the student in creating his or her own work. What is left of real value, then, to warrant the birth of yet another book on the subject?

Much. We have said no two people extrapolate from even their shared experiences quite the same meanings or see from the identical viewing point. We need and find ever fresh ways of looking at old questions, posing new ones, re-seeing and re-viewing the visual world from new vantage points. This was made clear to me in a dramatic way at an exhibition of Matisse's paper cut-outs at the Museum of Modern Art a number of years ago. A student asked what Matisse meant by saying only with scissors could he draw a line (**Fig. 0.7**). Dissatisfied with my own explanation (I had no idea what he meant), I began to investigate possible meanings of his profound remark and to analyze lines made by many people, not all calling themselves artists or designers. The realization that several unlike, even unrelated, visual products have all been classified in one seemingly irreducible term prompted me to search for the clearest possible example of each of the visual experiences called a line. Now, students and other readers of this volume will be able to immerse themselves in so vast an array of what-can-be-meant-by-a-line that their own works and studies cannot fail to become enriched. Whether you choose to create lines with scissors, an X-Acto knife, etching needle, pen, pencil, airbrush or computer, or in some other way, is not as important as the idea that you will be selecting through knowledge; you will be making use of the experience of others but in your own way.

When looking at the works of others, whether book illustrations, magazines, slides or actual objects in studios, galleries or museums, even in that constantly changing

Fig. 0.7 Henri Matisse, *The Lagoon*, 1947. Painted and cut paper, $16\frac{1}{8} \times 24\frac{1}{8}$ ins (41×61 cm). Plate 18 of *Jazz*. Courtesy: Museum of Modern Art, New York.

Fig. o.8 Graffiti, New York City, 1989.

Fig. o.9 Stencil graffiti, New York City, 1988.

"gallery of the streets" (**Fig. o.8**), you will have that much more in your memory bank upon which to draw for enjoyment and inspiration. New questions may come to mind. Is graffiti art or defacement (**Fig. o.9**)? Can it be both, sometimes one, sometimes the other?

Even the definition of what is two-dimensional and what is three-dimensional is worth exploring in detail, for the boundaries between these can be less than clear, as you will see. It is not so much the label you affix to a particular work, but the search, the voyage of discovery, that holds the real excitement, perhaps the truth. It has been said that a question holds the seed of its answer; also that questions are more interesting than answers.

"I think, therefore I am," said René Descartes. The specific subject of his thought is not mentioned; the very realization that he is capable of thought, of weighing options, making choices, arranging elements in his mind, defines his existence as a human being. It is this human ability to arrange, to seek, find and create order, to manipulate the elements of our universe to our own satisfaction in the visual world that drives some of us to make patterns, designs, art. It can also cause us to categorize, to break down and separate from the seamless fabric of life things we call subjects, elements, fundamentals. So you may find questions and commentary relating to geometry, history, philosophy, chemistry, language, and optics in this book. Recognizing that all human experience is of a piece and inseparable, we may focus on a specific aspect of this unity. Perhaps you will join me in applauding the Head of the Art Department at my first teaching assignment at the Baldwin School, who understood this very well. When challenged at a faculty meeting, "But you are only an art teacher..." Hilda Terry replied, "I don't teach art; I teach students."

A book, after all, is a conversation between author and reader (Whitman knew this), and the value of any book may be the extent to which it is used, questioned, even challenged. This is a book to use, to study and re-study, to put to the test; to be read at times slowly for intense, concentrated thought, at times to be skimmed quickly for a generalized overview. You may find it of value to return to a thought or an illustration already studied or to look ahead to an indicated passage or visual example before it is discussed at length. Do be a page-turner! See this book more as a salad bar or a smörgasbord than a formal, sit-down, soup-to-ice-cream dinner.

Although there are a number of definitions and facts you may have to accept as given (you are not about to redefine Bilateral Symmetry or change the primary colors—though you may be surprised to learn that experts haven't always agreed just which colors *are* primary), there are many questions and ideas you will wish to reconsider after investigation.

Until this century almost all serious *fine arts* (as opposed to acceptably *decorative arts*, diminished further by being termed *minor arts*) employed some aspect of pictorial, largely figurative subject matter. Today, however, it is not unusual to consider a pieced-cloth quilt or a Navajo weaving a work of art, a color-field geometric painting in fabric or textile. These works have not changed, but our perception of them as aesthetic objects has.

Many interesting questions are raised in considering such objects. Is their subtle, often sophisticated color a result of intuition or accident? Did the designers of such works really know what they were doing? Are the makers of these objects artists or merely "craftspeople?" What determines the identity of an object as an art object (**Fig. 0.10**)? Does some functional or utilitarian purpose reduce or remove the object's art designation? Can a non-artist create a work of art? Compare some of the pairs of "craft" and "art" objects assembled by Jean Lipman in her book "Provovative Parallels." Do you agree that questions raised are often more useful and revealing than answers reached? After all, a question opens a door; an answer closes it.

Which of these questions have you considered:
— Where is the line between art and design?
— What is the distinction between structure and decoration? Is one preferable in the arts?
— Does art serve a real purpose? Are physical functions more real than aesthetic, symbolic or expressive functions?
— Does form truly follow function? Should it?
— Is realistic art better (or even more real) than abstract or non-objective art?
— Besides beauty, are there other concerns that may be called "aesthetic?"
— How important for an artist is personal style? Must this be consciously attempted or does it happen of itself?
— Why do people make objects that have no clear use? Why do people want to own works made by others, especially non-functional objects? What makes one object better than another?

Fig. 0.10 Fabric sample, Wullschleger Sales Corp., 1988. Courtesy: Connie Crespo.

Fig. 0.11 Roy Lichtenstein, *Compositions III*, 1965. Oil and magna on canvas, 56 × 48 ins (142 × 122 cm). Collection of Irving Blum. Photograph courtesy of Blum-Helman Gallery.

— Should art have social value or content?
— Does subject matter matter?
— Is primitive art somehow inferior, or less civilized?
— Can sophisticated artists make primitive art?
— Is everyone an artist or designer in some sense?

Ideas you now hold firmly may be seen in a new light upon reflection. Do you agree that:
— You cannot draw a line with a pencil.
— Gray is not a color.
— Red and green make yellow.
— A painting is as useful as a pitcher.
— Every work of art or design must be carefully planned in advance.
— The difference between pattern and texture is scale.
— Art cannot be taught.
— Authentic artists make ''art'' mean the thing they do, rather than doing the thing meant by ''art.'' (Adam Gopnik's idea.)

Can you distinguish fact from opinion? Which depends on research rather than experience, taste, your own point of view, or the way you look at it?

Chapter One

SPOT, LINE, SHAPE AND FIELD: MARKING THE SURFACE

Fig. 1.1 Head and back of a deer. Unknown Paleolithic artist, perhaps 30,000 BC, from a cave at Lascaux, France. Courtesy: Caisse National des Monuments Historiques et des sites.

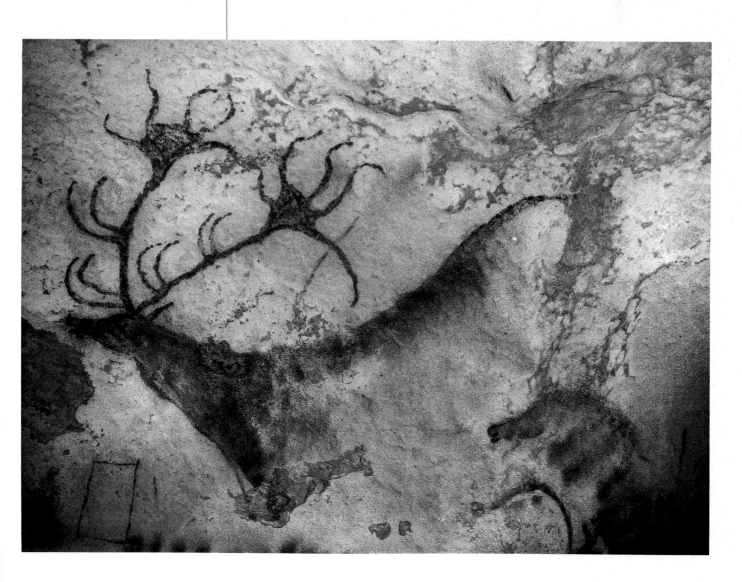

Fig. 1.2 (*top*) **Vincent van Gogh**, *Wild Vegetation in the Hills*, 1889. Brown inks, 18 × 24 ins (46 × 61 cm). Courtesy: Vincent van Gogh Foundation, Rijksmuseum, Amsterdam.

Fig. 1.3 (*bottom*) **Gabor Peterdi**, *Angry Sky*, 1959. Engraving with etching. Courtesy: The Borgenicht Gallery, with permission of the artist.

Making marks on surfaces

Markings have been made on every kind of surface since one of our distant ancestors blew a puff of sooty, russet earth onto the wall of a damp cave through a hollow reed or bone, or scratched into the dry or muddy earth itself. Some marks are as transient as footprints in sand; others last for ages, as have those made at Lascaux perhaps 30,000 years ago (**Fig. 1.1**).

Physical or visual two-dimensionality?

Any mark on paper or canvas must have some amount of length and width. If visible to the eye, all dots, spots, marks, squiggles, lines, shapes and fields are seen as two-dimensional, showing where material has been deposited or removed (**Fig. 11.9**).

A mark records the touch or movement of an implement as it comes in contact with or is pushed and pulled along the surface (**Figs. 1.2, 1.3**). There are exceptions, such as material released at a distance (**Fig. 6.5**), or computer-generated, electrically and chemically activated imagery. In this chapter we will look at the two-dimensional surface or picture plane and its component elements in a purely visual way, focusing on point, line and shape as they are seen. Necessary mathematical or scientific definitions will be investigated later. We will find here and throughout our study many differences between physical or measurable facts and their visual or perceived effects, a reflection of the multiple nature of "reality."

Blank space—empty or full?

Begin with a flat surface, the empty, undetermined page or canvas. Are we seeing "nothing," a blank emptiness, or "everything," an entire field filled with whiteness? Cartoonists make the humorous suggestion that such a space depicts a polar bear drinking a glass of milk during a snowstorm!

A word about words

INFINITY/UNDETERMINED SPACE → Point → Dot → Spot → Stroke → Squiggle → Line → Stripe → Area → Shape → Field → INFINITY/UNDETERMINED SPACE

This seamless sequence and similar verbalizations help categorize and identify aspects of two-dimensional works, but they must always be recognized as poor substitutes for visual experience. The word can never be that which it stands for; it is forever a symbol representing another kind of reality (**Fig. 1.4**). [1]

Words may be used differently in varied circumstances. At the risk of some confusion, try to become familiar with the spectrum of meanings of terms used throughout the history of the visual arts. Keep a card file of art words, adding new meanings and interpretations as you encounter them. No single text, glossary, or dictionary will be able to include the range you can collect from many sources over a period of time.

When a mathematical friend asks if you can really "draw a line," you can reply, "It depends on the definition being used at this 'point' in time!"

Fig. 1.4 **René Magritte**, *La Trahison des Images (Ceci n'est pas une Pipe)*, 1928. Oil on canvas, 23⅝ × 37 ins (60 × 94 cm). Courtesy: Los Angeles County Museum of Art. Purchased with funds provided by the Mr. and Mrs. William Preston Harrison Collection.

EXERCISES

Exercise 1:
Identify a specific visual example for each verbally expressible kind of *edge* you can "invent"; for example, cut edge, sharp edge, shimmer edge, jagged edge, fuzzy edge, smudgy edge, shaded edge, melted edge, soft edge, blended edge. Compare your examples with those of someone else. Do you agree with the other person's choices? Do you want to change any of your own?

19

A starting point

When even the smallest mark is made, the page suddenly assumes the role of background or environment for that focal point. How small a spot can be placed on our *tabula rasa* or blank slate? The merest touch of certain tools—a pencil, crayon, charcoal, pastel, ballpoint pen or felt marker—will be sufficient to deposit a trace of their component material on the surface. Other implements—pens and brushes—must be coated with a liquid or viscous substance such as ink or paint before their touch leaves its mark. Still others—scratchboard knives, etching needles and engravers' burins—remove material from a surface, often previously coated .

The minimal mark

In our search for the minimal disturbance or marking of a flat surface that can be perceived, the simple touch of a tool is used to produce a speck of ink, graphite or paint so small that its shape or configuration cannot readily be identified. This dot may be the "footprint" of a sharply pointed pencil or a fine brush or pen. [2]

Have you ever watched a photograph being "spotted" by the application of diluted points of India ink? The spotter tries to match the gray tone surrounding each white spot left by dust or air bubbles on the negative as the print was made. Can you imagine a mark less visible than a light tone of gray applied to a very small white dot on a near-white area of such an image? [3]

Varying pressure on the surface

Does the size or shape of the mark change as you apply pressure to the tool? If you use a sharply pointed, hard pencil or a stiff steel pen-point, pressure should not appreciably affect your result. Brushes and flexible split-point nibs will respond noticeably to variation in pressure. You may see several kinds of shapes appear, suggesting petals, raindrops, tadpoles or other associative subjects as they change in size and configuration (**Fig. 1.5**). [4]

Would the rhythm, mood and energy of music affect the same qualities in your work? What kind of music would you expect Piet Mondrian or Jackson Pollock to have chosen to accompany their painting "performances?" Are you surprised to learn it was jazz?.

EXERCISES

Fig. 1.5   *Brush "footprints"* by Art Education students, Long Island University, the Brooklyn Campus.

Exercise 2:
Experiment with various implements to find the minimal point below which a mark cannot be seen. Try a pointed steel pen, a crow quill, various hard and extra hard pencils such as 7F or 9F, and superfine brushes such as a photographer's 0000 spotting brush.

Exercise 3:
Create a design which hovers on invisibility using a variety of minimal marks.

Exercise 4:
Use a finely pointed bamboo brush—the kind designed for Asian calligraphy—to see how many differing kinds of simple footprints or

"brushprints" you can make, exerting almost no pressure at first, then slowly adding weight to your mark, causing larger areas of the brush to come in contact with the paper. Keep the brush pointed; do not push or pull it along the surface; simply let it leave its mark. Fill a page with a self-generated field of these marks, allowing the brush itself to lead the way, or directing the design consciously. Dilute the ink to add a variety of gray tones. Refer to sources of Asian painting, seeking only marks clearly determined by varying pressure on the brush. Can non-associative patterns emerge in this way? Try working to music, from Bach to Debussy or Prokofiev, from jazz to the latest popular sound.

Dot to field

A number of tiny dot-points can easily fill an area and assume a tonality or shape. In her series "Triadic" and "Triangulated Intaglios," Anni Albers has explored a variety of triangular shapes and patterns, never needing to draw an outline or edge to contain the many three-sided forms and clusters of forms that interact with their surrounding unfilled spaces (**Fig. 1.6**). Such fields are developed from the inside out, so to speak, stopping when they arrive at their periphery. **[5]**

Do you think Anni Albers' dot-field works might reflect her intense involvement with woven fabric at the Bauhaus (p. 166) and in later years?

Fig. 1.6 **Anni Albers**, *Triadic I*, 1968. Ink and gouache on paper, 14 × 17 ins (35.5 × 43 cm). Courtesy of the artist.

Stippling

Stippling—creating areas of tone by continuous application of points—is often used by illustrators, particularly in technical, scientific and medical work, to achieve precise rendering of detail. Variations in tone and texture result from increasing or decreasing the number or size of spots in a given space.

If spot-shapes are large enough and their pictorial associations compelling, an entire cluster of images may assume a strong sense of field while each component shape retains its identity (**Fig. 1.7**).

Fig. 1.7 **Antonio Frasconi**, *Migration # 2*, 1959. Woodcut, 4 × 14 ins (10 × 36 cm). From "Against the Grain." Courtesy of the artist.

Fig. 1.8   **Chuck Close**, *Leslie*, 1986. Color woodcut, $30 \times 25\frac{1}{4}$ ins (76×64 cm). Courtesy: Crown Point Press.

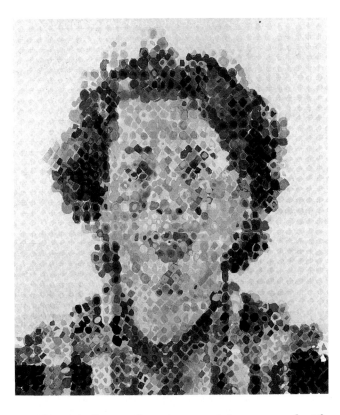

Fig. 1.9a   Detail from Fig. 1.9.

Although Georges Seurat was mainly concerned with optical mixture, and the interaction of color within the fields of dot-spots that cover his canvases, the all-over surface of touched color-points provides much visual interest and gives his works their distinctively flat yet tactile surface quality (p. 166).

The almost unseeable point is the single unit of a cluster, spray, spatter or constellation appearing as an unbounded field of tone or texture that can seem to melt into its surroundings. The cumulative effect through repeated application of a spray can be a solid textureless surface. A flat appearance also results from a screen of dots such as the Benday, used in printing, in which the individual unit is simply too small to be perceived. [6]

When does a spot become a shape?

Exaggerated enlargement of this kind of dot-shape pattern has been used by a wide variety of artists : for example, Chuck Close's *Leslie* (**Fig. 1.8**). In Pop Art, the dot-spot has grown in size to become a circular spot-shape (**Fig. 1.9**). Fields created in this way may not show clearly defined edges as they merge into other areas of color or tone. Or they may cover the entire work and provide an overall texture or plane.

Wassily Kandinsky suggests that the size of any point-dot, in relation to the size of its containing plane and to other marks nearby (such as dots and lines), determines whether it is to be read as a point or as a shape. A single focal dot-spot may appear as a point, dot, spot, shape or a combination of these (**Fig. 1.10**). Is our enjoyment of a painting enhanced or interrupted by pursuit of such questions?

EXERCISES

Exercise 5:
Create fields of dot-spots or spot-shapes paying attention to their accompanying tactility or texture.

Exercise 6:
Scrape the ink-laden bristles of a hard brush (toward yourself, not the receiving surface) so that ink-spots are sprayed onto your paper; if possible, apply an aquatint to an etching plate, or use an airbrush.

Fig. 1.9 Roy Lichtenstein, *Drowning Girl*, 1963. Oil and magna on canvas, 67 × 67 ins (170 × 170 cm). Courtesy: Museum of Modern Art, New York. Philip Johnson Fund and gift of Mr. and Mrs. Bagley Wright.

Fig. 1.10 Georgia O'Keeffe, *Black Abstraction*, 1927. Oil on canvas, 30 × 40 ins (76 × 101 cm). Courtesy: The Metropolitan Museum of Art, New York.

Using dots to create linear movement

As in a spider's web or the contrail of a jet plane, a line may be seen as the result of kinetic energy, something in motion, purposeful, going someplace.

A line may be created, or suggested, as the visual path between two or more dots, spots or other markings (**Figs. 1.11, 1.12,**). This is made possible, minimally, by placing a mark in just a few places, perhaps allowing the line to fade and reappear along its way.

The line suggested by the spiraling path of spot-markings on the alphabet cone shell might well have been placed there by a contemporary designer (**Fig. 1.13**). Can you find other examples of dot-line in nature?

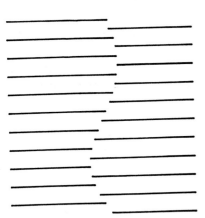
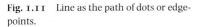

Fig. 1.11 Line as the path of dots or edge-points.

Fig. 1.12 **Yvonne Jacquette**, *Verrazano Horizontal*, 1981. Oil on canvas, $72 \times 52\frac{1}{8}$ ins (183×132 cm). Courtesy: Brooke Alexander. New York.

Fig. 1.13 Alphabet cone shell (*Conus litteratus L.*). Collection: Sylvia W. Gross.

Just as one point serves as a focus, two points establish a relationship, a kind of tension existing between them, creating a line of connection from one to the other even if it remains physically absent. Anyone who has completed a follow-the-dots picture knows that line may be seen as the path of a sequence of points, regardless of the width or thickness of material applied to the surface from dot to dot. Indeed, the line may merely be implied. [7]

Tactile perception of dot-line

In Braille, a system of dots is used to communicate letters of the alphabet through the sense of touch. Each letter is composed of one or more dots raised from the surface within a modular "domino," a six-dot grip. The resulting configurations are interpreted in a linear way as read by moving the fingertip along the page (**Fig. 1.14**). To speed the reading process an intricate shorthand of advanced symbols standing for groups of letters or entire words can be learned. [8] My personal secret code was devised simply by drawing lines between the Braille dots in a continuous cursive way. [9]

Many tactile, digitally perceptual experiences may be presented to those unable to receive visual information who study the visual arts. Instead of excluding those whose entire experience is non-visual from two-dimensional studies of dot, line and shape, inventive alternatives that can be devised by instructors as well as students themselves will be enriching to the entire group. [10]

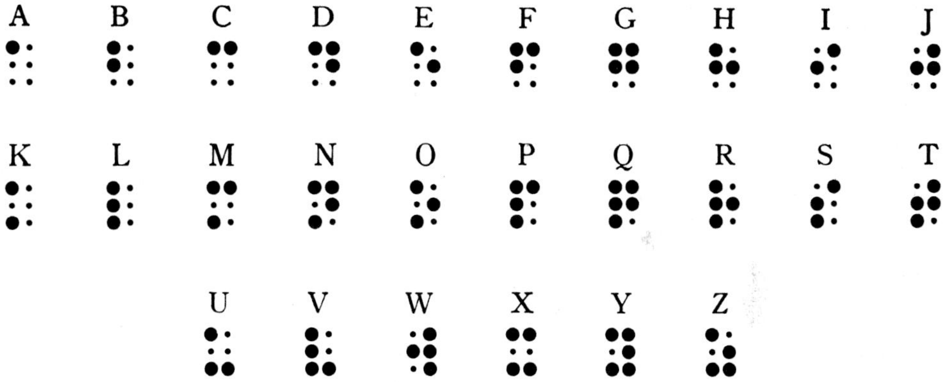

Fig. 1.14 Braille alphabet key, from "Standard English Braille in Twenty Lessons," 1934, by Madeleine Seymour Loomis.

Albers' dot and line exercises

To acquire greater control of the subtle interaction between eye, hand and brain, particularly in order to build skill in drawing, a progressive series of exercises was developed by Josef Albers. One end result of this sequence, based on the dot and line, can be a perfect circle drawn within a perfect square, entirely freehand!

To start this series, you place a small dot near the upper left corner of a sheet of paper, merely touching the surface to locate a "target" point. Then you bring your sharply pointed pencil down the paper an inch or two closer to yourself, touch it lightly to the page, pause briefly to "aim" at the first point, and "fire" a straight line directly up at the target. Don't change the direction of the line; if it misses, it misses. Make a second line to a second target, as parallel as possible to the first one. Keep a steady rhythm and pace of "shots" at your target; after a while your aim will improve, so that you can direct your line cleanly at any spot, in effect drawing a straight line without a ruler. This accomplishment brings a great deal of satisfaction. But it is only the beginning.

Next, visualize your line as half of a right angle, to be completed by a fourth step as you continue the line to the right after reaching the target point: "Ready, aim, fire, right angle." Slowly, as control develops, you can add the next step, a smooth curve, starting from the end of the right-angle line and fitting perfectly within the right angle. The curve returns to the "aim" point from which you started, creating a shape called a spandrel, a quarter-circle within the right angle. "Ready, aim, fire, right angle, spandrel."

A further sequence, starting at the original "aim" point but moving down the page toward yourself and then to the right, closes the second spandrel into a finished half-circle. Eventually you can add a symmetrical mirror-image sequence to describe the opposite half of the squared circle, and, with dedication and time(months if not years), you may well be able to delight small children by drawing a perfect circle within your perfect square. [11]

Linear fields

Related studies using parallel lines can produce handsome finished works. By placing each subsequent parallel line in the "ready, aim, fire" series slowly closer to or farther from the preceding one, you can achieve tonal and spatial modulation, controlled only by the weight of your line and the interlinear distances. Fields of lines can describe either flat planar shapes or carefully modeled suggestions of volume and form. Strongly optical effects may be achieved, with or without a three-dimensional illusion (**Figs. 1.11, 1.15, 2.34**). [12]

Creation of fields of tone through the use of more or less parallel lines is not only a twentieth-century convention (**Fig. 1.16**).

EXERCISES

Exercise 7:
Create a follow-the-dots linear design.

Exercise 8:
Use Braille patterns in a two-dimensional design.

Exercise 9:
Create a code of dots or lines and use this in a design.

Exercise 10:
a) Make simple rubbings of a variety of textured surfaces.
b) Make collages of tactile panels. (Use a single monochromatic tone to emphasize the non-visual focus.)
c) Use small palpable dot-modules (tacks, nails, punched heavy-paper dots, beads and other found objects, or shapes cut of thin corrugated board, sandpapers, embossed wallpapers, fabrics . . .) to build linear or surface-covering designs which can serve as blocks for relief printmaking as well as independent aesthetic objects.
d) Use glued line (string, wool, wire) to draw, or prepare shape-separating edges for the application of tone, color or texture.

Exercise 11:
Follow the sequence of Albers' "ready, aim, fire" technique to draw a straight line, a right angle and a spandrel. Add another spandrel to make a half-circle. Try other variations and patterns. Many students stop after the first spandrel, in itself quite a feat.

Exercise 12:
Experiment with linear fields to express tone and space. Pay particular attention to the edge-lines created by your starting and stopping points (a secondary linear component of these works), allowing forms to grow thinner where they are darker and wider where they are lighter.

Fig. 1.15 (*top*) **Julian Stanczak**, *Segmented Image*, 1965. Oil on canvas, $40\frac{1}{2} \times 54$ ins (103×137 cm). Private collection, permission of the artist.

Fig. 1.16 (*bottom*) **Jean Francois Millet** (French, 1814–1875), *Faggot gatherers returning from the forest*, 1854. Black conte crayon on wove paper, $11\frac{1}{4} \times 8\frac{3}{8}$ ins (28×20 cm). Courtesy: Museum of Fine Arts, Boston. Gift of Martin Brimmer, 76.437.

27

Kinds of line

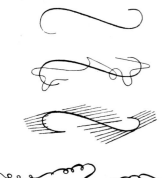

Paul Klee identified three kinds of line: the active or free line, moving not necessarily to a destination; the medial line, which describes or outlines a coherent form; and the passive line, in which form (shape) is filled in and line is only its edge. Do you agree with Klee's distinctions? Are all possible kinds of line included in his categories (**Fig. 1.17**)? [13]

Fig. 1.17 Paul Klee, *Lines* from "The Pedagogical Sketchbook," 1925. Reprinted by permission of Faber and Faber Ltd.

Parallel-edge lines

Since any line applied to a surface leaves a quantity of material in its wake between its two edges, the thickness of that line or track will remain perfectly constant if the edges are parallel and equi-distant; other lines can vary from near invisibility as the edges approach one another to fully developed two-dimensional shapes as the edges diverge. More rigid tools tend to produce parallel wire-lines while softer implements lend themselves to greater variety and possibly more expressive results.

Parallel-edge lines, seen by some as mechanical, wire-like or machine-made, offer the special qualities of depersonalization, consistency, non-objectivity or a hands-off unemotional visuality that provide an acceptable use of the decorative in abstraction. [14]

Although later (p. 78) we will show that a mathematical or "true" line has only the single dimension of extension, we have to agree with Robert Scott that "we cannot express this extension in material without giving it thickness. The amount of [thickness] this can have and still read as a line is a relative matter."

Artists such as Frank Stella, Al Held and Sol LeWitt carefully construct parallel-edge shape-lines (**Fig. 1.18**). Study the line-ribbon-stripe-bands of Piet Mondrian, Gene Davis, Barnett Newman and Morris Louis. Can you always distinguish line from shape (**Figs. 1.28, 4.2**)?

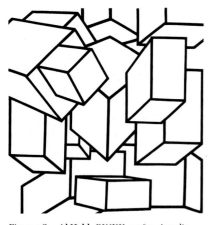

Fig. 1.18 Al Held, *BWXX*, 1969. Acrylic on canvas, 8 × 8 ins (20 × 20 cm). Courtesy: André Emmerich Gallery, New York.

Varied or calligraphic line

One specialized tool can create controlled variations in the width of its "ribbon" as it turns, or changes its angle, on the page. The calligrapher's pen-point or nib presents a chisel-shaped edge to the writing or drawing surface. If the nib is placed flat along a horizontal guideline and pulled straight toward you, a mark as broad as its full width will be made. When the tool is moved laterally, a thinner line, merely the thickness of the metal itself, results. As the pen is held at an angle to the page, approximately 45° to the perpendicular, both vertical and horizontal movements will show a certain amount of thickness. Later, keeping the pen at this constant angle, we will create a consistent ribbon-shaped alphabet in the Italic form (p. 291). [15]

Flexible varied-width lines

Intricate, elaborate examples of decorative line work were quite popular during the nineteenth century and even earlier. Virtuoso demonstrations of continuous line drawings, sometimes in one tight but variously swelling concentric spiral, often engraved by hand, have had their awe-struck admirers (**Fig. 1.19**). To some, a main criterion for visual work is its degree of technical proficiency or craftsmanship, the level of manipulative dexterity required for its execution. A word in favor of caution is suggested when evaluating works that rely on mere showmanship, decorative embellishment or empty form. [16]

Fig. 1.19 (*opposite*) **Claude Mellan,** *La Sainte Face*, 1649. Single-line spiral engraving. Courtesy: The Philadelphia Museum of Art, Charles M. Lea Collection.

Fig. 1.20 **Josef Albers**, *Sandpits*, 1916. Ink on paper, $8\frac{3}{8} \times 10\frac{1}{4}$ ins (21.5×26 cm). Collection: The Josef Albers Foundation.

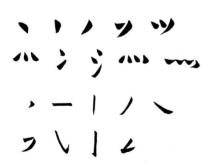

Fig. 1.21 *Brush-dancing* by Art Education students, Long Island University, The Brooklyn Campus.

Fig. 1.22 **Wang Chi-Yuan**, from "Essentials of Chinese Calligraphy", published by Grosset and Dunlop, New York, 1974.

Expressive line

As a tool is drawn over the surface, its track remains, leaving the markings we call the drawing itself. A focus on the free movement of the mark-making hand and arm (perhaps the entire body), regardless of associative or representational intent (**Fig. 1.20**), can lead in an almost choreographic way directly to the familiar action painting of the Abstract Expressionists. Asian painters traditionally heighten the expressive character of their work by emphasizing the dance of the brush and the responsive touch of the hand in interpreting the basic shapes of their calligraphic writing and pictorial art. Donald Anderson believes that the direct and bold strokes of Asian calligraphy "carve ... the path for Franz Kline, driving the brush in right cross and left hook". [17]

Asian calligraphy

Simply placing the responsive bamboo brush on paper, with almost no pressure, creates a distinctive petal-shaped footprint that can be made stronger and more emphatic by increasing the weight behind the placement. As the brush is moved even slightly along the surface in different ways, a whole palette of strokes results, some reading more as dots or spots, some as short lines, others as simple curves or shapes (**Fig. 1.21**), many having traditional significance when combined to create images and words by Chinese, Japanese or Korean artists (**Fig. 1.22**).

Similar markings may be written with instruments permitting no variation in thickness, such as a ballpoint pen. Though legible to readers of each Asian language, these offer limited expressive quality.

Asian calligraphic brushwork, not limited to verbal symbols, includes a rich tradition of conventionalized forms for animal, plant and human subject matter, made personal and expressive through the individual interpretation of each artist. There is no semantic or aesthetic distinction between the linear works Westerners might classify as "writing" or "drawing" (p. 137, 286). [18]

In-between categories

In Asian calligraphy we find markings that exist somewhere between a dot and a line, more than merely the touch of a tool to the surface, but less than a point drawn a considerable distance from its starting place.

The action of placing, then slightly pulling or pushing a marking implement to extend the original touch-spot and quickly lifting the tool creates a gestural mark, the "handwriting" of many artists, a major determinant of what is called "style." Vincent Van Gogh's agitated, slightly curved squiggle-strokes dance equally over the surfaces of his drawings and paintings (**Fig. 1.23**).

To what extent do you suppose artists adapt their natural, intuitive or chosen style to the requirements of a particular design or subject matter? Is this a question to be answered or considered? Can you gain insight by the very process of framing a question? [19]

Line quality

Does line quality depend on the tool employed as well as the sensibility of the artist? How is the exquisite sensitivity to detail in the drawings of Arnold Bittleman facilitated by the superfine tools he has chosen (**Fig. 1.24**)?

Would the same hand movements made by Josef Albers with his broad brush produce a drawing that retains its lively activity and joy with a less intense kind of surface marking (**Fig. 1.20**)? [20]

Fig. 1.23 (*left*) **Vincent van Gogh**, *Cypresses*, 1889. Reed pen and ink drawing, 24 × 18 ins (61 × 46 cm). Courtesy: The Brooklyn Museum, 38.123, Frank L. Babbott and A. Augustus Healy Fund.

Fig. 1.24 (*right*) **Arnold Bittleman**, *Untitled IV* (detail), 1970–74. Pencil and ink on paper, $22\frac{3}{4} \times 31\frac{1}{4}$ ins (58 × 79 cm). Courtesy: The Alexander F. Milliken Gallery and Dolores D. Bittleman.

Fig. 1.25   H. S. Blanchard, *Copperplate Script Birds* from "Ornate Pictorial Calligraphy," published by Dover Publications, Inc. New York, 1982.

EXERCISES

Exercise 13:
Make a collection of different kinds of lines.

Exercise 14:
Use different tools to create as many parallel-edge lines as you can.

Exercise 15:
Experiment with Speedball C-0, 1 and 2 nibs to create a variety of "ribbons."

Exercise 16:
Using a flexible, split-pointed pen, experiment with calligraphic lines to create drawings resembling the thick and thin curvilinear lines of Copperplate script (**Fig. 1.25**).

Exercise 17:
Experiment with a variety of pointed and chisel-edged brushes to create expressive lines. These may be transferred to a block of wood, or drawn directly on white pine to develop as a woodcut, or on to a linoleum block. They may also be used in etching (**Fig. 1.26**).

Exercise 18:
a) Create varied line through the movements of brush on surface.
b) Repeat these lines but with a rigid or ball-point pen.
c) Try to duplicate the Asian brushwork shown in this chapter or obtained through your own research. Create bamboo and other traditional images.

Exercise 19:
Study paintings for personal touch and style of brushmarks.

Exercise 20:
Study drawings and prints in this book in terms of their uses of line. (Consider specifically, the works of Hokusai, Altman, and Matisse **Fig. 1.27**.) Try to identify the tools or implements chosen and imagine how each work might look if the artist had made a different decision. Do you agree that appropriate instruments were used in each work?

Fig. 1.26   (*left*) **Jerome Burns**, *Jo*, 1984. Sugar-lift, soft-ground etching, 8 × 10 ins (20 × 25.5 cm). Gift of the artist.
Fig. 1.27   (*right*) **Henri Matisse**, page from *Pasiphaë, Chant de Minos*, 1944. Linoleum cut, $12\frac{7}{8} \times 9\frac{3}{4}$ ins (33 × 25 cm). Courtesy: the Museum of Modern Art, New York, the Louis E. Stern Collection.

Shaping space on the surface

As Susanne Langer, a philosopher who focused on aesthetic concerns, notes, "to give shape means (first of all) to set limits." We have seen that the fewest limits required to create a line are two, a starting place and a stopping spot. A line that curves or bends around to meet itself and enclose an amount of space may also be suggested by a few simple, compelling "clues," but no fewer than three.

Line as the edge of shape

"Lines that close to become shapes separate the inner, contained space of the shape or figure, from the outer, excluded or left-over space, the ground." Does this sound reasonable? Or do you prefer this more "equal" way of seeing the same idea: "Lines that close to become shapes create equal and opposite shapes on both sides of their edge?"

If you are not certain whether a particular mark should be classed as an applied line or as a shape, and if you think the distinction is important, what criteria may be used (**Figs. 0.7, 1.28**)? Consider: Has this line more than one edge? If so, is the space between the edges wide enough to compete with its length for visual importance? Is length the primary function of this line? Are its edges parallel? Can you "feel" or "sense" the varied pressure exerted on a tool by the artist in order to vary or widen the line? Can you always tell line from shape? (**Figs. 4.2, 4.11.**)

Fig. 1.28   Cynthia Dantzic, pages from "What can you see?", a book of woodcuts, 1963.

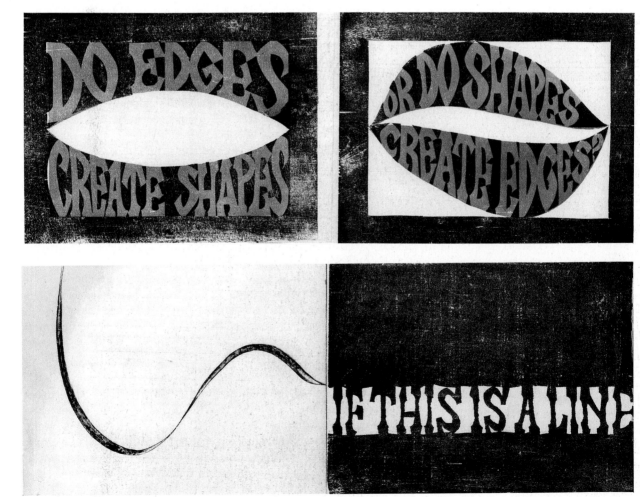

Fig. 1.29 Stone wall similar to one used for Bernard Chaet's exercise.

The figure/ground relationship

When a dot-spot is large enough so that its shape is clearly distinguishable, we begin to see not only that inner shape but the shape of the enclosing area around it; this is the beginning of the figure/ground relationship.

Chaet's double-edged brush study

A particularly valuable study, introduced by Bernard Chaet, makes use of the flexible pointed brush to depict the spaces between chunky rectangular stones in a campus wall (Fig. 1.29). In an effort to capture the subtle shapes of these interstices or so-called negative spaces between the solid rock forms, it is necessary to respond with sensitivity to the two contours described at once, by varying the pressure on the brush, in effect drawing the filled and unfilled spaces at the same moment. As each line develops, it describes the contour or edge-of-form seen around both surrounding objects and, as it is defined by them, it also defines them. In addition to showing clearly the way in which any applied line must recognize its two boundaries and what is happening in the filled space between them, this study also provides an introduction to the figure/ground concept. I have found no more excellent method of demonstrating the equality of the two shapes existing simultaneously on either side of any edge. Of course, it is possible to act as though only one of these is important or of interest, particularly if one of the interacting shapes looks like something, that is, if it is a representation of a recognizable subject. But the artist or designer must always see the total picture, the integration of all visual elements on the picture plane. There is no "empty" space, no "background" from this point of view. Any mark on the surface determines the structure, the identity, of the entire field. [21]

Equal figure/ground

Unfortunately the term "equal figure/ground" itself seems to perpetuate the mistaken notion that one of the two, the figure, is the real subject, and the other, the ground or background, is merely an environment to contain this more important component. Some effort to substitute terms such as "figure/figure" or "filled and unfilled space" has been made, but it is difficult to impose a new vocabulary. So long as an understanding of this problem exists, we may continue to speak of equal figure/ground or "the figure/ground exchange." The use of directly cut line-as-separating-edge by Matisse invariably elicits our admiration for his bravura performance. Think of figure skating when enjoying his cut-paper works, imagining the edges being sliced into the surface with energetic flourishes.

Fig. 1.30 (right) **Douglas Hofstadter**, *Recursive Figures*. Illustration from "Gödel, Escher, Bach: An Eternal Golden Braid," published by Vintage Books, a division of Random House, 1980.

Fig. 1.31 **Scott E. Kim**, *Figure-Figure*, 1975. Illustration from "Godel, Escher, Bach: An Eternal Golden Braid," published by Vintage Books, a division of Random House, 1980.

Douglas Hofstadter, Pulitzer Prize-winning mathematical philosopher, distinguishes what he calls "cursively drawable" shapes, "whose ground is merely an accidental by-product of the drawing act," from "recursive" figures or shapes "whose ground can be seen as a figure in its own right." As examples of recursive shapes, he presents the kind of figure/ground word and shape configurations familiar to students of psychology (**Fig. 1.30**). A strong design of repeated identical black and white shapes forming each other's "ground" in a clearly equivalent way is "Figure/Figure" by Hofstadter's colleague and friend, Scott E. Kim (**Fig. 1.31**). Hofstadter sees M. C. Escher as the artist employing this idea most successfully and most thoroughly .

Are these descriptions of equal figure/ground interchangeable?
     Equality of shapes sharing a common edge.
     Shape fitting into adjacent shape.
     Interaction of adjoining forms.
     Relationship of two areas with one boundary.
Often an idea such as "figure/ground" is understood but considered optional, perhaps to be saved for special projects. A transitional series of studies can be particularly useful in finding the exact point of equilibrium, and in showing the relationship that exists between the two—regardless of quantity. [22]

Although "seeing is believing," the actual doing and experiencing of a visual truth can provide far more meaningful, lasting knowledge than studying the most successful examples of the work of others through illustrations in books or slides.

In order to bring about a more equal sense of figure and ground, particularly with a representational subject, some designers or illustrators stress the area around the object to the point of eliminating *any* treatment of the "figure." This leaves a blank or negative space where the object would be, and all markings are placed in the supposedly empty "background" area (**Fig. 1.32**). [23]

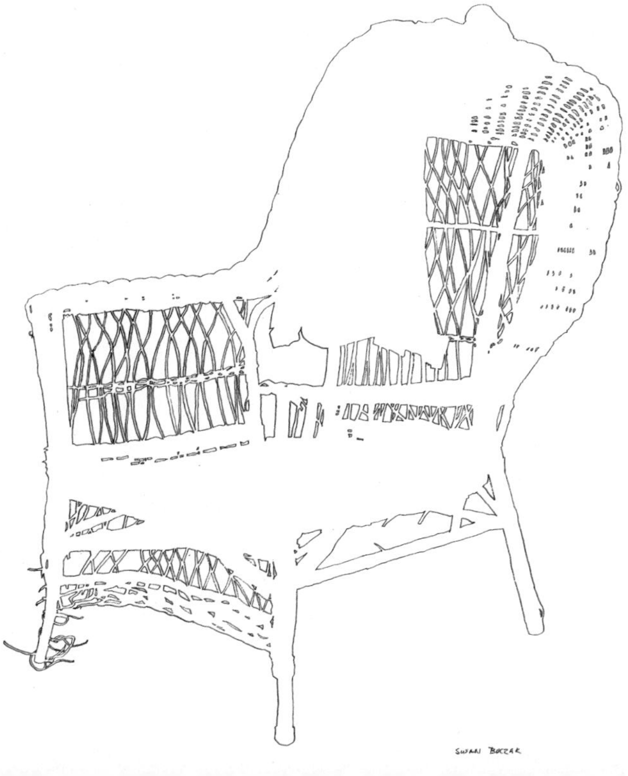

Fig. 1.32 *Drawing of the spaces around an object.* By a student of Irwin Rubin, The Cooper Union, New York.

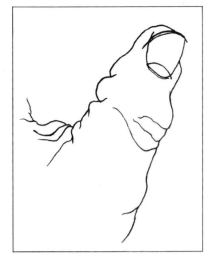

Fig. 1.33 Robert Kaupelis, *Diagram* from "Learning to Draw", published by Watson-Guptill, New York, 1966.

Fig. 1.34 Virginia Cantarella, *Drawing of a high-buckled shoe*, 1988.

Edges

The physical edge of the picture plane acts as an arbitrary cut-off for a pattern, texture or design that would otherwise continue beyond the page or canvas. A sample of wallpaper or fabric clearly conveys this.

It is often said that line as such doesn't exist in nature. Can you identify examples of edge or applied line found in the natural world (**Fig. 3.5**)? [24]

Perception of edges

Note the difference between *physical* edges, such as those at the periphery of a sheet of paper, and *apparent* edges, which mark the limit of our ability to see around the three-dimensionality of form. Observe the horizon, which continues to move away as you approach it, and even the contour of your hand as it turns before your eye. Such non-existent but clearly visible edges or outlines are often referred to as "contour" lines, changing with every movement between the eye and the object observed (**Fig. 1.33**) [25]

Drawing from the outside in and inside out

In her meticulous rendering of an old-fashioned high-buckled shoe, Virginia Cantarella proceeds from the outside edge to the interior area of a shape, the preliminary contour line disappearing into the finished drawing (**Fig. 1.34**). [26]

Compare this process with the highly criticized, yet widely, used coloring books which present an emphasized outer line for children to complete, usually with crayons, the predetermined outline remaining the strongest visual element even after the coloring-in.

Are children, exposed constantly to this type of work, likely to believe that a clear outline must precede any finished drawing or painting? Have you worked with teachers who require a completed drawing or sketch before permitting work on any canvas, plate or block?

Study the works of Helen Frankenthaler (**Fig. 10.16**) and Conrad Marc-Relli (**Fig. 1.35**) to consider the question: "Do edges create shapes or do shapes create edges?

Fig. 1.35 **Conrad Marca-Relli**, *Sand Brown*. Courtesy: Marisa del Rey Gallery and the artist.

Fig. 1.36 **Cynthia Dantzic**, pages from
"What can you see?", a book of woodcuts,
1963.

(**Fig. 1.36**)" Can either sequence work? Can a shape be created from the inside out to an edge (**Fig. 1.6**)?

Visual crossing of physical boundaries

Inseparable cluster-shapes with a common outline may be part of a complete rectangular picture plane, a total composition, or they may act as a central complex-figure to be seen against a supporting ground, as a kind of vignette (with soft edges) or silhouette (with sharper contours).

Shapes flowing across the edges of their five component panels help to unify the square format of the Modular Paintings. The visual edges of combined-shape areas are seen as more real than the physical structure of these works. [27]

Edgeless, unbounded fields

Markings on a surface need not be neatly enclosed by precise edges; soft, fuzzy, blended or melting fields of varying tonality are important parts of many artists' palettes or styles (**Fig. 1.37**). Have you encountered or worked with such "clouds" or fields that never resolve themselves within distinct bounded edges? Are there surface markings that defy categorization altogether?

Fig. 1.37 **Richard Mayhew**, *Mohawk Hills*,
1974. Oil on canvas, 44 × 48 ins
(112 × 122 cm). Courtesy: The Midtown
Gallery and the artist.

Fig. 1.38 Evelyn Yee, *The Flute Player*, 1980. Pencil, 8 × 10 ins (20 × 25.5 cm). Courtesy of the artist.

Fig. 1.39 Cynthia Dantzic, *Cathy as Anastasia*, 1979. Pencil on paper, 29¾ × 22 ins (75.5 × 56 cm). Collection: The Brooklyn Museum, New York. 79.229, Prints and Drawings Department and other Restricted Income Funds.

Naming marks that elude naming

If we truly acknowledge the non-verbal quality of the visual experience, shouldn't we expect there to be unnamable, intuitively grasped aspects to every work? Aware of the discrepancy between purely perceptual experience and the words we select to try to bridge this unbridgeable gap, we move through an inadequate verbal language in studying "the language of vision." Can we agree that *dot* and *spot* identify a location or touch a place on the surface, *line* marks the track or path of a spot in motion, filling in the space between its own physical edges, *shape* describes the filled areas on either side of a separating outline, while *field* refers to a general expanse covering a portion of the surface whether or not it exists within a clearly defined boundary?

EXERCISES

Exercise 21:
Using a pointed flexible brush such as the Asian bamboo, with India ink, try to achieve the double-edged line, as described above, in drawing an irregular, textured stone wall.

Exercise 22:
Place a white geometric shape on a black rectangle, and an organic or pictorial shape in black on a white rectangle. Then, in three transitional stages, move to and through the central "equal figure/ground" relationships, to the opposite design.

Exercise 23:
In pencil, or in cut paper, create a background-only study. A familiar subject for this is the many-spoked art-studio stool whose varied geometric spaces provide much visual interest.

Exercise 24:
Carry your camera for a week to collect examples of edge and line in nature.

Exercise 25:
To show the difference between physically existing edge lines and transient, changing contour lines, tack a large square of paper to the wall and move the tack gradually lower so that, as the paper begins to bend and curl over itself, a non-existent but visible contour line appears. In drawing this, how can you indicate the two different kinds of lines? Is this important? Study drawings of the figure and drapery to see different solutions (**Fig. 1.39**). Line may melt, even disappear, with no loss of contour or form (**Fig. 1.38**).

As a further development, make a complex looping of a long strip of wide brown Kraft or wrapping paper. Draw an unshaded, continuous contour line. Visualize the hidden portion of physical edges that continue behind the convolutions of your paper drapery, then include such unseen continuations of your line as though the entire subject is transparent.

Exercise 26:
Try making a drawing from edge to interior.

Exercise 27:
Create a modular rearrangeable design, or one in which the visual appearance differs from the physical structure.

Indirect markings

There is a large and historically rich area of two-dimensional design in which markings of every description, point, dot, line shape and field, are created indirectly on the surface. In the various techniques known collectively as printmaking, ink is transferred onto, or impressed into, paper from one or more original blocks or plates generally of wood (**Fig. 1.40**), stone, metal or plastic. In this way, a large number of "multiple originals" may be printed or "pulled." Much variation is possible during the printing process, so that every degree of uniqueness is seen from editions of virtually identical clones to highly individual one-of-a-kind monoprints and monotypes. Since many artists are now combining and modifying classical techniques and introducing new materials and methods, it may be more difficult to identify the way contemporary prints have been made.

There are excellent detailed texts, such as Gabor Peterdi's "Printmaking", for in-depth study of specific techniques, for which there is no space in this volume. [28]

EXERCISES

Exercise 28:
Make one print in any printmaking medium (This exercise may be delayed until you take a class in printmaking, although woodcuts and linoleum-block prints require no press or complex equipment.)

Fig. 1.40 **Antonio Frasconi**, *Woody Guthrie*, 1972. Woodcut, $23\frac{1}{2} \times 38\frac{3}{4}$ ins (59×99 cm). © Antonio Frasconi. Reproduced by permission of the artist.

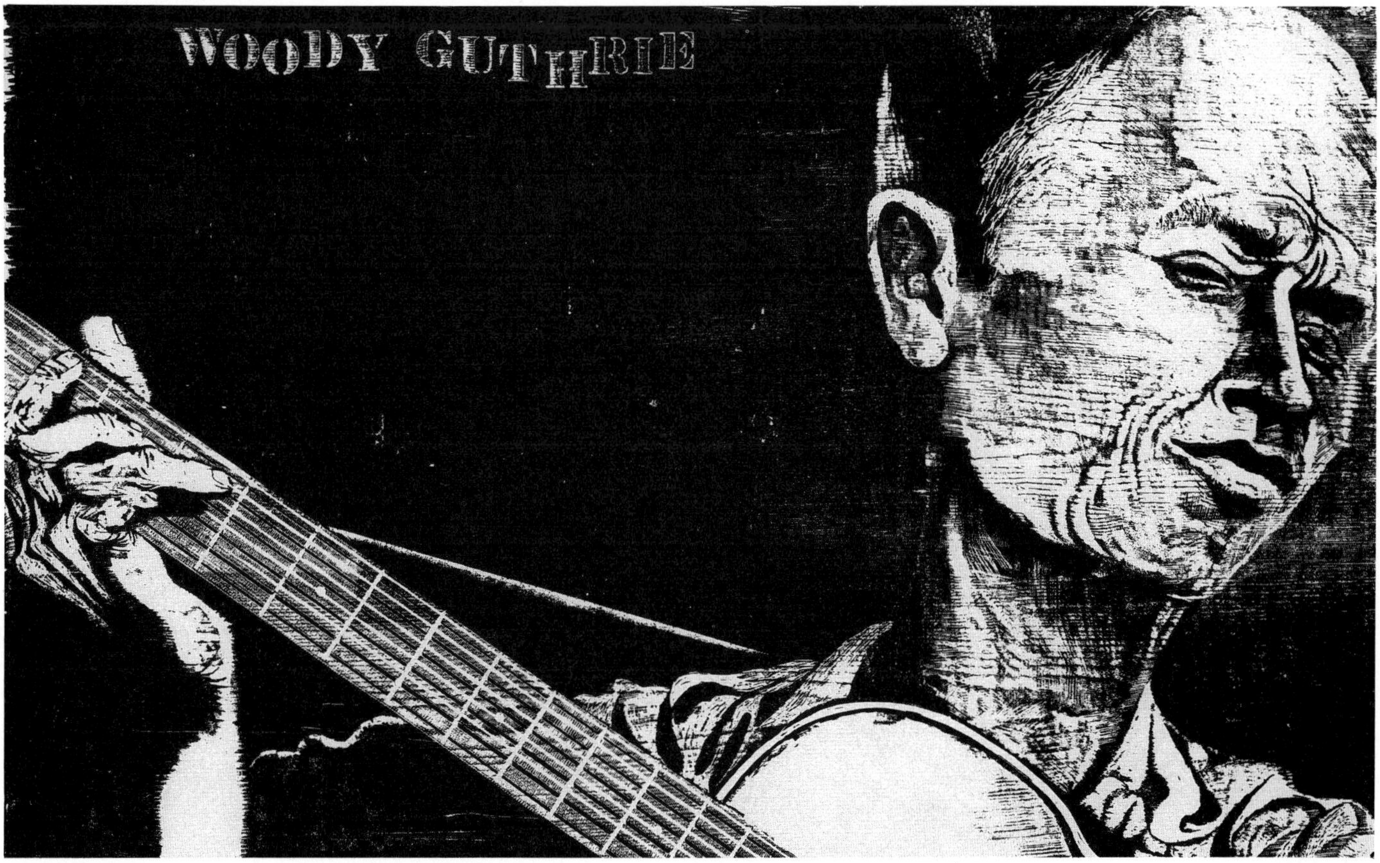

Limitless variety of markings

Each medium has its own distinct group of characteristics, each artist and designer a unique "handwriting" or style. The number and kinds of marks that can be achieved on the two-dimensional surface are therefore infinite. This realization adds to the importance of the visual arts as a major force for the advancement of human civilization, for recognition of the special value and distinction of each contribution to the total human experience. Of course, such a way of looking at design and art tends to encourage a broad, eclectic view in which the richness and variety of artistic styles, even eccentricities, are cherished and savored. This is not a viewpoint that encourages each student to produce works that are an imitation of the instructor's example or of any particular, even admired, exemplary models from the pages of art history, except as technical, skill-building studies.

Samplers

Often, artists present us with a veritable sampler of all the richness of markings they can devise, particularly in drawing. From point/dot to dot/spot, spot/mark, mark/squiggle, squiggle/line, line/shape, shape/field, dot/field, line/field and other nameless and unnamable inventions that hand, mind, eye, imagination and materials can fashion, the possibilities are surely as limitless as the individuals who create them. For, as much as we categorize and classify, describe and define them, every artist's and

Fig. 1.41   Henri Cartier-Bresson, *Seville 1933*. Photograph. Courtesy: Magnum Photos, Inc.

designer's markings have their creator's individual style, and the works *you* will make have not been made by anyone before you in exactly the way that you will make them (**Fig. 1.41**). No matter how exhaustive (and exhausting) any one author's charts of dots, spots, lines, shapes and fields may be, they cannot show every possibility. Study the examples presented here and in a wide assortment of good quality, generously illustrated art books and also in visits to museums and galleries. Then, with as many implements and tools as possible, make your own samplers and charts. [29]

Are you certain that each mark has been placed in the "right" category? Might some of your marks belong equally on two or even all three samplers? What does this mean about the marks? About the categories?

Compare your samplers with those made by others. There is always more to be seen, more to be shown, more to invent. As you work with ideas and suggestions in the chapters ahead, remember we never cover material, but *un*cover possibilities, *discovering* more about art, design and ourselves.

We are advised to avoid clichés or over-used configurations; yet many original and surprising interpretations of these shapes (such as the familiar heart) may be seen in ancient as well as contemporary works (**Fig. 2.11**). So beware all rules, including this one. You need not be concerned with making your mark; indeed only you can do so, no one else can make it for you.

EXERCISES

Exercise 29 (Three Part):
Suggestion: Make a *dot* sampler, using the widest variety of tools and materials available; on a sheet of the same size create a *line* sampler, and a *shape* sampler on a third sheet. Refer to your own samples frequently in studying the illustrations presented here and those you encounter in classroom, gallery, museum and elsewhere, making additions freely.

Chapter Two

SYMMETRIES

Fig. 2.2   **Ferdinand Hodler**, *Lake Thun*, 1909. Oil on canvas, 26 × 36 ins (67 × 92 cm). Courtesy: Musée d'Art et d'Histoire, Geneva.

The idea of symmetry

To some symmetry calls to mind beauty and harmony; to others it has a mechanical, decorative connotation. On the one hand, symmetry suggests regular placement of identical elements, repeated to produce a structural whole, bringing focus, strength, completeness, elegance, majesty, well-balanced, well-proportioned unity and order to works of nature as well as human invention. On the other hand, symmetry says rigid, formal, impersonal, predictable, tedious, mathematical, precise and ornamental—an accretion of evenly positioned modules, the antithesis of uniquely human creative expression.

In nature and art

In nature we recognize and delight in the perfect arrangement of parts encircling a central point to produce a snowflake (**Fig. 0.1**), flower (**Fig. 2.1**), or starfish—or two halves mirroring each other around a central line as in a butterfly, leaf, or reflection in the still surface of a lake (**Fig. 2.2**). Our distant ancestors were moved to respond to the symmetries in their environment and in their own bodies by employing various kinds of repetition in their works in every material. [1]

The same design unit often appears in the works of many different nations and people. In ceramics, textiles, mosaics, architectural adornment or other arts, variations of the meandering "Greek Key" (**Fig. 2.3**), (an example of translational symmetry as you will see), can be found in the work of nearly every civilization that has left a trace, as distinct as Chinese bronzes and Navajo weaving (**Figs. 2.4, 2.30, 2.35**). Meanders, still inlaid into parquet wood floors and tiled into the walls of municipal buildings and restaurants (**Figs. 2.30, 2.35**), continue to be used by artists in every medium.

Fig. 2.1   **Piet Mondrian**, *Chrysanthemum*, 1908. Pencil drawing, 12 × 9 ins (30 × 23 cm). Courtesy: Sidney Janis Gallery, New York.

Fig. 2.3   (*left*) Greek Amphora, geometric style. Courtesy: National Archaeological Museum, Athens.
Fig. 2.4   (*right*) Navajo wool blanket. From the Claflin Collections. Courtesy: Peabody Museum, Harvard University.

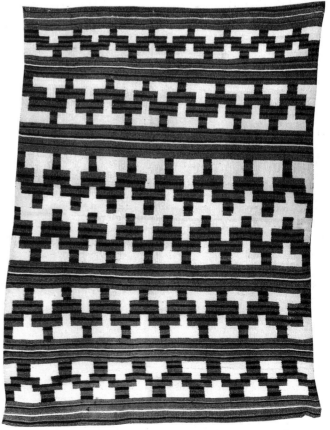

In science, math and philosophy

Symmetry is involved with far greater concerns than simple ornamentation. According to Hermann Weyl, author of the definitive study of the topic, "Symmetry is a vast subject, significant in art and nature. Mathematics lies at its root." Indeed, he explains, "the entire theory of relativity is but another aspect of symmetry ... It is the inherent symmetry of the four-dimensional space/time continuum that relativity deals with." A vast subject, indeed!

The mutual concerns of the sciences and the arts have served as a focus for many original thinkers, such as the naturalist D'Arcy Thompson, whose observations of countless forms of living creatures and their growth patterns led him to conclude that "the perfection of mathematical beauty is such that whatever is most beautiful and regular is also...most useful and excellent." More recently, Jay Hambidge has developed a description of what he calls Dynamic Symmetry, based on the proportions of living and growing plant and animal structures. Hambidge is convinced that no design is possible without symmetry. These writers and others have shown how different symmetries are the basis for much of the structure encountered in biology, botany, chemistry, crystallography and astronomy as well as in art. Weyl recognizes that all the standard symmetries act as a static force and are likely to produce a state of equilibrium. Among others, Islamic artists have long chosen such forms specifically to eliminate the personal or transient element from their work. Dynamic Symmetry, however, is seen as a spur to creativity, freeing the artist's mind as a springboard, using nature as inspiration, not as a model to copy. "As wide or as narrow as you may define its meaning," says Weyl, "symmetry is one idea by which [we] have tried to comprehend and create order, beauty and perfection."

EXERCISES

Exercise 1:
Collect examples of natural objects and designs you consider symmetrical in some way.

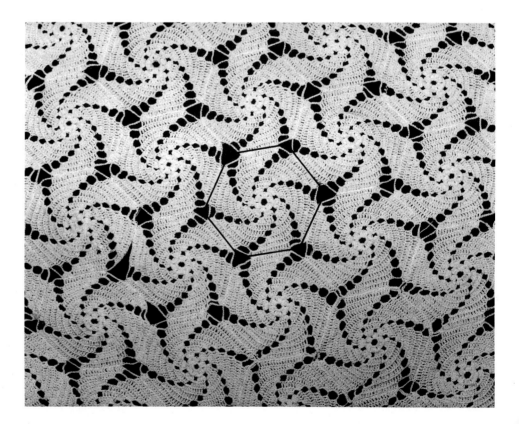

Fig. 2.5 **Anna Wiener**, *Crochet Piece*, c. 1940. Modular pattern of individual circles, cotton thread. Collection of the author.

A vocabulary of symmetry and related ideas

As in any discussion, the meanings of related, overlapping and extremely general terms must be made clear if our investigation of symmetry is to be of value. In his classic work, *Module, Proportion, Symmetry and Rhythm*, Gyorgy Kepes recognizes that these four terms "seem to justify being considered as concomitant factors." It is largely a varying of emphasis and focus on different "threads" of one indivisible fabric of design that gives us divisions into seemingly discrete topics and areas of study.

Try to sort out the extent of shared meanings, and of separable aspects, in the following terms. Some will be amplified in later chapters, as indicated. Which illustrations might also be used for a neighbouring category in the list?

Module (**Fig. 2.5**), a unit repeated in a regular way to create a larger configuration; may refer to the shape itself or to the design upon it.

Pattern, a surface covering composed of modules which extend up to or seemingly beyond the edges of a shape. In positioning repeated patterns, such as wall coverings, perfect matching must occur so that no unwanted joinings are seen between adjacent or overlapping areas.

Rhythm, stressing a beat, a pulsing alternation of elements and the intervals between them (p. 135).

Balance, a state of equipoise sensed in viewing a harmonious placement of parts, often symmetrical, as an image and its mirrored reflection on either side of a central line (p. 63).

Proportion, (**Fig. 2.6**), a relationship between parts of a totality, or of a part to the whole, in terms of size or quantity (p. 67, 68).

Size, a quantitative description of an individual on a scale or within boundaries; always relative (p. 65).

Scale, generally used interchangeably with proportion; suggests a more precise calculation (p. 71).

Ratio, expresses the relationship between one number or quantity and another (p. 185).

Unity, a concern with the totality of a work, an orchestration of its subdivisions (p. 74).

Symmetry, in two dimensions, the arrangement of modules around a central point, as in a snowflake, or on either side of a central edge, as in an inkblot. These may be combined in a variety of ways. Repetition of an element along a linear path, another kind of symmetrical structure, is mainly used as a decorative enhancement of a utilitarian object. A sense of symmetry may be achieved by regular placement of unlike but evenly balanced elements. "Dynamic Symmetry" is a special description of the ways in which a particular proportional relationship of parts, based on the Golden Mean, is found in the structure of many naturally occurring life forms and in art and architecture.

Repetition of modules is basic to any symmetrical structure, as is a tendency to a static, flat, formal reading, described variously as "reflections of unity" (Keith Critchlow), "that which governs the just balance of variety in unity" (Jay Hambidge), and "the series of ways in which a single motif can be repeated an exact number of times (within a given border or shape)" (Keith Critchlow). The absolute flatness of a symmetrical design can be opened, given a certain visual shift, a sense of alternating, fluctuating space and form, by introducing the spatial "flip-flop" of an optical illusion (**Fig. 2.7**).

Variety is limitless, one of the wonders of symmetry being its demonstration of "a

Fig. 2.6   (*left*) **Quilt square, Monkey Wrench pattern** (also called Virginia Reel, Indiana Puzzle and Snail Trail). Photo from the book "A People and Their Quilts" by John Rice Irwin, Norris Tennessee. Courtesy: John Rice Irwin.

Fig. 2.7   (*right*) **Quilt, Baby Blocks** (also called Illusion). Unknown Canadian artist, no date. Collection of the author.

Fig. 2.8   **William Blake**, *Angels Watching Over the Tomb of Christ*, c. 1806. Watercolour. Courtesy: The Trustees of the Victoria and Albert Museum, London.

single geometric organizing principle capable of providing infinite solutions" (Donald Anderson). This "mystery of multiplicity in unity . . . can be seen . . . retaining unity at the center of symmetry, yet flowering into multiplicity along its radii . . ." (Keith Critchlow). Such richness is often a result of combining several kinds of symmetry in one work, as a design can have more or less symmetry. It may clearly reveal its structure or eliminate its axis completely, blending the two mirrored halves (**Fig. 2.8**). One of the criteria often used to distinguish "design" from "art" has been the subtlety or softening of a structural armature. "Design" may reveal its secrets; "art" can suggest ways for the viewer to discover its message, privately.

One of the special values of symmetry has been called its "power of transition, or movement from one form to another. It produces the only perfect modulating process in any of the arts" (Jay Hambidge). Static symetry as used by the ancients was based on the patterning properties of such regular shapes as the square, hexagon and equilateral triangle. A serene equilibrium is exuded by symmetry, valued for its power in tribal, religious and other formal works.

Mere similarity of parts does not guarantee symmetry. Although a work may include a number of similar, even identical, elements, placement alone identifies the presence of that attractive yet mysterious influence we recognize as symmetry.

Although strict symmetry was out of fashion in Western art for centuries, many twentieth-century painters have used a centered, frontal format, which might suggest a simple, bilaterally symmetrical pattern. Certain modifications have made all the difference. In such works, rather than in natural or created designs, which may astonish and dazzle the eye with intricate detail and meticulous precision, a certain space is left for the viewer's creative participation (**Fig. 2.9**). Edges may melt (**Fig. 9.14**) or blend, shapes merge or shimmer, colors change and space appear to pull the eye into the painting or to thrust it out toward the viewer (**Fig. 11.1**), with the passage of time, as the work is studied. In these paintings, a symmetrical armature is chosen as the minimal means by which to present the active color and atmosphere speaking directly to the eye and sensibility of the viewer. The very neutrality and anonymity of symmetry provides these painters with the freedom to give full attention to their individual painterly concerns, with the least risk of associative connotations intruding.

Approximate or implied symmetry, a kind of left/right balance sensed in a work with no actual physical midline, can give a feeling of equality of weights, colors, lines, shapes, textures, even of associative, representational elements, distributed so that they appear to be at rest or at least in a momentary stasis—tension restrained. Since these qualities are non-measurable and subjective, a very wide range of individual examples is to be expected (**Fig. 2.10**).

Fig. 2.9 **Mark Rothko**, *Earth and Green*, 1954–55. Oil on canvas, 91 × 74 ins (231 × 188 cm). Courtesy: Museem Ludwig, Cologne.

Radial or rotational symmetry

Fig. 2.10 **Ashoona Pitseolak**, *Night Demons of Earth and Sky*, 1961. Stone cut, 24 × 36 ins (61 × 91 cm). From "Eskimo Graphic Art 1961." Courtesy: Dorset Fine Arts, a division of West Baffin Eskimo Cooperative. Photograph courtesy of Inuit Art Seetion, Indian and Northern Affairs, Canada.

Beginning with one central point, a second point is moved in a curved path a fixed distance away, to describe a circle. Since any radius of a circle is equivalent to any other, and there are numberless radii possible, the circle is the most symmetrical shape, having virtually infinite symmetry. This idea fascinated early Islamic designers and is the origin of their incredibly intricate, fluid, curvilinear, surface-covering patterning. The metaphysical and religious applications of such universality, plus the limitless ways in which a single motif can be repeated an exact number of times within a circle, combine to make a unique place in history for Islamic geometric art (**Fig. 2.11**).

As it turns, a circle presents the same face, so we are never certain whether the circle we see is at rest or in motion. This explains the choice of the rectangle or square by many geometric painters seeking neutrality and stasis. As an example of a circle that moves, constantly showing a different image, a kaleidoscope would seem to demonstrate simple rotational symmetry. But, on reflection(!), note that each edge is mirrored to the left and to the right. Therefore, every other wedge, or triangle, is reversed, and of the six visible design units, you see three repeats of one bilaterally symmetrical design. There is one module, reflected like an inkblot, repeated three times to complete the circle. What makes the kaleidoscopic image so fascinating is the mirror symmetry of both edges of each module, blending the whole into a fluid continuity. This can hardly be called simple rotational symmetry. A similar structure is seen in Pennyslvania "Dutch" decorative circular panels or "hex" signs. [2]

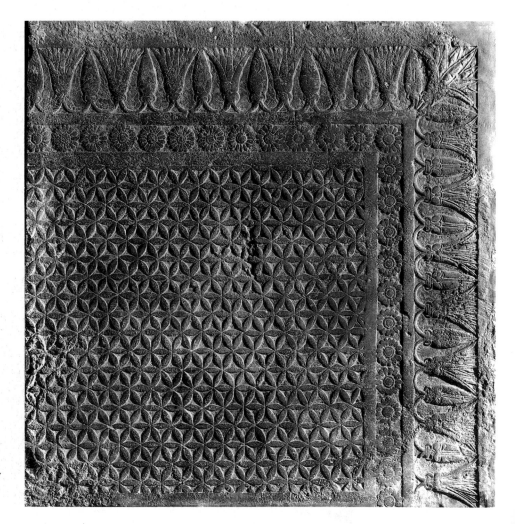

Fig. 2.11 Paving Slab, from the Palace at Nineveh, Assyrian, c. 700 BC. Reproduced by courtesy of the Trustees of the British Museum, London.

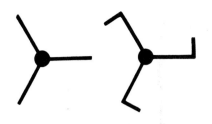

Fig. 2.12 Tripod and Triquetrum, from "Symmetry" by Hermann Weyl.

Fig. 2.13 Logo/corporate symbol of the National Westminster Bank.

Is it possible to show a radially symmetrical design without a reflection at each axis? A simple three-legged tripod can be seen as divisible into three pairs of legs, each half as thick (**Fig. 2.12**). To avoid reflective symmetry in a simple tripod, a small "foot" can be added to each "leg", creating a design famous in the history of art, the triquetrum. This oddly disquieting example of "incomplete symmetry" was credited with magical significance by more than one ancient civilization, and may be seen in the center of a familiar corporate symbol (**Fig. 2.13**).

A powerful design used for many thousands of years by people of nearly every culture as a symbol of good luck, as well as an attractive decorative adornment, has in recent years become so intensely associated with perverted, inhuman values that its off-balance four-legged symmetry can hardly be seen without creating a disturbing emotional response in any viewer. Even so objective a scientist as Hermann Weyl in his classic treatise, *Symmetry*, refrains from depicting the swastika. "The modification of the triquetrum with four instead of three arms is the swastika," he writes, "*which need not be shown here*...one of the most primeval symbols of mankind." One day we may again be able to come across this purely geometric structure, found so often in Egyptian, Greek, Chinese, Amerindian and other art, without feeling the taint of our own century marring our perception of these works.

Perhaps the most familiar and most beautiful class of natural objects combining rotational and reflective symmetry is the snowflake or snow crystal. Twelve separable units of design, or six pairs of right/left mirror-images, all of the same one module, define each radially symmetrical snowflake (**Fig. 0.1**). And no two alike!

A square has rotational symmetry, with four stopping places, which can be called the symmetry of four, four-symmetry, four-fold symmetry or four-part symmetry.

Rotational, radial, cyclical, circular symmetry, or symmetry around a point, whichever term you encounter, all have to do with the number of turns a module makes around a center or *vertex* before reaching its starting place and "mapping onto" itself in its original position. There are special attributes of several kinds of rotational symmetry, and a number of familiar examples can be found for each. Do not limit your inquiry to the few that can be shown here.

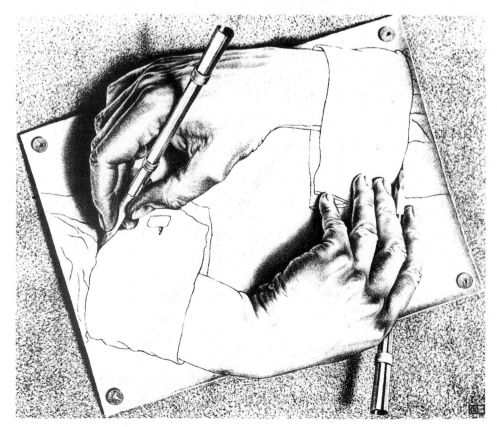

Fig. 2.14 Yin-yang circle designs. After Robert Lawlor's illustrations in "Sacred Geometry."

Fig. 2.15 **Maurits Escher**, *Drawing Hands*, 1948. Lithograph, 11 × 13 ins (28 × 33 cm). Courtesy: Cordon Art, Baarn. Holland.

Fig. 2.16   **André Kertész**, *Satiric Dancer*, 1926. Gelatin silver print. Courtesy: Estate of André Kertész.

Fig. 2.17 Logo/corporate symbol of The Chrysler Corporation (hood ornament).

The Asian "yin-yang" circle must be the simplest instance of two-fold rotational symmetry (**Figs. 2.14, 2.15**). The tripod and triquetrum clearly show three-part, as we have seen. The simple cross and footed cross, or swastika, divide a circle equally into four partitions around its center. By far the richest treasures, however, are to be found in the detailed study of five-fold pentagonal and six-fold hexagonal symmetry. In nature, pentagonal symmetry is largely reserved for living forms such as flowers and starfish. We have five fingers and toes on each limb, evidently a related development. Dynamic Symmetry, which creates the spiral of the nautilus shell (**Fig. 3.5**) and so many other life forms, is based on the symmetry of five. The pentagon with its five axes drawn from the center is a popular symbol (**Fig. 2.17**). With an inscribed star, called the star pentagon, this powerful image served as the secret device of the Pythagoreans in fifth-century-BC Greece. The simplest linear track that can produce a star is contained within a pentagon. [3].

Unlike five-fold symmetry with its organic applications, six-fold is the symmetry of crystals and inorganic structure. Because hexagonal patterns are also generally mirror-images, they have a greater degree of symmetry than odd-numbered rotational symmetries. The star hexagon, or double triangle, Shield or Star of David, considered the "most perfect" configuration in Islamic design, is also a symbol for the monotheism longest in existence, that of the Hebrew people. This interpenetration of two equilateral triangles cannot be drawn as a single "track", but is always a relationship of two separate entities (**Fig. 2.18**). It is also used to demonstrate the placement of the secondary colors in relation to the primaries (p. 183). The hexagon, the most complex polyhedron, or many-sided regular shape, can fill a flat plane completely with no space remaining (**Fig. 2.19**). Hexagonal structure may be discovered in many representa-

Fig. 2.18 Navajo Weaving, c. 1935, New Mexico. Wool, 14 × 40 ins (35 × 102 cm). Collection of Sylvia W. Gross.

Fig. 2.19 Hexagonal flooring tiles, with and without coloring to create star pattern.

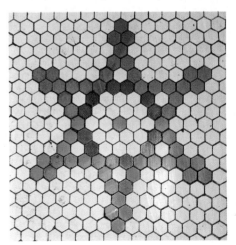

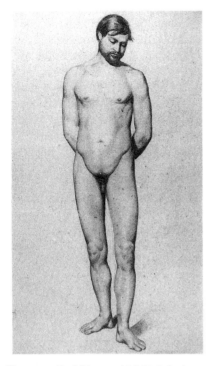

tional works (**Fig. 2.20**). Seven-part symmetry occurs unexpectedly in nature.

There are two kinds of star octagons possible: one drawn as a single continuous line, the other composed of two intersecting squares. [4]

One of the most historically significant rotational symmetries is the twelve-fold pattern of the traditional rose window, which, in addition to its shimmering complexity of form, offers a framework for such twelve-part ideas as the signs of the zodiac and months of the year (**Fig. 2.21**). The twelve-fold pattern of atoms in chlorophyll, considered the basis for the possibility of life on this planet, gives special meaning to this splendid form of symmetry.

Thus far, we have considered rotational symmetry as a totally flat idea, in which a module changes position but not its shape as it moves about its center. In a different usage, it can also signify an apparent change of shape, as a module is imagined moving physically through space, revolving about a central line or axis a full 180° until it comes to lie flat again against its original shape, but now seen as from its other side. Yes, this sounds like another way of describing a simple mirror-image or bilateral symmetry! An excellent picturing of this concept is the winged Sumerian design in which the raised *left* arm to the front of the figure, moving through the picture plane in imagination and back again so that we now see it from the other side, becomes hidden behind the now forward *right* arm (**Fig. 2.22**). To the eye this may not look "symmetrical" as we do not see "inkblot" mirror symmetry. But it is truly a special case of rotational symmetrical structure.

Fig. 2.20   **Paul Cézanne**, *Male Nude Study*, 1862. Fusain et crayon noir sur papier vergé, 24 × 18½ ins (61 × 47 cm). Courtesy: Musée Granet, Palais de Malte, Aix-en-Provence.

EXERCISES

Exercise 2:
Design one "wedge" of a kaleidoscopic image. Repeat as required to complete a circle. Use Xerox, collage, patience.

Exercise 3:
Number the points of a pentagon in sequence clockwise. Connect the "dots" in this order: 1 to 3 to 5 to 2 to 4 to 1.

Exercise 4 (Two-Part):
To make a one-line star octagon, number the points of an octagon sequentially and connect them in this order: 1, 4, 7, 2, 5, 8, 3, 6, 1. (Skip two points around the octagon as you draw the star.) To construct a double-square star octagon, skip one point as you go around. This sequence is: 1, 3, 5, 7, 1 and then 2, 4, 6, 8, 2.

Fig. 2.21   (*left*) Rose Window, West, Chartres Cathedral, 1216 AD.

Fig. 2.22   (*right*) Eagle-headed men, Sumerian. From "Symmetry" by Hermann Weyl, published by Dover Publications Inc., New York.

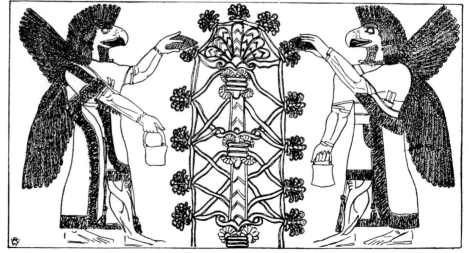

Date Dec. 21, 1908

Name Natalie Sleeper

Date Dec. 9, 1912

Name Mary Shields

Date January 4, 1970

Name Cynthia Maris Dantzic
on my thirty-seventh birthday

Fig. 2.23 Symmetrical inkblot signatures. From 1900 book "Your Hidden Skeleton."

Fig. 2.24 Mauricio Lasansky, *Self Portrait*, 1957. Engraving, drypoint, etching and roulette, printed in black and brown, $35\frac{5}{8} \times 20\frac{1}{2}$ ins (90 × 52 cm). Courtesy: The Museum of Modern Art, New York.

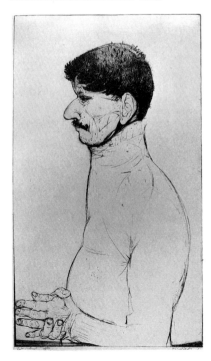

Bilateral symmetry

Bilateral or two-sided symmetry is easily created by reflecting any design or image between two mirrors at certain angles, 60°, 30° and 36°, or by folding a sheet of paper with a blot of ink in the crease.

An interesting pre-television pastime (very likely pre-radio from the examples I have collected), involved inkblotted signatures, made with wet ink along a folded page in a special kind of "symmetrical autograph album" (**Fig. 2.23**). **[5]**

The principle of repeating an element, reversed, by "hinging" it along an edge to its mirror-image, gives the form of symmetry most easily identified and seen as beautiful. Examples in nature include butterflies and moths, the leaves of countless trees, human and animal forms as seen from above and below or directly from the front and rear. (Side views, or silhouettes, do not present bilaterally symmetrical images of such three-dimensional structures [**Fig. 2.24**].) Visualize the subject of this intense portion of William Blake's poem:

Tiger! Tiger! Burning bright
In the forests of the night,
What immortal hand or eye
Could frame thy fearful Symmetry?

The central line or axis of symmetry, usually thought of as vertical, can be at any angle to the viewer's eye (**Fig. 2.25**), and is often found in horizontal compositions such as the reflected landscape at the edge of a lake. This axis need not be physically present in nature or in art (**Fig. 2.26**). As we have shown, great formality and subtle mystery can result from its absence (**Fig. 2.8**). Can you see why this type of symmetry has also been called "heraldic?" Another name, "right/left symmetry," is worth our special attention, as these designations, throughout human history, have not been considered quite equal in certain ways; am I right? (You have the right to remain silent . . . but you may be left behind.) What is left to say, but that there has long been a sinister connotation to one side, while the other has been called right as rain; the "right" angle is basic to Cubism and other geometric usage in art and design. To Christians, the perpendicu-

Fig. 2.26 **Lucien Clergue**, *Rice in Winter, Camargue*, photograph, 1960. Courtesy of the photographer.

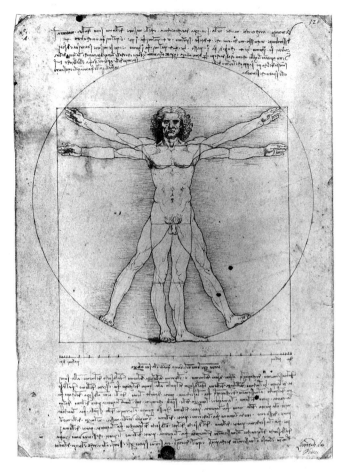

Fig. 2.27 (*left*) **Michelangelo Buonarroti**, *Ceiling mural*, Sistine Chapel (detail: The Creation of Adam) 1508–12. Fresco. Courtesy: The Vatican Museums, Rome.

Fig. 2.28 (*right*) **Leonardo da Vinci**, *Dimensions of the Human Body*, c. 1485–90. Pen and ink, $13\frac{1}{2} \times 9\frac{3}{4}$ ins (34 × 25 cm). Courtesy: Academy of Fine Arts, Venice.

lar cross symbolizes more than one kind of "right" angle (**Fig. 15.3**). Indeed, Michelangelo, in his "Creation of Adam", aims the life-giving dexterous right index finger of God at a perfect right angle to awaken the limp left hand of Adam (**Fig. 2.27**). The designations left and right were chosen arbitrarily, a human convention with no special merit to either side. They may derive in some intuitive way from the clockwise, right-hand, and counter-clockwise, left-hand, naturally spiraling tendencies of growth and motion at the subatomic, atomic, and galactic levels of structure in the universe. Could this be right?

Automatic two-handed symmetry

The satisfaction derived from bilateral symmetry is a reflection of our own structure (**Fig. 2.28**). An interesting demonstration can show just how inbuilt and innate this left/right drive is. [6]

Often mask-like "primitive" images will result, and other associative designs of surprising power and invention. Once you have played with this technique, it can be enlisted as an aid in the creation of less accidental works, particularly satisfying since they express your own "automatic" symmetry.

Could there be a relationship between our natural bilaterality and the success of so many symmetrical symbols and logos (**Fig. 2.29**), from the hexagonal star and the cross to the Shell shell and the Bell bell? On the one hand, you might be right, but on the other . . .

A more complicated kind of bilateral symmetry can result from curving the central axis. D'Arcy Thompson discovered this in the structure of several plants, such as the begonia.

Fig. 2.29 Bell and shell logo.

Fig. 2.30 Detail of Mitla Wall. Photographed by Sheila Hicks.

Fig. 2.31 Logo of the Atlantic Computer Company, Waltham, Massachusetts.

Translational symmetry

A running line is the key to a completely different symmetry, called translatory or translational. Here, modules are repeated at equally spaced intervals along a path to produce highly decorative patterns, useful as borders or separations in architecture, fabric design, ceramics and many other utilitarian arts, and in painting as well. Since the impulse for this continuous, additive process is movement from spot to spot along a line, it is called a "one-dimensional symmetry operation." The designs themselves are two-dimensional; it is their generating principle which has only directed length (in mathematical terms, a *vector*). Characteristic of this form is a pulsing rhythm, which adds to its value as reinforcement at an edge (**Fig. 2.30**).

Translations of a simple motif, not by itself a mirror-image, are rarely seen and are called "primitive." You are more likely to find examples of this linear, cyclic, translatory symmetry showing the "self-covering parallel shift" of a module which is a combination of elements. Equal spacing of the axes or centers of reflection make the units merge so that they appear inseparable. A frequent discovery within complex meanders (especially those in place before the 1930s) is the footed cross or swastika (p. 49). [7]

Sequential enlargement of each module along a path evokes a less static response in the viewer, building to a focus or climax (**Fig. 2.31**). In nature, a translation that adds proportionally growing units along an equally expanding curve produces the famous nautilus shell with its dynamic symmetry (**Fig. 3.5**).

To Western artists, accustomed to working within a predetermined frame or format, the potentially infinite continuous linear flow of translational design offers refreshing variation, as in works by Anni Albers and Richard Anuszkiewicz.

Fig. 2.32 Detail of Navajo Rug, Fig. 2.35.
Fig. 2.33 **Maurits C. Escher**, *Horsemen, Symmetry Drawing.* From "Escher – Fantasy Symmetry, The Periodic Drawings of M.C. Escher" by Caroline MacGillavry, published by Harry N. Abrams Inc.

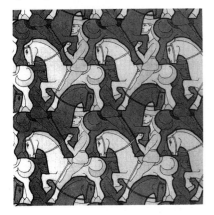

Meanders

The most universally known category of cyclic pattern, the meander, includes numberless individual interpretations (**Fig. 2.32**) [8]

In all of these, the basic translation is accompanied by an additional "flip," a shift called the "glide reflection." An imaginary center line, horizontally placed, divides the meander into upper and lower halves, identical in shape but placed in an alternating, "positive and negative" arrangement. In the simplest U-meander, U-shapes alternate with upsidedown Us in a continuous fluid line. (The U shape is itself a bilaterally symmetrical unit.) When an L-meander is repeated, however, the special "glide" feature is more evident, as the basic unit alternates with its background shape, generally in a different color and facing in the opposite direction, upside down! [9]

Can you identify the people who originated each of the examples shown, or the century during which each was created (pp. 43, 59)? [10]

Slip reflection

Similar to glide reflection, usually found along a horizontal line, is the botanically ubiquitous slip reflection, recognized in plants whose leaves alternate left and right along a stem at regular intervals. This movement of half a pattern along an axis is familiar to students of Cubism, who recognize the shift of a shape, with its accompanying ground, along an edge, dividing the surface of a painting into areas of flat space, known as the "slipped plane." It is also seen in the meticulously intricate work of M. C. Escher (**Fig. 2.33**), who combined many kinds of symmetry and space-filling patterning to cover planes with an incredible assortment of fish, birds, insects, people and architectural detail. Interestingly, Escher and the Cubists always used associative subject matter. Geometry alone or non-objective imagery did not satisfy their aesthetic needs.

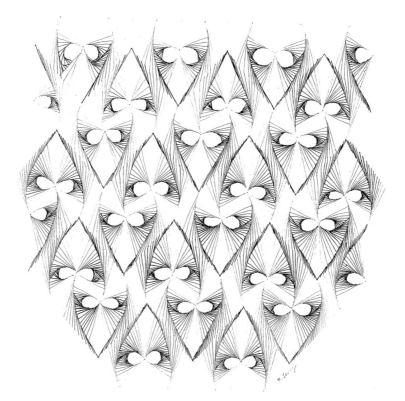

Fig. 2.34 **Module Creating Texture.** By a student of Irwin Rubin. Pencil on paper. Courtesy: The Cooper Union.

Slipped-middle patterns

In fabric design the "slipped middle" is a similar idea which makes it possible to cover an unlimited space with a continuous repetition of a pattern by moving every other row or column of the same module down one half-step (**Fig. 2.34**).

The edges of such patterns are often eliminated or camouflaged so that no sense of a precise module is communicated, and an all-over surface is achieved. [11]

EXERCISES

Exercise 5:
Make inkblots along creased sheets of paper. Try it with a wet ink signature in the fold.

Exercise 6:
Stand in front of a large sheet of paper attached to a wall or board. Place two crayons, one in each hand, at a spot above eye level directly in front of you on the drawing surface, relax for a moment and close your eyes. Allow your other hand to move as it will and slowly direct your dominant hand to draw a long, looping, linear scribble. (Be sure your other hand is also moving; inhibition sometimes prevents this crayon from leaving the starting spot!) As you gain confidence, you will swing both crayons in a perfect mirror-image duet, creating symmetrical patterns and forms.

Exercise 7:
To demonstrate a mix of left-right and translatory symmetry fold a length of narrow paper, accordion-style, into many equal "pages" and close it flat before cutting a few irregular shapes from the folded edges. If you make each cut shape quite different, the result upon opening the paper will show a regular placement of two sets of mirror-image shapes in a translational row. Use this method to create a number of classical meanders.

Exercise 8:
Photograph or copy on graph paper meanders encountered in a one-week period.

Exercise 9:
Study the examples of U-, L-, T- (footed and plain) (**Fig. 2.35**), S and even G meanders; then imitate at least two using graph paper, simulating the tiles often employed by the meandering artist.

Exercise 10:
In another use of the folded accordion strip, on graph paper design a pattern with an L along one fold and an upside-down reverse L along the other (not joining or your work will come apart). When opened, you will have a description of reflection on both vertical and horizontal axes. These studies can be developed into amazingly elaborate designs, particularly with clever uses of tracing paper or a reducing Xerox copier.

Exercise 11:
Design a slipped-middle textile pattern.

Fig. 2.35   Navajo rug, cotton and wool
weaving, 1885–95. Nine-section sampler,
135 × 135 ins (343 × 343 cm). Courtesy:
Tony Berlant, from his collection.

Symmetry groups

Of the basic regular geometric shapes, which ones can be used to cover flat space completely when repeated and touching with nothing "left over?" A circle will not cover space, when four come together, without leaving that concave curved diamond between or a concave triangle when three are packed even closer. Pentagons will not work either. Only the square, triangle and hexagon cover a plane completely. The hexagon is most often selected for this purpose, but keep in mind that a hexagon is actually six triangles meeting at a central point (**Figs. 2.19, 2.36**).

The seventeen different patterns or configurations composed of various combinations of the square, triangle and hexagon have been worked out by geometricians. They are called "symmetry groups," or familiarly, "wallpaper groups," by mathematicians as well as designers (**Fig. 2.37**).

Repeat patterns—metamorphosis

Islamic art is largely composed of ornamental surface-covering repeat patterns, derived from the three shapes we have noted as space-filling, often including the circle, with its extra interstitial shapes (**Fig. 2.11**). These patterns may be interpreted with considerable degrees of freedom (**Fig. 2.38**), Escher, as we have seen (**Fig. 2.33**), shared with the Islamic artist an absorption with space-covering symmetries, but in addition to associative subject matter, he introduced another element, which might be called metamorphosis, where one form can be seen slowly changing by subtle steps into another form, often becoming a positive image of the background shape around the original form. In another of his works fish with vaguely birdlike background shapes slowly turn into birds with vaguely fishlike ground shapes. When such transitions of form are accompanied by gradual changes in light and dark, amazing surreal effects are suggested and day can unexpectedly become night (**Fig. 2.39**). [12]

EXERCISES

Exercise 12:
Try a simple Escher-like repeat using triangles or hexagons.

Fig. 2.36 (*right*) Symmetry patterns (selected). Adapted from Matila Ghyka's "The Geometry of Art and Life," published by Dover Publications Inc, New York.
Fig. 2.37 (*far right*) Symmetry groups (selected). Adapted from Matila Ghyka's "The Geometry of Art and Life," published by Dover Publications Inc, New York.

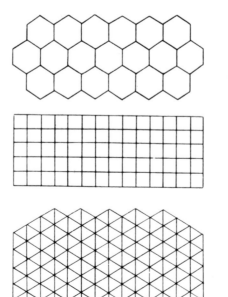

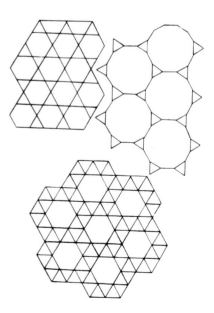

Fig. 2.38 (*opposite, top*) **Fred Gutzeit**, *Blue Glove Screen*, 1983. 5 × 8 ins (13 × 20 cm). Courtesy of the artist.
Fig. 2.39 (*opposite, bottom*) **Maurits C. Escher**, *Night into Day*. Courtesy: Haags Gemeentemuseum, The Hague.

Attitudes to symmetry in painting and design

Frontal, mirror symmetry, rarely selected by representational painters, confers stark power upon certain works of Georgia O'Keeffe. Combined with oversize scale, simplified form and clear color, a formal symmetry lent exaggerated importance and sometimes a touch of irony to the canvases of Pop artists (**Fig. 7.11**).

Pattern Painting, Systemic and other often symmetrical geometric styles tend away from the associative, avoiding even the "frivolity" of the curvilinear in a search for minimal means of expression and neutrality of image (**Fig. 2.40**). Series of closely related works are frequently seen—some with barely perceptible discrepancies, others showing dramatic sequential developments in physical form as well as surface treatment (**Fig. 6.21**).

Minimal art can carry the message "less is more" dangerously close to "less is less." The original statement, associated with the Bauhaus and Josef Albers, signifies an increasing concentration of visual content within an ever more purified, reduced context. Achieving the greatest "outget" with the minimal "input" is the goal: economy (**Fig. 2.41**). However, in nature and design no amount of precision or detail is necessarily excessive. Just as you may study the wing of a butterfly with ever-greater magnification to discover more detail and substructure, down to the atomic level, so the analysis of complex Middle Eastern carpet patterns or meticulously involved Islamic designs yields ever greater understanding of their underlying structures. John Dewey, the innovative educator and aesthetic philosopher of the twentieth century, believed the term "art" should convey a sense of the experience felt by the viewer in active engagement with a work, so that the work is itself re-created in each experiencing. In this sense, is there an irreconcilable difference between the finest in design and in art? Can the various symmetries, if used in wonderful ways, not result in "wonderful things!"

Fig. 2.40 (*left*) **Kendall Shaw**, *Happy Days with the Fire Chief*, 1979. Acrylic and mirrors on canvas, 84 × 84 ins (213 × 213 cm). Courtesy of the artist.
Fig. 2.41 (*right*) **François Morellet**, *Doubles Trames*, 1958. Courtesy: Bruno Facchetti Gallery, New York.

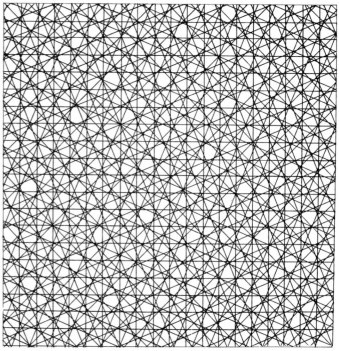

Asymmetry

Asymmetry must be distinguished from chaos or absence of structure; it always implies an underlying sense of symmetry, interrupted. In Kertesz' photograph of the actor Rouet (Fig. 2.42), the axis of symmetry falls to one side of the centerline of the picture, creating tension, as half of the figure is literally a reflected image of the other half. Asymmetry is also evident in the differing shapes behind the left and right sides of the figure. As a "given" from which the variation departs, a ("broken" or "interrupted") symmetry relies upon the implied armature, the tacit cushion, of the original theme (Fig. 2.44). Ceremonial Iroquois masks, cut from the living tree, show this visual rearrangement of physically symmetrical parts in a unique way (Fig. 2.45). A certain humor tempers their ferocity. The Asian god Šiva, with hands pointing alternately earthward and heavenward, shows a compelling asymmetry (Fig. 2.46) [13]

In depicting highly symmetrical biomorphic subjects in motion, so that their potentially mirror-image stasis is rearranged, strong rhythms, action and even sensuality can be conveyed. Warriors, dancers and lovers are among the most popular candidates for such asymmetrical imagery, in Eastern as well as Eurocentric art.

Uneven growth or placement of otherwise symmetrical elements along a central axis occurs in nature as well as in art; witness D'Arcy Thompson's begonia.

Visual asymmetry

Visual asymmetry can be introduced into a physically symmetrical pattern by unequal treatment in terms of color, dark and light placement, texture and other means (pp. 12, 185). Nineteenth-century quiltmakers, who doubtless "knew" better, often treated one square of a pattern as an interruption, made of an unexpected color, or shaped in a modified configuration. Contemporary grid-based paintings frequently use a similar asymmetry (p. 164).

Approximate symmetry

Approximate, felt or sensed symmetry may exist in a work without a discernible axis or center, when such a midline is somehow implied by the disposition of elements on either side (p. 48). [14]

Fig. 2.44 (*left*) **Marc Chagall**, *Self-Portrait With Grimace*, 1919. Etching and aquatint, $14\frac{11}{16} \times 10\frac{3}{4}$ ins (38×28 cm). Courtesy: The Museum of Modern Art, New York. Gift of the artist.

Fig. 2.45 (*right*) Iroquois mask. Courtesy: Department of Library Services, American Museum of Natural History.

Fig. 2.46 Siva. Cambodia; Angkor period, first half 12th century. Courtesy: The Asia Society, New York, Mr. and Mrs. John D. Rockefeller 3rd collection.

Freedom from symmetry

As symmetry suggests rest and a binding together, so asymmetry calls to mind movement and freedom. "In a perfectly homogeneous medium," says Matila Ghyka, "there is no sufficient reason for any change." A certain asymmetry in the structure of the universe gives the impetus for life and growth, according to a number of scientists.

The search for ways to free creative works from the "tyranny" or restraint of compulsive, mechanical repetition, of "automatic" symmetry, has engaged the imagination of artists and designers from the earliest recorded times. But methodical geometric patterning has also been a strong human concern, since ancient cave surfaces were marked by those intriguing grid patterns that accompany the more familiar bison and reindeer (**Fig. 2.43**). These resemble, to a remarkable degree, the very latest grid symmetries. How downright syncopated, asymmetrical and poised in tension do we see a so-called "pure plastic" work by Mondrian (**p. 155**) in comparison!

Further study suggestions

Symmetry, asymmetry and lack of symmetry exist in art and in nature in ways without number. Since you will want to recognize and use these design elements in your developing visual vocabulary, you may gain additional understanding through the study of geometry, crystallography, botany and comparative anatomy, among others. For this purpose, and for their sheer fascination and exuberance, the works of Weyl, D'Arcy Thompson, Ghyka, Hambidge, Lawlor, Kepes, Dewey, MacGillavry and Escher are strongly suggested. Some may wish to skip the mathematics and study the illustrations. But you may decide to go back for a second helping.

EXERCISES

Exercise 13:
Modify a symmetrical design asymmetrically.

Exercise 14:
Select asymmetric compositions or areas within a larger, symmetric whole by using two L-shaped pieces of cardboard to form a rectan-gular window, which may be opened or closed to create frames. In this way, you may also identify "unsymmetrical" arrangements, in which no elements seem to be equivalent to each other, or relate to any inherent order.

Chapter Three

RELATING TO PROPORTION

Fig. 3.1   René Magritte, *Delusions of Grandeur*, 1948. Oil on canvas, $39\frac{1}{8} \times 32\frac{1}{8}$ ins (99×81.5 cm). Courtesy: Hirshhorn Museum and Sculpture Garden, Smithsonian Institution. Gift of Joseph H. Hirshhorn, 1966.

Meanings and importance of proportion

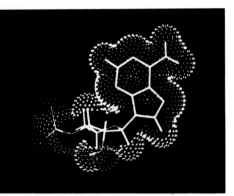

Fig. 3.2 DNA Molecule, a double helix (seen in an end-on view). Computer generated image. © 1985 Arthur J. Olson, Scripps Clinic Research Institute, La Volla, California.

Like symmetry, proportion is concerned with the structure of nature and design. When you ask, "Is my drawing in proportion?" or when you say, "I can't seem to get the proportions right," what do you mean? Is there something about your drawing that does not correspond with the model? Is there some agreed-upon standard, a correct or most pleasing arrangement of parts of the human figure which you do not know or cannot accomplish at your level of skill?

According to many scientists, the basis for the stability and constancy of form in living plants or animals (whose every atom of each cell is replaced every five to seven years) is the inbuilt tendency of DNA to form regular spirals resulting from a set of fixed geometric proportions (**Fig. 3.2**). "These proportions ... exist ... without any bodily counterpart, as abstract, geometric relationships. The architecture of bodily existence," Lawlor claims in his book *Sacred Geometry*, "is determined by an invisible, immaterial world of pure form and geometry." In this sense, the idea that proportion has to do with the proper relationship between things and their component parts assumes a powerful new importance.

Proportion, whether considered by philosophers, scientists or artists, suggests a weighing of different elements with regard to one another, but not necessarily a precisely measurable, static apportioning. In art, proportion involves the sensibilities of the perceiver, which are largely a determination affected by training, familiarity and acquired taste (**Fig. 3.3**).

For our study of this complex subject, some mathematics must be used, but that part will not get out of proportion! What *portion* of a chapter can be given to math, yet remain the right *size*? Can we keep the *ratio* of math to non-math content acceptable? On a *scale* of 1 to 10, how much math would give us the proper *proportion*? Are all these terms interchangeable?

Do the following definitions clarify their distinction? (Which of the illustrations in **Figs. 2.7, 10.6,** and **3.25** seem to be most appropriate for each term?)

Part, an amount less than the whole which may be separated from the whole physically or in the imagination.
Portion, one of a number of equal parts into which a whole is divided.
Size, the magnitude or quantitative degree of anything in relation to a particular standard of measurement. As we generally consider ourselves the measure of all things, we assume a human-sized sense of "large" and "small" (p. 65).
Ratio, a comparison of, or relationship between,two quantities. "One to three," written 1:3, means that of a group that can be divided into three parts, you are concerned with one (p. 71).
Fraction, a mathematical expression of a ratio. One-half, for example, means the whole is divided in two parts of which we are considering one. This can be written 1/2 as a fraction or 1:2 as a ratio.
Proportion, the equality of two ratios or the statement that they are the same. "One-half equals two-fourths" means $\frac{1}{2} = \frac{2}{4}$, or 1:2 = 2:4. that is "one is to two as two is to four." Less precisely, proportion has to do with the relative size of a part to the whole, involving comparison, analogy. According to scientists, the tendency of nature to develop according to a geometric spiral based on a particular proportional relationship makes life possible.
Scale, involves measurement by comparing a unit with the whole, composed of those units. By using diagonals within enclosing rectangles, or with different sized grids, an artist "draws to scale." In scaling "up" units are larger than in the original; in scaling

Fig. 3.3 Jacques Lipchitz, *Girl with Braided Hair*, 1914. Pencil, $7\frac{7}{8} \times 6\frac{1}{4}$ ins (20×16 cm). Collection: The Museum of Modern Art, New York. Mr. and Mrs. Milton Petrie Fund.

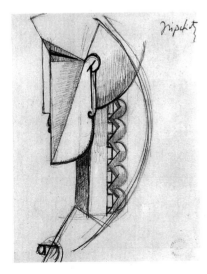

"down" they are reduced. Unbelievable, outsize scale can result in attention-grabbing focus, also in broad humor. [1]

Proportion is as important in non-representational as in pictorial art and design, for any work must exhibit some interaction between elements. Even a blank canvas presents a relationship or ratio of height to width.

The golden mean

For centuries philosophers, mathematicians, scientists and artists have considered the idea of ideal proportion, trying to identify in nature a numerical standard which when translated into human endeavors would assure perfection of form, harmonious balance, beauty. Independently and frequently, such searches have led to the discovery of a particular proportional relationship known as the Golden Section, Golden Mean, Golden Proportion or Divine Proportion. Using this measurement, a Golden Rectangle can be developed (it may surprise you to discover how easily) and the related Logarithmic Spiral as well (p. 68).

Creating the golden mean and golden rectangle

Fig. 3.4 Development of the Golden Mean and Equiangular Spiral. Adapted from diagrams in texts by Pedoe, Hambidge, Scott.

The classic Greek tools of geometry, the compass and straight edge (no inches necessary!) are all you need. Reading the following description without actually drawing the accompanying shapes and patterns cannot be very satisfying, so if you don't have materials at hand, return when you can join in. [2]

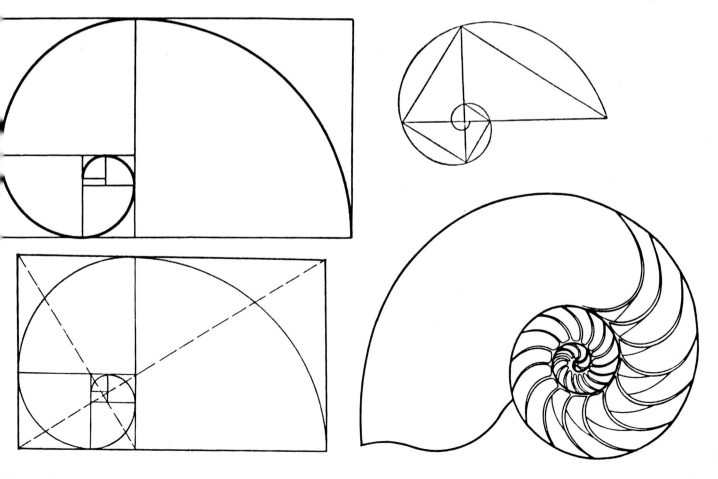

Fig. 3.5 Nautilus Shell. Photograph, American Museum of Natural History.

Fig. 3.6 Henri Matisse, *Design for proposed iron-work grille door*, 1953. Brush and ink, $107\frac{1}{2} \times 43$ ins (272×109 cm). Photograph courtesy: The Marlborough Gallery, New York.

Draw a square on graph paper using an even number of boxes. Place a compass point at the center of the square's base, then open it until your pencil touches the upper right-hand corner. Using this distance as your radius, draw a curve down (toward the right) until it stops at a line which is an extension of the base. From this point, complete a rectangle whose sides are the right side of the original square, a line parallel to this side at the distance marked off by your compass on the extension of the base line, the extension itself and a similar extension of the upper edge of the square (**Fig. 3.4**). You now have two Golden Rectangles, the new shape to the right of the square and the new shape plus the square itself. The base line of the square plus its extension give you a line which is divided at its joining point into two sections, that is, two Golden Sections meeting at their Golden Mean.

Now, draw in the upper part of your smaller Golden Rectangle a square whose side is the length of its smaller edge. The small rectangle left over below is ... another Golden Rectangle! This reduction can continue in theory indefinitely until you reach an imaginary "point rectangle" and infinity! In the other direction, you can add new squares and continue, also without end. This sequence, called "whirling squares" by Jay Hambidge, seems to spin about one central point, never actually reached.

Drawing the equiangular spiral

From the Golden Rectangle it is easy to draw a special curve, the "long slow curve" known as the Equiangular Spiral, Logarithmic Spiral or, in Latin, the almost religious-sounding *spira mirabilis* of the mathematician Bernoulli—the marvelous spiral! The number of natural forms which display this simple but powerful curving line may amaze you. From the nautilus shell (**Fig. 3.5**) to the sunflower (**Fig. 3.13**) and cactus, from our own bony skeleton (**Fig. 3.7**) to that of the dinosaur, the Golden Proportion and Spiral can be seen giving form, elegance and dynamic symmetry to organic life.

Draw a diagonal from the lower left to the upper right corner of your original square. From this point, which is also the top left corner of your next smaller square, draw the diagonal down to the bottom right of the smaller square. Continue to draw out this angled line as it makes an angular spiral through the successive diagonals of each smaller square. Notice that the diagonal of each square intersects the diagonal of its "reciprocal" (smaller in size, similar in shape) square at right angles. If, instead of a diagonal line, you draw a quarter-circle (using the lower right corner of each square as a center or vertex for your compass and the side as a radius, reducing the radius for each smaller square), you will have drawn a perfect, continuous in-curling curve, the famous Golden Spiral (**Fig. 3.5**). [3]

Greek temples and other classical and modern works of visual art and music have been based on the proportions of the Golden Mean and Equiangular Spiral (**Fig. 3.6**). To Vitruvius, without symmetry and proportion, there could be no principles on which to base the design of a temple. Fortunately, such designing was made easier by the beautiful simplicity of the size relationships of the sequential units in the Golden Proportion. The mathematical sequence, called the Summation Series or the Fibonacci Series, is so clear and self-evident you can never forget it. Simply add the first two numbers together to produce a third—for example, 1 plus 2 equal 3—drop the first number and continue; 2 plus 3 equal 5, 3 plus 5 equal 8, and so on. 1, 2, 3, 5, 8, 13, 21, 34, 55 ... to infinity.

This additive sequence has been considered special in the study of botanical and animal form and growth patterns—the size of rootlet in proportion to root, of stem to branch, vein to leaf, and the placement of leaves as they spiral around their stem. (Investigate the term "phyllotaxis.") Look at the proportion of the length of the first small bone in your index finger to the next bone, and of that to the next, and of the next to the metacarpal. Touch that fingertip to your thumb, curve your wrist—your hand folds into the Golden Spiral (**Fig. 3.8**). It is said that Buddha once gave a silent "sermon of the flower" by holding a blossom before his audience (**Fig. 3.9**). Using the Golden Propor-

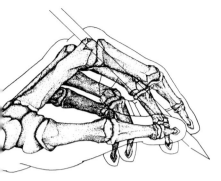

Fig. 3.7 Alix Rehbock, *Drawing of hand with skeleton*, 1978. Pen and ink, $4\frac{1}{2} \times 7$ ins (12 × 18 cm). Courtesy of the artist.

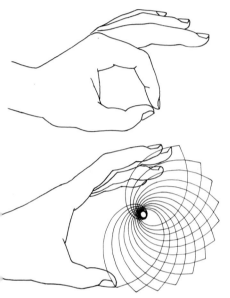

Fig. 3.8 and 3.9 Gyorgy Doczi, *The Hand of Buddha, Unfolding*, from "The Power of Limits" published by Shambhala Publications, Inc., 1981.

tion, architects and others have paid tribute to this ubiquitous, underlying dynamic structure, often with a sense of reverence. Alexander Pope's idea that "man is the measure of all things," the frequent statement that the human body is a temple, and Henri Fabre's finding in number "the key that turns the Universe," all attest to the powerful attraction geometry has held in human history. Among the many books that address this idea in different ways are Robert Lawlor's *Sacred Geometry*, Matila Ghyka's *The Geometry of Art and Life* and Doczi's *The Power of Limits*. Even ideas about reincarnation can be seen as springing from a life in which the unfolding of each new form out of a preceding one is a familiar experience. [4]

To keep this study "in proportion," it should be admitted that there are a number of cautionary pronouncements to be found relating to a too rigid application of the Golden Mean or any formula for beauty or perfection in art. Albrecht Dürer, whose proportional model for human structure is perhaps less familiar than that of Leonardo da Vinci (**Fig. 2.28**), advised us that "the boundary lines of the human figure cannot be drawn with compasses and ruler." In the nineteenth century, John Ruskin was at the forefront of a movement which spoke out against the use of the Golden Mean and other fixed standards in the arts. Rudolf Arnheim points out, "the norm of the oak leaf is not perfectly realized in any one specimen, so no rule of proportion can be expected to appear perfect in any thing ... we seek distinctions between the essential and the accidental ..." Pedoe seems to enjoy his revelation that Le Corbusier's Modulor of human proportions didn't come out "even" until he assumed a standard six-foot (English) height and not the shorter (French) height as the norm for a man. Hermann Weyl, warning us about the "aurea sectio, which has played such a role in attempts to reduce beauty of proportion to a mathematical formula," reminds us that "animals alter the relative proportion of parts as they grow, and so the golden mean is not an idea of a biological type." Kepes urges us to think of biological rules not as those of the module, but "of a kind (such as) the relatedness of neighbors." Oskar Schlemmer's *Man*, a collection of his notes and proportional studies made while teaching at the Bauhaus, can add valuable analyses and observations to this discussion.

After a large number of observers claimed to prefer, among a variety of rectangles, those whose proportions approached the Golden Mean, Fechner found when he measured hundreds of paintings that in practice a much shorter rectangle was chosen. Arnheim explains that in the empty rectangle the relation between length and width is "pleasant enough," but in a composition where every part of the area is to be related to every other, as part of a more closely knit whole, "the distance in the longer dimension would be relatively so large as to be unbridgeable."

EXERCISES

Exercise 1:
Create a simple cartoon whose "funniness" is a result of a discrepancy in scale.

Exercise 2:
Follow the description on p. 68 to draw a set of Golden Rectangles diminishing in size. It may be helpful to work on tracing paper over graph paper until you have made a start. Make sure your first square has an even number of boxes along the length of its sides.

Exercise 3:
Draw a set of "whirling squares" as you did in Exercise 2. Draw the diagonal of each successive square to create an equiangular spiral, starting with largest and continuing as far as you can. Draw another set of squares and draw a quarter-circle in each square, to form a Golden Spiral.

Exercise 4:
Design a representational composition using Equiangular Spirals and Golden Rectangles. Adapt your design using only geometric elements.

Spirals

Fig. 3.10 Archimedean spiral. From Amerindian and New Zealand designs, after Boas.

The special dynamic quality of the spiral derived from the Golden Mean can be seen when compared with the static, same-thickness "coiled rope" of the Archimedean Spiral (**Fig. 3.10**). The difference may be seen as that of a coiled cylinder rather than a coiled cone. The cylinder produces a surface like that of a woven mat, whose diameter grows larger as it increases at a steady pace arithmetically while the so-called Nautilus Spiral (the Logarithmic Spiral) builds in velocity as it grows geometrically. Actually the spiral of the nautilus shell itself is developed in an additive or built-up fashion, unlike

Fig. 3.11 Helix spiral and Penmanship loops, after Doczi and early 20th C. writing manual.

the transitory positioning of an elephant's trunk, to assume the shape of the Equiangular Spiral. "Shells and horns don't alter as they grow," writes D'Arcy Thompson, "each increment is similar to its predecessor, and the whole is just as before." Thompson calls this terminal or asymmetric growth, at one end only. "These forms are not bent into a spiral; they have grown into it. Their non-living parts are successively and permanently laid down." He sees the Logarithmic Spiral as a characteristic of non-living material. The nautilus and other shells build their spiral through accumulation, an accretion of residue resulting from growth and involving the duration that this process requires, adding the dimension of time.

Both kinds of spiral are found in two-dimensional work, the Archimedean being used more often as ornamentation where flatness and stationary position are to be emphasized. But both are true spirals starting from a center, whereas the helix turns like a screw at a constant rate of curvature, having no specific starting or stopping place. Although the helix is a three-dimensional form which can be visualized as a spring, a row of penmanship loops gives a good two-dimensional approximation (**Fig. 3.11**). [5]

On a flat surface, visualize a drawing of the Equiangular Spiral. A photograph of a sectioned Chambered Nautilus shows how clearly this three-dimensional form can be translated onto a plane. You can picture the Logarithmic Spiral either clockwise or counterclockwise as it turns, but can you see them together, overlaid upon one another, dividing a surface into many small rhomboidal modules? Nature has done this very neatly on the face of each sunflower (**Figs. 3.12, 3.13**)! This underlying double spiral structure is often seen in mosaic and paving stone patterns. Spirals may be composed of units, whether sunflower seeds or tesserae; they can also be fluid and continuous as in the snail and the scroll.

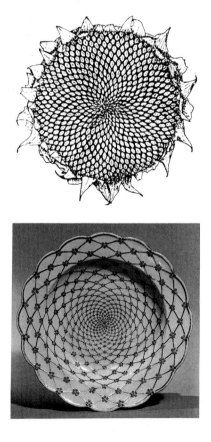

Figs. 3.12 and 3.13 Double spiral, seen in sunflower, model of sunflower and dinner plate. Dinner Plate for Empress Elizabeth I, made by the Imperial Porcelain Factory, St. Petersburg, Russia, c. 1760, porcelain, 10½ ins (26 cm) diameter. Courtesy: The Metropolitan Museum of Art, New York.

EXERCISES

Exercise 5:
Try to draw a smooth row of "Palmer penmanship loops." Then invent your own spiral designs, using all three types of spirals.

Scaling and transformation

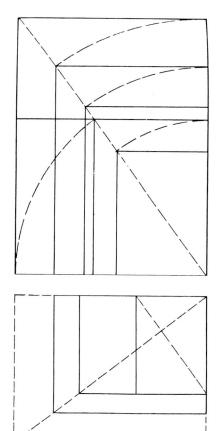

Scaling, or altering the size of a design, can be accomplished easily through the use of the diagonal (**Fig. 3.14**); altering proportions while maintaining some sense of similarity to the original is considerably more difficult (**Fig. 3.16**). Yet D'Arcy Thompson has shown that even this is not beyond the inventiveness of nature. Both ideas can be described in terms of subdivisions of a geometric shape.

To scale a design down thirty percent (or make a thirty percent reduction in its size), a diagonal line is made from lower left to upper right on a sheet of tracing paper placed over a drawing, say $6'' \times 10''$ in size. (Recalling that a proportion is a relationship between two ratios, note that the first ratio is 6:10, that is 6 to 10 or $\frac{6}{10}$.) To reduce one side by 30 percent, a right triangle or a T-square may be held along that edge (the $10''$ vertical) and slowly moved to the $7''$ mark. At this point hold your right triangle on, and perpendicular to, the $10''$ side and draw a horizontal line from the diagonal to the left-hand edge (parallel to the top edge). Moving the triangle to the left, draw a vertical down from the diagonal to the lower edge of your rectangle. The new shape is reduced by 30 percent. Although you know that the vertical length of the smaller shape is $7''$, the length of the smaller side is not immediately clear. So far, your second ratio is incomplete, though you can plainly see the newly scaled shape. You may solve an algebraic equation ($\frac{x}{7} = \frac{6}{10}$) or use a printer's prepared scaling key or chart which displays the math as you turn a wheel or slide a panel. [6] Graphic designers often make several different uses of a single image in this way.

Grids have been used for transferring drawings to canvas, walls and ceilings for centuries (**Fig. 3.15**). Traces of such grids may be seen on frescoes and other large paintings throughout the museums and cathedrals of Europe. Preliminary gridded drawings or sketches were called cartoons. Do you recognize these as the ancestor of our multi-paneled sequential picture story, the comic strip, or single-frame cartoon (p. 223)?

Complete transformation of the original proportions of a design may be difficult to imagine, but the idea came to D'Arcy Thompson toward the end of the nineteenth

Fig. 3.15 (*left*) **Tintoretto**, *Crucifixion*, 16th C. Charcoal on grey paper, $15\frac{1}{2} \times 10\frac{1}{4}$ ins (39×26 cm). Dyce 235. Courtesy: The Trustees of the Victoria and Albert Museum, London.

Fig. 3.16 (*top right*) **D'Arcy Thompson**, *Grid transformations*. From "On Growth and Form," published by Cambridge University Press, revised 1952.

Fig. 3.17 (*bottom right*) **Albrecht Dürer**, *Geometric Distortions of the Head*. From "Four Books of Human Proportions," as shown in Pedoe's "Geometry and the Visual Arts," published by Dover Publications Inc., New York.

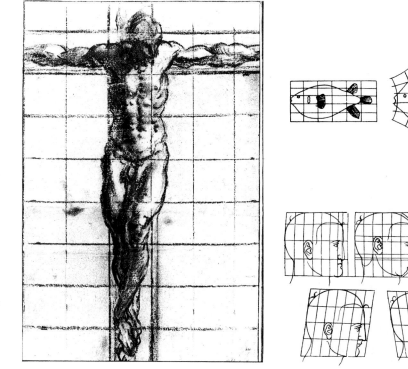

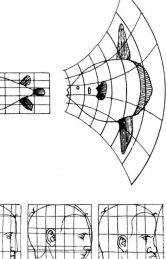

Fig. 3.18 (*right*) **Michael Snow**, *Five Girl Panels*, 1964. Enamel on canvas, 84 × 120 ins (213 × 305 cm). Courtesy: The Isaacs Gallery, Ltd., Toronto.
Fig. 3.19 (*below center*) **Suzanne Valadon**, *Maurice Utrillo and his Grandmother*, 1894. Charcoal on paper, $22\frac{3}{4} \times 15\frac{1}{2}$ (58 × 39 cm). Collection of Mrs. John Hay Whitney.
Fig. 3.20 (*bottom*) **Jean Metzinger**, *Tea Time*, 1911. Oil on wood, $29\frac{3}{4} \times 27\frac{3}{8}$ ins (75.5 × 70 cm). Courtesy: The Philadelphia Museum of Art.

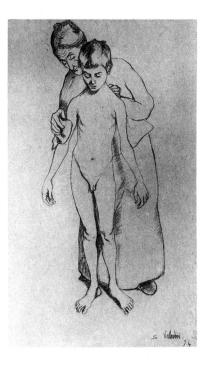

century, as the great naturalist, "to amuse children, would draw a puppy-dog on an in-diarubber and pull it sideways to make a dachshund." Today he might have used a computer. At the time, in studying the comparative anatomical structure of certain fish, he visualized a kind of "transformation of the whole," a change in the shape of one fish into another quite different-looking type by a kind of alteration of a grid on which the two different fish might be drawn (**Fig. 3.16**). He tried changing the rectangular format of the grid to a fan shape or other distorted contour as needed in an attempt to show the relationships between apparently only distantly related individuals. In this way, he showed a remarkable metamorphosis or change in shape, "all of a piece," so that a viewer could visualize the "same" individual, stretched or distended to create variations which were not mere fantasies, but actually to be found in nature. Thompson's remarkable transformations make us aware of the invaluable contribution to art and science that can result from courageous, even seemingly unthinkable, hypotheses. We marvel at the daring of Albrecht Dürer in the sixteenth century in proposing a system of oblique coordinates to construct a grid upon which to change and distort the facial angle of the human head (**Fig. 3.17**). Many modern "innovations," not only Cubism and Geometric Abstraction, owe a great deal to the imagination of such pioneers as Dürer and Thompson (**Fig. 3.18**). While today any design can be modified with precision and almost limitless variety by the "automatic pilot" of computer art, we should recognize the special contributions of those who in earlier times did it the hard way. Some still do. [7]

Consider an "ideally" proportioned figure, according to the "perfect" analysis of da Vinci, Dürer or Le Corbusier. Then visualize the "transformation" of that ideal to produce a figure typical of the proportion favored by a particular artist (**Fig. 3.19**). We can appreciate Lawlor's thought that "our perceived world is [made up] of ... differences that make a difference."

Particularly in Analytical Cubist works, the grid or the restructuring and de-structuring of an object with its surrounding space may be more discernible and dynamic than any specific representation of the subject (**Fig. 3.20**).

EXERCISES

Exercise 6:
Follow the method on p. 71 to make a reduction of 30 percent in the size of a drawing, your own or someone else's.

Exercise 7:
Transform the proportions of a simple design by drawing a grid over the work, then transferring it, unit by unit, to a differently proportioned grid. See how far you can modify your design while still retaining some sense of the original.

Anamorphosis

Fig. 3.21 Anamorphic street sign for bus lane, New York City.

If you have ever driven toward a seemingly random row of parallel lines on the road which all at once came into focus as the word, SLOW, you are familiar with the startling technique used as a secret device by many artists for centuries called "anamorphosis" (**Fig. 3.21**). Leonardo da Vinci may have been the first to attempt this carefully stretched, distorted reproportioning of a drawing so that it could be seen correctly only from an oblique angle with the eye close to the paper (**Fig. 3.22**). Extreme elongation, characteristic of such works, makes them appear meaningless to the uninitiated, but the proper viewing point brings a sudden integration of elements through contracting perspective and the normal proportions of the work appear (**Fig. 3.23**). Anamorphosis demonstrates the close relationship between proportion and perspective; if you apply the proper grid to any anamorphic rendering, you will have a result very like a D'Arcy Thompson "transformation." [8]

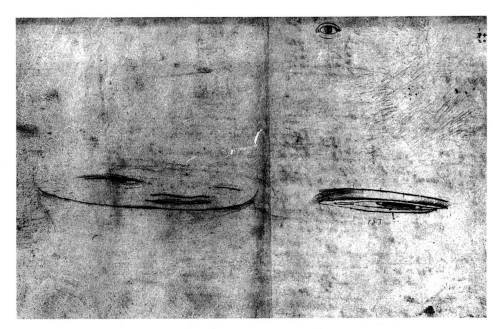

Fig. 3.22 **Leonardo da Vinci**, *Anamorphic Sketches of a Child's Head and an Eye.* Courtesy: Biblioteca Ambrosiana, Milan.

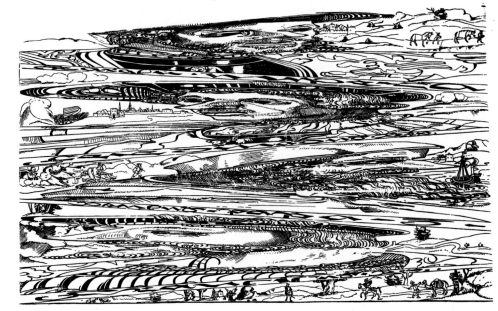

Fig. 3.23 **Erhard Schön**, *Anamorphic portraits of Charles V, Ferdinand of Austria, Pope Paul III and Francis I*, c. 1535. Woodcut, $17\frac{3}{8} \times 29\frac{1}{2}$ ins (44×75 cm). Courtesy: Graphische Sammlung, Albertina, Vienna.

Fig. 3.24 *(opposite, top)* **Hans Holbein**, *The Ambassadors*, 1533. Oil on panel, $81\frac{1}{2} \times 82\frac{1}{2}$ ins (207×209 cm). Courtesy: The Trustees, The National Gallery, London.
Fig. 3.25 *(opposite, bottom)* **Juan Gris**, *The Watch*, 1912. Oil and papier collé on canvas. Private collection.

Fig. 3.26 *(right)* **Wassily Kandinsky**, *Improvisation #30*, 1913. Oil on canvas, $43\frac{1}{4} \times 43\frac{3}{4}$ ins (110×111 cm). Courtesy: Art Institute of Chicago, Arthur Jerome Eddy Memorial Collection.

Hans Holbein used this technique as a way of adding a private message to an otherwise straightforward work, hiding a skull, symbol of mortality and transience, in his painting *The Ambassadors* (**Fig. 3.24**).

Some anamorphic designs are centered about a blank circle and can be condensed into focus by the use of a mirrored or mylar cylinder. The secrecy and concealment emphasized by this technique have made it popular with those whose messages were theological, political or erotic.

The secret of proportion seems to lie not in single shapes, but in the relationships between them. Such a "grasp of relations, at once intuitive," was sensed by the writer André Gide as a major factor in his art. Dürer himself, often admired for his precision and scientific approach to art, believed that, if an artist has "learned the art of measurement and therefore acquired theory and practice together . . . then it is not always necessary to measure . . . for thy acquired art endows thee with a correct eye."

A growing confidence in your own sense of proportion is vital. Measure and then put measurement aside, relying on your intuitive tendency toward satisfying visual relationships. You will know when the work "holds still," revealing its structure as complete—when together you and your work are "in synch," and everything does seem to be in proportion (**Figs. 3.25, 3.26**).

EXERCISES

Exercise 8:
Try to create an anamorphic drawing.

Chapter Four

DIMENSIONS OF SPACE

Fig. 4.1   Edouard Vuillard, *Seated Girl*,
1891. Brush and ink, traces of pencil,
$7\frac{1}{8} \times 7\frac{1}{8}$ ins (18 × 18 cm). Collection: Mr and
Mrs. Alfred R. Stern.

Dimensions of space: 1, 2, 3 and more

At this *point*, a few *lines* on space itself should help *shape* those features that distinguish one dimension from another. Since our concern is with two-dimensional design, it would be good to discover just what there are two of, but the boundary between one dimension and the next may not always show itself clearly (**Figs. 4.1, 4.4**). Indeed, several original thinkers have developed the idea of in-between, fractional dimensions, helpful in describing the structure of space.

Empty, undetermined, infinite space is a dazzling concept. The philosopher Kant thought it a creation of our own minds, "an ineluctable modality of our perception." Does every work of art create its own universe? The potentiality, the room in which to create, intrigues artists. Max Beckmann, the painter, revered "space and space again, the infinite deity, which surrounds us and in which we ourselves are contained." More scientifically, Hermann Weyl announced that "empty space has a very high order of symmetry, for every point is like any other, and at any point there is no intrinsic difference between the several directions."

The idea that space and time do not have actual existence, but are "forms of the mind and not external to it as they appear to be," has been made visual in much twentieth-century painting and sculpture, originally interpreted by the Cubists (**Fig. 5.42**). "Distance or nearness in actual space makes no difference, since all points are merely differentiations of a single space we hold within (our) mind as an always-present mental world" (Wilson). "Space then becomes something more than a void in which to roam about . . . [but] a comprehensive and enclosed [place], within which [we] engage" (Dewey). Not a passive receptacle, space may be seen as an element interacting with matter.

Eastern and Western ideas about space

In the East, space is seen as an extension, created by unfolding through the dimensions, involving varying degrees of freedom to move, to develop in a particular direction. Traditionally, the Western "three dimensions" describe three mutually perpendicular types of motion, three degrees of freedom. Any point in this space can be reached by combining these directions: up/down, left/right, advancing/receding.

Locating a point in space

How may we locate a specific point in space at which to begin? Some pre-existing reference, some landmark, must be established or we cannot say where our point is. On a rectangular piece of paper (this page, for example), we can specify a point: three inches below the top, two inches in from the left. The position of the paper in the universe does not matter. It could be tacked to the wall or flying out the window, but the spot *on the paper* is still in the same spot *on the paper*!

Since we accept the idea of the continuous orbital motion of the planets and our solar system throughout the expanse of the universe, there is no real pinning down of a particular point, *except in reference to a given place or object*. The point itself has no dimension and cannot be seen; it has no physical existence. As an idea it exists, perhaps with more permanence and meaning than a merely temporal being. We will return to this point.

The first dimension

The usual description of the first dimension, as the path of a moving point, is misleading, for we visualize a path or track as having a certain width (**Fig. 1.28**). If a line has only length, moving from one point to another, its degree of freedom is simply forward and back. With no thickness at all, how can a line be seen (**Fig. 1.28**)? Can an artist use this kind of intangible length? Although a line as such cannot be seen, any more than the elusive point, its exact place, direction and extent may be made visible by treating the space on one side of it differently from the space on the other side. [1]

Can we say that line, *purely*, may be seen as *the edge of shape* (**Fig. 4.2**) and we actually see the *space* on either side of the line, not the line itself? So, in order to see or create a one-dimensional line, we move into the next dimensional realm, that of plane shape or flat surface area. Matisse understood this perfectly (**Fig. 0.7**)!

Enclosing shapes within lines

If a straight line moves only in one "self-covering" direction with no curve or bend, it cannot enclose a shape. What is the smallest number of straight lines needed to contain a space? [2] If the lines are perpendicular? Of course, a single curved line can enclose a shape easily.

Between two points only one straight line can be imagined, but any number of curved or irregular lines may be invented. [3]

EXERCISES

Exercise 1:
Paint an area of color spreading out until it stops at what seems to be the inner edge (or outline) of a circle.

Exercise 2:
Enclose a shape with the fewest possible straight lines.

Exercise 3:
With an X-Acto knife or pair of scissors show how many ways you can connect or "draw a line" between two points a given distance apart.

Fig. 4.2   Cynthia Dantzic, page from "What Can You See?" a book of woodcuts, 1963.

The second dimension

Picture a line between two points in space, placed four inches apart. This must be seen with the inner eye. Move this line in one smooth motion away from itself, something like unrolling a window shade, and stop exactly six inches from your starting place, creating a two-dimensional shape, a rectangle four by six inches. This shape is still in your mind. Now that we have imagined a flat shape, are we in the visible world; can we draw or paint on the surface just put together? Not until that shape is at the outer surface of an actual three-dimensional form will we be able to touch, move, see it in a physical sense.

Moving into the third dimension

Again, we must move into the dimension beyond in order to appreciate the special qualities of the one being considered. When the third dimension or depth of an object is merely the thickness of paper, it is easily ignored, but we must acknowledge its existence as the carrier of the surface being seen and used. In fact, it is only through the power of sight that the two-dimensional world may be experienced. The texture or feel of a surface may be known through touch, but all differences of tone, color and linear subdivision that are two-dimensional have their identity through visual experience alone. In the words of Madison Avenue, they must be seen to be appreciated! In the dark, all paintings disappear!

The sequence of dimensionality

Since two-dimensionality is our subject, why not stop here, before we move into the sphere of the third dimension or, as indicated, more? To make sense of each dimension and to consider the new idea of possible transitional dimensions, we need to get a sense of the sequence of dimensionality, stepping from each to the next and looking backward to re-view the picture. This may carry us out beyond the third dimension to the Einsteinian fourth, but I promise we will stop this side of the Twilight Zone!

The journey from a single point through the fourth dimension can be shown rather simply, starting with one agreed-upon location. Imagine the intersection of two lines, anywhere; X marks the spot. If those lines are along the top and the right-hand edges of this page, our spot is at the upper right-hand corner. Move the spot to the left and stop at that corner to identify a one-dimensional line, along the top edge. Move that line down along the surface of the page to the bottom edge to give us the second dimension, perpendicular to the first, with length and width. Picture this plane at the level of the page, pushing slowly down through the book, a page at a time in imagination, until it rests at the surface of the back cover, and you will have produced a tangible, three-dimensional object, a volume.

Now you see why a book is known as a volume! It occupies or fills space, a rectangular solid of otherwise empty air. Each dimension clearly moves at right angles to the others. Holding the book still, can we see the back cover or sides? As with any three-dimensional form, this is not possible.

Adding the idea of time

The perception of point, line and shape can be accomplished from a single location. There need be no change of position between the eye and what it sees, except as we sweep our field of vision over the surface. This is not true of the perception of three-

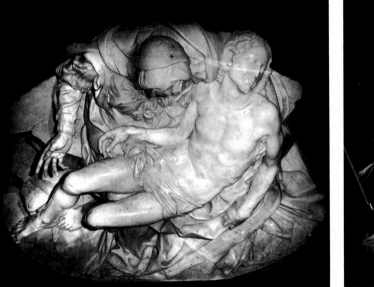

Fig. 4.3 Michelangelo's, *Pietà*, 1499. White Carrara marble, 68½ ins (174 cm) high. Photographs © 1975 by Robert Hupka from his book "Michelangelo, Pietà", published by Crown Publishers Inc., New York. Courtesy of the photographer.

dimensional objects in space. We can see one view or aspect of such a form, but there is no way to perceive its full three-dimensionality unless the form moves in space to reveal its other, hidden, aspects—or unless we move through space around it. Such movement will require a certain amount of *time* at a certain rate of speed, or velocity. Recognizing the inseparability of what we call three-dimensional space, existing as a unified field within a space/time continuum, brings us into the fourth dimension.

For the artist, the idea of a four-dimensional space/time continuum has opened new worlds, literally. In painting, the attempt to show objects more fully, from many sides at once, from many viewpoints at the same moment, gave inspiration first to the Cubists. Although the uninitiated may question a figure with three eyes or other parts that do not seem to align themselves correctly from a single focal point, the enlightened perceiver recognizes varying views of the subject and its surrounding environment, analyzed, edited, rearranged on a two-dimensional canvas. For perhaps the first time the viewer can sense in the round, and actual motion, on a flat surface (**Fig. 8.5**). [4]

Showing three-dimensional objects in two dimensions

Since a three-dimensional form must be seen all around as it or its observer moves through space, how can the single stopped view of a photograph communicate the totality of a work of sculpture? It cannot. How many believe they have seen Michelangelo's *Pietà*, when they are familiar only with one static, frontal image out of the fullness of the work's swirling spiral through space and time (**Fig. 4.3**)? In this context, how significant is the quest of the photographer Henri Cartier-Bresson for that critical "decisive moment" when, between the past and the future, one instant can be frozen at the peak of an action or the most expressive coming together of elements (**Fig. 15.46**)! [5]

EXERCISES

Exercise 4:
Analyze Cubist works for the inclusion of the idea of the fourth dimension. Then draw an object showing this idea.

Exercise 5:
Study a three-dimensional object from many viewing points. Select the "best" vantage point for a two-dimensional study and make the study. Change your "spot," and make another.

Partial dimensions

Three-dimensional works that need a new category

Fig. 4.4 *Tji Wara*, Bambara antelope head carving, wood, Mali, 20th C. 25 ins (63.5 cm) high. Collection: C. and J. Dantzic.

Would you agree that any work of art which can be shown satisfactorily through a single photographic image cannot truly exist as a sculptural form-in-space? Consider the carved Tji Wara antelope form, seen in profile or silhouette (**Fig. 4.4**). Can you visualize what this piece looks like from the other side? Easily. A reversed image, but the same. Front or back views reveal little but the thickness of the original piece of wood. Since the Tji Wara is worn on the head as part of a costume, no view is intended from below, and seen from above the form is not at all clear. This is a work of startling pattern and design, rich in visual qualities. Would you call it a fully realized three-dimensional object? Many so-called sculptures share its visually flat, one-viewpoint conception. With minimal thickness to support them physically, such stamped-out, cookie-cutter objects exist somewhere between the single surface of two-dimensionality and the completely continuous form-in-space identity of the three-dimensional world. May we propose the category of two-and-a-half dimensions for such works? [6]

Fully realized three-dimensional works

Compare the Tji Wara, in terms of dimensionality, with a construction by José de Rivera (**Fig. 4.5**). Would questions about the front or back of this work make sense? How many separate two-dimensional views might be shown without repetition? How many would be necessary to show the entire work? Is such a thing possible? Study the sequence of photographs of this form. Can you say which view shows the real or best picture of the sculpture? Does this question make any more sense than a search for front or back? The surprise, the constantly new and unexpected delight of unfolding form, marks a fully orchestrated work, aware of its existence within the space/time continuum.

Fig. 4.5 **José de Rivera**, *Construction #190*, 1980. Stainless steel, $27\frac{1}{2} \times 43 \times 33$ ins (70 × 109 × 84 cm). Private Collector. Photographs courtesy: The Grace Borgenicht Gallery, New York.

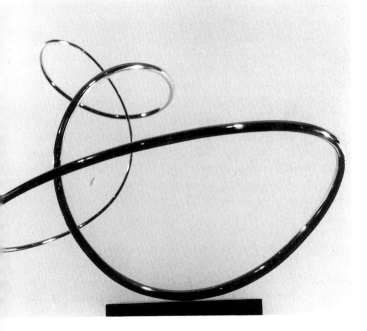

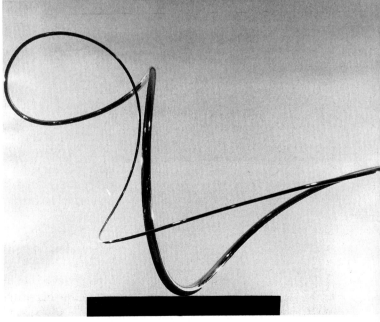

Fig. 4.6   Mask, Namua, Papua, New Guinea. Painted bark, cloth and cane, 8 ft (2.4 m) high. Courtesy: National Museum of Ireland, Dublin.

Fig. 4.7   Iroquois bone comb, late 19th C. Collection: C. and J. Dantzic.

Fig. 4.8   **Henri Matisse**, *The Back III*, 1916. Bronze, 74 × 44 × 6 ins (188 × 112 × 15 cm). Courtesy: The Museum of Modern Art, Mrs. Simon Guggenheim Fund.

Two-and-a-half dimensions considered

In our new two-and-a-half-dimensional space we might count works of bas-relief, which contain some elements that spring from the flat surface yet make no effort to complete their three-dimensionality (**Fig. 4.8**). The wall or panel support appears to intersect them, and if we could get behind them, we would see the rest. [7]

The idea of space-planes

The Tji Wara and Iroquois comb (**Fig. 4.7**) contain many openings, or shapes of "empty" space. These planes of space, the thickness of the wood or bone itself, are experienced as somehow different from the outer space surrounding the work, and are clearly part of the object. Instead of thinking of such space planes as *empty*, try to consider them as *unfilled* planes, interacting in an equal and opposite way with planes filled with material. This eliminates the judgmental connotation of terms such as Negative and Positive Space.

Where does the object end

At the outer edge of two or two-and-a-half dimensional forms, openings into the edge of the contour may introduce an ambiguous, transitional kind of shape for which it is not always possible to determine an exact boundary between contained and containing space. The interlocking of filled and unfilled shapes gives unity and cohesiveness to a work, holding its parts in place and determining the overall structure. In sculpture, the unfilled spaces within a work may subtly blend into the space around it (in theory the rest of the universe, but actually as much of the outer space as the eye can engage). Look for similarities in works that at first seem to be unrelated or to exist in different dimensionalities. Visualize the scissors of Matisse (**Fig. 0.7**) at work along the periphery of the Tji Wara, especially as the "background" becomes enmeshed in the forms of the antelope's mane and tail.

Other in-between dimensions

As the idea of a transition between two and three dimensions helps us to understand each dimension individually, it may be of value to consider other "in-between" dimensions. Starting as small as possible with no dimension at all, a point has no degree of freedom (unless we can think of it as a sort of on-and-off switch, now located in space, now vanished). Once we mark the spot, as with a pencil, no matter how small a dot we apply, if that spot can be seen, it must have extent, a shape, two dimensions.

A canvas or any picture plane contains many potential points, such as its center, corners, the midpoint of each edge. Although these are fixed and the corners may actually be identified, they have no measurable dimension. Any mark made on a surface must have some minimal shape, but the small point/dot—acting only to identify a place, not to occupy an area—could be considered as more than an incorporeal point yet less than a shape. We might assign to it the status of $\frac{1}{2}$D, half a dimension. A cluster of point/dots may create a sense of field or area of flat space without a clearly defined boundary or outer edge. Each point/dot may be a minuscule geometric shape, such as a circle, or an amorphous, shapeless thing, giving a diffuse texture rather than an even pattern. Aligned in a row or following a given path, a sequence of points/dots will delineate a line, drawing the eye from one spot to the next (**Fig. 1.2**).

A constellation of stars in the night sky, seen as a celestial follow-the-dots configuration, shows the importance of scale in our evaluation of visual elements. In a photograph of the night sky each luminous point represents an object whose size may be many times that of our sun, and the line we visualize connecting them, as a kind of cosmic drawing, would be millions of miles in width! It is in our mind's eye that meaningful size or dimension exist.

One-and-a-half dimensions

Somewhere between the "breadthless length" defined by Euclid as one-dimensional line and the contained, boundaried surface expanse called two-dimensional space, there is surely a special place for the kinds of linear, edged markings applied to paper and canvas by pen, pencil and brush. Shall we call these shaped line, applied line, or perhaps a transitional form having one-and-a-half dimensions? The subtle change from edge/line to shape/line to shape can be so gradual that line becomes shape without our awareness. In the woodcut shown in **Fig. 4.9**, follow the background shape between the bear's hind legs as it thins to become the outline of one leg. Find several other places in this print where shape thins to shape/line and melts to edge/line. Can you always tell line from shape (**Fig. 4.2**)? **[8]**

The shaped line in design

Artists often emphasize the variable thickness of applied line and use implements constructed to spread apart with the application of pressure, creating more space between their edges, and therefore a wider line. Since this principle is the basis for the pressure-sensitive modulations in Asian brush-writing or calligraphy, such drawn linear work is often said to display calligraphic line, regardless of size, material or imagery. Would you call the Coca-Cola logo (**Fig. 4.10**) calligraphic line, shape or both? What of the ribbon-like painting of the dimension-conscious de Rivera (**Fig. 4.11**)?

Tom Wesselman calls his laser-cut steel lines, "drawings," his combined shape-and-linear works, "paintings" (**Fig. 4.12**). If his "drawings" were placed freestanding in space, would they become "sculptures?"

Stripe/line

Are stripes shaped lines or linear shapes? Their very ambiguity may account for their frequent use by non-representational artists.

A field of stripe/lines can give a sense of shape, softly melting with the ground of the paper or canvas. In the drawings by Millet (**Fig. 1.16**) and Harold Altman (**Fig. 4.13**) we find a shared understanding of this graphic idea which transcends the century between their creation. **[9]**

Weaving as linear surface

Weaving has been called a *linear surface*, since it exists as the result of a continuous path, looping and overlapping in a single motion to cover a field or area (**Fig. 4.14**). Knitting and crocheting are other techniques for drawing one linear element into a field or a series of repeated designs, generally over a flat space. They may also extend over cylindrical and other rounded forms, in the third dimension. Just as in a spider's

Fig. 4.9 F. Morgan, *Polar Bear*. Woodcut, undated, Alaskan. Collection: C. and J. Dantzic.

Fig. 4.10 Logo of the Coca Cola Company.

Fig. 4.11 **José de Rivera**, *Untitled Painting*, 1945. Oil on canvas, 24 × 24 ins (61 × 61 cm). Collection of Marilyn and Lucian Krukowski. Photograph by Lucian Krukowski.

Fig. 4.12 **Tom Wesselman**, *Monica Lying on a Blanket*, 1988. Enamel on laser-cut steel, 21 × 40 ins (53 × 102 cm). Courtesy: Sidney Janis Gallery.

Fig. 4.13 (*right*) **Harold Altman**, *Matriarch*, 1961. Felt pen drawing, 16 × 20 ins (40.5 × 51 cm). Courtesy: Philadelphia Museum of Art.

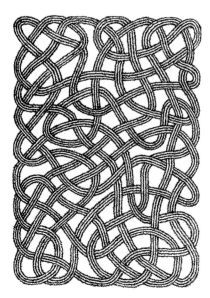

Fig. 4.14 **Anni Albers**, *Drawing for Nylon Rug*, 1959. Pencil, pen and ink on paper, 15 × 11 ⅛ ins (38 × 29 cm). Courtesy of the artist.

web, the thread is actually a miniature cylinder, but we may think of these as various kinds of line. [10]

Again, relative size, or scale, comes into the picture, and we can agree with the philosopher, Alfred North Whitehead that "accuracy essentially collapses at some stage of inquiry." Accuracy, after all, is not necessarily a concern of those fashioning art works—that is, accuracy of dimensional category. For those who have agreed to be frequent page-turners, see the discussion of fractals and the question regarding the length of the coastline of Britain (**Fig. 13.26**).

The surface of a sphere—how many dimensions?

Mathematicians such as Arthur Loeb see the *surface* of a sphere or polyhedron (a many-faceted solid figure such as a pyramid or cube) as two-dimensional. Even though these solids are not flat, movement upon them extends in only two perpendicular directions, never entering the depth of the form they surround. Such surfaces act as a planar skin. A painting may be seen as two-dimensional although it covers the surface of a sphere, if we think of space in this way (**Fig. 4.15**). After all, to locate a point on the surface of the ocean, a sea captain must find the intersection of two lines, longitude and latitude, at right angles, though the Earth is very like a globe. A deep-sea diver, however, enters the third dimension by leaving the surface of the sphere. [11]

Fig. 4.15 **Jacqueline Lima**, *Painting on a Sphere*, 1981. Oil on wood, sphere, 10 ins (25.5 cm) diameter. Courtesy of the artist.

EXERCISES

Exercise 6:
Consider the idea of two-and-a-half dimensions. Identify works in this new category.

Exercise 7:
Using geometric or other cookie cutters and slabs of clay, create two-and-a-half-dimensional forms.

Exercise 8:
Find examples of shape/line and edge/line in woodcuts of Nolde, Frasconi, Baskin.

Exercise 9:
Invent your own monochromatic or full palette stripe-line studies in design or in drawing.

Exercise 10:
Create a linear surface with any tools or materials. Or watch a skilled knitter or crocheter at work, and create a related image.

Exercise 11:
Create a two-dimensional work on the surface of a sphere, or polyhedron.

Islamic ideas of dimension

Dimensionality from a Western point of view emphasizes the perpendicular and the right angle. Having introduced the rounded form of the sphere, let us look at space from a different perspective, that of ancient Islam, where the circle, not the square or rectangle, is the primary two-dimensional shape, with its center symbolically the still, eternal focal point of the universe. To show this, the Islamic designer starts with the same "luminous point" with no dimensions, extending it in a single direction to stop at a second point, along a line. Holding the original point still, as a center, and moving the line from its outer point only in an arc, as with a compass, "rotation takes place, to encompass the next domain—an area," (Keith Critchlow) which is seen as a circle!

The mandala

The mandala, or circular "pattern of wholeness," has been employed as a format with mystical and religious associations by many different groups of worshipers and artists (**Fig. 2.21**). Microscopic images of organic and near-atomic structures reveal mandala-like design. Dante constructed his vision of Hell, Purgatory and Paradise on three inter-related mandala patterns, beginning with the sequentially deeper nine circles of the Inferno. The blossom extended by Buddha (**Fig. 3.9**) as his silent "flower sermon" re-iterates the mandala's circle. [12].

EXERCISES

Exercise 12:
With a compass create mandala patterns.

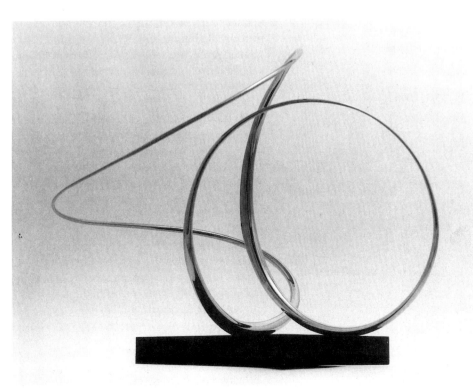

Fig. 4.16 José de Rivera, *Construction #1, Homage to the World of Minkowski*, 1955. Stainless steel, $19\frac{1}{2} \times 21\frac{1}{2} \times 15\frac{1}{2}$ ins ($49.5 \times 54.5 \times 39$ cm). Courtesy: Metropolitan Museum of Art, New York. Photograph courtesy: Grace Borgenicht Gallery, New York.

Fig. 4.17 Albert Kotin, *Modesty*, undated.
Oil on canvas, 40 × 48 ins (102 × 122 cm).
Courtesy of Charles A. Winter and of the
Artfull Eye Gallery.

A dimensional continuum

We can see a continuous flow from one dimension to the next. From the starting point to the partially realized dot with less than one dimension, to the first relationship, the connecting of two points, having the single dimensions of length and acting as an edge between separate areas, we move to the shaped line with perhaps a dimension and a half. Next, clearly within a containing edge, is the shape displaying two perpendicular, measurable dimensions. With a minimal thickness to lend physical support, we may then identify the freestanding but conceptually profiled two-and-a-half-dimensional shaped form, and finally, existing in a fully rounded space/time continuum, the three-dimensional form.

One of José de Rivera's most celebrated constructions, *Homage to the World of Minkowski* (**Fig. 4.16**), was dedicated to the mathematician who recognized that "Space and Time separation have vanished into the merest shadows and only a sort of combination of the two preserves any reality." Whitehead, educator and philosopher, knew that "we live in durations, not in points." The General Semanticist S.I. Hayakawa wrote, "reorganization of our visual habits [so that we] perceive not isolated 'things' in 'space' but structure, order, and the relatedness of events in space-time, is the most profound kind of revolution possible ... a revolution long overdue not only in art but in all our experience." [13]

It is often arbitrary to assign exact dimensionality to new kinds of works created by artists today. Does this matter? Enrichment of our perception and experience certainly is more to the point. This may be what the painter Al Kotin had in mind when he meticulously inscribed on one of his two-panel paintings (**Fig. 4.17**), "Scientists ... speak knowingly of the fourth dimension; I try for only one."

EXERCISES

Exercise 13:
Create a work showing the interdependence of
the many dimensions of Time/Space.

Chapter Five

APPEARANCE OF SPACE: THROUGH SIZE AND PLACEMENT

Fig. 5.1 **William Hogarth**, *Satire on False Perspective*, 1753. Engraving, $8\frac{1}{4} \times 6\frac{1}{4}$ ins (21 × 16 cm). Courtesy: The Trustees of the British Museum. London.

The look of space

The appearance of three-dimensional space on a plane surface can never give the actual "illusion" of depth experienced in viewing a hologram, 3-D movie (the kind you see through red and green glasses), or even an old-fashioned stereopticon viewer.

A picture is said to be worth a thousand words, but the novelist Ross MacDonald, in fewer than thirty-five words, paints a picture to open space before us in a wide swath, then abruptly flattens the picture plane in the reader's mind:

> *The living room commanded a broad view of the sea, which seemed from this height to slant up to the horizon. A few white sails clung to it like moths on a blue window.*

For the visual artist to achieve the look of deep space, or of a flat surface, elements on the page or canvas must be adjusted to work together to "release new perception." To some, "perspective" includes any means of creating the appearance of space. However, we can isolate many distinct ideas and techniques that may be identified in the works of others, or await one's own use.

You will rarely encounter any of these alone in a design or painting; in fact, it is difficult to select an example of one that doesn't show several others as well. In a delightful scene (**Fig. 5.1**), William Hogarth thoroughly confuses and amuses us by applying a number of perspective techniques just a bit incorrectly, misaligned, or of the wrong size, so that the work as a whole doesn't "work" in space as we would expect. He was surely the eighteenth-century counterpart of the painstakingly misleading M. C. Escher, our twentieth-century master of rearranged perception. Escher's staircase and waterfall (**Fig. 5.2**), remaining perfectly level at the same time that they ascend and

Fig. 5.2 Maurits C. Escher, *Waterfall*, 1961. Lithograph, $15 \times 11\frac{3}{4}$ ins (38×30 cm). Courtesy: Haags Gemeentemuseum, The Hague.

Fig. 5.3 Fritz Glarner, *Relational Painting*, 1949–51. Oil on canvas, 65 × 52 ins (165 × 132 cm). Collection: Whitney Museum of American Art. Photograph: Geoffrey Clements.

descend several stories, is an example of the kind of wit and wonder that would have delighted the experimental Hogarth.

Before investigating the several ways to break out of, or to push into, the level surface of the canvas, we might consider just what it is that creates the look of flatness, the belief that there is no depth into which we gaze, but that a kind of window shade has been drawn, on whose surface the painting exists. We are, in effect, looking not *through* but *at* the "looking glass" itself, upon which Lewis Carroll played with elaborately calculated adventures for the many-dimensional Alice of his Wonderland.

Visualize a three-dimensional cube in space, stopping directly before your eye so you see only one square face, the other five hidden from view. Close one mental "eye" to produce a monocular, two-dimensional effect. How can you tell that the rest of the cube is "there," if all you see is the surface perpendicular to your viewpoint? Flatness is experienced by a frontal, head-on viewing point which obscures the three-dimensionality of the object. You would see the same square drawn on a sheet of paper; but the moment the object is shown tipped or turned to reveal one of its other faces, its square shape must be modified to acknowledge perspective's converging parallels, and the flatness of perpendicular frontality is gone. This is the reason for the use of the square and rectangle by most geometric abstractionists, who recognize that any angle other than the right angle will produce an illusion of movement away from the frontal position and suggest space opening into the picture plane.

The term "picture plane" describes the flat frontal surface of a page or canvas with three-dimensional space extending in front of it and suggested behind it. We may either emphasize and reinforce that flatness or suggest the illusion of space so as to treat the canvas as a mirror or a window. The former treatment is called "respecting the picture plane," a major concern of many visual artists. Fritz Glarner introduces slight diagonals into his planar forms, so that, even with his allegiance to the pure primary colors and geometrically balanced structure of the "neo-plasticists" such as Mondrian, true picture-plane flatness eludes him (**Fig. 5.3**).

Overlap

If any flat, frontal view is to be maintained as completely two-dimensional, its entire contour or outline must be visible. Any portion shown as incomplete, such as that part of a square left over when a smaller square is placed in one corner, makes the complete shape (in this case the smaller square) seem to be in front of the incomplete (L-shaped) form, partially obscuring a corner of that larger square. The smaller shape looks as though it is overlapping and in front of the larger incomplete shape. For this reason complete rectangles and squares are used by most geometric abstractionists and the left-over L-shape is avoided. As a compositional challenge, the "L" may be resolved in a variety of ways.

In the earliest recorded two-dimensional works, cave paintings in Spain and France, there are numerous examples of incomplete outline, showing all or part of one animal's shape hidden or masked by the contour of another that is seen as in front of the unfinished individual. Space is sensed between the two animals, both of which are intended to be thought of as whole. This overlapping technique may be at least 30,000 years old!

Many centuries later, the Egyptians adopted a more literal approach to the blocking out of parts, particularly in representing the figure. They realized that in an incomplete outline unseen portions of the figure may seem to disappear. The religious significance of these figures required that there be no misunderstanding about their completeness and perfection. Therefore, even in a frontal view, feet are shown in profile, the maximally visible position, and in profile views the hands are depicted fully fingered. Faces are shown in profile with all features indicated, but in order to display the eye most completely, it is seen as from the front. Each figure is arranged to show as much of the body as possible (**Fig. 5.4**). All these requirements created a stylized, flat, abstract imagery, not seen again until the twentieth century with the work of Pablo Picasso and other "modern" painters (**Fig. 5.5**).

In his classic *The Natural Way to Draw*, Kimon Nicolaides shows how misreading of form may occur when, in placing one object "behind" another, blocking part of the more distant subject's outline, a new "double silhouette," tying together both contours in one continuous line, is inadvertently created (**Fig. 5.6**). When suggesting space by hiding part of a form, be sure to reinforce the use of overlap and not to counteract it, unless you intend a flat, decorative reading of shapes in an inlaid or jigsaw puzzle fashion.

Fig. 5.4 (*bottom left*) Egyptian banquet scene. Courtesy: The British Museum, London.
Fig. 5.5 (*bottom right*) **Pablo Picasso**, *Lady With a Fan*, 1905. Oil on canvas, $39\frac{1}{2} \times 32$ ins (100×81 cm) Courtesy: National Gallery of Art, Washington. Gift of the W. Averill Harriman foundation in memory of Marie N. Harriman.
Fig. 5.6 **Kimon Nicolaides**, *Two Apples, showing the difference between drawing the contour following the sense of touch, rather than the outline following the eye*. Figures 1, 2 and 3 in "The Natural Way to Draw", published by Houghton Mifflin Company, ©1941 and renewed 1969 by Anne Nicoläides.

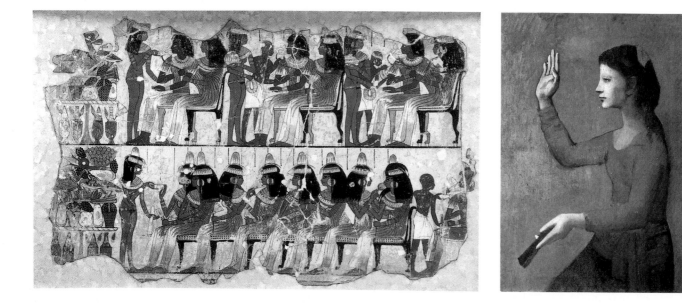

If the complete contours of two overlapping forms are depicted, how can we know which object is to be seen in front? In such X-ray views, quite often seen in Australian "aboriginal" art, not only is transparency suggested but also an ambiguity of spatial placement (**Fig. 5.7**). This so-called primitive idea appealed to the Cubists and others as a way to show two things, or two views of one thing, occupying the same space at the same time (**Fig. 5.8**). Overlap, either opaque or transparent, frequently combines with other techniques to create the appearance of an even deeper field of space, moving into the picture and off the flat surface of the plane (**Fig. 5.9**). [1]

Fig. 5.7 *Kangaroo*, X-Ray style Bark Painting, Australia. Unknown Jaako artist, undated. Courtesy: South Australia Museum.

Fig. 5.8 (*above right*) **Paul Klee**, *She Bellows, We Play*, (detail), 1928. Oil on canvas, $17\frac{1}{8} \times 22\frac{1}{4}$ ins (43.5×56.5 cm). Courtesy: Paul Klee Foundation, Museum of Fine Arts, Berne.

Fig. 5.9 **Peter Rigby**, page from "The Chinese Word for Horse and Other Stories" by John Lewis. Calligraphic illustration, published by Schocken Books, 1980.

He kept on hiding as he watched, but nevertheless, he began to enjoy watching.

The horse swished his tail admiringly, while the man swished his sword. The man heard the horse's tail and said what a beautiful echo.

Days passed, and the man was so happy swishing his sword that he didn't take heed of the change in the weather.

Reduction in size

When two same-size subjects are shown overlapping, they are seen as close in space, perhaps touching. Reduction in the size of the more "distant" figure increases the apparent distance between the two. This continues to be so even when both are depicted in full outline with no overlap, as objects appear to diminish in size as they move away from us (**Fig. 5.10**).

Even in abstract art, whether geometric or more loosely defined, similar shapes will tend to space themselves according to "size place," moving off into the distance. This effect is enhanced by others, particularly advancing and receding color, as in the works of Hans Hofmann and others (**Fig. 11.1**).

Often the Egyptians avoided spatial illusion by placing a row of adjacent figures of the same size along a horizontal line—something like a stage apron—or in bands or tiers, regardless of the activity being described (p.90). [2]

EXERCISES

Exercise 1:
Make two drawings of overlapping objects so that first one object then the other appears nearer.

Exercise 2:
Arrange similar shapes of different size in a composition to show maximum depth through size discrepancy.

Fig. 5.10 **André Masson**, *Haystacks*, 1946.
Chinese ink, $23 \times 18\frac{1}{8}$ ins (58.5×46 cm).
Collection: Annick and Pierre Berès.
Courtesy: Hermann, Paris.

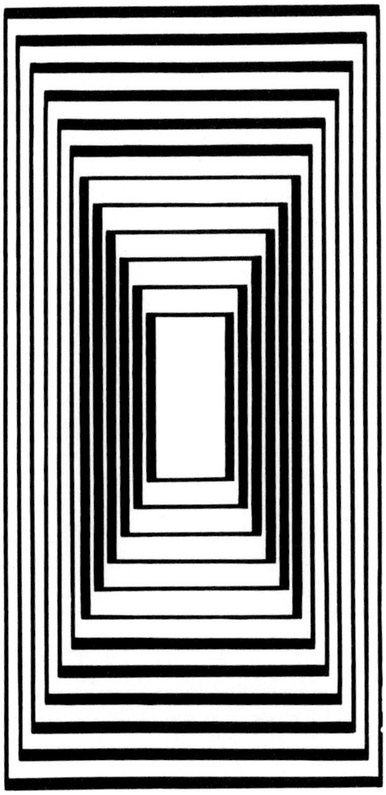

Fig. 5.11 **Josef Albers**, *Introitus*, 1942.
Lithograph, $19\frac{7}{8} \times 11\frac{1}{8}$ ins (51×28 cm).
Courtesy: the Josef Albers Foundation.

Placement

From edge of format to center

Placement within the picture plane also has a powerful effect on perception, related to our own position in space. Stand, or imagine you are standing, behind a picture window extending from floor to ceiling. Trace, on the glass or sheet of plastic held upright, the size and position of objects in your field of vision. The largest object you see, before you reach the "window," will be yourself, at the periphery of your inner eye, from the top of your glasses (if you wear them) to the bottom, and down to your own feet—with a slight tip of the head. *You* fill your own frame of vision. When Christopher Isherwood said, "I Am a Camera," inside the "stereo" screen of his eyes, he saw other objects, no matter how large in reality, smaller, within that space. In the same way, the edges of any flat format may be read as a window whose frame is nearest the eye, with other smaller objects or shapes receding into deeper space as they move away from the border toward the center of the area. In many geometric works, flat frontality combines with this spatial effect, often with subtlety of color action, to produce magic sensations of ambiguous space, alternating between the "tunnel" of depth receding from the edges of the painting to its center and the constantly reaffirmed flatness of the surface (**Fig. 5.11**).[3]

Vertical position within format

Look through the glass pane, this time to trace the relative size of objects at various distances from the eye. If we are looking at sailboats on the sea, as suggested by Ross MacDonald (p. 88), we will trace ever smaller "white moths" as we move higher on

Fig. 5.12 **Emil Nolde**, *Fishing Boat*, 1910.
Woodcut, 3×4 ins (7.5×10 cm). Courtesy:
Nolde-Stiftung, Seebull.

the window. Visual weight confers a sense of heaviness at the lower edge with airiness filling the upper part of a format. [4]

Artists acknowledge such apparently rigid constraints, but as we often see, the artistry of an individual is more powerful than any rule (**Fig. 6.28**).

Constant sensory bombardment by the visual imagery of television, films and photographs has made us all more sophisticated than any previous generation in the reading of shapes on a surface. We see galaxies pass at incredible speeds as we "fly by" in star ships, seated in our living rooms! The pyramids of Egypt fit neatly onto our six-inch screen. Yet a single dot on our screen may be read as a pyramid as we move away from it or as a microscopic creature if we zoom in closer to its minuscule size and watch it grow to fill our frame of reference. [5]

EXERCISES

Exercise 3:
Finish a composition suggesting deep space, based on your "picture window" study, in either a realistic or abstract style.

Exercise 4:
Stand at a window with a long view down a level, busy street. Trace the shapes of cars or people rising to the height of the horizon as

they decrease in size. Larger, nearer objects will tend to be those toward the bottom of your composition.

Exercise 5:
Design a "science fiction" space-scape with no earthly spatial clues. Try to show an otherworldly gravity.

The horizon

Through science fiction films and newsreels, we have learned to visualize space away from the earth with no horizon in view; still any horizontal edge dividing a picture plane tends to suggest sky and deep space above that line, even in works that are non-pictorial. If the area above the horizontal is blue, you can forget about convincing the viewer it is simply flat. When presented with two "horizons," we see the central band as sea and the lower area as earth; irregular horizontals like those in Lichtenstein's *Seascape* (**Fig. 5.13**) suggest mountains between earth and sky.

Along the horizon, critical in the study of perspective, objects apparently reduced in size as they move away from us become infinitely small and vanish completely at a point on this vanishing line. Since the viewer's eye level is always level with the horizon, interesting effects can be achieved by varying the position of the viewing eye (**Fig. 5.14**). The major horizontal line in a painting need not be located at the actual horizon, or even level, to serve as a visual "horizon" (**Fig. 5.15**). [6, 7]

Fig. 5.13 (*left*) **Roy Lichtenstein**, *Seascape*, 1964. Oil and magna on canvas, 30 × 36 ins (76 × 91.5 cm). Courtesy: Leo Castelli Gallery, © Roy Lichtenstein.
Fig. 5.14 (*center*) **Jerry Dantzic**, *Sidney Mines, Nova Scotia*, 1962. Gelatin silver print.
Fig. 5.15 (*right*) **Charles Viera**, *Beach 149th St.*, 1986. Oil on canvas, 10 × 14 ins (25.5 × 35.5 cm). Courtesy of the artist.

EXERCISES

Exercise 6:
Show the same scene with two spatial effects by locating the horizon differently in each.

Exercise 7:
Design a work with a horizontal band of blue at the top that does *not* read as sky (Good luck!).

Perspective

Seeing space from a point of view

Both the vanishing point and the idea of infinity with which it is linked were unknown in ancient times, even in Greece and Rome. According to Marshall McLuhan, the invention of printing with movable type in the Renaissance introduced the thought of indefinite repetition of an event. It became possible then to conceive of a limitless sequence, growing larger or smaller, without measurable number; and there you have infinity, where magnitude or minitude dissolve into indivisibility.

Since parallel lines seen from a single point of view seemed to converge, or approach each other in the distance, they should theoretically meet at the point of vanishing and infinity, on the horizon. A "perspectivity" could be projected by freezing all motion and diagramming the structuring of "points of three-dimensional space, mapped onto the picture plane by connecting them, by rays, to a fixed point, called the point of projection (or vanishing point) and determining where these rays intersect the picture plane," according to E. A. Lord.

As important as an understanding of perspective is, this is not a treatise on projective geometry, and so, reluctantly, we will briefly discuss its essential features and leave further research to those whose interest has been unsatisfied. To some, when you've seen one set of railroad tracks shrinking up to its point of disappearance, between two rows of decreasing telegraph poles, you've seen them all. To others, curiosity prompts a climb to greater heights or a push forward to a new vantage point, from which a new horizon may be discovered.

One-point perspective

In true one-point perspective, the infinite vanishing point is in the center of the picture plane with diagonals radiating to it from each corner (**Figs. 5.11, 5.16**). (In an amazing and rather humorous interpretation of center-focused perspective, Mantegna places the spectator in a bridal chamber below a circle of overhead observers [**Fig. 5.17**]. At the same time, the viewer may look far beyond them to the infinite space of the sky.) A

Fig. 5.16 Ralston Crawford, *Overseas Highway*, 1939. Oil on canvas, 28 × 45 ins (71 × 114 cm). Courtesy: The Regis Collection, Minneapolis.

Fig. 5.17 (left) **Andrea Mantegna**, *The Bridal Chamber*, c. 1472–74. Ceiling mural. The Ducal Palace, Mantua.
Fig. 5.18 (right) *Union Poster*, United Garment Workers of America, 1899. Lithograph, $16 \times 24\frac{1}{2}$ ins (40.5×62 cm). Collection: C. and J. Dantzic.

series of gradated quadrilaterals whose sides are parallel to the edges of the canvas gives a sense of an infinite hallway or tunnel or, seen in a different way, projects out of the picture toward the viewer (p. 93). This creates ambiguity of space, a push/pull effect, hypnotically drawing the eye in and out, always toward the center. Combined with the active color of Albers' many "homages" to the square or the near-invisible aura of Reinhardt's so-called black paintings, a mysterious, mystical magnetism attracts the senses as well as the eye. Power and majesty, quiet strength and effortless control have been ascribed to the often-religious portrait head placed in a frame in the flat frontality of single-point perspective. This effect is enhanced as we stand, physically lower than the image, where we must raise our eyes to meet those piercing us from its awesome face (**Fig. 1.19**). A similar effect is achieved in certain self-portraits.

Stark control and omnipotence are conveyed through ancient and tribal uses of central one-point perspective, far more dramatic than other, subtler, psychological messages. The idea of an individual having a one-to-one relationship with a caring deity is enhanced by the empathetic eye contact suggested in the never quite symmetrically central perspective of many Christian icons, though a slight asymmetry does not necessarily guarantee less strength or increased warmth.

Similar but less imposing effects can be achieved by stopping the rush to infinity at the center with a small rear wall or panel shown at the end of a "hallway." This may be achieved with some subtlety or with a naive charm as in the 1903 poster in **Fig. 5.18**—which displays almost every method we have described to increase its sense of space.

A modification of one-point perspective is shown by the famous railroad tracks, seeming to move uphill or down as the horizon is raised or lowered, always directly in

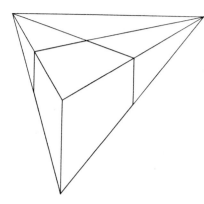

front of the eye. This in effect tips the picture plane's top edge toward the viewer, raising the corresponding lower rear edge of an imaginary cube of space behind the flat, frontal plane of the canvas. Tipping the top edge away similarly lowers the back edge of the painting space. The vanishing point remains in the center along the newly positioned horizon. Any tipping of the picture plane means it is no longer completely frontal and perpendicular to the eye, but we will overlook that fine point and construct our little box along the tracks in one-point perspective. Note that only the top (or bottom) and front of the cube may be seen if the box is solid or opaque. If transparent, then all six surfaces are shown. See Paul Klee's "Pedagogical Sketchbook" for a development of related ideas. [8]

Fig. 5.19 Dan Pedoe, *Two-point perspective description of rectangular solid,* 1976. From "Geometry and the Visual Arts," published by Dover Publications, Inc. New York.

Two-point perspective

Since all four parallels converge at one point in one-point perspective, there is no other focal spot to be considered. However, when an object is not viewed head-on in a frontal way, the picture is quite different. Imagine a cube in space placed at an angle, so that you see the top plus a left- and right-hand side (**Fig. 5.19**). No matter how you turn this solid form you cannot see more than three of its faces at once. How many sets of parallel edges can you visualize, growing smaller as they converge in space to meet at the horizon at the point where they appear to vanish? Remember to continue the actual edges by extending them with the "rays" proposed by Lord as a guide (p. 96). You should see three edges moving in concert off to the left, disappearing at one point, and a separate trio of edges diminishing together toward the right to vanish at another spot. If your cube were transparent, you could see two pairs of parallel edges moving toward their respective vanishing points in either direction, or four lines, meeting at each point. Using our picture window once again as a surface on which to trace in two dimensions what is actually seen in three, a straight edge or ruler may be placed along each line to help us locate the often distant vanishing point. Depending on the size and shape of the object shown in two-point perspective and the angle at which it is presented to the eye, the vanishing points may be well off the picture plane and the gentle diminishing of converging lines barely suggested. Exaggerated perspective and an insistence upon getting all vanishing points on the page can produce excellent mechanical drawings or patterns for objects to be constructed with precision (**Fig. 5.20**). [9]

The painter or printmaker uses two-point perspective with a certain latitude, if not disregard. After all, it is largely a Western convenience, one of several possible devices for depicting objects in real space according to many mathematicians and artists. "Linear perspective," says Anderson, "depends on some suppositions which violate experience." Marshall McLuhan, who taught us that often the "medium" is its own "message," regretted that we moderns "are shut off from Blake's awareness that we become what we behold." In India and China, as Pedoe points out, extra vanishing points are sometimes located behind the spectator; Kepes calls this viewer-focused technique "inverse perspective." In certain panoramic works, conventional two-point perspective is replaced by a viewer-focused 360° sweep of space.

Fig. 5.20 *Blocks drawn in two-point perspective.* By a student of Irwin Rubin, The Cooper Union.

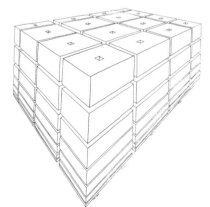

Still, it must have seemed almost magic for artists such as Albrecht Dürer in the early sixteenth century to trace the look of actual objects in space, using "mechanized devices for representing perspective (**Fig. 5.21**). Between [a sighting glass] and the subject, a glass plate or a frame divided into squares by a net of black thread is interposed." Using such devices, Renaissance artists created almost photographic likenesses of objects and scenes in space, several hundred years before photography. We may enjoy a similar experience allowing our eye to be fooled by a *trompe l'oeil* façade on a blank wall adjacent to an actual façade (**Fig. 5.22**). Can you tell which is the painting?

CHAPTER FIVE

98

Three-point perspective

In a three-dimensional object such as a cube, with not two but three sets of parallel edges, the vertical uprights are usually shown parallel while we send the other edges off to converge at their distant points on the horizon to the left and right. Cartoonists and the advertisers of tall buildings have long exaggerated this dimension by using a third set of converging parallels, placing the vanishing point well below ground level, diverging the verticals up toward the sky's infinity, or converging them at a point out in space.

Architects use this idea with discretion in rendering groups of buildings seen from above or below. Aerial photographs and others made with special lenses and from viewpoints not perpendicular to the vertical lines of a building, show this convergence of parallels in three-point perspective (**Fig. 5.23**). However, as theory and practice often diverge in art, a too faithful adherence to this may lead to over-emphasis of three-dimensionality and a kind of caricature. The very effort to be accurate may produce a lack of subtlety and understatement that works against the artistry of your art. [10]

Fig. 5.21 (*right*) Albrecht Dürer's Device for Representing Perspective. A network of black threads divides a plate of glass between the eye and the subject. From K. A. Knappe, "Dürer: the complete engravings, etchings and woodcuts," published by Thames & Hudson, 1965, and Dan Pedoe's "Geometry and the Visual Arts," published by Dover Publications, Inc, New York.

Fig. 5.22 (*left*) Trompe l'oeil facade, New York, 1987.

Fig. 5.23 **Peter B. Kaplan**, *Tickertape Parade # 2*, 1984. Gelatin silver print, © Peter B. Kaplan.

Fig. 5.24 (*left*) **Mary Cassatt,** *Woman Bathing,* c. 1891. Drypoint and aquatint in color, $14 \times 10\frac{1}{2}$ ins (35.5×27 cm). Courtesy: The Brooklyn Museum, Dick S. Ramsay Fund.

Fig. 5.25 (*right*) **Nishikawa Sukenobu,** *Young Woman Preparing Ink,* 17–18th C. Edo, Ukiyoe school. Silk, $13\frac{13}{16} \times 25\frac{7}{8}$ ins (35×66 cm). Courtesy: the Freer Gallery of Art, Smithsonian Institution, Washington, D.C.

Fig. 5.26 **Henri de Toulouse-Lautrec,** *The Jockey,* 1899. Lithograph, $20\frac{1}{4} \times 14\frac{5}{16}$ ins (51.5×37 cm). Collection: The Museum of Modern Art, New York. Gift of Abby Aldrich Rockefeller.

Isometric perspective

Without complex diagrams, it is possible to show the essence of this "pointless" perspective system through which objects in space are seen to grow smaller, although their parallels remain the same distance apart, never at any point to vanish. The "isometric," or same-measure, technique gives flatness to the picture plane, as its diagonals suggest movement back into space (**Fig. 5.24**). Individual figures or architectural elements are shown smaller and higher on the surface as they recede, but are rendered isometrically with adjustments where they meet. This planar kind of space, used in China and Japan for centuries (**Fig. 5.25**), was enthusiastically received in the West toward the end of the nineteenth century, inspiring Degas, Van Gogh, Cézanne and others to tip their floors and tables upward toward the viewer, to leave stretches of unfilled space in a composition, or to show objects whose sides did not appreciably converge in the distance. Cubism could not have developed without the isometric insights of Asian and African art.

Some contemporary painters combine Eastern and Western perspectives. Familiarity with the isometric idea should help identify works in which a Western picturing of space is not the aim. Isometric perspective also makes possible the ambiguous optical illusions we will investigate later (p. 103). **[11]**

Foreshortening, reverse and amplified perspectives

Objects very near the eye show an exaggerated increase in size. This can be treated in several ways. The apparent compression between the enlarged, close-up areas and suddenly reduced elements farther away gives a "shortened" look to the projecting portion as it moves to the "fore" ground. Amplification of such protrusions, even beyond the size recorded on our field of vision, can add strength, massive volume and expression, particularly to the graphic arts (**Fig. 5.26**).

The painter John Sloan advises a conscious effort to avoid this exaggeration. "If you are drawing a figure with the arm extended toward you," he advises, "reduce the size of the hand until it is its normal proportion in relation to the size of the face. The arm itself will be drawn in a condensed space ... Resist the size of the projecting features, and increase the width of receding parts." He urges us "to use foreshortening—resist perspective."

Carried to an extreme, this leads not only to a normalization of approaching

Fig. 5.27 (*left*) *Herod's Banquet*, Basilica of San Marco, Venice, 14th C. Mosaic. Courtesy: La ditta Bohm.

Fig. 5.28 (*right*) **Andrea Mantegna**, *The Lamentation*, c. 1490–1500. Oil on canvas, approx. 27 × 32 ins (68.5 × 81 cm). Courtesy: Pinacoteca di Brera, Milan.

portions of a subject but even to a diminution, so that they are shown smaller than they might be expected to appear (**Fig. 5.27**). It can reverse the angle of perspective as the parallel lines seem to converge in our direction, if not actually behind us! Mantegna's *The Lamentation* (**Fig. 5.28**) shows this with more force and eloquence than any verbal description of parallels and their vanishing point. [12]

Multiple or simultaneous perspectives

When objects or their parts are presented as though seen from several viewpoints, an effect of the viewer in motion is achieved (**Fig. 5.29**). This leads directly to Cubism, compartmentalizing separate areas of a scene into units of subject-plus-surrounding-space. The challenge of representing space in unique ways has led to works such as Lima's drawing on a continuous Moebius strip (**Fig. 5.30**) and Kotin's multi-panel *The*

Fig. 5.29 **Henri Matisse**, *Blue Nude*, (*Souvenir de Biskra*), 1907. Oil on canvas, 36¼ × 55¼ ins (92 × 104.5 cm). Courtesy: The Baltimore Museum of Art; The Cone Collection, formed by Dr. Claribel Cone and Miss Etta Cone of Baltimore, Maryland.

Fig. 5.30 **Jacqueline Lima**, *Life Everlasting World Without End Amen*, 1981. Pencil, 11 × 7 × 5 ins (28 × 18 × 13 cm). Courtesy of the artist.

Fig. 5.31   **Albert Kotin**, *The Crucifixion*, 1970–74. Many small panels. Oil on canvas. Photograph courtesy: Charles A. Winter and Artfull Eye Gallery.

Crucifixion (**Fig. 5.31**), in which the viewer, in Christ's place, looks out on a field of witnesses to the Crucifixion.

Earlier, twenty years or so before the first Cubist canvases appeared, Van Gogh created the distorted, convuluted forms of *The Church at Auvers* (**Fig. 5.32**), seen as though through the curved surface of a carnival mirror, stretching and pulling in different ways. As though several views of the church merge without separating edges, we see the subject through more than one "lens." (Compare this effect with the "stretched grid" transformations of D'Arcy Thompson in **Fig. 3.16**.) Does the photograph of façades in **Fig. 5.33**, skewed by reflection in slightly curved windows, relate more closely to the Thompson or the Van Gogh distention of form? Do you suppose Van Gogh's disturbance of the painting surface reflects the physical or emotional disturbances in his life? Can knowledge of a painter's experiences, environment, philosophy and other factors not revealed by studying the work itself be important to an understanding of the work? Are such details irrelevant to aesthetic content? To help resolve or even formulate such questions, consider the study of art history, aesthetics or philosophy.

Fig. 5.32   (*left*) **Vincent van Gogh**, *The Church at Auvers*, 1890. Oil on canvas, 37 × 29 ins (94 × 74 cm). Courtesy: Louvre Museum, Paris.

Fig. 5.33   (*right*) Neighboring Buildings to Javits Center, New York Newsday/Bruce Gilbert, 1986.

Fig. 5.34 **Josef Albers**, *Structural Constellation NN2*, 1962. Machine engraved vinylite. Courtesy: The Josef Albers Foundation.

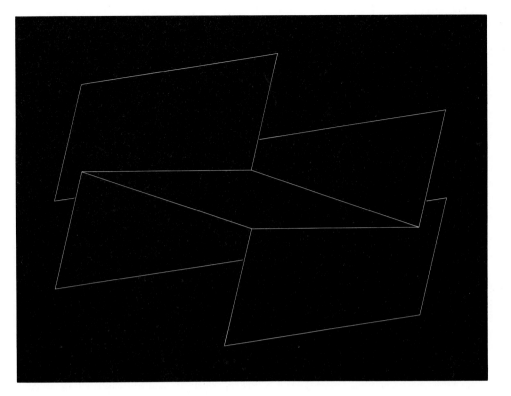

Fig. 5.35 Optical illusions: *Reversible staircase* by Schroder, in William Seitz's "The Responsive Eye," Museum of Modern Art, 1965; *Embedded Figure*, adapted from "Basic Design" by Richardson, Adkins, Coleman and Smith, published by Prentice-Hall Inc, 1984; *Triple-pronged fork* in "Sign, Image, Symbol," edited by Gyorgy Kepes (reprinted from "From Stimulus to Symbol; The Economy of Biological Computation" by Heinz Von Foerster, 1966).

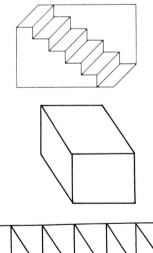

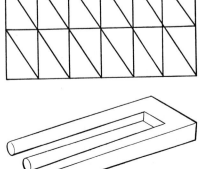

Optical illusion and fluctuating form

Isometric perspective, by maintaining an equal distance between parallels, permits a limited suggestion of space behind the picture plane, facilitating a quick shift of focus in designs that can be read in alternating ways. The non-converging lines in the baby-blocks pattern (**Fig. 2.7**), regardless of color, present no clue to tell the eye which trio of diamond shapes must be read as a solid form. As soon as one choice is made the eye begins to tire of it and another gestalt appears, either as a convex or concave form. A flat reading seems impossible. This is also true of the "double staircase" whose two readings continue to alternate. [13]

The complex line drawings of Albers owe their space-twisting magic to a highly imaginative development of this idea. Using only straight lines (or "Despite Straight Lines," the title of his 1961 volume of these graphic constructions), varying the width of some in relation to others and their position in symmetrical configurations, he delights us with an unexpected sequence of visual events (**Fig. 5.34**). François Boucher, in his analysis of these "intangible images of reality," notes "Albers chooses a system of orthogonal perspective whose parallel lines go 'through' the viewer ... the effect is one of dematerialization." Far from being simple descriptions of clever problem-solving, these works reveal "ceaseless investigation [which] contributes a new diagram of reality to the art of the present."

By "orthogonal," Boucher means the perpendicular framework of these drawings and the grid of parallel lines on which they have been constructed to "perform space and volume illusions of multiple images [and] interpretations." As far back as 1942, Albers wrote, "we cannot remain in a single viewpoint, we need more for the sake of free vision." [14]

For those who still insist that seeing is believing, a careful study of the triple-prong fork (**Fig. 5.35**) with two branches is recommended. Cover the left half of this "object" to see only the two branches; then (splitting the picture plane vertically) cover the other half to see only the three-pronged fork. Now, hands off, look at the two together! Can you tell the *figure* from the *ground*—the "filled" from "unfilled" space? Some illusions by Maurits Escher are more concerned with shifting shape than with the fluctuating appearance of (even shallow) space (p. 57). [15]

Perceptual abstraction—optical ("op") art

In the exhibition called "The Responsive Eye" of 1965, Curator William C. Seitz of the Museum of Modern Art put together works in several styles, all involving the viewer's eye in directly perceptual experience (**Fig. 5.38**). (The linear "isometric" drawings and engravings of Albers were featured.) Some of the most active, literally shimmering canvases in this exhibition used no chromatic color, simply an interlacing, intricate subdivision of black and white lines, stripes, checks, grids and other geometric arrangements. Seitz calls the eye-dazzling aura, said to have caused physical responses in sensitive viewers, "spatial radiation."

The pulsation, surface disturbance and pure energy that bombards the eye in Bridget Riley's works (**Fig. 5.36**) result from "systematic crowding or separating [of] units, [so that] effects of illumination and shade are created as either black or white dominates." When individual elements are very small, says Seitz, or at a distance from the eye, optical mixture occurs and they blend into one tone or texture. Sometimes a sensation of pale color—pink, gold or blue—is produced.

Visually responsive art is not a discovery of the twentieth century, or the "schooled" eye. Pieced quilts made throughout the United States during the nineteenth century, particularly in Amish communities, display strong graphic and optical effects. We may think of these as fabric paintings, their intricacies of pattern and color quite at home with optical art.

In another fabric-surface eye-dazzling art, Navajo weavers have created zig-zag lightning designs, using bright color accented by near-black to produce brilliant surfaces (**Fig. 5.37**). Even in black and white, these weavings still demonstrate how well they reflect their familiar name, "eye dazzlers."

Fig. 5.36 Bridget Riley, *Current,* 1964. Synthetic polymer on composition board, $58\frac{3}{4} \times 58\frac{7}{8}$ ins (149 × 150 cm). Collection: The Museum of Modern Art, New York, Philip Johnson Fund.

Fig. 5.37 Navajo Weaving, c. 1885–95. Wedge-weave style, handspun dyed and natural wool, 69 × 48 ins (175 × 122 cm). Collection of Tony Berlant.

Moiré patterns were first observed in double-layered watered silk, when the fine parallel lines of one roll were pressed into the other, slightly misaligned, as they passed through cylinders, in a process known as calendering. Moving "fringes" of dark and light and a splintered glow of irregular curves pulsate over the overlapping but not quite parallel linear designs, meeting at points that seem to merge and blur between open brighter spaces that expand with light (p. ii). The key to the moiré effect is the angle of its intersecting lines, according to Gerald Oster, "the most intensive investigator of moiré patterns," according to Seitz. In graphic reproduction, which reduces tones to dot patterns of black and white, unplanned moiré effects may occur, not always to the delight of the designer. Clever use of this perceptual illusion may result in fascinating, spatially active works, unattainable through careful planning. Play and experimentation will work better than excessive control in moiré patterns, although an almost compulsive precision marks other types of perceptual abstraction. [16]

Cubist perceptions of space

Background

Developments in science and painting led "inexorably" to the revolutionary canvases of Braque and Picasso, who introduced the analytic, geometricized, rearranged, shallow-spaced, abstracted and almost monochrome view of objects in space that amazed the art world under the name of Cubism, from about 1910 to 1914. The concept of the space/time continuum, uniting previously separable notions of time and space, presented by Albert Einstein in his 1905 paper "The Special Theory of Relativity," affected thinking people in every discipline. No longer did objects exist as positive elements in the emptiness of a negative space. The interaction and interdependence of substance, energy and light brought the "viewer" into an intimate relationship with the "viewed;" the total perception of an event over a period of time, moving through the universe, stimulated the imagination of artists everywhere.

Experiments in integrating "background" space with that filled by "figures" had been undertaken by painters who followed the Impressionists in the late nineteenth century, the diverse group referred to as Post-Impressionists. Each of these innovators worked in different ways to flatten the picture plane, structure space on the canvas, simplify form and push the use of color in new and individual ways (**Fig. 5.42**). When Cézanne suggested in 1904 that "everything in nature is formed in correspondence to the sphere, the cone and the cylinder ...", he did not mention the cube. Straight lines were the measure of the Cubists and their ·followers; Cézanne did not find them in nature.

Fig. 5.38 (*left*) **Paul Gauguin**, *The White Horse*, 1898. Oil on canvas, $55\frac{1}{2} \times 35\frac{3}{4}$ ins (141 × 91 cm). Courtesy: The Louvre Museum, Paris.

Fig. 5.39 (*right*) **Pablo Picasso**, *Bread and Fruit Dish on a Table*, 1909. Oil on canvas, $64\frac{5}{8} \times 52\frac{1}{4}$ ins (164 × 132.5 cm). Courtesy: Oeffentliche Kunstsammlung Basel, Kunstmuseum.

Cubist fragmenting of form and space

Although Cubism has been divided by many into "analytic" and "synthetic" styles, Pierre Daix prefers the terms "geometric" and "creative." Both incorporate geometric analysis of form and synthesis of structure and concept.

In fragmenting or dissecting form geometrically, Picasso and Braque often made no distinction between figure and background, or filled and unfilled space. On canvas every shape acted equally as part of the whole; every line separated two equally active areas (**Fig. 5.40**). A sense of space moving through the work was often heightened by overlapping lines and forms, creating a kind of loose transparency of planes and broken contours, sometimes to be read more as a crowding together of chunks of matter-plus-surround, sometimes more as sliding panels.

Several techniques for achieving Cubist space can be distinguished, though they are often used together. Splitting Cubism into "parts" is only justified if it achieves a new understanding of their underlying unity. Almost every example presented here shows several aspects of structuring Cubist space. Study a wider variety, certainly more than can be included in one text or museum.

Splitting the picture plane

A composition may be divided at any angle by one or more lines or axes, permitting different treatment of the shapes on either side, giving a greater flatness and equivalence to every part of the surface (**Fig. 5.40**). Such splitting of the picture plane, with the general contours of the subject unchanged, provides the opportunity for varying

Fig. 5.40 Robert Delaunay, *Rhythm without end*, 1935. Gouache, brush and ink, $10\frac{5}{8} \times 8\frac{1}{4}$ ins (27 × 21 cm). Courtesy: Musée National d'Art Moderne, Centre Georges Pompidou, Paris.

line, tone, texture, color and spatial indications, lending unity to the whole—but also, especially in late "synthetic" Cubist works, more decorative, poster-like, graphic use of these elements, especially a brighter palette. Juan Gris made frequent and varied use of the split plane.

A variation of this idea involves splitting a single object plus its portion of surrounding "space," minus the missing part, or placed at a distance from it, in a kind of sliver or stripe. When several splits occur at different angles, new shapes may be enclosed, restructuring the entire space of the work.

Splitting the plane is a first step to visualizing the time/space continuum. As interpreted by McLuhan, "Cubism sets up an interplay of planes and contradictions . . . that drops the illusion of perspective in favor of instant sensory awareness of the whole . . . Sequence yields to the simultaneous." Cubist surface divisions "compartmentalize" an image, so that it may be seen from "the inside and outside, the top, bottom, back and front and the rest," suggesting not a static view of the third dimension from a single position, but all the way to the "fourth!" [17]

Slipped plane

By sliding the image on one side of a split plane along its edge, a repositioning of the space around a form, along with the form itself, is achieved, and the viewer sees the subject from different locations at one time (**Fig. 5.41**). The joining of slipped portions of a plane may be emphasized or minimized so that the total space either subdivides with geometric regularity or shimmers and blends into a continuously moving rearrangement of planes and forms (**Fig. 5.42**). Lines may be stressed along planar edges, or barely suggested simply by ending one shape and beginning another (**Fig. 5.43**). [18]

Tipped plane

The most dramatic spatial shift in Cubist work is prefigured by Cézanne's tilted tabletops, increasing the surface seen, and flattening the picture plane (**Fig. 6.11**). Influenced by Japanese woodblock prints using isometric perspective, Cézanne, Van Gogh, Degas and others changed the way space was shown in Western art. But the Cubists developed the idea to show objects from every viewing point, at different distances, tipped at steep angles, all at once, yet always retaining a plastic unity, respecting the planar nature of the canvas (**Fig. 3.20**). [19]

Fig. 5.44 **Albrecht Dürer**, *Two Heads Divided into Facets*, 1512–19. Drawing, 4½ × 7½ ins (11.5 × 19 cm). Courtesy: Sachsische Landesbibliothek, Deutsche Fotothek, Dresden.

Modifying the size of parts of an object combined with splitting, slipping and tipping the picture plane allowed the Cubists a wide latitude for individual expression, although this was not among their goals. Many early Cubist works were unsigned, indicating that they might as well have been painted by Braque as Picasso, who wrote, "most of those that are signed we signed years later ... we felt ... the hope of an anonymous art ..." Individual styles are evident even in these early works; the curvilinear, more lyrical, light-fragmenting concerns of Braque led him along a different lane of the same road taken by the more geometrically minded, volumetrically analytical Picasso. Heir to the rich early experimentation of these pioneers, Juan Gris created some of the most elegant synthetic Cubist works, which, unfortunately for all of us, ceased with his early death in 1927.

Cubing volume

In analyzing and simplifying the depiction of solid form, the early Cubists tried such techniques as subdividing spheres into flattened, planar facets and reducing parts of the body to angular, often irregular, many-sided or polyhedral volumes (**Fig. 3.20**). To keep our study in perspective, look at **Fig. 5.44**. This illustration of the same concept was drawn by Albrecht Dürer in 1512 when he was experimenting with "rounded forms, analyzed in terms of planes." Centuries before his time in this investigation, Dürer never incorporated these prophetic studies in his paintings. Dürer's "Cubist" drawings share with their distant descendants a strict allegiance to representational inspiration. Abstract, in the sense of eliminating unwanted detail, yes, reduced to bare-bones simplicity at times, but never non-objective, Cubism remained firmly in the "associative" camp of modern art. [20]

Fig. 5.45 Log Cabin pattern variation. Crib quilt, pieced cotton and wool, $43 \times 25\frac{1}{2}$ ins (109×65 cm), early 20th C. American. Collection: C. and J. Dantzic.

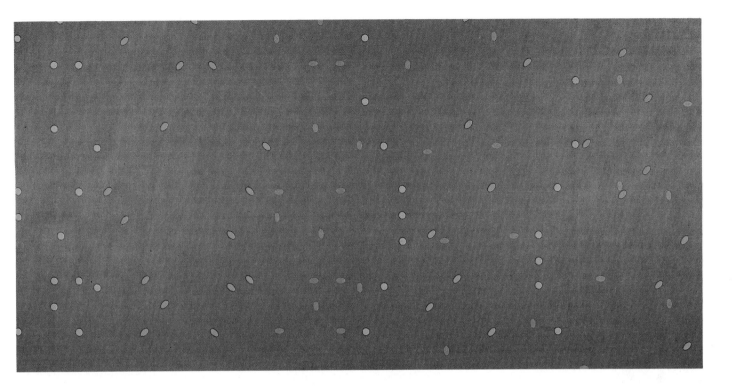

Fig. 5.46 Larry Poons, *East India Jack*, 1976. Acrylic on canvas, 144 × 78 ins (366 × 198 cm). Courtesy: Yale University Art Gallery, Gift of J. Frederick Byers III.

The floating field

An almost magnetic attraction of the classic "log-cabin" quilt pattern is the sense of an overlaid, floating field, created by a visual grouping together of the central squares, often bright red, in each patch or module (**Fig. 5.45**). Such a field appears to spring forward, hovering in space.

Although the painter Larry Poons was mostly interested in creating a shimmer of swimming, after-images in a painting shown in the "Responsive Eye" exhibition and similar works, a floating field is created as well (**Fig. 5.46**). Similarly the sense of a network moving over the surface is conveyed in Matisse's 1947 serigraph of the aerialists, *The Codomas*, included in his bouncy volume, *Jazz*. In this case, the net provides a physical surface for the trapeze artists to spring back from, as well as a springboard for the eye.

Recurring ideas are often found in seemingly unrelated works and categories, such as crafts, and fine, minor, primitive and graphic arts. In a particularly inventive variant of the floating field, Roy Lichtenstein's pierced white grid (**Fig. 5.47**) floats over a field of disconnected dots containing indications of a scene at a distance, behind the picture plane.[21]

EXERCISES

Exercise 8:
Using as a subject the railroad track and telephone pole cliché, design an interesting and original variation. Then quickly mail it to me, care of the publisher!

Exercise 9:
Draw a rectangular solid, or an object which resembles this, such as a book, in two-point perspective. First keep both vanishing points on the picture plane; then suggest vanishing points at a distance from your page.

Exercise 10:
Design an "extravagant" view of a building in three-point perspective, perhaps as the basis for a humorous cartoon.

Exercise 11:
Design a variation of Exercise 9, using isometric perspective.

Exercise 12:
Cover your face with one hand while stretching the other out as far as possible, noting their immense discrepancy in size. Then draw a reclining model whose "huge" feet practically touch your easel while the head appears as a smaller, more distant form. Using a trans-

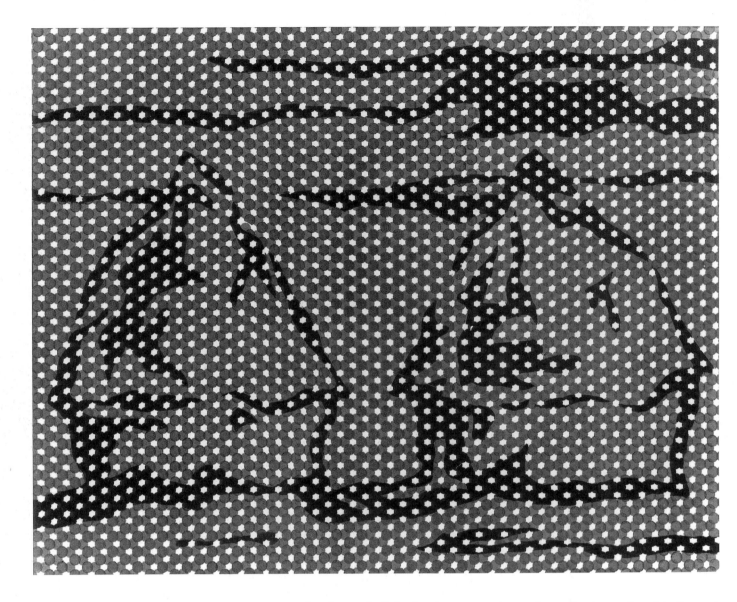

Fig. 5.47 Roy Lichtenstein, *Haystacks*, 1969. Oil and magna on canvas, 18 × 24 ins (45.5 × 61 cm). Collection: the artist. Courtesy: Leo Castelli Gallery.

Fig. 5.48 Jay Maisel, *Building Facade and Reflections*. © 1989, Jay Maisel. Courtesy of the photographer.

parent overlay, "normalize" the foreshortening of your drawing according to John Sloan's suggestion.

Exercise 13:
On graph paper design an isometric linear form. Trace, turn the tracing paper over and upside-down, then merge the images, eliminating as many lines as possible.

Exercise 14:
On graph paper, design a flip-flop optical illusion.

Exercise 15:
Create an "impossible" object with isometric perspective.

Exercise 16:
Select one technique of "optical art" and create an eye-dazzling work using only black and white.

Exercise 17:
Draw a still-life arrangement; then split the

picture plane at least once. Complete the work by varying surface treatment on either side of the axis (or axes).

Exercise 18:
Develop your previous study (Exercise 17) by introducing at least one slipped plane.

Exercise 19:
Draw a simple container, such as a cup, pitcher or vase, from several viewpoints in a still-life composition. Then integrate these, incorporating a top view, in a Cubist study including the tipped plane.

Exercise 20:
Draw a simple object from observation; then analyze its structure in planes, "cubing" its form in a faceted, geometric way.

Exercise 21:
Using any technique, compose a design in which individual elements cohere into a unified field appearing to float in front of the picture plane.

Flattening volume compressing space

With so many methods for suggesting the appearance of depth and volume, you may wonder how (or if) it is possible to maintain a look of flatness when a three-dimensional object is shown. An artist may easily "create an imaginary space, either similar to or different from [that] we ordinarily experience" (Lowry). Can such clues to the appearance of space be somehow "neutralized?" Photographer Jay Maisel, by removing the context of his shapes through careful placing of physical borders to conceal the surrounding environment, and by avoiding spatial hints, such as vanishing-point perspective, presents us with an image at once flat, yet seemingly geometric to the point of non-representation (**Fig. 5.48**). The close-value colors, pale blue and rose, encourage such a reading, but that is another chapter!

Chapter Six

UNIFYING ELEMENTS: STRUCTURE AND SURFACE

Fig. 6.1 **Philippe Halsman**, *In Voluptate Mors, (Dali's Skull)*, 1951. © Yvonne Halsman 1989.

The whole and its parts

In looking at a painting or any two-dimensional work, what first attracts your attention—color, arrangement of shapes, mood created by tone, texture or surface? Do you identify the subject before deciding to investigate further? Is an overall unity, an orchestration of elements first apprehended and only then dissected into component parts for enjoyment and understanding? Can this very analysis destroy the appreciation, the savoring of art? Or, does art reveal new levels of meaning upon study and contemplation? Consider these terms, used to describe the "visual glue," the holding together of parts on the page or canvas. Do they share meanings or have they slightly different connotations:

Composition	Organization	Layout
Arrangement	Configuration	Format
Structure	Plastic Equilibrium	Form
Harmony	Design	Wholeness
Plan	Unity	Order
Pattern	Gestalt	Orchestration

Which of these words emphasize oneness, a totality of visual experience communicated by an artist or felt by a viewer? Which stress the coming together of separate elements in a planned placement by their designer or in the eye of a beholder? Which suggest that the resulting effect provides pleasure, beauty or satisfaction to the eye? Which indicate specifically human creations rather than natural occurrences? Are there associations—"commercial art," "crafts," "psychological," "scientific"—that keep you from using some in a general, neutral, all-inclusive way? Can you apply any of them to other arts such as music, dance, architecture, poetry? If one term seems most universal, most all-encompassing, choose it for your own vocabulary, but be sure you recognize how the others are used, often interchangeably.

"There is in nature, even below the level of life, something more than mere flux and change. Form is arrived at whenever a stable, though moving, equilibrium is reached. (John Dewey)" "The artist's design seeks to impose enduring unity and order on the undifferentiated content of experience. (Suzanne K. Langer)" "'Plastic' [designates] the formative quality, the shaping of sensory impressions into unified, organic wholes. (Gyorgy Kepes)" "Form [is] the synthesis or fusion of all plastic means ... their harmonious merging. (John Dewey)" "Gestalt [means] the theory of form as a whole, indivisible. We do not study a tree ... by beginning with its roots, then trunk ... leaves; ... it is the tree as a unity that must be the center of our attention. (Molnar, in Kepes' M.P.S.R.)" "Gestalt [suggests] grouping into a configuration of few 'clues' ... perception of patterns from few suggestions. (Donald Andersen)" "... Before knowing what the picture represents, you are seized by its magical accord ... its harmonious ensemble. (John Dewey, quoting Delacroix)" "In a work of art, different acts, episodes, occurrences melt and fuse into unity, yet do not disappear and lose their own character. (John Dewey)" "Does the word 'art' not intimate discipline over formless, chaotic material, thus giving expression to [human] longing for order, to the healing power of art? (Lendrai, in Kepes' M.P.S.R.)" "Unification—the glorious response to a living diversity. (Suzanne K. Langer)" "... The fulfillment which calms ... (John Dewey)" "... The simplicity of order, which reveals itself rather than its origins. (Brewster Ghiselin)" "... The order in which ... elements are placed is more important than the elements themselves. (Brewster Ghiselin)"

Gestalt communicates the inseparable oneness of a visual whole, in art, considerably more than a mere sum of parts. Indeed, the "parts" may be used to create more than a single whole (Fig. 6.2)! Are all arrangements of these panels views of one work? Is one "modulation" the theme and the others variations? How many must you see to have seen the entire painting? [1]

In certain complex geometric patterns, the eye continues to group and regroup units into wholes or gestalts, then to see them as parts of even larger wholes. According to Kepes, "These larger wholes form with other groups until all possible relationships

Fig. 6.2 **Cynthia Dantzic**, *Modular Painting (Dawn)*, 1983. Acrylic on five panels, canvas over masonite, 24 × 24 ins (60 × 60 cm) overall.

Fig. 6.3 Group of small pocket mirrors. Celluloid or enamel on metal, distributed as advertising premiums, c. 1920s to 1940s. Collection: C. and J. Dantzic.

are exhausted to the point of saturation,[when] a uniformity of surface is produced on a new level." Stare at a hexagonal tile floor for an extended period; it is impossible to keep one configuration from turning suddenly into a completely different one (**Fig. 2.19**). How does Halsmann's image-shifting photograph (**Fig. 6.1**) make use of the gestalt effect?

With the Log Cabin quilt square (**Fig. 5.45**), many pattern variations can be created by varying placement and color of the individual modules. **[2]**

Unity in variety

"Unity in variety" is often called the "formula for beauty in nature and art." John Dewey used this expression to stress the dynamic relationship of interacting energies in a work. Others interpret the phrase as an identification of some shared characteristic in a group of related objects. Which uses of the term seem appropriate for the objects shown in **Fig. 6.3**? Might both definitions be applicable in some cases? Can you also find "variety in unity?" Consider the variety achieved through use of different inks with the same woodblocks (**Fig. 6.4**). Does design as well as science need a "unified field theory?"

All the terms signifying a relationship of elements involve the relationship itself and

Fig. 6.4 Naomi Bossom, *Mother and Daughter*, 1986. Multi-block woodcut, printed with two different palettes, Courtesy of the artist.

Fig. 6.5 **Jackson Pollock**, # *14*, 1948.
Enamel on gesso on wove paper, 22 × 31 ins
(56 × 78.5 cm). Courtesy: Yale University
Art Gallery, the Katharine Ordway
Collection. Copyright The Pollock-Krasner
Foundation/ARS N.Y., 1989.

the elements integrated within the total structure. These may include line, shape, color, texture and tonal value, as well as weight, direction, size, proportion, balance, rhythm, focus and emphasis. If we recognize that our analyses and unravelings aim to increase understanding, valuable insights may result. Only when each work is seen as a puzzle to be solved, a message to be decoded, are we impatient with paintings that do not quickly reveal their secrets, fit into categories, or subdivide into structures and styles with which we are familiar.

As you study each of the illustrations shown here and throughout this book, much more than the subject of our investigation may be discovered and enjoyed. If you avoid looking for specific features where they may not be found, you will not fault works failing to meet inapplicable criteria. Would you look for a full range of tonal value in a Mondrian or a balanced tension of plastic energies? Will the same ideas about color be found in works by Rembrandt (**Fig. 14.18**), Matisse (**Fig. 11.31**), Wyeth (**Fig. 11.28**), Picasso (**Fig. 8.20**) and Albers (**Fig. 11.7**)?

The paintings of Pollock (**Fig. 6.5**) or Reinhardt (**Fig. 9.14**), inappropriate choices in a study of dominance or focus, clearly show rhythm and movement (Pollock), and a subtle modular structure, close tonal values, atmosphere and integrity of the picture plane (Reinhardt). Would you expect to find orchestration, focus, movement and proportion in all the works shown? Are these criteria which may be appropriately applied to any visual work, regardless of individual characteristics of an artist's style? D'Arcy Thompson speaks of nature when he says, "the form of an object is a diagram of forces." Would such a definition apply to any two-dimensional work? Cubist and subsequent geometric, grid, pattern and modular art display their structural armatures in emphatic or subtly diagrammatic ways. But can we identify such underpinnings of form deep within works that seem completely naturalistic or spontaneous, even asymmetrical, or those without apparent composition? Are there clues to underlying structure in even the most random visual statements?

The need for unity

Biological needs for order, completeness, clarity, simplicity and closure of outline into shape have been identified and catalogued by perceptual analysts such as Kepes, Dewey and the gestalt psychologists. For those of us who cannot bear to leave an uncompleted crossword puzzle until the last letter has been fit in place, this is no surprise. The appeal that the long-discredited coloring book or follow-the-dots image holds for even the most creative child surely has something to do with a need for finishing an experience. Once this need is separated from the inventive, originating impulse, and clearly distinguished as such by the perceptive parent or teacher, "coloring in" takes its place as a mild therapeutic satisfaction and loses much of its supposed power to subvert creativity.

Kepes says the "drive toward spatial order tends to shape optical units into closed compact wholes," but he also criticizes the controlled geometry of the "'pure plastic" painters for making "order ... an end in itself, instead of a guiding principle." He quotes Goethe, who wrote, "the eye especially demands completeness," yet he emphasizes that "the eye needs action and repose ... a measuring and relating [of] visible differences." In his classic work "The Language of Vision," Kepes explains that "sight [means] more than pure sensation, for light rays reaching the eye have no intrinsic order as such ... As soon as they reach the retina, [the] mind organizes and molds them into meaningful spatial units ... [However,] one cannot look at a static relationship long without losing interest. Only changing variety can provide the stimulus necessary for holding attention on the picture surface ... Every image is based on [this] dynamic dualism, the unity of opposites." Dewey feels that "equilibrium comes about ... out of, and because of tension." He notes that "continued variation makes a picture or any work of art wear ..." From the Pythagoreans, who referred to the "simultaneity of opposites," to the contemporary Aesthetic Realists, who use Eli Siegel's phrase, "the making one of opposites," the importance of contrasting visual elements in a constantly active interrelationship has been seen as a most important criterion in determining such elusive qualities as beauty or artistry.

EXERCISES

Exercise 1:
Design a multiple-unit modular work and see how many "wholes" can be created.

Exercise 2:
Design and make many copies of one Log Cabin Square (Xerox will do), to see how many patterns you can devise.

Elements of unity—reading the picture plane

Fig. 6.6 Arabic restaurant sign, Brooklyn, New York.

Fig. 6.7 **Ben Shahn**, *Alphabet of Creation, (Hebrew Calligraphy)*. Courtesy: Bernarda Shahn.

Just what elements are contrasted or placed in a relationship on the visual field? As Robert Scott noted, "any field has certain 'potentialities'." Before these are studied, the eye must first be attracted to the work, the attention held and directed along a path on the surface. At what point along the edge of a rectangular format does the eye enter the picture plane? Compare reading a painting with reading a printed page. Your eye entered this page at the upper left-hand corner; then sweeping in horizontal bands from left to right, lower and lower, it will eventually cover the surface and exit at the bottom right-hand corner. To the Western-trained eye, this path is familiar and comfortable; it looks right. But those oriented to Arabic (**Fig. 6.6**) or Hebrew (**Fig. 6.7**) enter a page at the upper right and travel in right-to-left horizontal rows, exiting at the bottom left-hand corner. These forms of reading share with the Asian languages a sense that the beginning is located at the upper right, but they differ in a most important respect, for the written Chinese, Japanese and Korean traditionally move in vertical rows from top to bottom, ending at the lower left.

An awareness of one's own pre-judgment, or prejudice, in reading two-dimensional work facilitates an understanding of the uses of spatial direction and movement across the surface of works created from differing viewpoints. A Japanese painting or print, for example, with figures close to the right-hand edge, facing left into an area of unfilled space, may appear to show the subject "backed against the wall" in an uncomfortably enclosed environment to the Western eye (**Fig. 6.8**). From the Asian point of view, the same work can be seen providing the figure with ample airy "breathing space." Are such qualities as balance and weight also affected by this factor? When the Plains Indians were taught English, they had difficulty in distinguishing M from W, since they saw these as the same shape approached from a different place. Similarly when adults try to simulate the writing of children, they often draw the S or N backwards to show an unfamiliarity with the adult way of seeing the world. Such dysfunctional conditions as dyslexia, in which the brain seems to scramble signals seen in reading, and dysgraphia, which creates similar problems between the brain and the hand in writing and drawing, have often been misinterpreted as related to intelligence or to educability, though they are actually malfunctions of the patterning and configurational system, the gestalt tendency itself. Through skilful retraining and specialized techniques including art therapy, these disabilities can frequently be overcome and, in the visual arts

Fig. 6.8 Jar, Ching te chen ware, Ming, 14th C. China (detail of warrior on horse). Courtesy: The Museum of Fine Arts, Boston. Bequest of Charles B. Hoyt.

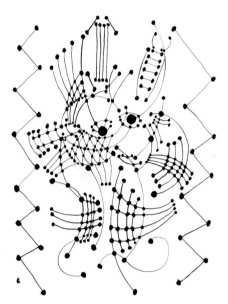

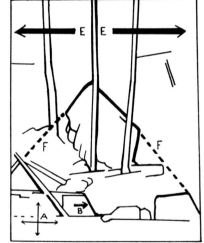

especially, turned into assets. Leonardo da Vinci's facility in, and reliance on, mirror-image writing may have had as much to do with a natural dysgraphic predisposition as to a desire to keep his notes from the eyes of the Inquisition.

Much remains to be learned about the way the mind and brain work to arrange and comprehend the immense number of signals and impulses received.

Reading the two-dimensional surface refers to the path taken by the eye in moving over the picture plane, pausing to rest at points of emphasis, returning along directional lines to previous points of rest or focus, sweeping over the entire field as directed by subtle or powerful clues and enjoying a kind of silent symphony of visual counterpoint. This "reading" has nothing to do with literary or verbal messages intended. Pathways for the eye may be created by a sequence of dots or short markings (**Fig. 6.9**), by a graduated change of hue, value or color, or by the linear edge of shapes or groupings of shapes (**Fig. 9.3**). Frequently a combination of these elements is at work (**Fig. 13.28**). Erle Loran's excellent analysis, *Cézanne's Composition*, is an invaluable resource in the study of this idea (**Fig. 6.10**). In his book "A Primer of Visual Literacy," Donis A. Dondis provides clues to reading the picture plane, counseling against ambiguity of forms ("they should harmonize or contrast, attract or repel, relate or clash"), showing how weight and placement can be used to effect "leveled compositions with minimum stress."

In representational work or even in associative abstraction, the degree of rapport between visual (or "formal") and story-telling content may be a criterion for success of the artist's effort.

Without actually drawing triangles and grids or variously looped curvilinear lassos and pretzels over the paintings you study, let your eye find pathways and armatures that reveal underlying structure. In Cézanne's *The Basket of Apples* (**Fig. 6.11**), enter the painting at the upper left with a small circular loop at the basket's handle, follow the round opening of the basket several times to "wind up," repeat the circular motion around each fruit within the basket's oval, then swing down and around the edges of the drapery along the table top to the right, imitating the original large curve of the basket, up and back to the left around the plate of buns in a kind of continuous figure eight, pinned down near the center of the painting by the heavy vertical of the wine

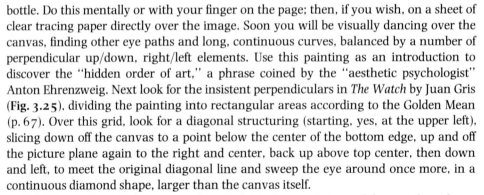

Fig. 6.12 **Piet Mondrian**, *Fox Trot A*, 1942. Oil on canvas, 43¼ ins (109 cm) × diag. Courtesy: Yale University Art Gallery, Connecticut. Gift of the artist for the Société Anonyme Collection.

bottle. Do this mentally or with your finger on the page; then, if you wish, on a sheet of clear tracing paper directly over the image. Soon you will be visually dancing over the canvas, finding other eye paths and long, continuous curves, balanced by a number of perpendicular up/down, right/left elements. Use this painting as an introduction to discover the "hidden order of art," a phrase coined by the "aesthetic psychologist" Anton Ehrenzweig. Next look for the insistent perpendiculars in *The Watch* by Juan Gris (**Fig. 3.25**), dividing the painting into rectangular areas according to the Golden Mean (p. 67). Over this grid, look for a diagonal structuring (starting, yes, at the upper left), slicing down off the canvas to a point below the center of the bottom edge, up and off the picture plane again to the right and center, back up above top center, then down and left, to meet the original diagonal line and sweep the eye around once more, in a continuous diamond shape, larger than the canvas itself.

Further analysis will uncover a level of circular repetitions of the watch. Did you notice the meander and transparency of forms that appear to overlap, occupying the same space? The more you look the more you see. [3]

In the works of Mondrian and other "pure plastic" painters, it is easy to identify the geometric structure holding each work in exquisitely poised balance, as a sort of stretched membrane, often containing within black-barred white spaces one or more areas of primary red, yellow or blue. A special tension exists in lozenge or diamond-shaped works, in which perpendicular linear elements oppose the diagonals of the outer edge of each canvas, seeming to continue (as in the Gris) outside the picture plane but always returning to it (**Fig. 6.12**).

EXERCISES

Exercise 3:
Choose other paintings from this book or elsewhere and follow the visual paths you can find in them.

Focal points

Center-focused unity

A special pictorial organization is seen in da Vinci's *Last Supper* (**Fig. 6.13**), which shares with Albers' *Homage to the Square* and his *Introitus* (**Fig. 5.11**) a central-focused one-point perspective, in which the picture plane is entered in a circumferential way along its entire periphery, then moves from its corners toward the center by actual or sensed signals. The frontal images of Rothko, Reinhardt, Anuszkiewicz and others may be read in this way, with no associative connotations to distract the viewer. Many representational (even allegorical and surrealistic) works employ a strong plan of organization, often overlaid with so much other information and detail that the "hidden order" is difficult to extract. Can you find such structure beneath the surface of the alternately flat and open *False Mirror* of René Magritte (**Fig. 6.14**)? (He also uses the reverse effect, based upon the same spatial idea, to convey a sense of enclosure to the point of claustrophobia.)

The idea of vanishing-point perspective, first seen in the fifteenth century (**Fig. 6.15**), was thought to introduce a revolutionary way of depicting real space on the painting surface. Many contemporary analysts, noting that it shows a stationary observer's monocular view of a motionless subject, consider perspective a useful convention but unrelated to reality. Philip Pearlstein, whose teaching is as intensely considered as his painting, discovered through efforts to explain perspective that "it is impossible to make a correct perspective [drawing] of something ... while you are looking at it." He believes one-point perspective is "an intellectual construct that is not true to empirical

Fig. 6.13 **Leonardo da Vinci**, *The Last Supper*, 1495–98. Fresco mural, 173 × 336 ins (439 × 853 cm), Santa Maria delle Grazie, Milan.

Fig. 6.14 René Magritte, *The False Mirror*, 1928. Oil on canvas, $21\frac{1}{4} \times 31\frac{7}{8}$ ins (55×81 cm). Courtesy: The Museum of Modern Art. New York.

vision," developed to "put across [Renaissance] materialistic attitudes about the world."

The diagonally converging lines of center-point perspective give us a good model for other kinds of aimed directional signals, readily identified in contemporary advertising design and abstract or geometric art, but more difficult to discern when woven into the general texture of complex, story-telling compositions. In David's *Oath of the Horatii* (**Fig. 6.16**), follow the paths indicated by extended fingers, arms, legs and feet, sweeping across the canvas in lines that unify the entire work as a triangulated pattern, changing direction at every intersection, flowing around curved architectural elements and drapery to stop abruptly and pick up the sharply angular geometry, leaping from the glance of an eye to a waiting focal point, and all together pinned down at the apex

Fig. 6.15 (*left*) **Masaccio**, *The Holy Trinity*, c. 1425. Fresco, Santa Maria Novella, Florence.
Fig. 6.16 (*right*) Jacques-Louis David, *Oath of the Horatii*, 1784. Oil on canvas, 130×168 ins (330×427 cm). Courtesy: The Louvre, Paris. © photo RMN.

Fig. 6.17 (*left*) **Paul Cézanne**, *The Large Bathers*, 1906. Oil on canvas, 82 × 98 ins (208 × 249 cm). Courtesy: The Philadelphia Museum of Art, The W. P. Wilstach Collection.

Fig. 6.18 **Edgar Dégas**, *The Musicians of the Orchestra*, 1868–9. Oil on canvas, 22 × 18 ins (56 × 46 cm). Courtesy: Musée d'Orsay, Paris.

or joining of the "asterisk" of criss-crossed, upraised arms, hands, swords. In this work, inspired by a ballet (whose theme was the dedication of Horace and his sons to the defense of the Roman Republic), the "choreography" cannot be experienced at a glance but calls for a period of concentrated attention for its structure to unfold, much as a dance performance would require. [4]

Off-canvas focal points

A curved line looping through the limbs of trees and figures in a broad "tear drop" encloses Cézanne's *The Large Bathers* (**Fig. 6.17**) within a single gestalt whose focal point, the intersection of converging lines, is off the canvas, above the center at the top. This innovative work was completed near the end of Cézanne's career when pre-Cubist ideas were beginning to appear in the works of Braque and Picasso.

In its daring suggestion of allowing forms and movements to intersect the edge of the canvas before they achieve completion, a painting such as this may have provided Pearlstein with a precedent, a representational instance of incomplete form working harmoniously within the picture plane. In an earlier work, Degas cropped his composition to eliminate the heads of a row of dancers, yet in the total balance of the painting we do not sense any incompleteness (**Fig. 6.18**). Pearlstein regularly crops away portions of the body, to focus attention on the remaining form and give strength, importance and intimacy to his compositions (**Fig. 11.18**). Visualize how you might move an imaginary frame about to reveal additional, presently hidden features of this figure or its environment. Do you find the frame moving back to hold its original position?

Letting a work find its own unity

Experimenters such as Kurt Schwitters and Jean Arp tried to remove themselves from the conscious creative process, allowing torn and cut shapes to fall "according to the laws of chance." The resulting collages are often indistinguishable from works whose elements were carefully arranged and designed. Do you think Pearlstein's compositions

Fig. 6.19 Winslow Homer, *Study for "The Undertow,"* 1886. Pencil, $3\frac{1}{2} \times 5\frac{1}{4}$ ins (9×13 cm). Courtesy: Sterling and Francine Clark Art Institute, Williamstown, Massachussets.

are planned precisely or that the cropped edges are simply accidental? Look again.

Placement of elements within a format, whether accomplished with great effort or allowed to occur apparently spontaneously, determines to a large extent the way we read the final work. What choices can be made in the placement or positioning of visual material?

Focal point, placement and planning

On an empty field the introduction of any mark attracts the eye and acts as a focus. The space around this "magnet" is seen as negative or a background, perhaps not consciously seen at all. Many students begin to depict a subject with no thought to its placement within the rectangle of the page or the relationship of the object's size to the size of the paper. The paper may end in the middle of the drawing if sufficient space has not been allowed. As the edge of the sheet looms closer than expected you may begin to reduce the proportions of the subject, shrinking it to fit the paper. In order to allow a drawing as much space as it needs, some instructors encourage the addition of a second sheet of paper. I am one of these and recommend the use of micro-pore surgical tape to attach the additional sheet (or sheets!) invisibly. [5]

When "finished," the work may be cropped or even extended further. If you plan ahead, drawing with regard to the available space will result in compositions which acknowledge no empty, background or undetermined space but exhibit a fully interactive relationship of all parts of the field. In earlier ages when the scarcity and cost of paper was a factor, many artists attached separate sheets to form a larger surface. In preliminary sketching for paintings, composite multi-sheet studies are frequently seen since they are not intended as finished works, the paper merely acting as a physical support for the developing idea (**Fig. 6.19**).

EXERCISES

Exercise 4:
On tracing paper, investigate the visual choreography of David's *Oath of the Horatii* (**Fig. 6.16**), then develop a non-representational study of this "dance" or that of another painting.

Exercise 5.
Start a drawing which cannot fit the page. Add a sheet (or more) as described on this page.

Additive compositions

Another add-a-sheet approach produces large, even mural-size, drawings which might otherwise intimidate those who think of an 18″ by 24″ sheet as large and anything larger as out of the question.

Use a non-spiral-bound drawing pad whose sheets are easily removable. As a subject select a large plant, such as a pandanus or split-leaf philodendron. Observe the plant in its entirety before selecting a single leaf to draw slowly, life size, more or less in the center of your page. Then, selecting a second leaf which touches the first one, concentrate on that object in relation to the first one, including any necessary connecting branches or stems. Continue, one leaf at a time, adding additional sheets with the tape. Fold away any sheets you are not working on at the moment. Butt the pages together end to end carefully to keep the entire project under control. When you unfold the completed drawing, you may be surprised to see how many sheets you have used. It may be necessary to complete a rectangular field by adding several blank pages.

You may be amazed to see how well the entire composition works and how consistently in proportion the plant remains throughout. The most valuable discovery you are likely to make is that you have been able to create such a gigantic drawing painlessly (though not without considerable time and effort). If you had been given a single paper the size of the completed multi-sheet drawing, would the result have been the same? Would you have had the courage to attempt the project? [6]

EXERCISES

Exercise 6:
Use your very large drawing as the basis for a very large painting.

Forces acting on the picture plane

Perpendicular forces

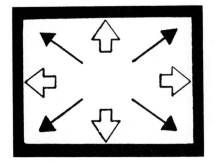

Fig. 6.20 Gyorgy Kepes, *The Picture Field*, 1964. From "The Language of Vision," published by Paul Theobald & Co., New York.

Returning to our hypothetical empty canvas, what forces activate or affect the positioning of elements on its surface? If the canvas is a rectangle, there are, even before the introduction of a single mark, several strong influences already at work, vying for attention, directing our eye along predetermined paths. Two vertical edges along the sides slide our eye movement up and down along parallel tracks, competing for interest with the pair of left-right horizontals along the top and bottom edges. Points of intersection at the corners abruptly terminate these perpendicular tensions, pinning down the format, affirming its size and proportion and drawing the viewer's eye, like four visual magnets, to the corners of the field (**Fig. 6.20**). Imagine the surface as "a field of potentialities" covered with a kind of texture of visual "iron filings" responding to the forces we have described. Suddenly the "empty" picture plane is no vacant void, but an active, even interactive, set of relationships, a unity given at the start. Edges and corners provide sufficient visual interest and activity for some artists who seek to achieve maximum "outget" with minimal input. When, in 1918, Malevitch placed one

Fig. 6.21   Lucian Krukowski, *Complex II*, 1978. Oil on canvas, multi-panel work. Courtesy of the artist.

Fig. 6.22   (*left*) Will Barnet, *Singular Image*. Courtesy of the artist and the Kennedy Galleries.
Fig. 6.23   (*right*) Keith Haring, *Untitled*, 1985. Acrylic on canvas, 10 × 12 ins (25 × 30 cm). Courtesy: Tony Shafrazi Gallery, New York.

white square, tilted, within a slightly different white square, he felt he had achieved a supremely minimal visual statement. The square eliminates tension between unequal length and width as in a rectangle. More recently some minimalists have eliminated even the second interior square, presenting the viewer with a field of uniform color, often quite large, upon which the eye and the imagination are free to discover and play individual games of mental perception. A field of potential parallels echoing the vertical and horizontal framework of the picture plane may give rise to various grids (**Fig. 6.21**). A number of "minimal" artists limit their enhancement of the basic visual field to such grids and checkerboard configurations.

From the earliest cave art to the twentieth-century and minimal painting, the perpendicular, or right angle, has held a special significance. This intersection, as the cross, has long served a multipurpose function as a symbolic and visual support, providing psychological, spiritual, plastic and graphic structural qualities to two-dimensional works in every medium (**Fig. 6.22**).

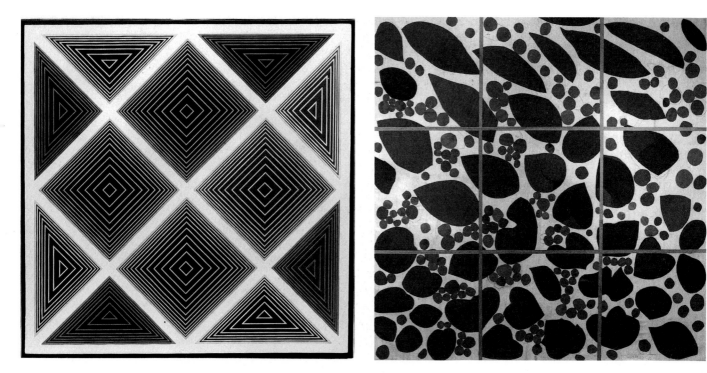

Fig. 6.24 (*left*) **Richard Anuszkiewicz**, *Multicolor B*, 1968. Liquitex on board, 17 × 17 ins (43 × 43 cm). Courtesy of the artist.

Fig. 6.25 (*right*) **Henri Matisse**, *Ivy in Flower*, 1953. Collage, 112 × 112 ins (284 × 284 cm). Courtesy: The Dallas Museum of Art.

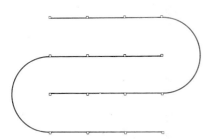

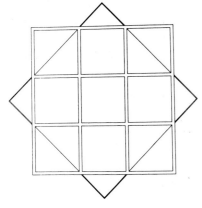

Fig. 6.26 and 6.27 Development of 9 squares indicated by 16 columns. The Cooper Union School of Architecture, students of John Hejduk, from " The Education of an Architect," 1971.

Diagonal forces

Diagonal tensions on the canvas pull opposite corners of the rectangle to one another, intersecting at the center of the picture plane, to create perhaps the most powerful focus of all at that point (**Fig. 6.23**). A central vertical and horizontal axis, also meeting in the middle of the canvas, will be seen to divide it into four equal rectangles, whose corners and diagonals add new points and lines of emphasis (**Fig. 6.24**). Variations are often seen, sometimes curving, drooping, asymmetrical or almost lost in a myriad of detail, but clearly developed from diagonal axes (**Fig. 2.25**).

Nine-square compositions

Another familiar division of the plane, into thirds along each side, gives us the nine-square or nine-rectangle grid often selected by painters, quilt designers and Navajo weavers (**Figs. 2.43, 6.2, 6.25, 9.14**). In each of these we visualize the field alive with the attraction and tension of minute units of surface energy, particularly at intersections and corners. Additional elements, lines, shapes, fields of texture or color, must respect and work with those structures present on the surface at the start. An element placed at the center of the field will be read quite differently than if it were placed in or near a corner. Any object located at the actual or implied intersection of directional indications must be seen as a focus. [7]

An interesting variation, developed at Cooper Union's School of Architecture, calls for linear development of sixteen points (which determine nine squares (**Figs. 6.26, 6.27**).

Other directional and qualitative factors

Generally, objects near the bottom will be seen to respond to gravity and "weigh" more than if they had been placed higher on the field. The power as well as the mystery of Magritte's floating *Castle of the Pyrenées* (**Fig. 6.28**) rests upon an elaborately delineated disregard for the *gravity* of the situation.

Fig. 6.28 René Magritte, *The Castle of the Pyrenées*, 1959. Oil on canvas, 79 × 57 ins (200 × 145 cm). Collection: The Israel Museum. Courtesy: Mr. Charly Herscovici.

According to Robert Scott, forms take on the values of rest, stability (with potential movement) and action, according to their linear outline or the direction of their dominant axis. Stasis, or rest, is suggested by a horizontal, the vertical is poised for action, while actual movement is implied by the diagonal. Elements placed close to one another may be read as a single shape or unit, particularly if they seem to share a common contour or outline. Clearing the field of distracting elements surrounding a focal object may isolate and thus emphasize it.

EXERCISES

Exercise 7:
Design a nine-square composition using a specific theme, palette or geometric shape. Then rearrange the nine units.

The textural surface

Repeating a shape or linear element at regular intervals will create texture or pattern, depending upon the size of the unit. The smaller the element the more it appears part of an all-over surface covering and the less each discrete element maintains its identity.

This distinction in scale is the criterion for texture as opposed to pattern. Examples showing continuous texture as well as individual units of design can be discovered throughout the book (**Figs. 2.19, 2.37, 6.29, 6.30**). If you were nearer and could distinguish individual parts of those you see as *texture*, would they at some point become *patterns*? If you moved away from the *patterns* so that each unit merged with its neighbors into one field of *texture*, would the category change? Do you consider mosaics as pattern or texture?

Although it is difficult to visualize an entire human being as a mere spot in a textural pattern, the photographer Arthur Mole made amazing images by placing hundreds (sometimes thousands) of individuals, frequently in military dress, to form representations of the Statue of Liberty and other patriotic themes (**Fig. 6.30**). Carefully arranging tonal value and interval to correspond to the distortions of perspective and the requirements of contour and field, Mole created works that stand at the brink between pattern and texture. [8]

Many works, otherwise quite different from each other, revel in texture. In the 1970s several painters developed a number of styles loosely related to the structure of weavings, textiles, carpets and other finely moduled traditional works, given the

Fig. 6.29 **Neil Welliver**, *Storm's End and Sunlight*, 1983. Oil on canvas, $48\frac{1}{2} \times 48\frac{1}{2}$ ins (123×123 cm). Private collection. Courtesy: Marlborough Gallery, New York.

HUMAN STATUE OF LIBERTY
18,000 OFFICERS AND MEN
AT
CAMP DODGE, DES MOINES I
COL. WM. NEWMAN, COMMANDE
COL. RUSH S. WELLS, DIRECTI

© MOLE & THOMAS
15 MEDINAH BLDG.
CHICAGO, ILL.

Fig. 6.30 (*opposite*) **Arthur Mole**, *Human Statue of Liberty, Camp Dodge, Des Moines, Iowa*, 1918. Photo by Mole and Thomas, ICKi-16808. Courtesy: Chicago Historical Society.

Fig. 6.31 (*top left*) **Pablo Picasso**, *Still Life With Chair Caning*, 1912. Oil on canvas with collage elements, $10\frac{5}{8} \times 13\frac{3}{4}$ ins (26 × 35 cm). Courtesy: Musée Picasso, Paris. © photo RMN.

Fig. 6.32 (*bottom left*) **Georges Braque**, *Violin and Pipe*, 1914. Collage and charcoal. Courtesy: Centre National D'Art et de Culture, Georges Pompidou, Paris.

Fig. 6.33 (*right*) **William Harnett**, *Old Models*, 1892. Oil on canvas, 54 × 28 ins (137.5 × 71 cm). Courtesy: Museum of Fine Arts, Boston, Charles Henry Hayden Fund, 1939.

general name Pattern Painting. Kendall Shaw later included small mirrored units in his paintings, adding another level of light, space and texture (**Fig. 2.40**).

Although texture is usually thought to apply only to irregular and rough surfaces, the word refers to any surface, glassy as well as lumpy in look or feeling. Since the term has the same origin as textile, the heavier woven connotation persists. As William Ivins Jr points out, tactile experience only exists in the close, touchable human world. "We never say anything 'feels red'," he notes, "as we do say things 'look heavy, dry, cold' . . . We give visual expression to tactile qualities, but not the reverse."

Collage

Between 1910 and 1912, the incorporation of actual texture glued to canvas was introduced by Braque and Picasso, with linoleum printed to look like wicker caning, scraps of wallpaper, words clipped from newspapers and other materials (**Fig. 6.31**). Two new techniques, *papier collé* and collage, seem to have been a consequence of the

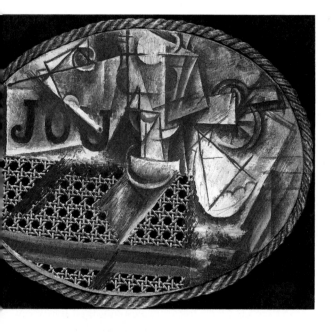

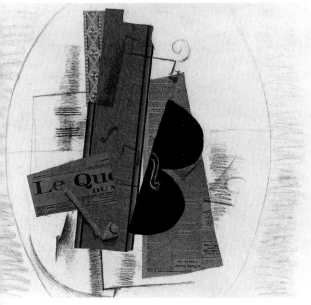

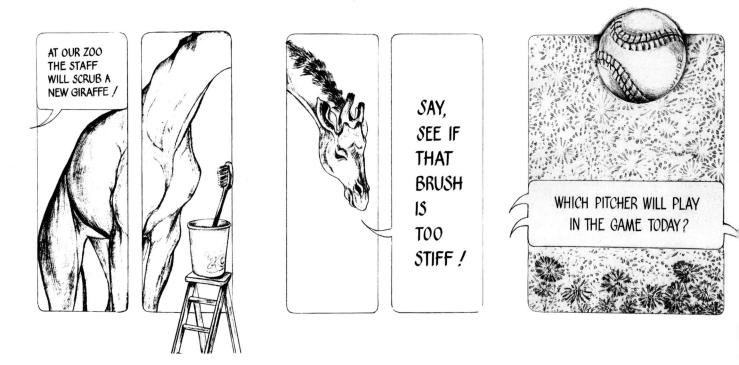

Fig. 6.34 Cynthia Dantzic, pages from "Sounds of Silents". Pencil, crayon rubbings and calligraphy, published by Prentice Hall, New York, 1976.

super-realistic or *trompe l'oeil* skill mastered by Braque as a decorator early in his career (**Fig. 6.32**). The idea of re-creating the appearance of actual texture in a painting was not new; from the earliest days the representation of materials such as fur, satin, jewelry and lace enhanced portraits of personages deemed worthy of being immortalized in paint (**Fig. 3.24**). During the late nineteenth century, William Harnett showed in his highly realist works, precursors of photo-realism, that despite the claim of some, even for the extremely faithful copyist of the look of nature, painting was not dead after the introduction of the camera (**Fig. 6.33**). [9]

Rubbings

Pattern or scale can appear altered for special graphic effects, as in the illustrations in **Fig. 6.34**, whose textural areas are all rubbings reproduced in their actual size. In this children's book the giraffe's blocky pattern is taken from hexagonally tiled bathroom flooring, and the flower garden is from a panel of florentined glass. Rubbings, frequently incorporated into collages and works of mixed media, were used extensively by Max Ernst in a series called *frottages*. [10]

EXERCISES

Exercise 8:
Set up an arrangement of modules and photograph (or draw) them à la Mole. Then readjust and rephotograph until you are satisfied. Small items (marbles or sea shells) may be used.

Exercise 9:
Using relatively flat textured surfaces and paper, wallpaper, wrappings, paper ephemera, fabrics ...), compose a simple collage. Try to re-create this work using paints alone.

Exercise 10:
Rub a crayon or chunk of cobbler's wax over a sheet of rice paper to pick up the raised portions of carved, incised, embossed or otherwise textured surfaces. Complete the shape of the original object, or rub a selected portion within a new outline. Use your rubbings, alone or with other materials, in a collage.

Chapter Seven

UNIFYING ELEMENTS: RHYTHM AND SYNTHESIS

Fig. 7.1 **Ray Metzker**, *Europe: Venice*, 1960. Photograph courtesy: Laurence Miller Gallery, New York.

Rhythm

Repetition of elements plays a major role in unifying design, beyond definition of texture and pattern. The quality of duplication and interval, duplication and interval, exactly replicated again and again or modified in some regular way, gives to the completed work a sense of rhythm (**Fig. 7.1**) (as important in writing as in the visual arts!). We easily identify "overt," exaggerated rhythm, such as a repetition of parallel curves, exactly repeated shapes (although these may take different specific object-forms) and an even distribution of similar elements throughout the picture plane. "Covert," hidden or subtle rhythms, more difficult to detect, may give a feeling of satisfaction and harmony, not easily traceable to a source. As in music, visual rhythms can incorporate changes in amount and quality of components, often in a sequentially incremental way, building or softening, rising or falling. Repetition and interval are the impulse of rhythm. [1]

Rhythm satisfies our human need for confirmation and reaffirmation of the cyclical nature of life and the natural world. We expect seasons to return, the sun to reappear, seeds to generate and grow, rest to refresh us for activity in a never-ending rhythmic flow.

Brushstrokes, stitches, spots and markings on any surface recall the repeated movements of our own pulse and heartbeat, of the tides under lunar influence, or the larger swing and orbit of planets and stars. Dewey sees the alternation of elements, dawn/sunset, night/day, rain/sunshine, spring/fall, as the basis for human creative expression. "Rhythm is the ordered variation of changes," he writes. "With no variation, there is ... stagnation ... Rhythm [must not be] superimposed upon material, but ... an essential property of form."

Robert Scott identifies a rhythmic sequence as at least three repetitions of an element, assuring at least two intervals between units.

Kepes is among those who separate "mere recurrence" or "excessive pattern" from the carefully ordered "fusion of sameness and novelty," "the touch of disorder," "energies resisting each other," "accumulated tension," the "not quite regular periodicity" referred to by Scott, Dewey and Whitehead in an effort to describe in a verbal way profound, elemental, unspeakable aspects of experience.

Although balance suggests a resting place, it can be a subtle, momentary pause in a poised network of tensions, more like a bird alighting on a loose wire than one dozing on a nest. In approximate balance, elements in one area of a work, in a general way, share qualities with unequal elements in another area, so that a sort of stasis is attained. Balance involves comparison and resolved equality.

Balance and proportion are inextricably linked to rhythm; either too much sameness, as in a crystal or grid—or a "patternless confusion of irregular detail" as in a fog—may be seen to lack rhythm through excess or insufficiency of repetition and structure. In the first, called the "tick-tock" theory by Dewey, identical "beats" either put us to sleep or exasperate our senses. "At the moment of reversal [between resisting energies] an interval [occurs] ... by which the interaction of opposed forces and energies is defined and rendered perceptible. The pause is balance, or symmetry of antagonistic forces." Monotonous sameness results without the pulse, or impulse, of rhythmic response. [2]

Modifying the module—uses of the alphabet and Asian writing

The importance of variation within structural elements extends to the idea of modularity. As Kepes explains: "The world is atomic ... modular; yet it never repeats. [Modularity] indicates order, discipline, freedom, [and] should represent a conceptual framework to operate in, rather than a specific dimension ..." Uses of the twenty-six-character alphabet and the larger number of distinct brushstrokes of Asian calligraphies show the limitless variations and recombinations of these modular systems (pp. 30, 291). [3]

The eighty-eight-Key piano offers the same kind of structure in the field of music, but stringed instruments can be "stopped" at any point, even between the notes on our Western scale. Is the violin as modular as the piano?

Is Asian writing (in which the brush may emphasize, connect, draw its components freely, blending elements in expressive ways), less modular than Western writing? Many contemporary Western calligraphers and painters reflect this understanding and freedom, most dramatically in drawing and the graphic arts. [4]

Rhythms in action

Look for an almost musical visualization of rhythmic concerns in abstract paintings, particularly those using the geometry of rectangular or flowing curvilinear form. Since music is primarily involved with the relationship of similar and varied units of textured duration and interval, independent of associative or naturalistic references, the rhythmic affinities of music and the visual arts should not come as a surprise. We have noted that Pollock and Mondrian painted to the accompaniment of jazz and other strongly rhythmic music. [5]

In graphic and advertising design, strong, compelling rhythmic relationships are quite effective and popular. Subtlety is not the "name of the game." Repetition of identical elements in a clear rhythmic way is almost a guarantee of graphic success (Fig. 7.2). [6]

Arrangement of units is critical, as is seen in the dramatic changes necessary to create an acceptable pattern of stars for the American flag as the number of states grew in stages from thirteen to the visually harmonious forty-eight, then to the present difficult fifty. When did the design change from a linear arrangement of modules (a circle of stars on a flat rectangle placed as a contrasting foil to the bands of stripes) to become a competing, equally active second textural field? Graphic elements of the flag have been adapted by Amerindian artists, often with little concern for accurate representation of the star shape (Fig. 7.3). Navajo weavers also responded to the flag's stripes closely resembling their chief-pattern blanket style.

The pulsing rhythms of Escher's elaborate enlarging and reducing modules provide as much of their almost hypnotic appeal as their inexorable regularity and precision. Except for the exaggerated size of units in central or corner positions, texture is as insistent as rhythm in these intellectual and technical demonstrations of virtuosity. In these scaled patterns, the individual module is often subordinated to the whole.

Fig. 7.2 Logo, Arista Air Conditioning Company, Long Island City, New York.

Fig. 7.3 Navajo Weaving With Flag, 1870–85. Handspun natural and dyed wool, $23\frac{3}{4} \times 56\frac{1}{2}$ ins (60×143.5 cm). Courtesy: Millicent Rogers Museum, Taos, New Mexico.

EXERCISES

Exercise 1:
Using tracing paper, mark the repetitive, rhythmic elements in some of the works in this chapter.

Exercise 2:
Create a "tick-tock" repetitive pattern; then vary it to add an interesting rhythm.

Exercise 3:
Compose a rhythmic design using several letters of the alphabet as visual not literal elements.

Exercise 4:
Using basic strokes of Chinese or other non-Western calligraphy, compose new words or images, then develop freely as abstract or pictorial rhythmic design. This idea can frequently be found in Islamic art.

Exercise 5:
Try painting while experiencing some kind of rhythmic music, selecting your sound environment with great care. You may find yourself dancing instead of painting, or perhaps, as in the case of Pollock, combining the two arts at once.

Exercise 6:
Design the logo for a product or organization using one element repeated.

Broken rhythm

Interruption of pattern, or broken rhythm, is often employed in the graphic arts, especially in the design of posters and cover art (**Fig. 7.4**). Interruption of a regular structure by the irregular placement of color or texture may be seen in otherwise even grid and checkerboard configurations (**Figs. 9.1, 10.13**). A work may thus demonstrate a discrepancy between its physical and its visual structure in ways other than those shown in Albers' color interaction studies, where it is most frequently pointed out. [7]

EXERCISES

Exercise 7:
Make a simple black-and-white striped or checked pattern; then, beneath a carefully concealed flap or window, interrupt the design in a marvelous, unexpected way. A special effect is achieved by displaying the results of a group's efforts, first with the interruptions concealed, then revealing them one at a time.

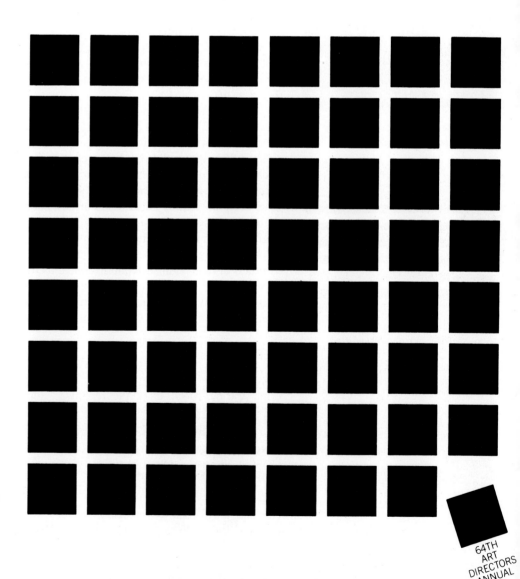

Fig. 7.4 Cover design, "64th Art Directors Annual, 1985–6." Courtesy: The Art Directors Club of New York.

All-over pattern and repositionable modules

A question often asked is, "How do you know when a work is finished?" An equally intriguing decision confronts those using modular, grid or multiple units of any kind: How many units or repetitions must be included to show the complete design, pattern or painting, but not to become simply wallpaper or texture which has no relationship to its frame and may extend limitlessly to cover any surface? As we have noted, a nine-square grid is frequently the basis for such modular but not all-over configurations. In *Dawn* and the other "Modular Paintings" of the series (**Fig. 6.2**) I have used a composition of five repositionable canvases (two squares, two double squares and one triple square) whose visual orchestration into a single nine-square unity may be modulated in a great many different ways, achieving freedom, asymmetry and variety. Through various groupings and the flow of shape, line and color, these paintings always present a new gestalt, visual structure and rhythm to the viewer. In these works, what is the importance of the concept of up or down?

The idea of repositionable compositions is not without precedent. In 1933, Albers

Fig. 7.5 (*top*) **Hélène Manzo**, *Reversible Landscape*, 1985. Etching 4 × 6 ins (10 × 15 cm). Courtesy of the artist.
Fig. 7.6 (*bottom*) **Ann Jonas**, page from "Round Trip," published by Greenwillow Books, a Division of William Morrow & Company, Inc., 1983.

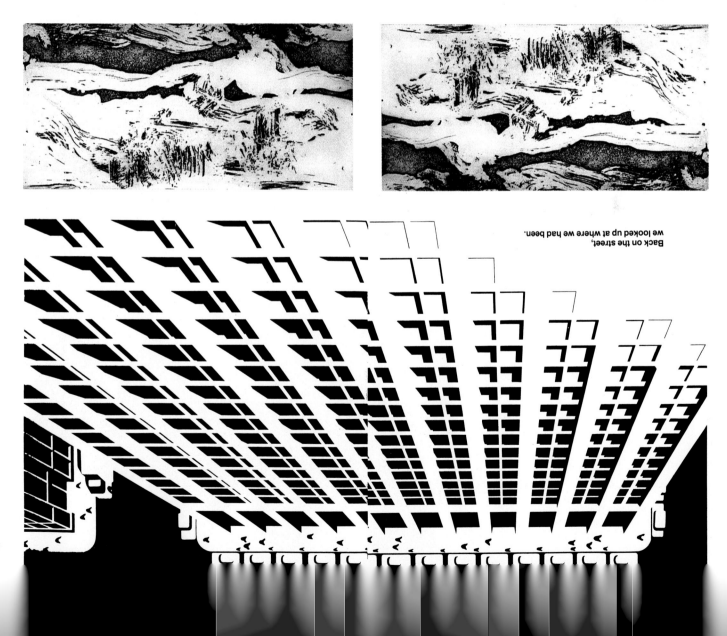

Back on the street,
we looked up at where we had been.

Fig. 7.7 Cynthia Dantzic, *Tangrams*, 1963. From a series of etchings.

created *The Aquarium* to be seen from any perpendicular attitude. Reversible landscapes have been attempted by artists in many mediums. Placement of the horizon and distinction of sky from land or sea surfaces provide choices without limit in such works (**Figs. 7.5, 7.6**). [8]

Tangram variations and shaped canvas

The tangram, a seven-shape division of the square, said to have been devised in China thousands of years ago in a prison cell, has provided a challenge to countless individuals creating animals, figures, objects of all sorts and geometric formations with its five triangles, one square and the parallelogram called a rhomboid. The tangram etchings shown, using seven separate plates, involve the white ground as line or shape working within the inked, positive areas. The tangram is particularly useful in consideration of the shaped canvas, for its component structures may be arranged to form conventional square or rectangular formats, or an apparently endless variety of associative, abstract or non-objective configurations (**Fig. 7.7**). [9]

Fig. 7.8 Jasper Johns, *Map (based on Buckminster Fuller's Dymaxion Airocean World)*, 1967–71. Encaustic, pastel, charcoal and collage, 186 × 396 ins (472 × 1006 cm). Courtesy: Museum Ludwig, Cologne.

Shaped canvases may urge the viewer to complete a kind of gestalt, enclosing the work within a simple geometric shape in the mind's eye. This is most evident in photographs which, unless they silhouette the irregular shaped canvas, make it appear as part of the rectangle of the photographic image (**Fig. 7.8**). It also influences our perception of square canvases presented on end as diamond shapes. Do you see Mondrian's *Fox Trot A* (**Fig. 6.12**) as a diamond-within-a-square, its four "empty" triangles filling out a sensed rectangular format? (Remember that questions posed here are just ideas for you to consider—not a subtle method of advising you what to think.)

Multi-unit formats

An alternative to the traditional single-panel rectangular format involves adjacent, often similar, separate units which only together unite as a single visual structure.

Fig. 7.9 (*top*) **Henri Matisse**, *The Dance II*, 1933. Three-panel mural installed at The Barnes Foundation as lunettes above entrance windows. Photograph © 1990 by The Barnes Foundation.

Fig. 7.10 (*bottom*) **Stuart Nudelman**, *Homage to Hockney*, 1986. Courtesy: The photographer © Stuart Nudelman.

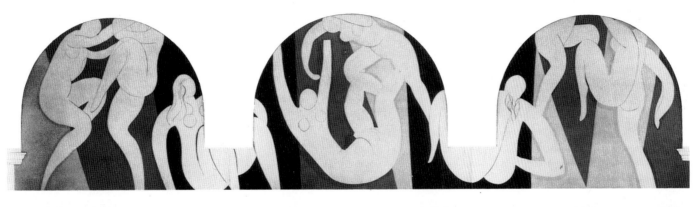

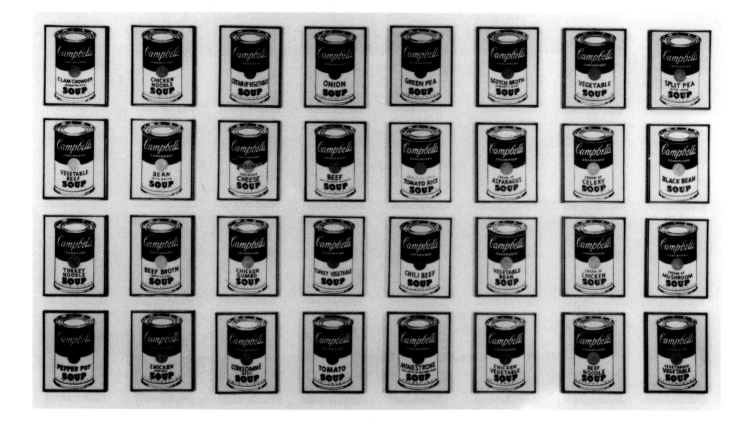

Fig. 7.11 Andy Warhol, *Soup Cans*, 1961–2. 20 × 16 ins (51 × 41 cm). Collection of Irving Blum. Courtesy: BlumHelman Gallery, New York.

Each component may stand as a fully realized design, but all assembled are required to achieve the total harmony of the work (**Fig. 7.9**). Panels of stained or leaded glass windows, two-panel diptychs or three-panel triptychs, and the uniform format of Polaroid images comprising certain of David Hockney's composite photographs may be seen as examples of this historically recurring concept (**Fig. 13.14**). The complex organization in Nudelman's physically single, visually modular *Homage to Hockney* was created through a series of glass bricks (**Fig. 7.10**). Compare this picture with the almost-identical replication of units in the *Soup Can* series by Andy Warhol (**Fig. 7.11**). Is Warhol using this technique to make a social as well as aesthetic statement? **[10]**

EXERCISES

Exercise 8:
In any medium, design a reversible (perhaps four-way) landscape or other composition.

Exercise 9:
Cut the tangram shapes out of a sturdy material. Then rearrange into several associative and non-associative designs. Use one in a finished work.

Exercise 10:
Using a linoleum- or woodblock, print several multi-image works, some using identical repetition, some varying the treatment of your unit.

Decoration and structure

In the consideration of structure as opposed to decoration, so-called authorities often take extreme and very different positions. To some, opposed to any embellishment of pure form, only pristine arrangements of formal elements qualify as art. Mondrian eschewed green as a "fugitive," impure color, the overlapping, so to speak, of yellow and blue, and is said to have faced away from the window at restaurants to avoid such visual imperfection.

Decoration has been equated with excess. "Form is ... a setting of boundaries ... limits, the whole extent of an idea, *but no more* ... [It] is the abolishing of excessive materials ... a constant elimination of nonpertinent matter, both of content and of shape ... If extreme simplicity is an objective, an artist's whole effort must be bent toward casting aside extra matter." Ben Shahn believed form is "The Shape of Content"—and no more. To John Dewey, the distinction between decorative and expressive is "one of emphasis ... There are objects with values that must be rendered decoratively and others that must be rendered without it ... An excess of decorative quality ... has an expressiveness of its own—Goya carries it ... to a point where [court] pomposity is made ridiculous ... in some portraits. [However,] in the degree in which decorative effect is achieved by isolation, it becomes empty embellishment ... ornamentation ... external bedecking. [Such] adornment [may be used to] conceal weakness and cover up structural defects." He distinguishes this fault from being wrongly ascribed to works from other cultures where "decorative quality takes on a new value, [because] patterns whose original value was ... religious or political—as tribal emblems—expressed in decorative semi-geometrical figures [are not grasped by] the Western observer. The plastic elements remain and sometimes give a false sense of the separation of decorative from expressive (**Fig. 7.12**)."

The painter Robert Gwathmey says, "Beauty never comes from decorative effects, but from structural coherence." He warns against the "humble ornamentation of surface pyrotechnics." Critchlow believes that "Western conditioning on the validity of

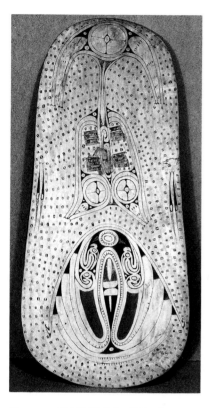

Fig. 7.12 Shield, Trobriand Islands, undated. Courtesy: Cambridge University Museum of Archaelogy and Anthropology. Copyright The Estate and Foundation of Andy Warhol, 1989, courtesy ARS N.Y.

Fig. 7.13 Joyce Kozloff, *Topkapi Pullman*, 1985. Glass mosaic at suburban station, Philadelphia. Courtesy: Barbara Gladstone Gallery, New York.

perspective and chiaroscuro has been the basis of the condemnation of Islamic art as decorative." He describes Islamic art as "concentrating on geometric patterns [which] draw attention away from the representational world to one of pure forms, poised tensions and dynamic equilibrium." The term *horror vacui*, or fear of emptiness, characterizes much Islamic art, which may seem, to the unfamiliar eye, crowded with competing intricacies and detail. This active approach to the picture plane is evident in the lively tiled wall murals of Joyce Kozloff (**Fig. 7.13**).

Carol Jopling, explaining that Navajo blankets would be as useful if they lacked "the meticulous outlining ... which costs much time and labor," feels "the separation of creation and decoration is arbitrary. It would be more correct to say that a function, which we do not fully understand, has been added to utility."

Do you agree with any of these assertions:
— Decoration is ornament affixed to an object.
— Good design is built into, not added onto.
— A test would be to remove the decoration and see what is left.
— Decoration may be a negative quality if it ignores or overpowers structure, trivializes or fails to respect form or restates elements in excessive, unsubtle ways.
— What's wrong with a little decoration—even Cleopatra used eye-shadow. (Would you restate the question?) [11]

EXERCISES

Exercise 11:
Design the most elaborate decoration you can invent; then simplify it until you feel that only structure remains.

Camouflage: dissolving of form

Consider a very different kind of surface treatment. Instead of trying to enhance or adorn a surface to make it more attractive, how would you understate, even conceal or visually destroy form? Taking a cue from nature, we can learn the secrets of camouflage. Is a bird resting almost invisibly among the identically colored, similarly textured, equally light-dappled grasses in the photograph shown in **Fig. 7.14**? Without contrasts of tone, color or shape, discrete forms become difficult to perceive. Camouflage patterns for military use are designed to confuse the eye, to provide false shape-separating clues by exaggerated contrasts bearing no relation to physical structure, creating a false gestalt. Instead of component visual elements unifying such forms, they may render them formless, chaotic or unseeable by the human mind, whose driving concern is to establish closure, economy, structure—the "unity in variety" noted earlier. See Roy R. Behrens' "Art and Camouflage: Concealment and Deception in Nature, Art and War" for valuable insights and examples, making a convincing case for the relationship between "dazzle" or form-destructuring camouflage and Cubist spatial devices. [12]

EXERCISES

Exercise 12:
Draw or paint an object or design, first alone on a contrasting ground, then camouflaged within an environment.

Fig. 7.14 Bird camouflaged in ground cover.

Fig. 7.15 **Georges Seurat**, *La Chahut*. Courtesy: Otterlo Museum.

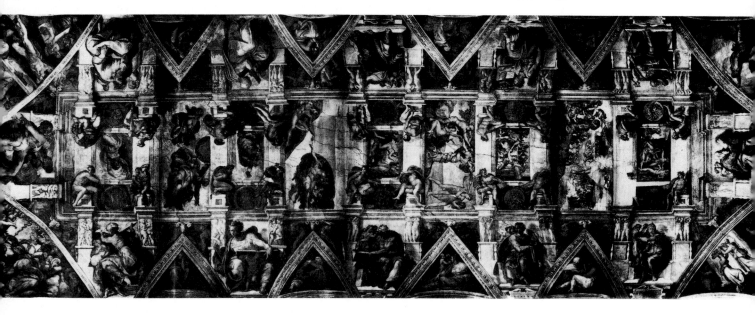

Fig. 7.16 **Michelangelo Buonarroti**, *Sistine Chapel Ceiling (overview)*, 1508–12. Fresco. Courtesy: The Vatican Art Collection, Rome.

Synthesis

A valuable suggestion regarding the understanding of "spatial sensations ... acting on the picture plane" comes from Gyorgy Kepes, who virtually defined "The Language of Vision." He recommends "storing up ... the greatest possible variety of ... experience [as] the most important part of the training for visual expression ... A playful manipulation of each element: points, shapes, lines—varying them in position, in color, in value, and in texture ... is the shortest way to understanding their interrelationships.... The variations to be achieved are endless ... for, while the elemental signs of the English language are twenty-six, the number of elemental forces with which the machinery of sight is provided is prodigious."

As you study and enjoy the works shown in this chapter (and elsewhere in this book), identify as many separable unifying elements as you can (see pp. 29, 132, 301). Do you feel such analysis hinders or heightens understanding and delight? Is it easier to discern formal qualities in representational works, or in non-associative works (**Fig. 7.15**)? Quite a few of Albers' most prominent students are now distinguished representational painters (for example, Bailey, p. 230, Fish, p. 195, Welliver, p. 131). Should there be any difference in training, preparation or study for realistic and for abstract artists? Is anyone at the age of twenty (or thirty) certain of the goal or even the paths that lie ahead?

In 1508, a thirty-three-year-old Florentine artist accepted a commission, against his inclination, to design and paint an immense fresco, 44 by 132 feet, for the ceiling of the Sistine Chapel in Rome (**Fig. 7.16**). Although Michelangelo considered himself a sculptor, this amazing work stands as perhaps the most complete synthesis of geometric structure and figurative rendition in the history of painting. He completed the four-year project at the age of thirty-seven and the adjacent *Last Judgment* twenty years later, all the while thinking himself a sculptor who ought to have been doing his *real* work. Without early training in every kind of artistic skill and knowledge—studies of the figure from every conceivable angle, anatomical investigations beyond that of his contemporaries, architectural, philosophical, poetic and other intellectual pursuits— even the unbounded raw talents of such a figure as Michelangelo might not have blossomed so thoroughly and richly, providing us, in one human being and his work, with a consummate expression of unity in variety at the highest level.

Chapter Eight

ABSTRACTING ESSENTIALS

Fig. 8.1 **Audrey Flack**, *Gambler's Cabinet*,
1976. Oil over acrylic on canvas,
83 × 78 ins (211 × 198 cm). Courtesy: Louis
K. Meisel Gallery, New York.

Many meanings of abstraction

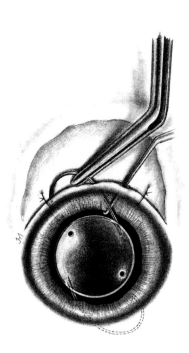

Fig. 8.2   Virginia Cantarella, *Medical Illustration (The Eye undergoing Microsurgery)*, 1987. Pencil, 3 × 5 ins (7 × 1 3 cm). Courtesy of the artist. Illustration from "Microsurgery of the Eye," published by C. V. Masby.

In even the most realistic works—tack-sharp photographs, photo-realist paintings (**Fig. 8.1**), the minutely perceived imagery of Caravaggio (**Fig. 11.17**), Vermeer or Eakins (**Fig. 12.9**), the hair-by-hair rendition of a Dürer hare, the almost microscopic depiction of detail achieved by medical illustrators (**Fig. 8.2**)—choices are made, aspects of the subject omitted, altered or arranged in one way rather than another. To this extent every visual image is an abstraction, selected from all that might be chosen by the artist. Just as a lawyer extracts from all the documents in a case the most essential, from which to prepare an abstract or summary, so an artist "abstracts" from the fullness of observation, memory and imagination a visual statement showing or expressing aspects of a subject or an idea. John Dewey realized that "every work abstracts—or it would create the illusion of the presence of actual things. The very attempt to present three-dimensional objects on a two-dimensional plane demands abstraction from the usual conditions in which they exist." Artists concerned with visual content unrelated to the physical appearance of reality use numerous expressions to convey this:

Non-Figurative, a term rejected by Picasso, since "there is not a figurative and non-figurative art … A person, an object, a circle are figures …" When we speak of "figure/ground relationships," we agree.

Non-Representational, unwieldy and incorrect, as " 're' signifies back … again … over; 'non' means not. Together … [they] cancel each other."

Presentational, a term Albers tried to introduce as it presented "positively, what non-representational says indirectly." He liked its sense of "directly apprehended by the mind."

Non-Imitative or **Non-Associative**, include "non" and are therefore unacceptable, for "adjectives [which negate] should be seen as improper for something as positive as art."

Non-Objective, particularly odious to many, for as Albers found, "it implies not only 'no object,' [but also, somehow] 'subjective;' both … misleading … [and] wrong." Since object can mean *aim* as well as *thing*, artists who involve themselves in semantics and philosophy often reject such a term.

Neo-Plastic and **Pure Plastic Art**, Mondrian's contributions, defining "the objective expression of reality … established [by] reciprocal action of determined forms and determined space … constituting the dynamic movement that expresses intrinsic life." He sought a "universal emotion, indescribable, therefore constant." [1]

Most artists accept "Abstract" as the all-inclusive term for other than realistic art. Mondrian grudgingly concedes, "…Abstract Art is right … it is concrete." Albers regrets that "'Abstract' … the first term applied to this art … and probably, so far, the best … over-emphasizes departure from nature and therefore does not adequately emphasize departure solely from vision or emotion."

Do *you* have a preference, based on terms used by a favorite artist or teacher? Can you distinguish the concept from the words in which it is clothed? Or, do you agree with the General Semanticists that language, far from merely expressing thought, determines the nature of the thought expressed? The editing or selective elimination of details can take many forms and has been responsible for numerous styles and categories of painting and design. In this chapter, some historical background is essential.

Historical background

Cézanne first referred to the "sphere, cone and cylinder" as the basis for the form of "everything in nature." He incorporated a sense of these curvilinear geometric solids into his paintings through the use of color facets to show the structure of fruit and

Fig. 8.3 Paul Cézanne, *The Basket of Apples* *(detail)*, 1890–94. Oil on canvas, 25 × 32 ins (63.5 × 81 cm). Courtesy: The Art Institute of Chicago.

other still-life objects (**Fig. 8.3**), and landscapes, and through the placement and simplification of trees and figures.

But in Western art the Cubists, Braque and Picasso primarily, first conscientiously eliminated reference to a particular object seen at a moment in time from one static point of view. What elements of reality can be so eliminated from a painting, or altered by the artist while retaining some allegiance to an original subject?

Ben Shahn wrote in "The Shape of Content", "abstraction uses content as a point of departure." He believes that although a work's "content" may seem trivial, no one may "pronounce either upon the weight or triviality of an idea before its execution into a work of art." Form, he says, can make any content "rise to the heights." His title says it all.

Selective Elimination

If selective elimination of non-essentials is the key to abstraction, we may, for the purpose of study, separate elements relating to *form* from those relating to *content*. Use the following terms to help identify formal or structural factors intentionally altered or removed in the accompanying works. Often several may be identified in a single work.

Suggestion of Three-Dimensional Space may be replaced by isometric or absent perspective, adjacent, non-overlapping shapes; flat, non-modulated tones (pp. 180, 129).

Full-Palette Color may be replaced by a limited palette such as primary color, black and white, or close-value monochromatic harmony (pp. 113, 154).

Fig. 8.4 **Jean Dubuffet**, *The Cow with the Subtile Nose*, 1954. Oil and enamel on canvas, 35 × 45¾ ins (89 × 117 cm). From the Cows, Grass Foliage series. Collection: The Museum of Modern Art, New York. Benjamin Scharps and David Scharps Fund.

Fig. 8.5 (*left*) **Robert Delaunay**, *The Eiffel Tower*, 1910–11. Oil on canvas, 78½ × 50¾ ins (199 × 129 cm). Courtesy: Kunstmuseum, Basel, Emanuel Hofmann Foundation.

Fig. 8.6 (*right*) **Paul Cézanne**, *Pines and Rocks*, 1895–1900. Oil on canvas, 32 × 25¾ ins (81 × 65 cm). Courtesy: The Museum of Modern Art, New York. Lillie P. Bliss Collection.

Single-Focus Point of View may be replaced by multiple viewpoints or combined partial views (pp. 108, 150).

Opaque, Solid Depiction of Objects may be replaced by transparent or X-ray views (pp. 91, 175).

Complete Rendition of Natural Details may be replaced by elimination of details and simplification of form to basic geometric or biomorphic shape (pp. 66, 158).

Sophistication, or skillful technical finish, use of correct proportion and anatomy may be replaced by "primitive" or naïve exaggeration, childlike lack of proportion or technique, sometimes stick-figure simplification (pp. 128, 150).

Curvilinear Form (Fig. 6.5) may be reduced to intersecting perpendiculars or other angular linear transitions (pp. 46, 155).

Specific Details Identifying an Individual (Fig. 4.4) may be replaced by a general type or symbol (pp. 81, 161).

Presentation of Forms in Their Expected Spatial Environment (Fig. 8.5) may be modified by a distortion of the spatial dimension, bending of the visual plane or individual objects (pp. 101, 102).

Emphasis on the Subject with reduced concern for forms around it, may be replaced by a more equal figure/ground relationship or elimination of the idea of negative space (pp. 72, 154).

Decorative Surface Adornment may be reduced or eliminated in favor of structural description alone (pp. 66, 154).

Realistic Modulation of Tonal Values, Chiaroscuro or Shading (Fig. 8.6) may be replaced by the arbitrary application of light and dark, alternate shading, or elimination of an indicated light source (pp. 160, 197).

Capturing of Chance Nuance of Form and Surface may be replaced or minimized in favor of elimination of the accidental and reduction to the general or average (pp. 90, 158).

Fig. 8.7   Willem de Kooning, *Woman I*, 1950. Oil on canvas, 64 × 46 ins (162.5 × 117 cm). Courtesy: The Museum of Modern Art, New York. purchase.

Precise Depiction of Observed Detail (Fig. 8.7) may be replaced by freely expressed suggestion, a sketchy or calligraphic response to a subject or idea, communication of feelings about a subject or idea, symbolic or personal interpretations of a theme, often without clearly delineated shapes, separable areas or distinct edges (pp. 151, 189).

Showing the Entire Subject in an Environment with an amount of space around it, may be replaced by a close-up, cropped portion of the subject (pp. 156, 246).

Separation of an Object from its Environment may be replaced by a camouflage effect, concealing the edge of form using close values and colors or similar patterns (pp. 72, 151).

Can you think of other qualities that may be altered, simplified, stylized or eliminated in these and other works called abstract? (*Stylized* means an exaggerated application of one or more generally recognizable simplifications, such as those derived from realistic biomorphic design, as in Art Nouveau, a curvilinear elongation, and Art Deco, a decorative geometric use of minimal contour.) [2] See book illustrations by Aubrey Beardsley and many wallpaper designs of that period.

Abstract expressionism

Reduction to geometric minima failed to satisfy the Abstract Expressionists, whose involvement with emotional, kinetic and kinesthetic impulse, as well as symbolic content and meaning, brought calligraphic gesture and "action" directly onto the surface of their often oversize canvases. The "Action" paintings shown are a small sampling of this diverse style, which displays as many variations as practitioners (**Figs. 8.8, 8.9**). Another form taken by Abstract Expressionists, a kind of "soft geometry," presents fields of almost melting color, softly fused or jagged at the edge, striped or stained, to reveal new kinds of configurations and expression (**Fig. 10.16**).

Would Abstract Expressionists agree with the critic Lawrence Alloway that "what is missing from the formalist approach to painting is a serious desire to study meanings beyond the purely visual configuration?"

Fig. 8.8   Franz Kline. *New York*, 1953. Oil on canvas, 79 × 50½ ins (200 × 128 cm). Courtesy: Albright-Knox Art Gallery, Buffalo, New York. Gift of Seymour H. Knox.

Fig. 8.9 Robert Motherwell, *Elegy to the Spanish Republic # 132*, 1975–85. Acrylic on canvas, 96 × 120 ins (244 × 305 cm). Collection of the artist. Courtesy: M. Knoedler & Co., Inc., New York.

The General Semanticist S. I. Hayakawa believes we are "object minded, and not relation minded." He calls for a "reorganization of our visual habits to perceive not isolated things in space, but structure, order, and the relatedness of events ... long overdue in all our experience." Representation in art, according to John Dewey, suggests either the "imitation or agreeable reminiscence" of what has been seen or remembered. The ancient Greeks questioned this aim. Art was considered imitative, therefore a falsehood, by Plato and Aristotle. The introduction of photography moved many who equated painting with realism to agree with Delaroche in the 1830s that "from today, painting is dead;" but there are those who share Matisse's view that the camera is a great boon to painters, relieving them of the necessity of copying objects. Ben Shahn summarized the transition from representational to non-objective art: "First, the object with no shorthand, and at last, the shorthand with no object."

EXERCISES

Exercise 1:
Add meanings of kinds of abstraction to your art vocabulary and update regularly. Note at least one example of each.

Exercise 2:
Identify each of the characteristics listed on pp. 151–2 in at least two works, one with the "realistic" quality and one with its "abstract" counterpart.

Development of geometric abstraction

We can easily envision a Mondrian-esque spatial division in Monet's 1891 placement of four trees (**Fig. 8.10**). In 1900, Cézanne also structured trees geometrically, but he included diagonals (**Fig. 8.6**). Georges Braque employed almost the same composition of vertical trees, stopped by a horizontal band. Plant forms and buildings, seen as geometricized shapes in a shallow planar space, help establish a formal, intellectual approach to painting, derived largely from Cézanne, but departing from any attempt to give an impression of nature.

Cubists, well into the 1930s, continued to "use content as a point of departure," never eliminating association with pictorial subject matter (**Fig. 8.11**), but some painters had made the break with representational content earlier. "Around 1913," claims Theo van Doesburg in the *De Stijl* magazine, "Piet Mondrian first arrived at Neo-Plasticism . . . as a logical continuation of Cubism."

The development of Mondrian's pared down, perpendicular, "relational" canvases, using pure primary colors placed precisely within bands of black among unequal white rectangles, shows one of the clearest progressions in painting's history. In retrospect, it seems easy to know exactly where Mondrian was headed, but our admiration for his accomplishment is enhanced by an awareness that each painting was at one time the farthest step taken into the unknown reaches of Abstract Art. If we think of realism and abstraction on a scale of 1 to 10, as suggested by Anderson, could Mondrian be considered a "perfect 10?"

Starting with his 1902 series of trees, remarkably reminiscent of the Monet *Poplars* (**Fig. 8.10**) in composition, Mondrian became interested in the intersection of branches, seen dark against the light sky. Study the small selection of his works (**Fig. 8.12**), though we might as well show a sequence moving from *Dunes* and *Sea* through his famous oval *Pier and Ocean* studies, the so-called plus-and-minus compositions, or

Fig. 8.10 (*left*) **Claude Monet**, *Poplars (Les Quatre Arbres)*, 1891. Oil on canvas, $32\frac{1}{4} \times 32\frac{1}{8}$ ins (82×81.5 cm). Courtesy: The Metropolitan Museum of Art, bequest of Mrs. H. O. Havemeyer, 1929. The H. O. Havemeyer Collection, New York.

Fig. 8.11 (*right*) **Paul Braque**, *House at L'Estaque*, 1908. Oil on canvas, $28\frac{3}{4} \times 23\frac{3}{8}$ ins (73×59.5 cm). Courtesy: Museum of Fine Arts Berne, Hermann und Margrit Rupf-Stiftung.

a

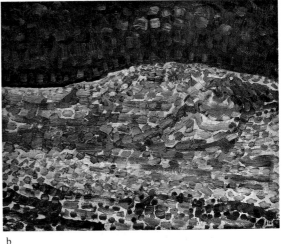

b

Fig. 8.12   Works by Piet Mondrian. a *Dune*, 1910. Oil on canvas, $55\frac{1}{2} \times 94\frac{1}{8}$ ins (141×239 cm). Collection: Haags Gemeentemuseum, The Hague. **b** *Dune II*, 1909. Oil on canvas, $14\frac{1}{4} \times 18\frac{1}{4}$ ins (37×46 cm). Collection: Haags Gemeentemuseum, The Hague. **c** *Flowering Appletree*, 1912. Oil on canvas, $30\frac{3}{4} \times 41\frac{3}{4}$ ins (78×106 cm). Collection: Haags Gemeentemuseum, The Hague. **d** *Oval* *Composition (Tableau III)*, 1914. Oil on canvas, $55\frac{5}{16} \times 40\frac{1}{8}$ ins (140×101 cm). Courtesy: Stedelijk Museum, Amsterdam. **e** *Composition 2*, 1922. Oil on canvas, $22 \times 21\frac{1}{8}$ ins (56×53 cm). Courtesy: The Solomon R. Guggenheim Museum. **f** *Victory Boogie Woogie*, 1943–44. Oil on canvas, $49\frac{5}{8} \times 49\frac{5}{8}$ ins (126×126 cm). Collection: Mr. and Mrs. S. I. Newhouse, Jr.

c

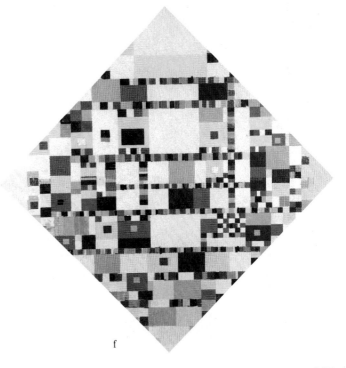

d

e

f

Fig. 8.13 **Piet Mondrian**, *Calla Lily*, 1916. Oil on canvas, 31½ × 19¹¹⁄₁₆ ins (80 × 50 cm). Collection: Haags Gemeentemuseum, The Hague.

various lighthouses and church façades, dissecting into perpendicular intersections leading to small color planes, checkerboards and even grids before resolving into the "pure plastic" mature Mondrian style. Toward the end of his life, Mondrian re-introduced associative titles, identifying cities as thematic inspiration. Is a new direction suggested in his last painting, *Victory Boogie-Woogie* (toward the end of World War II), through its pulsing spots of color, prefiguring the after-image responses of Op art? This final, unfinished work, placed in the diamond or "lozenge" position of several of his earlier studies, shows that Mondrian had not reached a stopping place in his quest for the essence of visual experience.

Study Mondrian's early drawings of chrysanthemums, gems of fluid, descriptive, linear representation. By 1916, an oil study of a calla lily, almost reduced to a perfect diamond shape, marks the end of his concern with such subject matter (**Fig. 8.13**). In 1918, in an amazingly similar composition stripped to its skeleton, Kasimir Malevitch tipped one white square inside another, in a supreme effort to minimize his means, creating the sense of a second white by placing his brushstrokes at different angles inside and outside the tilted square. Later efforts to reduce elements on the picture plane "about as far as they can go," in works almost but not quite invisible, seem to increase the importance of the pioneer Malevitch's contribution to the oft-quoted goal, "Less is More."

Fig. 8.14a **Georgia O'Keeffe**, *Green-Gray Abstraction*, 1931. Oil on canvas, 36 × 24 ins (91 × 61 cm). Courtesy: The Regis Collection, Minneapolis.

Fig. 8.14b **Georgia O'Keeffe**, *Jack-in-the-Pulpit # 11*, 1930. Oil on canvas, 40 × 30 ins (101 × 76 cm). Courtesy: National Gallery of Art, Washington, D.C., Alfred Steiglitz Collection. Bequest of Georgia O'Keeffe (1987.58.1) 1887–1986.

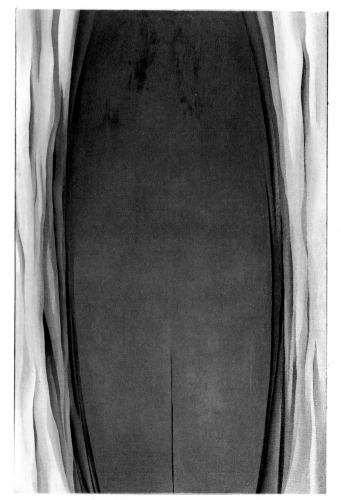

Development of biomorphic abstraction

Abstraction also flourishes in non-geometric directions, whether associative/geometric as in Cubism, or non-associative/geometric as in De Stijl, Neo-Plastic and Minimal Art.

Increasingly close-up, enlarged and simplified views of flowers and floral elements by Georgia O'Keeffe show a biomorphic, or growth/form development, reduced to such essentials as make recognition of their source unimportant (**Fig. 8.14**). The flowing curves and modulated color of even the most abstract of these works maintain an allegiance to nature. We always see O'Keeffe abstracting *from* the living source of her inspiration.

The invention and playfulness of Matisse's cut-out forms, looping and curving in and out of organically derived contour, recall the barest essence of actual referents (**Fig. 0.7**). The quintessential leafiness they convey is not compromised by association with any merely real individual plant. Familiar shapes on the seat for a folding stool from the tomb of Tutenkhamun of Egypt (**Fig. 8.15**) might lead us to believe it had been designed by Matisse except for the fact that Tut lived over three thousand years ago!

Perhaps Jean Arp succeeded in reducing the biomorphic curves of nature to their most pristine state. Called "a one-man laboratory for the discovery of new form," by Alfred Barr, Arp involved himself in the Dada and Surrealist Movements. Influenced by the Cubists, he was dissatisfied with the results of his search for unattainable perfection. Later, after accepting then welcoming the "laws of accident and chance" into his work, Arp reduced associative forms to a kind of "universal alphabet of basic shapes," psychologically as well as visually inspired, whimsical, witty and, to use his own term, "liberated." His chief concern became a minimal yet comprehensible iconography, bringing "elements of geometric as well as organic structure into equilibrium." His subjects, ranging from semicolons, navels, eggs, mustaches, leaves and shirt fronts to

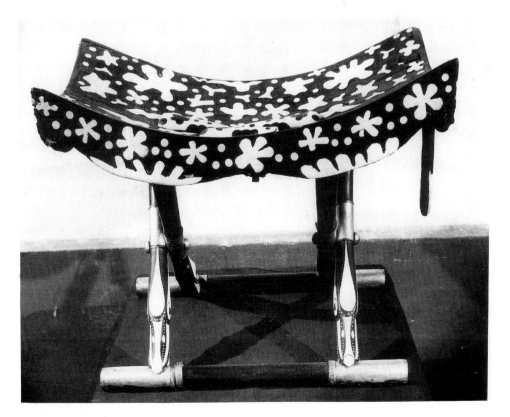

Fig. 8.15 Folding Stool from the Tomb of Tutenkhamun, XVIII dynasty, Egypt. Courtesy: The Egyptian Museum, Cairo.

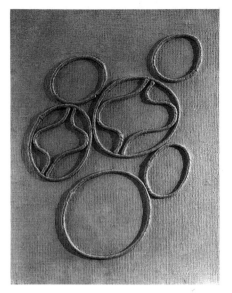

Fig. 8.16 (*right*) **Jean Arp**, *Leaves and Navels*, 1929. Oil and string on canvas, 13¾ × 10¾ ins (35 × 27 cm). Collection: The Museum of Modern Art, New York:

(*left*) *Skeleton and Moustache*, 1958. Tapestry, 59⅞ × 49¼ ins (152 × 124.5 cm). On exhibition with other works by Arp at Galerie Denise René, Paris.

forks, clouds and "star seeds," show that "the same law [unifying all natural processes] orders the fundamental process of artistic creation." His unique fusion of geometric and biomorphic sources of inspiration eventually "diverged, to become the two decisive directions of Abstract Art" (**Fig. 8.16**). Spontaneity, intuition, and a mystical sense Arp shared with Kandinsky and Klee, prefigured Abstract Expressionism, and are seen by some as sources of the "grafitti" and "neo-expressionist" styles in evidence well into the 1980s. "Reason," said Arp, "has cut man off from nature."

In six weeks during December 1945 and January 1946, Pablo Picasso produced a series of lithographs, actually progressive states of an image on a single stone, by which he intended to show the sequential abstraction-in-stages of one idea. This is an extraordinary glimpse into the visual thinking of an artist and his step-by-step simplification, geometricization, and elimination of three-dimensional suggestion until a single, irreducibly linear, essential "Bull" remains (**Fig. 8.17**). It should be studied and restudied by anyone seeking to understand abstraction in art or ways in which it can be achieved. The final, eleventh, print, the "least" in measurable quantity, becomes the "most" in terms of economy, elegance, unity and, to our delight, wit.

NOTE: We have looked briefly at the development, progressively abstract, of the work of several major artists. Nothing has been said of their sculpture, which, being three-dimensional, is outside the scope of this book. Look for sculptural works by Arp, Picasso, Matisse and others to enrich your understanding of their complete *œuvre*, or body of created work.

Fig. 8.17 **Pablo Picasso**, *The Bull, (3rd, 5th, 8th, 11th State)*, 1946. Lithograph on Arches paper. Courtesy: National Gallery of Art. Washington.

Applications of abstraction

Fig. 8.18 Prostrate Man, unknown Paleolithic artist, perhaps 30,000 BC., from a cave at Lascaux, France. Color photo by Hans Hinz.

Abstraction provides an opportunity for many related, valuable studies. Although an entire group's efforts can provide insights and comparisons unavailable to the person working alone, an individual may discover a surprising richness through completion of these sequential studies. [3]

"Primitivism"

Numerous similarities may be seen in works showing degrees of abstraction and in those exhibiting qualities often called "primitive." Just as "abstract" may embrace a large number of divergent styles, so "primitive" has also been used as an umbrella term covering a multitude of ideas, techniques and appearances, extending throughout the history of recorded art. It is amazing to note similarities between works created hundreds, if not thousands, of years apart, such as the earliest cave-wall markings and the latest products of the so-called graffiti artists on walls, trains and even canvas.

Fig. 8.19 (*left*) **Paul Klee**, *Handbill for Comedians*, 1938. Gouache on newsprint, 19⅛ × 12⅝ ins (48 × 32 cm). Courtesy: The Metropolitan Museum of Art, New York.
Fig. 8.20 (*right*) **Pablo Picasso**, *Les Demoiselles d'Avignon*, 1907. Oil on canvas, 96 × 92 ins (244 × 234 cm). Collection: The Museum of Modern Art, New York. Acquired through the Lillie P. Bliss Bequest.

Compare the depiction of human form in **Fig. 8.18** and **Fig. 8.19**, trying to avoid identifying or labeling each work beforehand. Can you distinguish intentional naiveté, mannered innocence and the reduction of details to archetype or symbol, lack of skill, training or sophistication? Is it important to know the visual conventions of societies that produce traditional designs, patterns, drawings or paintings before choosing to label them "primitive?" On first seeing an African mask, Picasso remarked not "How primitive," but "How rational." His first clearly Cubist-directed work, *Les Demoiselles d'Avignon* (**Fig. 8.20**), painted in 1907, the year after Cézanne's death, shows strong

archaic Iberian influence, as well as that of African mask sculpture (**Fig. 8.21**). Is this a primitive work because it employs symbols associated with Primitive Art? Why should a literate person, familiar with the worldwide artistic expression of many people during many ages, choose to work in a "primitive" way? Is the work of children purely primitive? Is it perhaps time to retire this much disputed term and to see each type of art grouped together as Primitive, separately, with no passing of judgment on the works as a whole? May we not apply the criteria of a group or civilization to its own achievement? Or must we believe in absolute standards of artistic excellence, according to our own cultural traditions?

Each of the many styles labeled "primitive" (by another group of people) is likely to demonstrate one or more of the characteristics we have identified as abstract. These include:

Children's Art (**Fig. 8.22**), which often shows exaggerated, symbolic, simplified form, no vanishing point perspective, flattened ambiguous space, omission of details felt to be unnecessary, proportion based on psychological rather than observable factors, and a fanciful bringing together of unlikely subject matter.

Folk Art or **Contemporary Primitive** (**Fig. 8.23**), often by self-taught artists concerned with remembered or allegorical urban or rural outdoor scenes, highly detailed but ornamental, flat, unconcerned with accurate perspective though frequently displaying a decorative use of perspective-like shapes, often without color modulations or atmospheric perspective, frequently relying on outline and clear distinction of edges throughout.

Tribal Art, using stylized forms of ritual nature, developed through long-established tradition, largely in non-technologically centered communities among people whose civilizations have been recorded and transmitted without written language, relying on powerful symbolic forms and spiritual values, created to serve ceremonial or functional purposes.[4]

Fig. 8.24 (*left*) Figure, Chokwe, Angolan wood carving, undated, location unknown. From Carl Einstein's ''Negerplastik,'' 1915.

Fig. 8.25 (*right*) **Fernand Leger**, *Back cover design of ''Little Review,''* 1923. Gouache and ink on paper, 12 × 8 ins (30.5 × 20 cm). Collection of Kay Hillman. New York.

Fig. 8.26 **Gerry Noyes**, *Navajo Art, U.S. Postage stamps*, 1986. © 1986 U.S. Postal Service.

Although not strictly *Tribal* as defined by anthropologists, many groups whose art has been so designated share the qualities described. William Rubin addresses the question of categories and names for this art at length. While acknowledging the misunderstandings likely to detract from the value of any term chosen, Mr Rubin prefers ''tribal'' to designate works originating in the nations and cultures of Africa (**Fig. 8.24**), the many groups into which the Amerindian people divide themselves, and the island civilizations in the Southwest Pacific areas known as Polynesia, Oceania or Micronesia. Instead of ignoring these traditions for lack of a satisfactory designation, let us celebrate with Kirk Varnedoe ''the inventive power of tribal artists, humbling in its denial of Western presumptions linking human potential to technological progress.'' He honors ''modern artists who, subverting their received traditions, forged a bond between intelligences otherwise divided by barriers of language, belief and social structure'' (**Fig. 8.25**). In noting ''the power of art to surpass its cultural confines,'' he asks us to celebrate ''the unpredictable potential of human creativity wherever found.'' The relegation of so-called primitive works to obscure halls of ethnology seems to have been happily reversed by such exhibitions as the Rubin/Varnedoe triumph, ''Primitivism,'' held at the Museum of Modern Art in 1984 and the earlier exhibition ''The Navajo Blanket,'' at the Brooklyn Museum in 1972. A sign of our increasing sensibility is our awareness that today this exhibition would have another title, perhaps ''Navajo Weaving'' or, as seen on the 1986 series of these works on United States commemorative postage stamps, simply ''Navajo Art'' (**Fig. 8.26**).

Fig. 8.27 **Lisa Collado**, *Rosa Mexicana*, 1988. Mixed media collage painting, $24\frac{1}{2} \times 25$ ins (62×63.5 cm). Courtesy of the artist.

Graffiti—art?

Within the scope the intentionally unsophisticated, often using words and numbers as graphic elements in a kind of comic-book-derived "bubble-script," cartoon or stick-figured to depict the human form, work comparable to present-day graffiti was originally seen on walls of ancient caves and in ancient Rome and has been acknowledged ever since. Now, in urban areas particularly, this form of self-expression is seen everywhere. During the 1980s, it began to receive the dignity of major exhibition coverage as certain practitioners applied their markings and designs to canvas instead of concrete. The "outline" graffiti of Keith Haring and others has found its way into fabric and other commerical design as well as several styles of painting (**Fig. 8.27**).

Created with cans of spray paint or wide-edged marking pens, can these same works on the side of a train be vandalism and on the wall of a gallery be art? There is no denying the strong graphic appeal of some of this work or its social value in providing an outlet for the anger, frustration and despair of individuals who see no chance for an improved life style within our society. But is it art, and whose definition is "definitive?" Norman Mailer has described the graffiti phenomenon "as if we are cast back into the emotional imperative of . . . cave painting . . . trying to make some scratch in the world . . . the cave painting is now collective." Referring to "the ambiguity of meaning in the twentieth century," he wonders whether "the nature of the painting has become less interesting than the . . . relation of painting to society—we can even . . . get the artist out of it altogether, and it is still art." [5, 6]

Stencil graffiti

An interesting variation originating in the mid-1980s is the stenciled, stylized, witty silhouetted figure and symbol on abandoned urban buildings and on sidewalks (**Fig 0.9**). These possess a certain charm which places them apart from the ubiquitous sprayed "name and number" markings. [7]

Have *you* ever written, carved or scratched your name into the surface of a wall, desk, tree or book? If so, was it a record of your existence, a declaration of territoriality, an identifying mark, a purposeless doodle—or a work of art? Does intention determine the nature of an act, or the results it produces? Can "Fine" Art include "Primitive" Art? Can answers to these and similar questions be found? Regardless of your response, do you believe that questions must be asked and reconsidered by artists and designers of every generation and style? Through constant refinement and elimination of non-essentials we approach a core of understanding, to help achieve a meaningful synthesis, following in the brushstrokes, if not the footprints, of the originators of abstraction.

The powerful, even magic, aspect that the most civilized among us attribute to the visual image is demonstrated by the "primitive" device of sticking a pin into the eye of a photographed face. Although intellectually we understand that the "map" is not the reality or "territory," we recoil from feelings associated with such an act. How perfectly Matisse understood a similar confusion of "levels of abstraction." When approached by someone complaining that she had never seen a woman who looked like the one in his painting, he replied: "Madam, that is not a woman; that is a picture."

EXERCISES

Exercise 3:
Develop a single representational image in three separate series of at least five steps each, creating sequences leading to biomorphic, geometric and expressionist final works.

Exercise 4:
Develop a drawing of a human or animal subject in three separate ways, representing Children's, Folk and Tribal Art. Ask others to identify each "primitive" style. Make necessary modifications.

Exercise 5:
Find an abandoned or otherwise appropriate building, wall or fence. With the owner's permission, design and execute a large-scale graffiti-style mural, as a group exercise preferably. Socially meaningful themes are recommended. Do include words or numbers.

Exercise 6:
Design a poster or fabric pattern using graffiti-derived imagery.

Exercise 7:
Design and cut a simple stencil to be incorporated in the previous exercises or completed as a separate work.

Summations

Fig. 8.28 Jean Arp, *Leaves and Navels*, (detail), 1929. Oil and string on canvas, $13\frac{3}{4} \times 10\frac{3}{4}$ ins (35×27 cm). Collection: The Museum of Modern Art, New York.

John Dewey, whose philosophy of art is summarized in his title "Art as Experience," found the solution to the question of abstraction in the words of his mentor Dr Alfred C. Barnes: "Reference to the real world does not disappear from art as forms cease to be those of actually existing things, any more than objectivity disappears from science when it ... substitutes for earth, fire, air and water hydrogen, oxygen, nitrogen and carbon ... When we cannot find representation of any particular object in a picture, what it represents may be the qualities which *all* ... objects share, such as color, extensity, solidity, movement, rhythm, etc.... Hence [art] serves ... as a paradigm of the visible essence of all things ... [by holding] in solution the emotions which individualized things provoke in a more specialized way."

Susanne K. Langer, the distinguished philosopher, will have the last word from her volume "Reflections on Art": "Abstraction from nature still is a mode of representation whose relationship with reality is stretched, but never snapped" (**Fig. 8.28**).

Chapter Nine

COLOR IN ACTION

Fig. 9.1 **Ellsworth Kelly**, *Sanary*, 1952. Oil on wood, $51\frac{1}{2} \times 60$ ins (131×152 cm). Courtesy of the artist and Blum Helmann Gallery.

"Color is the most relative medium in art," said Josef Albers, but in this ever-changing world, isn't the constancy of color one thing we can count on? Red is red, or is it? Because of the highly experimental nature of these color studies, you will find that exercises in this chapter have been incorporated into the text.

Cut a small rectangle of red paper into two equal pieces. Try to find a red with no trace of yellow (an orange), blue (a violet), white (a tint), or black (a shade). Collect many reds before you choose one for this study. The more you refine your eye, the larger your collection will grow.

Place one red rectangle on a ground of white paper, the other on black. Focus on an imaginary point between these two fields and slowly allow your peripheral vision to fill with the two physically identical red shapes. Immediately you will see a difference between the reds as each field acts to drain its qualities from the central figure. The black ground, draining darkness, will seem conversely to add light, while the white ground will cause its figure to darken perceptibly. The longer you observe this effect, the stronger it becomes. (This study is called "1 = 2" [p. 170] in the series we will develop.)

Which is the "reality," the physical fact that the reds are the same, or the visual effect, showing them to be very different in relation to their different environments? Much of Albers' work focused on this now familiar discrepancy. Perhaps the question should be rephrased: Which reality, the physical or the visual, is more useful or meaningful in the arts (**Fig. 9.2**)?

Fig. 9.2 Jeff MacNelly, *Shoe*, newspaper cartoon feature, 7/10/1985. Reprinted by permission: Tribune Media Services.

The nature of color: several views

Although many believe Albers has given the clearest contemporary expression to the interactive, relativist view of color, similar ideas have been expressed throughout the long history of art.

Da Vinci advised, "To give figures a great effect, a light figure must be opposed with a dark ground . . . In general, all contraries—because of their opposition—give a particular force and brilliancy of effect."

Goethe, the German poet and philosopher, who spent much time investigating the nature of color, found that "by purely juxtaposing color, complete paintings can be created, and without shadow." Even Picasso acknowledged, "Actually, you work with few colors. But they seem like a lot more, when each is in the right place" (**Figs. 9.1, 9.3**).

Faber Birren, still perhaps the leading color theoretician of our day, believes that "many visual sensations, alike to the physicist, may well be unalike to human experience." He realizes "the study of colors is generally confusing. Discrepancies found in physics, art and psychology offer no end of complication to the student . . . Color charts appear to offer no solution."

Fig. 9.3   Georges Seurat, *Sunday Afternoon on the Island of La Grande Jatte,* 1884–86. Oil on canvas, 81 × 120¾ ins (206 × 307 cm). Courtesy: The Art Institute of Chicago, Helen Birch Bartlett Memorial Collection, 1926.224 © 1989 Art Institute of Chicago. All Rights Reserved.

Therefore, although in the following chapter we will consider traditional concepts and see how to construct classic color wheels, it is more useful to begin by experimenting with perceptual studies, to build a personal vocabulary of color and develop visual sensibility. Only the process of selecting, placing, adjusting, making changes, making the search and discovery your own over a period of time, will ensure real learning or meaningful application of the principles behind any illustrations. Make every effort to verify, duplicate, or improve upon each color effect studied.

Josef Albers

This approach to the study of color interaction under observation is based on the work and teaching of Josef Albers. Called the "father of color theory" by many, he left Germany in 1933, after studying and teaching at the famous technical art and design institute, the Bauhaus. With his artist wife, Anni Albers, he emigrated to the United States, many years of teaching taking him first to Black Mountain and then to Yale, as Chairman of the Art Department. In addition to his celebrated course in color, he also taught painting and a perceptual approach to linear drawing. Albers' monumental 1963 work, *The Interaction of Color*, contains some two hundred serigraphed illustrations of his own and his students' solutions to the color problems introduced in his classes.

He believed in the importance of each student's discovery of the truths to be learned through investigation of the studies presented. Ideas would be dis-covered or un-covered; he would never simply "cover" them by telling too much. Presented in book form, what might be an epiphany through personal discovery may simply become a nod of agreement as you "see" each point intellectually. It is up to you.

The color studies: methods and materials

It is advisable to use opaque papers rather than paints for these studies. Unevenness of color, inconsistency of surface, differences between the color of wet and dry paint, and a general need to concentrate on the manipulation of pigment and brush, neatness of edges and matching of tones, rather than on the study of color action, can be avoided by using a rich assortment of colored papers. A set of commercially prepared papers in gradated steps such as the Color Aid assortment may be supplemented by colored and printed papers of every description, from junk mail to the theater tickets, bus transfers, envelopes and ephemera used by collage artists since Kurt Schwitters (**Fig. 9.4**). Too costly for the individual but a splendid resource for a department or studio is the Natural Color System Index, published by Färbinstitut, the Scandinavian Color Institute, containing several thousand subtly graduated and brilliantly printed samples of colors, modulated according to nuance, shades, tonality or hue.

You will need this equipment:
— An X-Acto pencil knife with #11 blade.
— A 12″ steel rule to use as a cutting edge.
— A small steel right angle and a clear acrylic right angle.
— Rubber cement in a small brush bottle or can.
— A self-healing plastic cutting board (optional, expensive).
— A supply of lightweight backing boards.

If you are fortunate enough to be in an area where the deciduous leaves turn color in the Fall, collect a great variety before they become brown or wet and press them in a telephone directory under a heavy weight for as long as possible. (I recently discovered a bookful several years old—thin, almost waxy-flat and translucent—full of fiery, smoky, unprintable hues.) These are excellent, particularly in free-study collages (**Fig. 9.5**).

Fig. 9.4 (*left*) **Kurt Schwitters**, *Merzbild (Entrance Ticket Collage)*, 1926. Collage, 7 × 5¼ ins (18 × 13 cm). Private Collection.
Fig. 9.5 (*right*) **Marcia King Speier**, *Leaf Study*, 1954. Collage with pressed autumn leaves, 5 × 4 ins (13 × 10 cm). Courtesy of the artist.

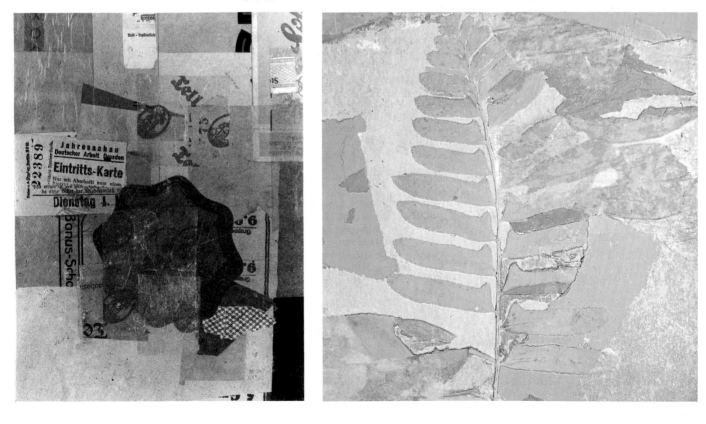

Inlaying areas of color, level and adjacent, as in a jigsaw puzzle, will produce works without the thin edge-shadow caused by placing one sheet on top of another. Accomplish this by cutting through several sheets at once, reserving duplicate areas for later use.

Neutral, geometric shapes such as squares and rectangles help you focus on color effects without being distracted by other associations.

Fig. 9.6 A gray scale, seen against a middle gray tone.

Identifying a particular color

Select a sample of any color, then try to identify it so that you might order a yard of cloth by telephone without showing its color at all. Can this be done? The identification of any color is an elusive, subjective effort at best, and it should be no surprise to learn that there is much disagreement as to the use and meaning of terms to describe and explain what color "is" and how it works. You may assume that you know the primary colors (red, yellow, blue, of course), but even this "fact" is open to further consideration as artists and scientists continue to investigate.

Hue

Start with a small piece of paper, say some kind of green. As any green contains at least some blue and some yellow, on an imaginary scale of nine choices, from yellow as # 1 to blue as # 9, locate your green:

1	2	3	4	5	6	7	8	9
Yellow	Y–Y/G	Y/G	G–Y/G	Green	G–B/G	B/G	B–B/G	Blue

This should give you a sense of the blue/yellow proportion of your green, the mix of primaries that make up this "secondary" color.

You have located your green on a scale of color, hue or chroma, the color-name quality, easiest to identify. (Many greens have a trace of the third primary, red, as well, but we will overlook that here.) To locate examples of the other secondary colors, use different scales, one moving from red to yellow (for orange), and one moving from red to blue (for violet). What kind of scales would you use to locate the hue of a brown, gray or primary color? (Look ahead to the discussion of Complementary and Analogous Colors for a way to approach these questions.)

Value

Make or imagine a photograph of your color sample with black-and-white film. All signs of green are gone; what remains is a tone of gray. Locating a color on a gray scale, moving from white to black, is not difficult; we are accustomed to achromatic, colorless tonality in photographs and film and, to a lesser extent in recent years, on television (**Fig. 9.6**).

1	2	3	4	5	6	7	8	9
White		Light Gray		Middle Gray		Dark Gray		Black

Prepare a stepped gray scale (guided by the Weber-Fechner Law, described on p. 186), and use it for this exercise, trying to locate your green in terms of its light value. The greater the amount of light, or white, the higher the value is said to be.

Photography students might wish to use a light meter for this determination, but a light color in the shadow will read very differently than it will in bright light, and a dark color will also read quite differently under varying types of illumination. It is better to train your eye than to rely on a meter at this point.

Intensity

The third quality of a color relates to its brightness, richness, luminosity, saturation or intensity. The variety and verbal color of the many efforts to pinpoint this quality

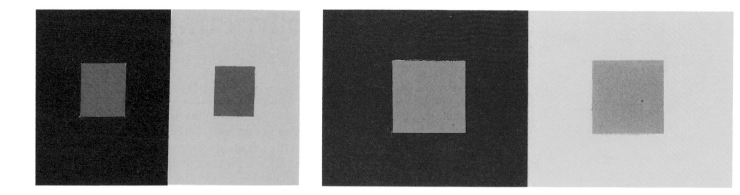

Fig. 9.7 *I = 2*, one physical color appearing as two, seen against different grounds. Inlaid Color Aid Paper collage.

Fig. 9.8 *Reversal*, one physical color appearing to be the same as its opposite ground. Monochromatic solution.

suggest that it is the most elusive to identify in words. In the middle ranges it is often difficult to tell whether two colors are of the same intensity, particularly if they are close in light value (**Fig. 9.13**), when extremes of intensity may be eye-dazzling and electric or faded and almost melted in appearance. You can create dramatic changes in intensity by juxtaposing colors of contrasting hue and brightness, for a color may show a vibrant, fluorescent edge in one environment and virtually melt away in another. As intensity diminishes, a color appears increasingly dulled or grayed, an effect which is produced in paint by the addition of a touch of a color's complementary hue or a mixture of black-and-white gray. This is a physical graying, having nothing to do with a color's place on a value scale, as a light green can seem bright or dull, and a dark black can appear flat and washed-out or patent-leather bright.

Locate your original green sample on a scale of intensity.

1	2	3	4	5	6	7	8	9
Bright, Eye-Dazzling		Brightish		Normal		Dullish		Dull, Washed-Out

In locating your sample, we have ignored the color's relationship to its neighbor colors. The exercise is therefore imaginary, an intellectual pursuit.

All three qualities of a color can be made to change, often quite remarkably, if you keep the effect of a visual sponge in mind, allowing the ground color to subtract or drain its three qualities from the central figure. When you have completed the studies, look for these color-active combinations in paintings and graphic works. (This is a lifelong "exercise"!)

I = 2 (color change)

In our first study you saw the ability of black and white to affect the apparent light-and-dark quality, the light value, of a color. This is not a true color change, as there has been no modification of the red-yellow-blueness, the actual *color* of the original hue (**Fig. 9.7**). A black-and-white photograph may capture every tonal nuance of an image, with no chromatic color at all. To create a true color change, the grounds surrounding the figure must contain chromatic color as well as tones of light and dark.

Place two shapes of physically identical color on different grounds so that their chromatic nature is altered. Repeat, with modification(s).

Reversal

For a subtle but satisfying study, try to make each of two small figures (squares) of physically identical color, seen on different backgrounds, appear to match the ground of the opposite figure. With fields of very different light value, but close hue and

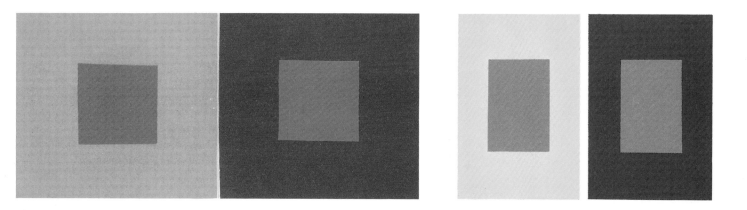

Fig. 9.9 Toward a reversal; colors moving in the direction of their opposite ground.

intensity, this is not too difficult, if the two identical figures are of a middle value (**Fig. 9.8**).

Try a monochromatic palette at first. Then use a secondary color (of middle value and intensity) on fields of its "parent" colors (an Albers term.)

This will work best if a touch of each primary is added to the other. You will never get a green to look pure yellow or pure blue (I should say, "hardly ever"), but it may easily look light yellow-green or dark blue-green against the other of these grounds (**Fig. 9.9**).

2 = I

This study is invaluable in fabric design and interior decoration for showing two objects of the same color in two different places—say a pillow on two different pieces of furniture. Since choice of ground affects the color of a subject, whenever you wish to show the "same" color in two different environments, it will be necessary to use two different mixtures.

Try making two physically different colors move closer together, or even appear identical, by the careful selection of grounds (**Fig. 9.10**). Modify your first intuitive choices until you succeed in creating the appearance of (almost) identical hue, value and intensity.

Fig. 9.10 2 = I, two physical colors appearing the same. on different grounds.

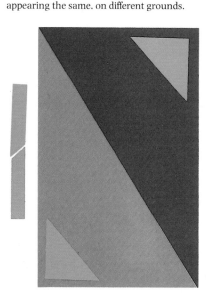

Stripe study

The effect of "fluting" in stripes, or the illusion of carefully stepped light values, can give a sense of shading or even color reversal. Gene Davis and other twentieth-century painters have found the stripe a sufficient subject for an extensive and ever surprising body of work (**Fig. 9.11**).

Design a stripe study so that each edge of every stripe is affected by its neighbor, giving the illusion of split stripes, each divided into two distinct, narrower bands of visually different colors. Try sequences from successful previous studies to start.

Fig. 9.11 **Kenneth Noland**, *Up Cadmium*, 1965. Acrylic resin paint on canvas, 72 × 216 ins (182 × 549 cm). Courtesy: André Emmerich Gallery, New York.

Vibration

A physical explanation for the seeming magic of vibration has to do with the additive mix of light waves. (See the discussion of light mixtures, additive and subtractive, on p. 184.) Although many find this electric effect disturbing if not irritating, it has been used handsomely by Stuart Davis, Matisse and most of the "Op" artists, particularly Anuszkiewicz (**Fig. 9.13**), who continues to investigate its possibilities. This prolific artist bases most of his shimmering, subtly structured work on the use of thin stripes and lines of vibrating color (**Fig. 9.12**).

As Matisse has shown, vibration may be used to advantage in the graphic arts, especially poster and advertising design.

Create a study in vibration by placing complementary colors (of the same or very close light value and intensity) at an edge, to give off a brilliant line of a new and unexpected hue. Try violet and green to excite the eye into seeing a thin line of neon blue. (The blue or cyan is a mixture of green and blue-violet light rays which spill over at the edge.)

Fig. 9.12 Student studies. Vibration (*left*), Melt (*right*).

Melted edge

The soft or melted edge all but makes invisible the boundary between adjacent colors, a quiet effect that can bring a special, almost mystical, quality to paintings or graphic work.

The paintings of Ad Reinhardt, especially his "black" series, show this subtle use of color (**Fig. 9.14**). At first viewers may see only black, but after a time the eye will fill with color; soft traces of violets, blues and grays seem to appear as though from within the painting, and the black will vanish! (No printed page can reproduce this effect.) A suggestion of nine-square structure and chromatic richness moving in and out of focus informs these paintings, called minimalist by some, as they attain their goals with the most economical means.

Experiment with placing colors of very similar hue, value and intensity near one another, to make their inner separation almost disappear.

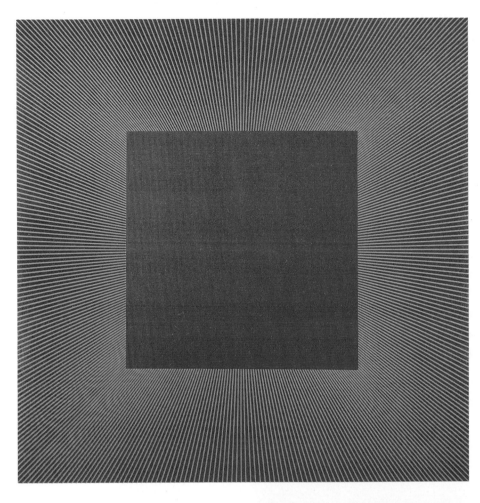

Fig. 9.13 Richard Anuskiewicz, *Magenta Square*, 1978. Acrylic on canvas, 48 × 48 ins (122 × 122 cm). Private Collection.

Fig. 9.14   Ad Reinhardt, *Black Painting*, 1952–54. Oil on canvas, 54 × 54 ins (137 × 137 cm). Photograph courtesy: The Pace Gallery, New York.

After-image

Following a period of intense focus or staring at a color, an after-image is produced when the eye is directed to a white area on which to "project," as on a screen, the original image in its complementary colors. Again there is a simple explanation for those who prefer their magic tricks revealed. In this case, the cone receptors, within the fovea of the retina, become saturated and refuse to accept further signals of a particular wavelength. The over-stimulated cone cells transmit only the wavelengths of the rest of the spectrum, seen as the complementary color.

Start with a simple red circle to project a green circle on a nearby white surface. Then study the reverse American Flag by Jasper Johns (**Fig. 9.15**) or the almost living field of oval images and after-images by Larry Poons to suggest the broader possibilities of this amazing effect. Create an amazing after-image.

Transparency

One of the most important and frequently employed color "deceptions" (as these studies have been called by Albers) is the ability to make us appear to see through an opaque area of color to another color beneath, as though it is physically transparent (**Fig. 9.16**).

The illusion of shallow planes of overlapping space and color can be suggested in a number of ways and is a special study of Chapter 11 (p. 192).

Fig. 9.15 Jasper Johns, *Flag*, 1965. Oil on canvas, 72 × 48 ins (183 × 122 cm). Photograph courtesy of Leo Castelli Gallery, New York.

Fig. 9.16 Laszlo Moholy-Nagy, *A II*, 1924. Oil on canvas, $45\frac{5}{8} \times 53\frac{5}{8}$ ins (116 × 135 cm). Collection: Solomon R. Guggenheim Museum, New York. Photograph by Robert E. Mates.

Free studies

Free studies, which do not fit neatly into any of the previously described categories, or which combine several ideas in new ways, are always to be encouraged. Often small and exquisite, these are sometimes referred to as gems when they sparkle with intense points of brilliant light and color. Torn as well as cut shapes may be used.

With pressed autumn leaves, Color Aid and recycled papers, find unexpected color relationships by "listening" as well as looking, and permit colors to suggest their own palettes and harmonies. Let the papers guide color choices rather than imposing a pre-determined set of colors or shapes upon them. Experiment, with the motto "Less is More" as a guide.

A word about systems

Return now to that piece of a green paper you have identified and located on all three scales of color quality. Will it be possible to order a quantity of that (or any) color through verbal description alone? What would you expect to receive if you ordered "a square yard of a Yellow/Green on the fourth level of the gray scale at about a third-level intensity?"

There are a number of systems which, at least in theory, make this perfectly possible. Both the Munsell Color Tree and the Ostwald System of color nomenclature use a three-way structure to locate a particular color, according to two different sets of criteria. In the Munsell Tree, a three-dimensional arrangement of colors is used to locate over four hundred different gradations of five primaries, according to hue, value and chroma (Munsell's term for intensity).

In the Ostwald System, some 680 gradations derived from four primaries may be found in a triangulated color solid, ringed in the center by twenty-four hues, coming to a point of white at the top and a point of black at the bottom.

Although scientists, producers of dyes and pigments and others who require exact color standardization have relied on such systems of classification, they are of limited value to the artist or creative designer. Of what use is a system or structure that can pin a color up, down and sideways when an artist can change it beyond recognition simply by placing it in a new environment? The effects of simultaneous contrast, as you have seen in each color study presented, point us toward a practical, experiential approach to the study of color, and truly convince us that color *is* the most relative medium in art (**Figs. 9.2, 9.17**). Regardless of our loyalty to any particular color theory, we would do well to carry with us the urging of the painter Harvey Dinnerstein, "Stay amazed."

Fig. 9.17 Jeff MacNelly, *Shoe*, newspaper cartoon feature, 2/22/1986. Reprinted by permission: Tribune Media Services.

Albers' students—a footnote

Many artists who currently teach color theory are former Albers students and colleagues, as are many contemporary artists who make use of his interactive, relativist ideas (**Figs. 9.18, 9.19**). What may be unexpected is the number of his former students who have adapted these theories to representational, realist points of view. But this should not surprise us; the theory holds. Its use and interpretation have been developed uniquely by different artists, an individuality of artistic sensibility that would surely have been applauded by their mentor.

Fig. 9.19 **Charles Francis Tauss**, *In the Family; Terrestrial*, 1971. Acrylic polymer on panel, 30 × 30 ins (76 × 76 cm). Courtesy of the artist.

Fig. 9.18 (*above*) **Lois Swirnoff**, *Desert Light*, 1983. Acrylic on aluminum, 22 × 26 × ¾ ins (56 × 66 × 2 cm). Photograph courtesy of the artist.

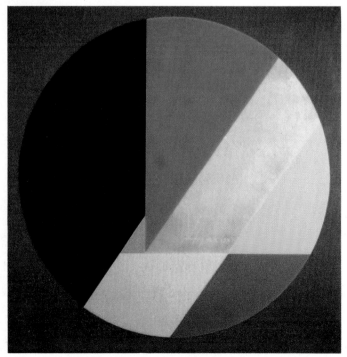

Chapter Ten

COLOR IN THEORY

Fig. 10.1 **Kees van Dongen**, *Modjesko,*
Soprano Singer, 1908. Oil on canvas,
$39\frac{3}{8} \times 32$ ins (100 × 81 cm). Collection: The
Museum of Modern Art, New York. Gift of
Mr. and Mrs. Peter A. Rübel.

A little light on the subject

Colors exist not physically within or on the surfaces of objects, but in the eye (or more accurately the mind) as they are interpreted by the brain, a wide assortment of subjective factors affecting what is seen. Like beauty, color may truly live only in the eye of its beholder.

Color is the name given to the mind's response to stimulation, by rays of light, of certain extremely small nerve cells within the retina. However, light is not always necessary to the experience; dreams and pressure on the eyeball can give a vivid sensation of color.

Light is part of the energy generated by the sun, radiating in great waves or pulsations permeating our earth's atmosphere, filling the "empty" expanse of space with vibrating electromagnetic energy. As Isaac Newton demonstrated in 1666, a glass prism splits clear "white" light into a rainbow spectrum, a band of soft-edged hues moving from the shortest (violet) to the longest (red) wavelengths (**Fig. 10.2**). This visible light is a small portion of the entire electromagnetic spectrum, from the shortest, narrowest X-rays and gamma rays (less than sixteen millionths of an inch in width) to the longest radio and video waves (greater than thirty-two millionths of an inch in width) which can be miles in length but occur less frequently or have low frequency. At the short wavelength edge of the visible spectrum is invisible ultraviolet; at the long wavelength edge is infra-red, also unseen by the unaided eye, although these waves have many scientific and photographic uses.

Rays of light act as though composed of minuscule particles (photons), which make sight possible by striking and activating nerve endings of the rods(at the edge) and the cones (in the center) of the fovea, at the middle of the rear retinal screen of the eye's inner camera or chamber. This causes chemical changes which, converting to electrical impulses, affect the magnetic polarity of elements in the color-sensitive cones and the dark-and-light-sensitive rods, and turn on our mental "picture tube." The brain interprets or sees the images produced as shape, form, tone and color.

When some light rays are absorbed by or taken into an object, only the non-absorbed rays reflect back to the eye, and the sensation of particular colors is produced. Surfaces seen as white absorb no rays and are therefore cooler; surfaces seen as black "drink in" almost all visible rays and are warmer. Since seeing is possible only in the presence of light, true black may not be seen. Yellow, the thinnest color band in the spectrum, is highest in light value, while violet, the widest band, is by far the lowest.

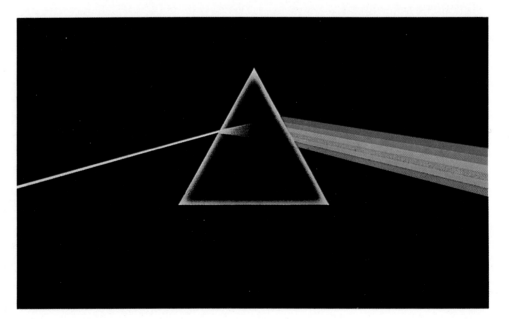

Fig. 10.2 Album Cover for "Dark Side of the Moon," by Pink Floyd, 1973. Harvest Label; design/Photo Hipgnosis, artwork George Hardie NTA, EMI Records UK.

Color in nature and human nature

In nature, color is a powerful, evocative factor, serving many purposes—from concealing and disguising animals and plants in their environment, protecting them from predators, to focusing attention on and targeting particular features. These opposing qualities, as camouflage or emphasis, are often used for aesthetic purposes by artists and designers, particularly through Melted Edge and Vibration techniques (pp. 172, 173). Not only artists have aesthetic needs, a hungering for elegant, harmonious relationships and visual enhancement, considered by some optional or impractical. Others recognize these to be as important as any sustenance to our human quality of life.

Not only the psychological primaries (blue, green, yellow, red), but all color affects mood, our sense of the physical environment and our emotional response to events. Many shared clichés refer to colors coloring feelings: I was GREEN with envy. He was so mad he saw RED. I felt BLUE. You're YELLOW. I'm in the PINK. She was born to the PURPLE. He's a WHITE-knuckle driver. I'm in a BLACK mood.

Fig. 10.3   Jacob Lawrence, *Self-Portrait*, 1977. Gouache on paper, 23 × 31 ins (58.5 × 78 cm). Courtesy: National Academy of Design, New York City.

Fig. 10.4 **Garry Trudeau**, *Doonesbury*,
12/28/1986 © 1986 G.B. Trudeau.
Reprinted with permission of Universal Press
Syndicate. All rights reserved.

Fig. 10.5 Still photograph from the film
"Citizen Kane," © 1941 RKO Radio
Pictures, Inc, Ren. 1968 RKO General, Inc.
Courtesy: Turner Entertainment Co.
Photograph courtesy: Museum of Modern
Art. New York. Film Archives.

In the Luscher Test, eight color samples are placed in order of preference, twice. The colors, blue (peaceful), green (assertive), yellow (expansive), red (exciting), violet (mystic), brown (physical), black (negative) and gray (neutral), indicate, in combination, personality type and areas of stress, to the trained analyst. [1]

Besides mood (sorrow, joy, sensuality, fear, tranquility), qualities such as climate (wet/dry, warm/cool, airy/oppressive), time of day or season, depth or shallowness of space, transparency or opacity of surface are influenced by often subtle color shifts and distinctions. How do you think (or feel) each palette was selected for the portraits shown in **Fig. 10.1** and **Fig. 10.3**? [2]

Color v. black-and-white

If you watch a film or television program prepared in color on a black-and-white set, you may feel you have not really seen the film. Your aesthetic needs will have been unfulfilled, although the factual content was transmitted to you. Films such as *Citizen Kane*, however, in which black and white is used to convey the full range of achromatic tonalities in exquisite richness, only gain aesthetic success by omitting color (**Figs. 10.4, 10.5**). [3]

Those working with color have been freed from many previously limiting restraints. Combinations once thought not to "go" together or to clash (orange/magenta or yellow/orange) are now used commonly in fashion, advertising and painting, often specifically because of the retinal action they can create. [4]

Fig. 10.6 **Robert Slutzky**, *Palazzo Fuga*. 1974. Acrylic on canvas, 70 × 80 ins (178 × 203 cm). Courtesy of the artist.

The subject is color

Color itself can be the subject of paintings, not paintings of something else representing (or presenting once again) another subject, but presenting color and color interaction directly to the viewer (**Fig. 10.6**). Such non-associative relationships of elements are more easily accepted in music than the visual arts, perhaps because so much of our seeing is used for identifying and responding to objects. Does the introduction of sounds-from-life (such as bells and roosters) enhance or diminish music's form and quality? Can you explain this?

EXERCISES

Exercise 1:
Investigate color symbolism and association in heraldry, church liturgy, theatrical lighting and costume, and academic garb, among others.

Exercise 2:
Divide a large rectangle into sectioned columns, then fill each with bands of colors selected to suggest a specific mood, climate or other subjective quality. Do not label these, but ask others to guess their meaning. Compare responses, reconsider your colors, then use one palette in a finished work, and again consider reactions to it in terms of your original intent.

Exercise 3:
Try to observe a color film or video presentation simultaneously on two sets, one black and white, one color. Study the difference, then try this exercise with a "color-enhanced" originally black-and-white film. Observe and discuss your responses.

Exercise 4:
Choose a visually unappealing or disharmonious palette, design two works, one reinforcing this view, one refuting it. See if others can tell "which is which." Expect to be surprised.

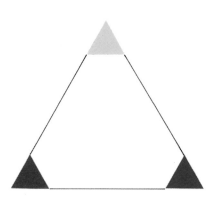

Fig. 10.7 The three primaries in pigment, or opaque color.

Fig. 10.8 The three secondaries in pigment, or opaque color.

A spectrum of theories

For centuries, scientists, philosophers and artists have attempted to explain color by for-mulating theories, identifying basic or primary colors from which they develop elaborate patterns showing light and color mixtures and relationships. To Goethe and Chevreul, the three primaries are Red, Yellow and Blue; to Ostwald, the four primaries are Red, Ultramarine, Sea-Green and Yellow; to Munsell, the five primaries are Yellow, Red, Purple, Blue and Green; to Faber Birren, the four are Yellow, Red-Violet, Ultrama-rine and Turquoise. Some bend the colors of the spectrum into a circle, the shortest wavelength, violet, meeting and blending with the longest wavelength, red, in a non-spectrum purple, a convenient though scientifically fictitious continuous flow of rainbow hues. Goethe prefers the triangle as a framework, subdividing it into smaller triangles of secondary and tertiary mixtures (see Helen Gardner's "Art through the Ages," eighth edition). Those favoring a three-primary view find this description self-evident, while those who see a four- or five-primary world choose the more indeter-minate circle, evenly divisible into any number of pie slices.

In Faber Birren's elaborate circle, the three-primary pattern of the physicist and the artist (R, G, B/V for the former; R, Y, B for the latter) overlaps the four-color structure of the psychologist (R, Y, G, B). In addition, the complementary hue of each color is indicated. This makes an amazing chart with its thirteen principal hues plus Black and White. There is poetry in Goethe's six-hue, nine-color triangle composed of Y, R, G, B, V and Peach Blossom! For years, students using Newton's seven main hues (to approximate the musical scale) have searched in vain for Indigo.

One feature of every color wheel or chart is the picturing of complementary colors, seen across from one another through the center of the pattern. These pairs contain some amount of all the primaries and mix to form a neutral grayed tone, often brown in pigment.

The clearest description may be seen in a triangulated placement of the three primary pigment colors, R, Y, B (**Fig. 10.7**), intersected by a reversed triangle of the secondary colors O, G, V (**Fig. 10.8**). Since each secondary is a mixture of the two primaries other than its complement, each pair of complementaries contains all three primaries in differing proportions. In Slutzky's painting (**Fig. 10.6**), pairs of complemen-taries spiral about the center.

The negative of a color photograph, in theory, shows the direct complementaries of the colors seen. Careful planning may result in striking "reverse palette" images (**Fig. 10.9**). [5]

Fig. 10.9 **Cynthia Dantzic**, *Little Green Apples*. Color photograph and its negative, showing complementary colors in film.

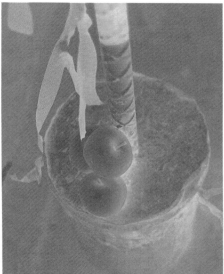

Fig. 10.10 Tertiary or intermediate mixture colors, on triangular diagram.

One interesting view of primaries is that it doesn't matter which group of three colors is used, so long as they combine to produce the total spectrum. In light, these must create clear or "white" light, in pigment as close to black or the total filtration of light as possible. [6]

In mixing paints you combine not only hues but light values. Although only a small amount of blue adds greenness to yellow, considerably more yellow must be mixed with a given amount of blue to affect that much darker color and move it toward green. A reduction of light occurs in mixing pigments, as those rays of light we do not see are blocked or filtered out of the mix absorbed by the paint which reflects the balance of the spectrum. Such mixtures are called *subtractive*. For example, red paint added to green paint, containing all three primaries (red plus blue-yellow), filters out almost all the rays of the spectrum and produces a deep brown. In theory, if all the light were filtered out, the result should be black, the absence of color. But since actual pigments are far from the pure colors in anyone's wheel or chart, a mixed black is very difficult to achieve.

Try to mix violet using standard red and blue paints to see the discrepancy between the idea of color and its actuality. Compare your results with those of several others.

Many attempt this blend with school temperas and produce a goodly amount of imitation chocolate. You will do better with artist-quality paint but may choose to buy your purples, greens, oranges and earth colors ready-made.

EXERCISES

Exercise 5:
Try having your color negative printed as a slide, by means of an "inter-neg" or, in this case, a "positive" transparency!

Exercise 6:
Within an up-pointed triangle, place the primary colors as in **Fig. 10.7**. On an overlapping transparent sheet, place the three secondary colors in a down-pointed triangle. Retain for further elaboration in subsequent exercises.

Fig. 10.11 (*right*) Special Color Chart.
Triad name:
Y¹—Y¹— Aquatec Cadmium Yellow Light
(an alternative, shown in text illustration)
Y²—Y²—Liquitex Cadmium Yellow Medium
    OY—Liquitex Azo Yellow Orange
YO—YO—Liquitex Value 6 Yellow-red
    O—Liquitex Vivid Red-Orange
    RO—Liquitex Indo Orange-Red
RO—OR—Liquitex Cadmium Red Light (Acra
    Red in triad)
R—R—Liquitex Cadmium Red Medium
    (Naphthol Crimson in triad)
    PR—Liquitex Deep Brilliant Red
    RP—Liquitex Naphthol Crimson
RV—P—Liquitex Deep Magenta
    UP—Liquitex Prism Violet
    PU—Shiva Violet Light
M————Lascaux Permanent Lilac (or
    Liquitex Medium Magenta)
B—U—Liquitex Ultramarine
V————Liquitex Dioxane Purple
    TU—Liquitex Phthalocyanine Blue
BV—Liquitex Brilliant Blue Purple
    UT—Liquitex Cerulean Blue
C—T—Liquitex Brilliant Blue
BG—ST—Liquitex Turquoise Blue
G—TS—Liquitex Permanent Green Deep
    S—Liquitex Emerald Green
    LS—Aquatec Permanent Green Light
    SL—Shiva Cadmium Green
    L—Liquitex Permanent Green Light
    YL—Liquitex Vivid Lime Green
YG-LY—Liquitex Brilliant Yellow Green

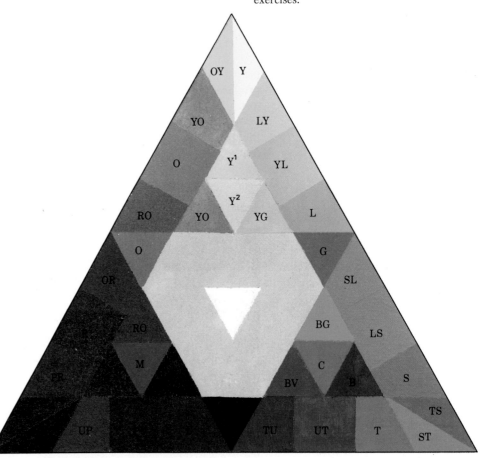

Fig. 10.12   Location of light-additive secondaries on Special Color Chart.

A special color chart: additive and subtractive mixes

The color chart on page 184 should be studied, as it integrates several sets of primaries in one comprehensive structure. Since it contains only unmixed areas of specifically identified paints, you may duplicate this chart for your own use; even the best printing cannot reproduce actual paint qualities (**Fig. 10.11**). [7]

   To the traditional double triangle of primary and secondary colors are added intermediate, tertiary mixes shown in each "primary triangle" with its adjacent analogous trio (**Fig. 10.10**). Three or more colors are said to be analogous when they contain one primary plus adjacent mixtures in sequence, like a flush in gin rummy! Yellow is at the top, bordered by yellow-orange and yellow-green; red lies between red-orange and red-violet; and blue is found between blue-green and blue-violet. Triads can be selected at any three equal intervals. [8]

   In the centers of the three primary triangles are three colors of special concern to those who work directly with light—in photography, video, computer art, theatrical lighting or printing. These are cyan, magenta and yellow, the basic colors used in many contemporary media as well as printing (**Fig. 10.12**). Each of these is acutally a secondary hue, produced by mixing the three light primaries received chemically by the minute cones in the fovea: Green, Red and Blue-Violet. It is easy to believe that red light plus blue-violet light creates magenta, a purplish pink. We can easily visualize green light and blue-violet light producing cyan, a clear bright blue. But when asked to believe that red light added to green light makes yellow, our credibility may be strained. Nevertheless, with red and green acetates covering a pair of flashlights that are aimed to overlap on a white wall or screen in a darkened room, you can show that this is true.

   Do you feel comfortable about such apparently irreconcilable mixtures existing in science and art? If an additive mixture means light added to light, you should not be surprised that any blend produces a lighter combined color than either color being

Fig. 10.13   **Robert Swain**, *Untitled Painting*, 1983. 9 × 17 ft (2.74 × 5.18 m). Courtesy: Johnson & Johnson.

mixed. In photography and other light-additive media, filters of cyan, magenta and yellow, or inks and dyes of these colors, are used to block out undesired light rays, permitting others to pass through and be seen. For example, overlapping yellow and cyan will block out the red contained in the yellow and the blue-violet in the cyan, but will pass the green contained by both the yellow and cyan. This is a subtractive mix. So, though you may have believed that "yellow plus blue makes green," to be scientific you might think that red-green (yellow) blocked by green-blue/violet (cyan) leaves over and therefore transmits only the green light rays contained by both! [9]

Although absence of light leaves darkness or black, the addition of black paint or pigment to a color adds darkness in the form of *shades*. The mixture of all colors in light creates the clear transparent colorless light we call "white." In paint, the addition of white creates lighter tones of a color, called *tints*. Are grays tints of black or shades of white? (Use your "little gray cells" here.) [10]

To place a color on a gray scale according to its light value, make a black-and-white photograph of the color or squint to reduce cone-related color perception and increase rod-related light-dark vision. Better yet, with practice you can train your eye to "override" the hue and see only the light value. These apparent exercises can be used as the basis for very subtle paintings (**Fig. 10.13**).

To make any of these tonal scales with a visually equal sequence of steps so that each tint or shade seems to be the same distance from its neighbors, it is necessary to use a physically unequal progression, known in honor of its discoverers as the Weber-Fechner Law. Simply, this discovery explains how, in order to achieve the appearance of an arithmetic sequence (1, 2, 3, 4, 5, 6, etc.), a physically geometric progression (1, 2, 4, 8, 16, etc.) is required in paint or transparent overlays. Otherwise, the eye will fail to perceive the rapidly diminishing distinction between the darker steps as the sequence progresses. [11]

More notes on the special color chart

In the chart on page 184, the central area is shown as white to emphasize the mixing of light. Generally this central area is reserved for the mixture of complementaries.

The largest, outer triangle suggests the twenty-four colors of the Ostwald Color System, with its emphasis on several types of green, in this sequence:
Yellow, Orange/Yellow, Yellow/Orange, Orange, Red/Orange, Orange/Red, Red, Purple/Red, Red/Purple, Purple, Ultramarine/Purple, Purple, Purple/Ultramarine, Ultramarine, Turquoise/Ultramarine, Ultramarine/Turquoise, Turquoise, Sea-Green/Turquoise, Turquoise/Sea-Green, Sea-Green, Leaf-Green/Sea-Green, Sea-Green/Leaf-Green, Leaf-Green, Yellow/Leaf-Green, Leaf-Green/Yellow, and back to Yellow.

Ostwald used four primaries, Yellow, Red, Ultramarine and Sea-Green. His secondaries are Orange, Purple, Turquoise and Leaf-Green. It is surprising to see how closely we may approximate his color sequence using unmixed commercially available acrylic paints. Although I am providing a list of the paints used (**Fig. 10.11**), you may improve upon this selection by your own experiments. A major problem with this or any demonstration showing adjacent analogous colors is the simultaneous contrast of colors at each edge. As you have seen in Chapter 9, this interaction is the reason I do not dwell on the various systems of primaries, secondaries or other patternings of color. It is one thing to say the primaries are red, yellow and blue, or X, Y and Z; it is quite another to say (or to show) precisely which red, which yellow and which blue—and then what color that red, yellow or blue is touching and being affected or changed by. Indeed, it is possible to select a color from this chart, say the magenta, and see it as deep violet (against yellow), as light pink (against violet), neon-bright (against sea- and leaf-green), as a faded rose (against red), and any number of others, without modifying the physical color at all. [12]

EXERCISES

Exercise 7:
Trace or make an enlargement of the sub-divided triangle you made in Exercise 6. Share colors with others in your class to increase your palette. Retain for study and use.

Exercise 8:
On additional overlays, add tertiary colors to your studies from Exercise 6.

Exercise 9:
With three acetate-covered flashlights or spotlights, overlap shapes of red, green and blue-violet on a white surface in the dark. Use your discoveries in a design.

Exercise 10:
Prepare evenly-stepped color and tone charts showing a progression of tints and shades between such opposites as black and white (a gray scale) (Fig. 9.6), blue and yellow (a green scale), red and yellow (an orange scale), red and blue (a purple scale) plus tints and shades of individual primary or secondary hues. For these "monochromes," place your starting hue at the appropriate step on an equivalent gray scale. On a yellow tonal chart, there is room for only one or two tints higher in light value than the starting hue; but as many as seven or eight shades lower. On a green tonal scale, there might be an equal number of tints and shades, while there would be little room for shades on a violet scale.

Exercise 11:
Using transparent overlays of a 10% gray acetate, demonstrate the Weber-Fechner Law. Layer the acetate the specified number of thicknesses to create each tonal value.

Exercise 12:
Place four physically identical squares of a "loud" or "strong" color, such as magenta, orange or chartreuse, in the center of four larger white rectangles. Then change grounds until you have completely altered the original central color.

Fig. 10.14 Paul Cézanne, *Green Apples*, 1873. Oil on canvas, $10\frac{1}{4} \times 12\frac{5}{8}$ ins (26 × 32 cm). Courtesy: The Louvre, Paris. © photo RMN.

Charting color

Classification of color can help in obtaining a consistent and predictable replacement for a particular sample of paint on paper. However, one manufacturer's ultramarine may be very different from another's. For this reason, a personal color chart of all your paints is a useful resource.

Use masking tape to mark off equal-sized rectangles in rows and columns. Keep and add to your chart. As each sample added dries, remove the surrounding tape for a neat gridded chart. You may prefer to write identification, color name or brand name, on an acetate overlay. Over the years, it will also show you permanence or fading quality of specific paints.

Full circle

How much does the student of art or design need to know about the nature of light and color? Knowledge gained through personal investigation and discovery will have more meaning than memorized lists and patterns of theory or even a detailed history of the experiments of artists and scientists throughout the ages. Such ideas as monochromatic (**Figs. 9.7**), analogous (**Fig. 10.06**), and complementary (**Fig. 10.15**) colors may help you to recognize the palettes used in particular works.

Until recently, it might have been possible for an artist or student, unaware of differences between additive and subtractive color mixtures, to ignore such facts since all paint-blending consistently utilized subtractive mixture. Now students of the light-additive arts must learn and use another set of primary and secondary hues. The cyan, yellow and magenta so familiar to the darkroom seem at first unrelated to the painter's palette. Yet, these two systems are different aspects of the same facts about the nature of light and perception. It is hardly possible to make use of today's simplest technology

Fig. 10.15 Vincent van Gogh, *Sheaves of Wheat*, 1890. Oil on canvas, $19\frac{7}{8} \times 39\frac{3}{4}$ ins (51 × 101 cm). Courtesy: Dallas Museum of Art.

Fig. 10.16   Helen Frankenthaler, *Sugar Blues*, 1988. Acrylic on canvas, $90\frac{1}{2} \times 107\frac{1}{4}$ ins (230×272.5 cm). Courtesy: The André Emmerich Gallery. Collection: Mr. and Mrs. Stuart M. Christhilf.

without a working knowledge of both. Some schools include photography in the Fine Arts, the Media Arts or the Communications Arts, but every student in any of these visual arts would be well advised to include a knowledge of basic camera skills in a well-balanced course of study. Since many formerly fixed distinctions between disciplines, mediums and media are changing and overlapping and many new career-related areas are developing and adding technologies, it is worthwhile to prepare as completely as possible. Original, creative uses of any theory will always triumph over the tedium of charts, systems and "facts" (**Figs. 10.16, 11.8**).

Color is the most challenging and ultimately rewarding medium in art as well as the "most relative;" it will always give you more than you expect if you pursue it in an active, participatory, experimental and personal way rather than simply learning a system of nomenclature or memorizing anyone's set of rules.

Chapter Eleven

APPEARANCE OF SPACE: THROUGH COLOR AND LIGHT

Fig. 11.1   Hans Hofmann, *The Golden Wall*, 1961. Oil on canvas, 60 × 78 ins (152 × 198 cm). Courtesy: © The Art Institute of Chicago, all Rights Reserved, Mr. and Mrs. Frank G. Logan Prize Fund, 1962.775.

Creating space through color

Color and light can create powerful spatial effects on the picture plane as diverse as Turner's vortexes of virtually abstract color and light, painted before such an idea had been identified, Hopper's canvases filled with light-struck form, never relinquishing pictorial subject matter (**Fig. 11.2**), and Diebenkorn's barely associative *Ocean Park* paintings (**Fig. 2.25**).

Push/pull color space

Space and color are inseparable, taught Hans Hofmann, and proved it through the freely brushed rectangular areas defining his large canvases, which are vigorously involved with the push/pull energy of warm and cool colors (**Fig. 11.1**). Warm colors (yellow/orange/red) are said to advance toward the eye, and cool colors (green/blue/purple) to recede, but Hofmann showed how subtle factors of size and placement can alter or even reverse that axiom. His electric chartreuse yellow/greens, hot-pink/magentas and glassy blues swim, float, shift and glide around slabs of deep purple, orange or clear red with such energy that viewers need not inquire about other subject matter. Just as a symphony is an orchestration of sounds and intervals, these paintings exist as symphonies of color in space. For viewers unaccustomed to enjoying non-pictorial or abstract art, "listening with the eye" to Hofmann's paintings can truly be an eye-opener. Do you think he had the golden rectangle in mind or the planar dimension when he entitled this major canvas *The Golden Wall*? [1]

EXERCISES

Exercise 1:
In collage or paint, place different-sized areas of warm and cool colors at random in a rectangle to study the push/pull effect. Modify and adjust until this study "works" in space.

Opaque color transparency

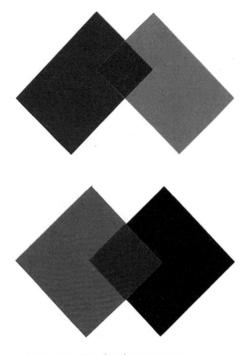

Fig. 11.3 Simple color transparency, created as a collage of opaque Color Aid papers.

The seeming contradiction between the terms "opaque" and "transparent" above underscores a discrepancy between physical fact and visual effect.

Draw (lightly) two simple shapes, overlapping. Using pencils, crayons or paints, fill the overlapped area with a secondary color such as green and the outer two shapes each in one appropriate primary, in this case blue and yellow.

The blue and green will read together as one combined blue shape, the yellow and green as a larger yellow form, and the green will appear as a shape created by the overlapping. (This perception of yellow and blue as separate from green in the mind is what Mondrian referred to as "fugitive" color, which he rejected in favor of "pure" primary red, yellow and blue.) Does the blue or the yellow appear on top, nearer the eye, or can you read the study either way, as an ambivalent optical illusion—now the yellow nearer, now the blue? Without color, the drawing may be read spatially in three ways: one combined shape nearer, the other nearer, or in perpetual equivalence, the central area seeming a kind of fusion, a "merger of gases" on the same plane. Even without color, such an overlapping fluctuates in space. Once a color choice has been made, what was a linear optical illusion is "set" in one "place," and the ambiguity (usually) seems resolved. Clearly words alone cannot convey such magic (**Fig. 11.3**).

To make use of this illusion in your own work and recognize it in the works of others (a frequent occurrence), the best study method is that taught by Albers, cut paper pieced in inlaid, "intarsia" collage. My college studies have dried like autumn leaves or come apart, because the best rubber cement is not permanent, but for investigation, not enduring works of art, I have found nothing better. (A melted-wax technique has been developed at Yale, but I have not tried it.)

Use rectangular shapes; their "neutrality" least affects color reading, and their right angles facilitate technique. Work with your X-Acto #11 pencil knife, straight metal edge, Color Aid papers and rubber cement.

Show two larger rectangles intersecting to produce a third rectangular shape. Select two primaries as the original colors, imagine them blending as a secondary color, then find and fill the overlapped section with that mixture. Remember, physically you are working with three adjacent shapes of solid color.

A development of this requires making three identical sets of "parent" colors, then selecting three "mixed" areas so that in two studies a different primary reads "on top," and in the third an ambivalent reading occurs. This is the easy way (**Fig. 11.4**).

Try a more challenging method by choosing the mixed color first (not necessarily a secondary), and, after careful observation and study, imagining what two colors might

Fig. 11.4 (*left*) **Cynthia Dantzic**, *Three-way Transparency*. Using primary colors, changing the "mixed" color to create the illusion first of one, then the other primary "on top," then an equal spatial "flip-flop" effect. (*right*) **Robert Speier**, Light Overlay Study, *Sisquoc*, 1988. Acrylic, $6\frac{1}{2} \times 7$ ft (1.98×2.1 m). Courtesy of the artist.

somehow fuse to produce it. Much trial and improvement will provide not only a solution to this problem but a refinement and development of your perceptual sensitivity. (There is no trial and error; all your efforts bring understanding.) In this approach, it is not choosing the colors to overlap that causes difficulty. Often different pairs will seem to produce the same mixture. The challenge is to find three sets that will give the desired illusion: one nearer, the other nearer, then both level and intermingling; yet all appearing to be derived from one central, physically unchanged color.

Before describing any hints and guidelines to assist in this investigation, I recommend that you put off reading them until you have made your own efforts at their discovery. Only then can such verbal assistance interact with your experience. Visual examples of results achieved by others mean more after you have made a similar search.

In the transparencies shown (**Figs. 11.3, 11.4**), select the one with the lighter color on top and follow the outline of the shape that appears nearer to the eye, a complete rectangle, including the central mixed area. Now read the contour of the darker, more distant shape. Does your eye turn the corner and separate this shape from the mixed portion so that you read a kind of "L?" This is an example of the gestalt effect in which we read the easiest visual path, trying to complete the simplest enclosure of field or shape. Seen in this way, accurate choice of colors is not so important as the relative hardness and softness of edges in giving a transparent reading. Those studies or finished works in which ambiguous alternation appears show almost equal strength of edges, so that the viewer must make a choice, not always consciously, in order to read with the mind what is received on the retina. Alternating such readings, sometimes very quickly, produces fluctuating spatial sensations carried to almost disturbing extremes in the optical or retinal works featured in the "Responsive Eye" exhibition.

Art creates a reality more believable than fact. In pictorial works the artist invents any story desired and makes us "see" it on canvas. Surrealist works present fantastic, impossible relationships we accept with willing suspension of disbelief. But when a square of red is seen to overlap a square of yellow and "create" an area of chartreuse or magenta, we are amazed! Careful study, daring guesswork, patience and a willingness to make incredibly small revisions will reward your diligence. (Neatness counts if you want to fool the eye.) Many illustrations selected by Albers for his classic book, "Interaction of Color," were solutions to class assignments by students. In the accompanying space you are invited to affix your best miniature color transparency. Such tiny "gems," often only two or three inches across, were the treasure of many in the famous color course, and I hear they still are.

Compose a small "gem" using one "impossible" but believable transparency. Carefully attach it to this page (**Fig. 11.5**).

Fig. 11.5   Affix your own collage.

Fig. 11.6 (*above*) **Ben Cunningham**, *Corner
Painting*, 1948–50. Oil on canvas,
$25\frac{1}{2} \times 36\frac{1}{2}$ ins (65×93 cm) and $25\frac{1}{2} \times 21\frac{1}{2}$ ins
(65×55 cm). Courtesy: Mrs. Ben
Cunningham.

Fig. 11.7 (*left*) **Josef Albers**, *Homage to the
Square*, 1962. Oil on masonite, 24×24 ins
(61×61 cm). (*right*) 1976. Oil on masonite,
$23\frac{7}{8} \times 23\frac{7}{8}$ ins (61×61 cm).

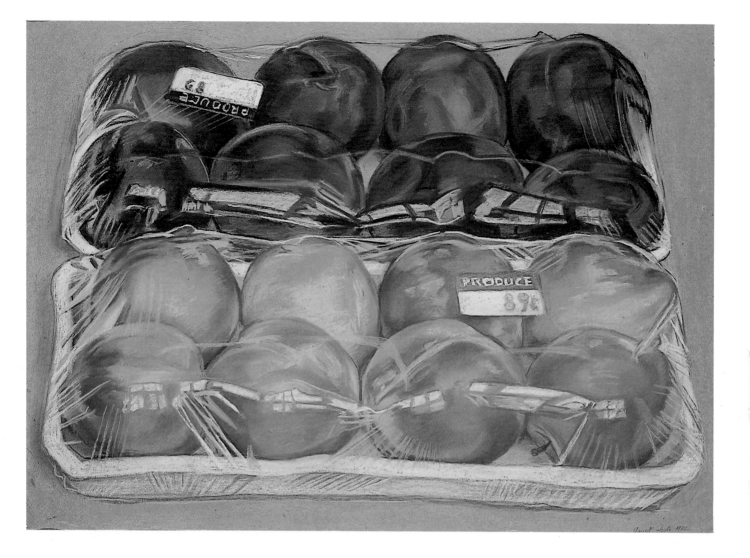

Fig. 11.8   **Janet Fish**, *Fruits*, 1972. Pastel on paper, 22 × 30 ins (56 × 76 cm). Photograph courtesy: Robert Miller Gallery, with permission of the artist.

Is your understanding and enjoyment of the Laszlo Moholy-Nagy painting in **Fig. 9.16** enriched by technical explanation of its transparent illusions? Do the complex choices Ben Cunningham made (**Fig. 11.6**) convince us we are looking into the intersection of transparent walls, plunging deep into pictorial space—or are they mirrors?

Can you see thin transparent space in Albers' *Homage to the Square* paintings (**Fig. 11.7**), where the inner squares push, pull or glide above, beneath or right through the outer squares?

Using glass, cellophane, sheer fabric and liquids as "containers for the light," Janet Fish started painting realistically "to get away from theory." Many of her early canvases celebrate the observation, then re-presentation, of transparent objects. Is this less magic when clothed in the forms of bottles, glasses or supermarket wrappings than in the geometry of squares and rectangles (**Fig. 11.8**)?

The appearance of transparent space on paper and canvas remains one of the most intriguing, delightful illusions the visual artist can conjure up for personal pleasure or that of the mystified viewer.

The appearance of light

Since most paper and canvas present us with a field of white, we approach the drawing and painting of realistic subjects as though we were required to add the appearance of darkness. We say we are "adding a shadow" to show a form seen in light. Of course, the opposite is true.

"The condition of space around us, when no objects are perceived ... is called darkness ... an abstraction ... We become aware of [light] as the activity on a specific object." Matthaei wrote this in 1790, explaining the color theories of Goethe! More recently Gyorgy Kepes explains, "... [an] image begins with light energy, flowing through the eye into the nervous system." Robert Scott simplifies: "In seeing, the cause is light." John Dewey adds, "... through light ... the world becomes visible." And Jay Hambidge says, "In the [painter's] palette, 'white' is the substitute for 'light'." In Ibsen's symbolic drama *Ghosts*, poor clouded Oswald calls for "The sun—the sun," recalling the last words of Goethe, "Light ... more light."

The creation of the world is symbolized in the command, "Let there be light," by the prime mover, the first cause, God. Have artists and designers misunderstood the idea that out of darkness comes light, that shadow is given and what we do is shed a little light on the subject? Could such an idea have inspired the white on black illustration shown in **Fig. 11.9**? Does it help us understand the sprinkled light emanating from Renoir's *The Swing* (**Fig. 11.11**)?

Fig. 11.9   Leonard Everett Fisher, *Candle Makers*, 1973. Ink on scratchboard, 5 × 7 ins (13 × 18 cm). From "The Homemakers", published by Macmillan Publishing Company.

Fig. 11.10 **Juan Gris**, *Fruit Bowl, Glass and Newspaper*, 1918. Pencil on paper, $14\frac{1}{8} \times 21\frac{1}{8}$ ins (35.5 × 53.5 cm). Courtesy: The Kroller-Müller Foundation. Otterlo.

The photographer prints an image in reverse from a negative. Similarly, anyone drawing with shading must think backwards, visualizing light falling on an object as a coating of its surface with volume, in the guise of white, leaving the light (white) alone and "adding" what is already present, shadow. Your drawing will not look like a "negative" or reversed image; this is simply a way to assist in visualizing light on a surface. Traditional oil painting, applying a dark ground as an underpainting on which to build volume through lighter and lighter tones up to the highest lights or highlights, may be seen in this context as quite correct. In contemporary *alla prima* or direct, from-the-first painting methods, this idea is not considered.

Achromatic, black-and-white tonality gives definition to monochromatic, single-hue work as well as drawing and other "colorless" media using black ink, graphite or black-and-white film. In full-palette painting, as the Impressionists showed, shadows may hold color as brilliant as the most vivid surfaces.

Drawings and paintings may suggest extremely subtle spatial volume and distance, as light and dark tonal values play across their surface. The most important consideration may be the relative hardness and softness of edges defining form and its shadows. A gradual tapering or diminution of light around the contours of a form and the sudden "horizon" at the edge beyond which we cannot see must be shown with exquisite sensibility in super-realistic styles sometimes minimized as illustration. There are as many ways to represent light and shadow on the two-dimensional surface as there are artists to create them. Some may look more "realistic" than others, but credibility is not necessarily related to the depiction of what actually is seen. One of the most convincing methods is unrelated to the perception of light as it shines on an object.

Fig. 11.11 (*opposite*) **Auguste Renoir**, *The Swing*, 1876. Oil on canvas, $37\frac{1}{4} \times 28\frac{3}{4}$ ins (94×73 cm). Courtesy: The Louvre, Paris. © photo RMN.

Fig. 11.12 Alternate shading giving form to otherwise flat oval lines. Blue crayon. Courtesy: Elaine A. Zimbel Logo and Stationery, Montreal.

Fig. 11.13 (*right*) **Jean Auguste D. Ingres**, *Study for the Grande Odalisque*, c. 1814. Pencil on paper, $4\frac{7}{8} \times 10\frac{1}{2}$ ins (13×27 cm). Private Collection: Photograph courtesy: The Courtauld Institute of Art, London.

Fig. 11.14 (*bottom*) **Giotto di Bondone**, *Vision of San Giovacchino*, (detail of fresco), c. 1305. Courtesy: Arena Chapel, Civic Museums, Padua.

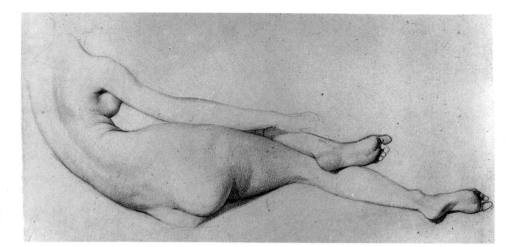

Alternate shading

This technique for suggesting roundness of form is absolutely arbitrary, an intellectual contrivance. But it works beautifully, suggesting dimension and fusing figure into ground—compressing the planar surface, yet suggesting fullness of form. Look for alternate shading in many Cubist drawings and paintings, particularly those of Juan Gris, sometimes handled softly, with hardly any apparent shading, and sometimes heavily—almost crudely—with an additional outline applied (**Fig. 11.10**).

Successful alternate shading uses the idea that line as edge has no width and any line you apply has two edges separated by the line's thickness. By softening one side of the applied line, melting it into the white of the paper, its entire thickness *becomes* the shadow either inside or outside the form being drawn. If you alternate this procedure, melting away about half the shaded portion inside and half outside the object, only one continuous edge/line will remain, with a suggestion of shadow partly on and partly off the form. With skill, the most delicate modulating of the blended edge may be accomplished, beginning virtually at the place it seems to fade, giving the sense of a single line running around the contour of the form, implying volume and space in some all but undetectable way (**Fig. 11.12**).

Recognizing the quiet strength of alternate shading, you may hesitate before adding an extra unnecessary outline around any form, effectively separating that object from its environment. In painting, the effect of alternate shading can be achieved by mixing the darker color at an edge with lighter tones, again half on and half off the form. This alternation of dark and light can occur several times and be of different colors and strengths, so long as the single one-dimensional line describing contour is respected. A form need not be enclosed by any out-line, but almost woven into the surface by subtle variations of the alternating idea, with contours flowing from the edge into the interior portions of the structure (**Fig. 11.13**). Drapery is an excellent subject for demonstrating this. Study renderings of drapery with heavy "modeling," all on the "in-side" of the form. What is the function of the dark area behind the figure in Giotto's *Vision of San Giovacchino* (**Fig. 11.14**)? [2]

EXERCISES

Exercise 2:
Draw a line with a soft pencil, then lighten and "vanish" one side of it with as little additional pencil work as possible, switch sides about halfway and continue, melting away the other edge. After a few experiments, try this on a drawing of a rounded form, say a potato, apple, circle or geometric figure. Compose an entire still life in this way.

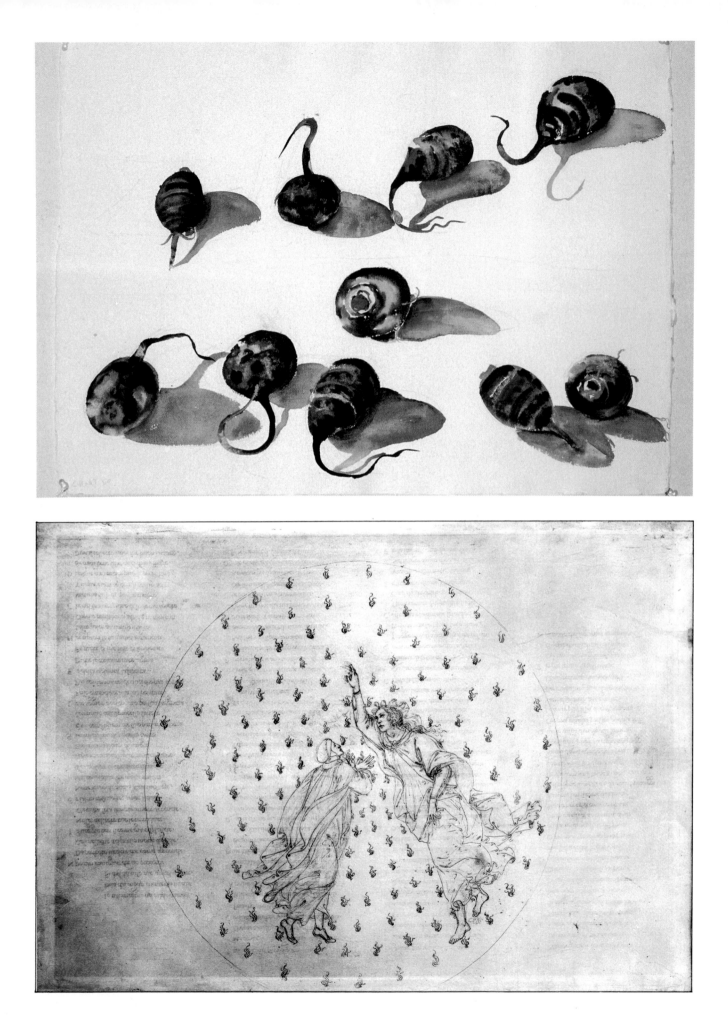

Ideas of darkness: the absence of light

As total blackness means complete absence of light, existing only in theory on Earth, areas we consider to be in "shadow" vary in darkness as differing amounts of light reach them. It is unlikely that you will encounter depths of inkiness under ordinary conditions, viewing a still life arranged in a well-lighted studio, a cityscape or landscape (even at night), or a figure model under almost any circumstances. A classic beginner's mistake is the "puddle-of-India-Ink" shadow, carefully placed beneath every object, solid black with a sharp edge all around. With subtlety this can be skillfully avoided (**Fig. 11.15**).

The lasting popularity of Dante's *Inferno*, written over 700 years ago, as a subject for illustration must be at least in part a response to the challenge of creating the awesome blackness of Hell with the limited, imperfect art materials available. Rich etchings and engravings in the most intense inks, pale silver-point drawings, and mixed media collages, have all been used to interpret light, darkness and other themes inspired by the *Divine Comedy* (**Fig. 11.16**). [3]

Shading: from a source of light

Scientists cannot agree if light, because it sometimes acts in waves, is composed of waves or, because it sometimes acts as individual particles, is composed of particles. Either way, light moves at an incredible speed, in fact at "the speed of light," and, at the distances with which we are concerned, in a straight line. A light beam, striking and illuminating an object, say a sphere, is stopped by it and, not reaching beyond the point where it is stopped, leaves a shape of darkness there.

Since an object is illuminated by many beams of light, approaching it from more than one angle, the shape and darkness of areas "in shadow" will vary.

In a darkened room, shine a flashlight on a white sphere centered on a flat white surface. Lower the light beneath the edge of the surface, and you will not see the sphere. Raise the light to the edge and begin to see, beyond the bright sphere, a diffused shapeless wash of light on the flat surface, as the sphere blocks most of the rays beyond itself. A little higher, and the flashlight will seem to project on the white surface a shadow, its shape changing, becoming shorter as the light source is raised and the angle between it and the edge of the sphere decreases. When directly "overhead" (noon) almost no shadow remains, but as the light moves lower and lower on the far side of the sphere, a shadow reappears on the near side, growing longer and longer as the angle increases, becoming diffuse again at the edge (twilight), and disappearing beyond the horizon (sunset).

You may test this sequence outdoors, at the beach, with the sun as your flashlight. The shadows will be sharper in your table-top experiment because the Earth itself is shaped something like a sphere, tending to scatter the rays at its horizon.

If you use a white cube in this experiment, you will see its three visible faces, each receiving a different amount of light, reflecting three differing tones of gray. As the light source moves, the amount of light reaching each surface changes, as will the gray tones. At extreme angles, those approximating dawn and twilight, the shadows will be longer and deeper, and the faces of the cube away from the light will grow darker. Similarly, but less dramatically, this shadowing, or modeling, will appear to define form on the irregular surfaces of component parts of any object, or group of objects, in a setting.

Late sixteenth- and seventeenth-century painters such as Vermeer, Caravaggio (**Fig. 11.17**) and Rembrandt achieved amazing effects of light and shadow, which,

Fig. 11.15 (*opposite, top*) **Bernard Chaet**, *Black Radishes*, 1950. Watercolor, 22 × 30 ins (56 × 76 cm). Courtesy: The Marilyn Pearl Gallery, New York.
Fig. 11.16 (*opposite, bottom*) **Sandro Botticelli**, *Dante and Beatrice in Paradise*, c. 1495. Silverpoint and pencil on parchment, $12\frac{3}{4} \times 18\frac{3}{8}$ ins (32 × 47 cm). Courtesy: Staatliche Museen zu Berlin.

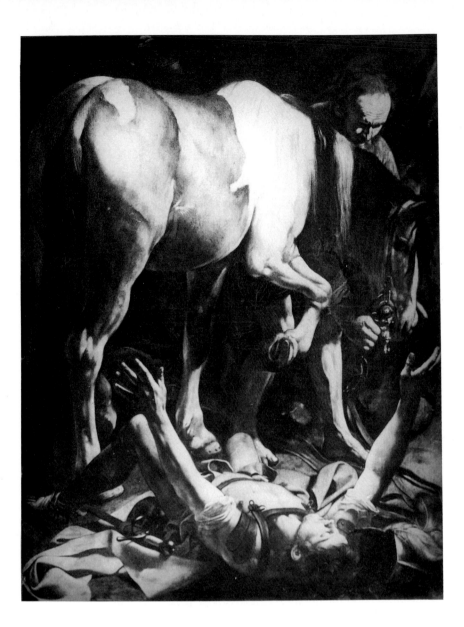

Fig. 11.17 **Michelangelo Merisi da Caravaggio**, *The Conversion of St. Paul*, 1600–01. Oil on canvas, 90½ × 70 ins (230 × 178 cm). Courtesy: The Cerasi Chapel. Santa Maria del Popolo.

Fig. 11.18 (*left*) **Philip Pearlstein**, *Female Model on Platform Rocker*, 1978. Oil on canvas, 72 × 96 ins (183 × 244 cm). Collection: The Brooklyn Museum, New York. 79.17, John B. Woodward Memorial Fund, A. Augustus Healy Fund, Dick S. Ramsey Fund, and other restricted income Funds.

Fig. 11.19 (*right*) **Alfred Leslie**, *Alfred Leslie*, 1974. Lithograph, 40 × 30 ins (102 × 76 cm). © Landfall Press Inc., Publisher. Chicago.

perhaps because we have seen so much photography, are not always met with the awe and incredulity they once elicited. It must have seemed nothing short of magic for the substance and aura of light to be fixed to a canvas, even to appear to flicker and glow.

Some contemporary painters find fascination in different aspects of light and shadow. Philip Pearlstein uses patterns created by multiple shadow forms on the surfaces of his human subjects, the surrounding floor and walls (**Fig. 11.18**). In this painting he shows the penumbra, or secondary shadow, resulting from more than one light source, often a series of overlapping, related shapes with clearly defined interior divisions in several tones of modulated grayed color.

Alfred Leslie, flashing almost blinding light sparingly at his otherwise darkened subjects, evokes exaggerated, dramatic, highly three-dimensional illusions of volume and space (**Fig. 11.19**).

Shading and chiaroscuro

The gray scale (**Fig. 9.6**), a graduated sequence of tones from white (the absence of dark) to black (the absence of light), is shown against a middle-value gray without any gradation. Of course, it is impossible to see it that way; as the central tone becomes darker, the ground grows visually lighter, and as the gray scale moves toward the lighter tones, the same ground apparently becomes darker. Which has more value to the visual artist, the fact that the gray is everywhere the same, or the evident perception that it stays nowhere the same? On the picture plane all tonal values are relative to one another. [4]

Use of a middle-gray ground

Traditional artists and illustrators, to assist in modulating light on form, often use a gray drawing surface, on which shadowing is indicated in darker grays or blacks and lighter areas in a whiter material, softly applied at first, then more opaquely to show the highest lights. Just as a uniform ground tone for the gray scale adjusts its light value in response to the adjacent area, so the gray ground of Prud'hon's drawing changes from light to dark, seeming to melt into the figure where values meet (**Fig. 11.20**). [5]

Modeled tonality

The term *chiaroscuro* has been used since the time of da Vinci to refer to the modeling of form through a fluid modulation of light (clear) and dark (obscured) tones. The selection of works in **Fig. 11.21** suggests the range of personal styles that can be expressed through tonal value as related to a single subject. Rembrandt's works seem to exist in the flicker of candlelight, their mastery of *chiaroscuro* undiminished even with the loss of golden color in black and white.

Black-and-white photography has made it possible to see immediately the *chiaro-scuro* structure of paintings with no chromatic color. El Greco and others built up tonal compositions in monochromatic tints and shades, before adding transparent washes or glazes of color. Until photography, this was the only possible method, other than preparing preliminary tonal studies, to see a painting's spatial dimension purely in terms of light value; it could never be recalled after the fact. Since spatial structure is also created by color, any painting seen in black-and-white reproduction alone has not been seen *as a painting* at all, but as an achromatic guide to its *chiaroscuro* aspect. Even so-called black-and-white paintings, such as Picasso's *Guernica* (**Fig. 11.22**), reveal a particular *kind* of grayness, lost in print. Did he use Ivory Black, Lamp Black or Mars Black? Each gives a different quality and a different range of grays. Frank D. Russell notes that *Guernica* is "not purely colorless, but ... through the grays, [there is] filtered a very slight bluish coloration ... [This] contrasts with the naked ocherish sizing of the canvas." The overwhelming power of the *symbolic* use of light in this painting is seen as a series of planes, increasingly lighter in value, advancing from depths of (political and

Fig. 11.20 **Pierre Paul Prud'hon**, *Bust of a Female Figure*, 1814. Black and white chalk on blue-gray paper, $11 \times 8\frac{3}{5}$ ins (28×21.5 cm). Courtesy: The Philadelphia Museum of Art.

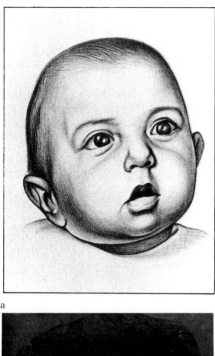

a

b

c

d

Fig. 11.21a (*top left*) **Unknown Mexican artist**, *Head of a Baby*, c. 1920. Lithographic pencil, 12 × 9 ins (31 × 23 cm). Collection: C. and J. Dantzic.

Fig. 11.21b (*top center*) **Pablo Picasso**, *Head of a Young Man*, 1923. Grease crayon, $24\frac{1}{2} × 18\frac{5}{8}$ ins (62 × 47 cm). Courtesy: The Brooklyn Museum, New York.

Fig. 11.21c (*top right*) **Kathe Kollwitz**, *Self Portrait*, 1924. Lithograph. Courtesy: Fogg Art Museum, Harvard University, Massachusetts. Gift of Friends of the Fogg Art Museum.

Fig. 11.21d (*left*) **Rembrandt van Rijn**, *Self Portrait*. Courtesy: Kunsthi Storisches Museum. Vienna.

Fig. 11.21e (*bottom left*) **Harvey Dinnerstein**, *Mercedes*, 1976. Silverpoint, $10\frac{1}{4} × 9$ ins (26 × 23 cm). Courtesy of the artist.

Fig. 11.21f (*bottom centre*) **Jean Antoine Watteau**, *Three Studies of the Head of a Young Negro for "Le Concert Champêtre" and " Les Charmes de la Vie,"* (detail) 1716–18. Chalk and watercolor, $9\frac{9}{16} × 10\frac{11}{16}$ ins (24 × 27 cm). Courtesy: The Louvre, Paris.

Fig. 11.21g (*bottom right*) **Albrecht Dürer**, *Head of a Black Man*, 1508. Charcoal, $12\frac{5}{8} × 8\frac{9}{16}$ ins (31 × 21.5 cm). Courtesy: The Graphische Sammlung, Vienna.

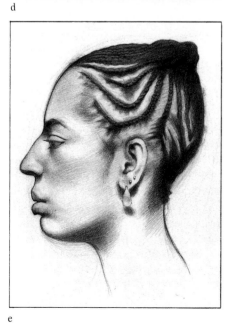

e

f

g

Fig. 11.22 Pablo Picasso, *Guernica*, 1937. Oil on canvas, 138 × 308 ins (350 × 782 cm). Courtesy: The Prado Madrid.

visual) darkness, under the all-seeing eye, the electric glare, the lamp of liberty and of history. The many levels of meaning that can be elicited from such a work add to the richness of the viewer's experience and in this way add to the overall light, or enlightenment, of the world. [6]

EXERCISES

Exercise 3:
After studying a variety of Dante illustrations, here and elsewhere, create one of your own, depicting the depths and blackness of Hell or the brilliant light of Paradise, as described in this epic poem.

Exercise 4:
Make two gray scales, first moving from white to black in equal, clearly separated steps, then as a continuous, edgeless flow. Consider an appropriate solution for the "background" in each study. Try a long torn-paper collage in many bits and pieces as well as a fluid wash in ink or paint.

Exercise 5:
On a middle-gray ground, use dark and light tones to show light modeling the volume of a form.

Exercise 6:
Select a reproduction of a painting in full color, and re-create its tonality in a black and white study. Compare your work with a black and white reproduction of the painting. Make necessary adjustments.

Fig. 11.23 George Grosz, *Untitled portrait*, c. 1932. Ink drawing. Illustration for "Der Speisser-Spiegel," published by Carl Reissner Verlag, 1932. Courtesy: Mr. and Mrs. Jerome Burns.

Using line to create light and form

Width and weight of line alone may define form and suggest space (**Fig. 11.23**). Sensitive adjustments, achieved by varying pressure on responsive pens and brushes, move edges closer or farther apart, the essence of "calligraphic" line (**Fig. 11.24**). Western "Action painters," no less than generations of carefully trained Asian calligraphers, express ideas about mass, delicacy, distance, flatness, pattern and disorder through lines revealing the very motion (and emotion) of the hand holding the brush (**Fig. 8.8**). [7]

Fig. 11.24 (*left*) **Hokusai**, *Tuning the Samisen*, c. 1820–25. Brush and ink, $9\frac{1}{4} \times 8\frac{1}{4}$ ins (25 × 21 cm). Courtesy: The Freer Gallery of Art, Smithsonian Institution, Washington, D.C.
Fig. 11.25 (*right*) **Giovanni Battista Caracciolo**, *Head of a Baby*, 17th C. Pen and ink, $8\frac{1}{2} \times 6\frac{1}{2}$ ins (21.5 × 16.5 cm). Courtesy: Kunsthalle, Hamburg.

Parallel-line tonality

A clustering of parallel lines can create a field much like a continuous tone, growing darker, perhaps heavier, as the lines move closer together and lighter as they spread apart, perhaps to disappear and leave a field of white. When form is defined by a group of these lines, curving, swelling, constricting to build shadow and contour as well as suggesting underlying structure, it may be difficult to separate the shading from the definition or description of the subject. [8]

Crosshatching

A similar technique, developed during the Renaissance, involves two series of form-building "hatching" lines, the second more or less perpendicularly crossing the first, and called, of course, "crosshatching" (**Fig. 11.25**). Used in engraving, etching, woodblock printmaking and drawing as well as in finely brushed tempera and oil painting, some examples seem nearly woven in a netting of criss-crossed "threads;" in others the device is applied with great restraint.

Crosshatching has been unsurpassed for rendering form and shadow in engraving, an additive, one-line-at-a-time procedure. It also appeals to artists who want each stroke of the hand or tool accessible to the viewer, a sentiment close to that of the "Action painters" or calligraphers just described. [9]

Prints and drawings may show techniques blended so skillfully we cannot easily unravel them for analysis and study.

EXERCISES

Exercise 7:
Draw the same subject twice using no tonal shading, but varying line quality in each for differing spatial effects.

Exercise 8:
Select a textured subject, such as a knitted hat or ball of string, and make a modeled drawing using parallel lines for tonality.

Exercise 9:
On a transparent overlay, add strokes to your parallel-line study to create the effect of crosshatching. Avoid excess!

Diminishing contrast: atmospheric perspective

As objects move into the distance, they appear to lose clarity of outline or sharpness; contrasts of color and light value diminish. Da Vinci wrote that these visual experiences, plus reduced size of objects seen from afar, constitute the field of perspective. Even today they are called Aerial or Atmospheric Perspective. Objects may be extremely small and remain sharply in focus if near the eye, yet merge and fade into a vague haze, as trees or mountains do, at a great distance. To re-create or re-present the image of nature in land-, sea- or cityscapes, it is necessary to acknowledge this graying and softening of colors and edges. A pale blueness created by dust particles in the air causes not only the sky but generally everything approaching the horizon out of doors to appear bluish. This has been noted and respected by painters wishing to represent the "mirror of nature" (**Fig. 11.27**). The Impressionists, who recorded subtle hue changes caused by time of day, season and weather, often shattering distant edges in a shimmer of radiant but close-valued, muted color, also acknowledged aerial perspective (**Fig. 11.26**).

Fig. 11.26 Claude Monet, *Grand Canal, Venice*, 1908. Oil on canvas, $29 \times 36\frac{3}{8}$ ins (73.5×92.5 cm). Courtesy: Museum of Fine Arts, Boston.

Fig. 11.27 **Jean Francois Millet**, *The Gleaners*, 1857. Oil on canvas, 33 × 44 ins (84 × 112 cm). Courtesy: The Louvre, Paris.

Fig. 11.28 (*left*) **Andrew Wyeth**, *Christina's World*, 1948. Tempera on gesso panel, 32¼ × 47¾ ins (82 × 121 cm). Courtesy: The Museum of Modern Art, New York, purchase.

Fig. 11.29 (*right*) **Dorothea Lange**, *Tractored Out, Childress County, Texas*, 1938. Gelatin silver print. Courtesy: The Library of Congress.

In the long-debated question regarding distinctions between so-called illustration versus so-called fine art, one of the criteria often used to determine whether a work succeeds as "art" has to do with its treatment of atmospheric perspective. In Wyeth's *Christina's World* (**Fig. 11.28**), the basic color of each area of the field remains constant all the way to the horizon, as does the contrast between the darker drawing over the ochre ground. The crisp horizon is the strongest edge in the painting, and the houses show no diminution of tonal or color value with distance. In paintings where realism is not a concern, these factors might not be significant, but in this work with its superb drawing and detail, we receive mixed messages. For these and other reasons, Wyeth is considered by many to be firmly established in the "illustrator" category. What criteria would you consider in making such a distinction—if you made such a distinction at all? Would a camera see this in the same way as the eye, the photographer the same as the painter (**Fig. 11.29**)?

Fig. 11.30 (*left*) **Edvard Munch**, *The Scream*, 1893. Oil on canvas, $32\frac{3}{4} \times 26\frac{1}{8}$ ins (83×66 cm). Courtesy: The Munch Museum, Oslo.

Fig. 11.31 (*right*) **Henri Matisse**, *The Window at Collieurs*, 1905. Oil on canvas, $21\frac{3}{4} \times 18\frac{1}{8}$ ins (55×46 cm). Courtesy: Mrs. John Hay Whitney.

A close second to the puddle-of-ink shadow is the too-hard horizon line, which flattens the picture plane unintentionally. However, such an effect may be desired and successful, as in Edvard Munch's *The Scream* (**Fig. 11.30**), where a sinuous, looping form beginning at the horizon swirls forward to engulf the tormented subject, compressing space symbolically and visually.

In his *Window at Collieurs* (**Fig. 11.31**) Matisse uses a heavy lavender line as the horizon, fitting it into the perpendicular structure of the window frame and other compositional elements just to act as a space-flattener. The context of an individual visual decision plays an important part in its success. No one element can be disengaged from the total interaction without affecting the whole. Yet we continuously focus upon this or that element in our study. It is helpful to remind ourselves that such analysis is only justified by the promise of synthesis at a new and higher level of understanding.

Look again at the Wyeth painting. Has your opinion changed? [10]

EXERCISES

Exercise 10:
In any medium, develop a landscape composition in two ways, one with an emphatic horizon line, the other employing atmospheric perspective.

Special effects of light

Backlighting

With the source of light behind the subject, a soft halo may appear at its edges while the part facing the viewer is seen in shadow, creating the effect called backlighting (**Fig. 11.3**). Pre-photography painters, relying solely on their own perceptions and familiarity with other artists' interpretations, may have approached the challenge of capturing the illusion of light with greater excitement and urgency than we can hope to recapture today. Oversaturation with visual imagery can reduce our determination to seek firsthand experience and satisfy us with secondhand seeing. The study of photography encourages direct confrontation with light and shadow, a fine supplement to other visual training. [11]

Offset shadows

Offset shadows give a strong sense of separation between an object casting a shadow and the surface receiving it. It is used in contemporary paintings and graphic design, to

Fig. 11.32 Mary Cassatt, *Lydia Seated in a Loge*, 1879. Pastel on paper, $25\frac{5}{8} \times 17\frac{3}{4}$ ins (65×45 cm). Courtesy: The Nelson-Atkins Museum of Art, Kansas City, Missouri, (anonymous gift).

Fig. 11.33 **Virginia Cantarella**, *Three drawings of an egg*, 1988. Pencil on paper, each 5 × 6 ins (13 × 15 cm). Courtesy of the artist.

suggest that objects (sometimes neon tubes forming words) are located in front of the picture plane, jutting out into space, the shadow appearing to fall on the surface of the canvas (**Fig. 15.39**). [12]

More about shadows

When a light object is seen against a light ground, the darkest shadow generally appears at one edge, immediately beginning to soften until it reaches the roundest contour, where it may appear to gain some strength as it meets the even lighter ground on the other side. As seen in these drawings, this logical modeling of form and shadow can be created on canvas or paper convincingly whether the illustrator has worked from the model, memory or invention (**Fig. 11.33**). Observe a dark object, say a green pepper, on differing surfaces, including the blackest paper available, and the picture is not so clear. A shadow may appear lighter than the object itself, with unpredictable light values meeting at the edge. The "black" paper may turn quite gray. Instead of simply varying in tone, the flowing lights and darks may assume a luminosity and glow that you can paint on the surface by "bouncing" and "reflecting" actual light onto the pepper from different angles. The edge between substance and shadow may melt away, leaving voluptuous, waxy-contoured, almost abstract nature-shaped, or biomorphic, forms. "Twenty years of effort have gone into the making of this pepper," wrote Edward Weston of his photograph (**Fig. 11.34**), "... a pepper—but more than a pepper." In his celebration of form, made visible through a collaboration between artist and nature, Weston saw the camera as a tool. "The camera does not reproduce nature, not exactly as seen with our eyes, which are but a means to see through as impersonal as the lens, and must be directed by the same intelligence that in turn guides the camera." [13]

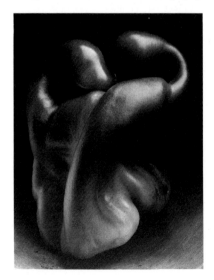

Fig. 11.34 **Edward Weston**, *Pepper*, 1930. Gelatin silver print. © 1981 Arizona Board of Regents, Center for Creative Photography.

Painting with light

Early photographers were apt to speak of their new medium in rapturous, poetic imagery, aware that they were witnessing a revolution. "Mirror with a memory" was one description. William Henry Fox Talbot entitled his 1844 book, the first on photography, "The Pencil of Nature." "I have chained the sun to serve me," proclaims a studio portrait card by a zealous photographer of the late 1800s.

By the 1930s Weston was making hundreds of photographs of peppers, shells, nudes, dunes and other natural subjects. It had become evident that the artist contributes the most important light to the chemistry producing a print, whether etched, carved or photographed.

Painting with light was the compelling drive that spurred the Impressionist Claude Monet to begin canvas after canvas of the same subject at different times of day,

Fig. 11.35 (*left*) **Claude Monet**, *Rouen Cathedral, The Facade in Sunlight*, 1894. Oil on canvas, $41\frac{7}{10} \times 28\frac{7}{10}$ ins (106 × 73 cm). Courtesy: Sterling and Francine Clark Art Institute, Williamstown, Massachusetts.
Fig. 11.36 (*right*) **Claude Monet**, *Rouen Cathedral (Morning Effect)*, 1894. Oil on canvas, $39\frac{3}{10} \times 25\frac{1}{2}$ ins (100 × 65 cm). Courtesy: Museum Folkwang, Essen.

different seasons and weather. The task of somehow translating the "diamonds and precious stones" of color seen by the eye into the substance of a painting, of making eternal the individual instant of perception, suggesting the speed of observation, yet maintaining the "envelope" or "total, unbroken fabric of appearance," took slow, difficult, dedicated effort. The illusion of spontaneity was as elusive as the illusion of space and light. Monet, with his sequential studies of haystacks, trees, the Rouen Cathedral façade (**Fig. 11.36**), and other repeatedly re-seen and re-painted "motifs," must be acknowledged as the single most devoted seeker after the quintessential orchestration on canvas of the unity of space, color and light. In the words of Kenneth Clark, "Monet undertook to prove that the object painted was of no importance, the sensation of light was the only true subject." Fifty years later, using a different kind of "brush" and painting directly with light, Weston, with a palette limited to black and white, in a related kind of serial dedication, addressed himself to this timeless quest.

EXERCISES

Exercise 11:
Illuminate a previously arranged still life with backlighting and develop a study in any medium.

Exercise 12:
Move a light tracing over a drawing until the original floats above the page, leaving the tracing as an offset shadow on the picture plane. Try tubular lettering or a geometric design.

Exercise 13:
Place a dark object on a like-value ground, observe and make a study in any medium, showing three-dimensionality and an appropriate shadow.

Chapter Twelve

SHOWING, SLOWING AND STOPPING MOTION

Seeing a world in motion

Still-life arrangements and posed human models are familiar subjects in the studio. Yet life is never still. A living model is constantly active, moving visibly with each breath, and invisibly as life functions continue, involving the movement of parts too small or slow to be seen. Fruits, flowers and vegetation undergo subtle and dramatic changes with time.

Artists have long sought and found ways to show, slow and stop motion, to acknowledge the passage of time on the flat, still canvas (**Figs. 12.1, 13.2**). The suggestion of time is inseparable from the illusion of motion, movement, change (**Fig. 12.2**). Kepes advises that "what should be grasped and given form are things in flux ... [for] all elements in nature are in perpetual interaction ... Matter is kinetic ... Earth rotates, sun moves, trees grow, clouds move ... light and shadow hunt each other in indefatigable play ... forms appear and disappear ..." Henri Cartier-Bresson, who sought to capture "the decisive moment" in each event he photographed, says in his book of that title, "the world is movement, and you cannot be stationary in your attitude toward something that is moving." [1]

Fig. 12.2 **Salvador Dali**, *The Persistence of Memory*, 1931. Oil on canvas, $9\frac{1}{2} \times 13$ ins (24×33 cm). Collection: The Museum of Modern Art, New York. Given anonymously. Copyright Dernart Pro Arte/ARS N.Y.. 1989.

Fig. 12.4 **Vincent van Gogh**, *The Starry Night*, 1889. Oil on canvas, 29 × 36¼ ins (74 × 92 cm). Collection: The Museum of Modern Art, New York. Acquired through the Lillie P. Bliss Bequest.

Motion, time and change

Motion implies a change of relationship, though some changes are too slow, distant, large or small for us to perceive as movement. The growth of plants and living beings, moving hands of a clock, changing daylight and shadow, sunset and moonrise, paths of stars and changes of seasons—these are movements we generally experience without being aware of them (**Fig. 12.3**). Yet artists can imbue even these events with active, pulsing motion (**Fig. 12.4**). Other actions pass too quickly for our eye to "hold" for an instant—moving blades of a fan, spokes of a wheel, frames of a motion picture, pattern of dots on a television screen, the continuous dance of athletes and ballet performers, the fleet of racing horses. Many are familiar subjects of brush, pencil or camera, their movement frozen at an instantaneous split-second, stopping time in its tracks, or conveying the continuous flow and passage of time and motion together (p. 218).

EXERCISES

Exercise 1:
Collect works suggesting motion in differing mediums and group them according to such qualities as technique, speed, kind of motion and number of subdivisions of movement. Compare with the collections and categories of others.

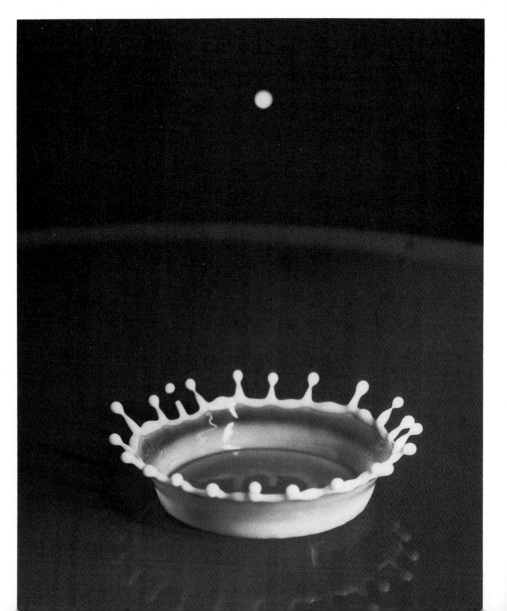

Fig. 12.5   Harold Edgerton, *Milk drop coronet*, 1957. Courtesy: Gus Kayafas, Palm Press, Massachusetts.

Relativity of motion, time and place

Motion is seen as objects alter their position in relation to one another or to an observer. A photograph or any rendition of a high-speed object may not clearly show whether it is stationary or moving without an indication of its relationship to an environment (**Fig. 12.5**). On a train, we cannot focus on the track just ahead as it passes beneath us at an incredible speed; yet objects at a distance appear to move normally, and things near the horizon look completely still, though they may be proceeding at the same rate of speed. Is motion a relative idea? "Nobody ever noticed a place except at a time or a time except at a place," said Minkowski.

Representational two-dimensional works must either acknowledge and somehow depict what the Japanese call *ukiyo-e*—the passing or floating world—or else they must, in the vocabulary of the photographer, "freeze the frame," stop the moment, and "snap" a single image out of the seamless flow of time/space. Since this moment may be chosen at any point, we can imagine an infinite sequence of potentially selected instants from which the artist decides which decisive moment is to become a "moment preserved" (**Fig. 12.6**). [2]

In the game of "Statues," you are propelled in a dizzy spin and told to "freeze" at a sudden unplanned signal. Would a photograph of such a pose look the same as a high-speed shot of the same moment made during a continuous performance of the activity? Certain works posed to resemble a glimpse of natural movement fail to convey a sense of life, but ring an artificial, unnatural note. Why?

"Perception [requires] a process developing in time," according to Dewey. Saul Bass explains that "when a painting surface has objects placed upon it, a sequence in time must be assigned [to them] ... albeit with infinitesimal time duration between each step."

Imagine a work in which sequential images are seen in a continuous flow, overlapping and merging in our awareness to produce the sense of a picture in motion, a

Fig. 12.6 John James Audubon, *Sooty Tern*, 1832. Watercolor, $29\frac{1}{2} \times 39\frac{1}{2}$ ins (75×100 cm). Courtesy: The New-York Historical Society.

Fig. 12.7 Gjon Mili, *Picasso Drawing a Centaur with Light*, 1949. Gelatin silver print. Courtesy: Life Magazine © Time Inc.

motion picture, a movie! Moving across the screen of our eye, such a fluid ''film'' creates the illusion of movement and carries us directly from the perception of individual still frames in a kind of leap, bypassing the solid reality of the third dimension, directly transporting us to the experience, the look, the illusion of the merging of space and time into the space/time continuum, the fourth dimension (**Fig. 12.7**)!

EXERCISES

Exercise 2:
Observe a figure, vehicle or animal performing a repeated motion; decide which ''moment'' most decisively suggests the entire action; make a photograph or drawing of that ''decisive moment.'' Repeat as necessary!

Achieving the look of motion or rest

Although on the picture surface there is usually no physical movement, every degree of apparent stasis and movement has been shown, from repose, permanence and enduring sameness through all levels of action, including the illusion that the viewer is moving while observing the subject (from a number of vantage points or a single "traveling" point). We see in every two-dimensional work at least one of these qualities:

— A split-moment stopped during motion (p. 216).
— Forms arranged at rest in changeless light (p. 230).
— Movement taking place as we observe it (p. 213).

Scenarios, allegories, filmic themes

These different ideas may appear in one work, as in allegorical, story-telling depictions of historic or fictional events. With selected moments often far apart in time, these may

Fig. 12.8 Sassetta and assistant, *The Meeting of Saint Anthony and Saint Paul*, c. 1440. Tempera on wood, $18\frac{3}{4} \times 13\frac{5}{8}$ ins (47.5×34.5 cm). Courtesy: National Gallery of Art, Washington; Samuel H. Kress Collection.

Fig. 12.9 Thomas Eakins, *The Swimming Hole*, 1883. Oil on canvas, 27 × 36 ins (68.5 × 91.5 cm). Courtesy: The Modern Art Museum, Fort Worth.

not be thought of as "frames" in a sequential, linear flow. The artist must use compositional, rhythmic devices to make us see the path along which such a story unfolds. An actual path is often shown, so we enjoy a sense of moving through the entire experience. Visually, the work is composed in perfect harmony—at rest (**Fig. 12.8**).

In a related filmic way, Dante opens his "Divine Comedy" with the narrator suddenly finding himself "amidst the journey of our life, in a shadowy wilderness, where the direct way [path] was uncertain," a fine instance of things in motion caught at an instant in time. Dante's adventures lead him, guided by the spirit of Virgil, to the "true way," providing many vivid moments for artists to illuminate—during the last 650 years!

In *The Swimming Hole* (**Fig. 12.9**) Thomas Eakins subdivided an activity into a series of moments, selecting six "frames" from what might be a film of a young man, rising, pausing and diving into the water, in a continuous loop of movement. The artist made photographs of his students in preparation for painting. He had studied sequential photographs of the figure in motion by Eadweard Muybridge and made several himself. Understanding this artist's intentions helps us see the work as a statement about the continuity of human movement. Eakins used poses from classical sculpture for several figures, and included a self-portrait as the swimmer. We are emphasizing kinetic aspects of the painting here, so additional details must be left for individual investigation or further study of art history.

Sequence, animation, films

Muybridge

Eadweard Muybridge's studies began in response to a challenge—to determine whether all of a racehorse's legs leave the ground together during its fastest run. By setting up a series of still cameras at equally spaced points along the horse's path with an automatic tripping system, Muybridge made a sequential study of the animal's movements, showing all four hooves clearly above the track (**Fig. 12.10**). The year 1872 marks the earliest unit-sequence camera record of an activity. You might compare this series with results attained by E. J. Marey and his celebrated "Marey wheel" (**Fig. 12.11**). Several years later, Marey predicted a new field of "animated zoology" developing from Muybridge's work. In 1893, Thomas Edison attached a sequence of Muybridge's individual frames to a celluloid ribbon, producing the first recognizable motion picture. Even earlier Muybridge had perfected his zoopraxiscope, a sophisticated variation of the zoetrope using the concept of the "persistence of vision" to fuse a sequence of silhouettes in the eye and mind as they pass a given slot, moving rapidly along a circular path. [3]

Fig. 12.10 Eadweard Muybridge, *The Race Horse*, 1879. Instantaneous photographs. Courtesy: The American Museum of Natural History, Department of Library Services.

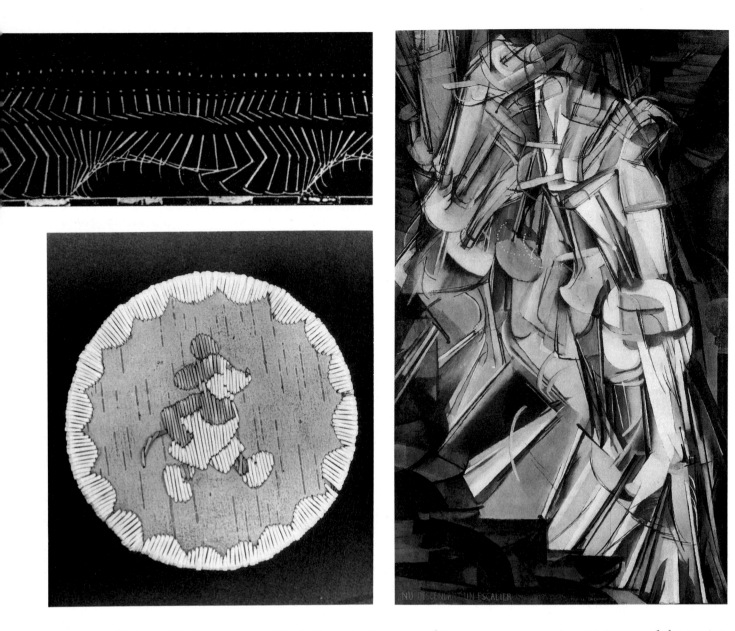

Fig. 12.11 (*top left*) **Etienne-Jules Marey**, *Running Man (self portrait)*, 1880. Chronophotograph. Courtesy: Musée des Techniques, Paris.

Fig. 12.12 (*bottom left*) Porcupine quill-work on birch bark box cover, with Mickey Mouse, c. 1935. Amerindian, 4½ ins (11.5 cm) diameter. Collection: C. and J. Dantzic.

Fig. 12.13 (*right*) **Marcel Duchamp**, *Nude Descending a Staircase*, 1912. Oil on canvas, 58 × 35 ins (147 × 89 cm). Philadelphia Museum of Art.

Muybridge actually projected images on a screen in anticipation of the motion picture. He completed thousands of sequential studies of humans, domestic and wild animals in "Animals in Motion." His books are classic reference sources for students of animation. Whether we enjoy an early Mickey Mouse cartoon (**Fig. 12.12**) or the most recent computer-generated graphic animation, we pay homage to the seminal contributions of the compulsive, eccentric Edward Muggeridge, who changed far more than his name during an inventive, dramatic lifetime.

Time and motion in painting—Cubism

Two years after Muybridge's death in 1904, Braque and Picasso were creating their first Cubist studies. For the first time, the ideas of multiple viewpoints, time sequence and the dissecting of images into repositionable units were introduced into painting. By presenting, on a single surface, the suggestion of the passage of time during which the eye moves about a subject, a new dimension was added to the artist's palette. Thus, photography may have stimulated the major innovation of twentieth-century painting, by providing an impetus for Cubism, in the words of Martin Ries, "the cornerstone of Modern Art."

In 1912, Marcel Duchamp, by shifting rhythmic, nearly parallel planes in a swinging, athletic sway, painted the movements of a figure descending a staircase (**Fig. 12.13**). It has been said that this painting reveals the "descending" but neither the nude nor the staircase! Again, the period of time occupied by the action brings us to the illusion of the fourth dimension.

Activating the field: environment, imagination

Activation of the environment surrounding a subject, in the form of material in motion (dust, air, adjacent objects) or brushstrokes and action lines continuing the contours of moving parts, can be quite subtle, merely enhancing a sense of activity. Through exaggeration and emphasis, however, they may suggest strong action or broad, comical humor (**Fig. 12.14**). Absence of parts in motion can be effective if the activity off the picture plane is graphically suggested. Speed or velocity may also be conveyed by sequentially altering the size of similar objects or spaces between them. An unusually "modern" sense of continuous action, reminiscent of animation, is often seen in ancient Egyptian work.

Simple animation—flip pads

Repetition of elements altered sequentially in form or position, found in much contemporary art and design (**Fig. 12.15**), is a key to cartooning and animation. Many effects of motion may be achieved, some whimsical, even witty.

Fig. 12.14 (*top and center*) **Dik Browne**, *Hagar the Horrible*, 4/9/86, 10/14/86. Reprinted by permission: King Features Syndicate, Inc., (*bottom*) **Tom Peters**, *Mother Goose*, 3/27/86. Reprinted by permission: Tribune Media Services.

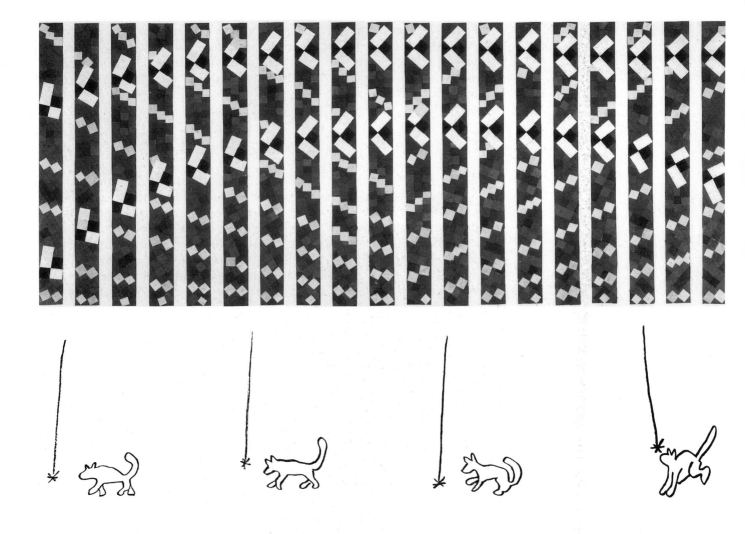

Fig. 12.15 (*top*) **Henri Matisse**, *The Bees*, 1948. Preliminary maquette for stained glass windows, $39\frac{3}{4} \times 94\frac{7}{8}$ ins (101×241 cm). Courtesy: Musée Matisse, Nice.

Fig. 12.16 (*bottom*) **Cynthia Dantzic**, pages from flip-pad animation, "Cat and Spider."

To create a simple animated sequence—for instance, on a flip-pad—great skill in drawing is not essential; a free, sketchy technique may be preferable (**Fig. 12.16**). [4]

Animated sequences often show fantastic transformations from one object or animal to another, limited only by imagination and courage. A charming flip-pad shows a stick figure catching a large fish which turns around and, as it is reeled in, opens its mouth very wide and swallows figure, fishing pole and all! It was drawn by a student in her first art course. [5]

Any results you may care to send will be added to my growing collection. Thank you.

Freezing the frame—at the decisive moment

The books of Muybridge's studies offer an opportunity to experience both movement, as we scan each series to read its filmic action, and the stopped gesture, seen in any single image. This double reading of time may account for the increasing popularity of the "freeze frame" or suddenly stopped motion picture image. Generally, in films there is no one decisive moment as activity unfolds in a continuous flow of movement with rhythm, pacing and even intervals of rest. The freeze frame stops an ongoing motion at its peak as we anticipate continued action.

The "decisive moment" is explained by the originator of the phrase, Cartier-Bresson himself: "Above all, I craved to seize the whole essence, in the confines of one single photograph, of some situation that was in the process of unrolling itself before my eyes" (**Fig. 15.46**).

Fig. 12.17   Jerry Dantzic, *Mambo*, 1953.
Gelatin silver print. Courtesy: the
photographer.

Representations of fast-moving action caught in the act of taking place risk
appearing frozen, instead of communicating motion. The faster an action is apparently
stopped by an artist or actually stopped by a photographer, the less likely it is to convey
a sense of movement taking place. Frozen time does not read the same as passing time.
Sharp focus and painstaking detail may not offer the sense of motion provided by
softened, blurred edge and contour (**Fig. 12.17**). (Another instance of "less is more.")
Reduced detail and diminished precision increase the sensation of motion. Stephen
Dalton, photographing insects in flight (at speeds of up to one ten-millionth of a second)
shows these never-still creatures seemingly motionless in air. Some might as well be
models of insects placed cunningly in diorama settings; they convey no sense of

Fig. 12.18 **Stephen Dalton**, *Common sympetrum dragonfly*, 1975. High-speed photograph, from "Borne on the Wind, The Extraordinary World of Insects in Flight," published by Chatto & Windus, Ltd., London. Courtesy: Photo Researchers, Inc.

movement. One of the more "moving" insects looks like an animated cartoon; we read its alternating up-and-down thrusting pairs of wings as a single pair in motion (**Fig. 12.18**). [6]

Stroboscopic sequence

Very small intervals exist between the steps of an action shown on a single stroboscopic frame permitting analytical study of the path of movement during extended continuous gesture or action (**Fig. 12.19**).

Is the multi-armed figure (**Fig. 12.20**) in Asian art truly intended to show the Hindu deity in possession of many limbs, or rather, in a kind of stroboscopic symbolism, the

Fig. 12.19 (*left*) **Harold Edgerton**, *A Back Dive*, 1954. Stroboscopic photograph, 30 exposures a second. Courtesy: Gus Kayafas, Palm Press.

Fig. 12.20 (*right*) Vajrasattiva (or) Bodhisattva Prajnaparamita. Female deity with many arms. Courtesy: The Asia Society, New York, Mr. and Mrs. John D. Rockefeller 3rd.

Fig. 12.21 (*top left*) **Harold Edgerton**, *Wes Fesler Kicking a Football*. High speed photograph. Courtesy: Gus Kayafas, Palm Press.

Fig. 12.22 (*top right*) **Kjell Sandved**, *Fan worm on coral reef*, 1984. Courtesy: of the photographer, and the Smithsonian Institution, Washington.

Fig. 12.23 **Andrew Davidhazy**, *Untitled "stretched" figure on a single photograph*, 1988. Courtesy of the photographer.

many simultaneous attributes she personifies? The numerous arms are often seen as a swinging flow of movement, encircling the figure in a flower-like spiral or the gesture of a dance. Compare the sequence of stopped movements during the dance with the action of Eakin's *Swimming Hole* (Fig. 12.9).

Harold Edgerton's experiments in stopping action as quickly as one ten-millionth of a second with his stroboscopic camera reveal previously unseen beauties of natural movement. Many of his progressions, showing the ordered movement of parts of figures in motion, bring to mind the works of Muybridge, Marey, Eakins, Duchamp and Balla. Examples may be as recent as the silhouettes of Trova or as distant as the swimming reindeer at Lascaux (Fig. 13.2). [7]

Exaggeration, distortion and gesture

By showing the effect of powerful forces on the very structure of a subject, a photograph may dramatically indicate that movement has occurred, is captured briefly, and will continue without interruption. Since we know that the distorted form in this photograph represents a momentary, changing situation, we see and feel the movement (Fig. 12.21). We add what we know to what we see and see what we expect. (Didn't you "read" the undersea fan worm in Fig. 12.22 as a stroboscopic photograph?)

In photography, as in painting, there are many ways to stretch, distort and otherwise modify the appearance of reality. Some alter the normal movement of a subject in front of the lens or the lens itself. Figures may revolve before the camera at varying speeds while the lens records the effect on one continuous piece of film,

227

Fig. 12.24 Henri Matisse, *The Dance II*, 1916. Oil on canvas, 8′5⅝″ × 12′9½″ (2.6 × 3.9 m). Courtesy: The Hermitage Museum, Moscow.

Fig. 12.25 Sheila Schwid Milder, *Matisse Madness*, 1983. 16 mm. film, animation cut-out with music, (sequential frames). Courtesy of the artist.

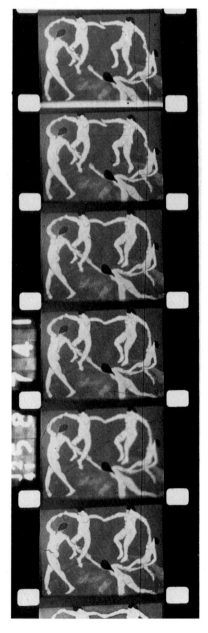

resulting in strangely pulled and expanded dance-like forms (**Fig. 12.23**). Some strobo-scopic photographs blend images to achieve a related stretched effect.

One telling moment during an action can convey the full flow of motion. The rounded movements of the circling dancers in **Fig. 12.24** encourage the eye to dance in time with Matisse's painting. Animator Sheila Milder created an animated film (**Fig. 12.25**) in which these figures move separately as cut-outs coming together to join hands and assume the inevitable, perfect position of Matisse's composition. A work such as this helps filmmaker and viewer imagine the creative impulse behind a painting.

Showing, slowing and speeding motion on film

Animators and cinematographers may suggest movement by relying on gestalt princi-ples, the viewer's determination to make sense of incomplete visual information. When the background behind a still subject is changed sequentially, the observer reads a still background with the subject in motion! Flying superheroes and animals merely pose with limbs outstretched while cities and landscapes "travel" by. No sensation of motion is possible without a discrepancy in the velocity of two events. Science says it better, but seeing is believing! [8]

On film the apparent speed of subjects can be controlled by the number of images made or projected per second. Normal activity is suggested by shooting and showing twenty-four frames a second. This can be accomplished in motion-picture photography by adjusting camera settings, but for the animator it can mean hundreds (or thousands) of drawings for each minute seen on the screen. Despite certain advantages provided by the computer, many animators prefer to draw each frame (or cell) by hand. Tracing and moving parts in "stroboscopic" progression can simplify the procedure.

Early silent movies used sixteen frames per second, which accounts for the stilted "Charlie Chaplin" walk; eight to sixteen frames projected at the normal pace give the effect of speeded-up "Keystone Cops" humor. But, "more is less" in slow-motion photography, for the more frames made per second, projected at normal speed, the slower the action appears. In filming growing plants or changing seasons, single frames, made hours, days or longer apart give a continuous condensed sense of time passing. Stems, roots and other "inanimate" forms of life twist in spirals, as the time elapsed between frames disappears, compressed, in time-lapse photography.

EXERCISES

Exercise 3:
Design a zoetrope by drawing a simple sequence of any action on a continuous loop or circle of paper which is moved past a stationary window in its container.

Exercise 4:
On the last page of a small unlined, non-spiral-bound pad draw a simple shape (geometric or representational) near the open end, using the cardboard as a support. Release the next page (so that you can see the drawing through the inexpensive paper), and almost trace the image, making some modification in size or position. Continue, making progressively altered drawings, until you have completed the action or you have come to the top sheet of paper. To add another "reel of film," remove the cardboard from a second pad, attach it with a rubber band and keep drawing. Use techniques outlined in Chapter 7.

Exercise 5:
For your next, "Technicolor," animation, use colored pencils or markers. No projector is required.

Exercise 6:
Design a simple, two-step action (a ball thrown back and forth, a dance movement, a winking eye) and see how many (or few) times it must be repeated to read smoothly in flip-pad animation.

Exercise 7:
Observe a figure executing a continuous movement (skipping rope, swinging a bat) and, on a series of transparent overlays, draw the fewest transitions needed to convey the action.

Exercise 8:
On a loop of paper to be placed inside your zoetrope, draw a slowly changing background or landscape, and move it behind a stationary subject drawn, opaquely, as though in action, on a transparent overlay.

Stopping time and change on canvas

Surrounded by moving film and video imagery as well as still photographs, we have difficulty imagining a time when there was no such visual documentation. We may fail to appreciate the power and magic attributed to artists who in earlier times with their eye, skill and imagination alone could apparently stop time and fix an image forever, so that observers might experience the subject re-presented directly to their own eye and mind. In the case of portraiture, such depiction conferred a kind of immortality

The fleeting life span of more slowly changing forms, such as fruit or flowers, was emphasized by introducing drops of dew, a candle flame, butterflies or other quick-moving, fast-disappearing insects into the picture. In seventeenth-century Spain and Holland, such works reached a peak of perfection, rivaling later *trompe l'oeil* (fool the eye) and photorealist paintings with which we are more familiar. In these works, the clock stops, the moving finger no longer writes, and, as we contemplate the moment being preserved, we experience the triumph of Art over inexorable, all-consuming Nature and time.

Stilled permanence is seen in Cézanne's *Card Players*. Monumental solidity informs these figures (gives them form). Cézanne selected his "decisive moment" only in choosing a viewing point and framing the visual elements—these figures are not about to move.

The still-life paintings of William Bailey offer peace to the eye and mind (**Fig. 12.26**). Whenever we return to them, nothing will have altered; no living forms will have suffered decay or changed position; the light will hold, and the gentle counterpoint of color, light and volume will still play its quiet melody. Any movement in these elegant works is intellectual, ethereal and of the spirit.

Fig. 12.26   **William Bailey**, *Still Life, Hotel Raphael*, 1985. Oil on canvas, 40 × 50 ins (102 × 127 cm). Collection: Equitable Real Estate Group, New York. Photograph courtesy: Robert Schoelkopf Gallery, with permission of the artist.

Fig. 12.27   **James Abbott McNeill Whistler**, *Nocturne in Black and Gold, the Falling Rocket*, c. 1874. Oil on oak panel, $23\frac{3}{4} \times 18\frac{3}{8}$ ins (60 × 47 cm). Courtesy: The Detroit Institute of Arts. Gift of Henry M. Ferry, Jr.

Action!

The Cézanne and Bailey canvases stand in contrast to the raw action paintings of de Kooning, Pollock or Hofmann, which seem to embody and transmit actual movement, their very surfaces alive with motion and the passage of time.

In freely brushed or poured kinetic gestures these painters bring physical activity directly to the canvas, the work's virtual documentation of motions made by their arms and bodies releasing pigment onto the surface with no thought of additional subject matter. Diagonals, loops and acute angles aimed at focal targets and other graphic devices keep these painting surfaces in motion.

Sensitivity to visual imagery is known to everyone who has seen a roller coaster drop steeply into the void on film—the response of one's own stomach cannot be denied. This extreme example should not mask our awareness of more subtle physiological responses that occur in the presence of any visual stimulus.

Never-still motion on canvas

In interpreting the incessant motion of natural phenomena (sea, storms, fire, windswept clouds, sunlight seen through trees, the changing color and quality of sunlight on landscape) painters have experimented widely. Monet's solution, in his famous haystack and cathedral series, was a frequent change of canvas, as differing light altered color, value and even the structure of forms observed. Renoir seemed to melt patches of moving sunlight into shadowy colors seen beneath heavy foliage (**Fig. 11.11**). Turner may have prefigured Abstract Expressionism in his concern with the sheer exuberance of color in action, paying the merest allegiance to subject matter as amorphous swirls of sea, storm and sky.

James A. M. Whistler also offered acceptable "representational" subjects and titles to accompany experimental studies (**Fig. 12.27**). His contemporaries, the Impressionists, depended on a close relationship with the seen aspect of nature; broken brushstrokes, close-value palettes, shimmering edges and soft-focus forms emphasized their aim of capturing the moving impression of light and color, alive with change and motion.

Fig. 12.28 Joseph Raffael, *Blue Pond, Winter Shore*, 1977. Oil on canvas, 78 × 114 ins (198 × 290 cm). Courtesy of the artist and Nancy Hoffman Gallery, New York.

Fig. 12.29 (*left*) **Ma Yuan**, *A Wave Under the Moon, (one of twenty scenes of water)*, Sung Dynasty 12th C. handscroll. Ink on silk. Courtesy: National Palace Museum, Taipei, Taiwan, Republic of China.

Fig. 12.30 (*right*) **Vija Celmins**, *Long Ocean 3*, 1979. Pencil, 31 × 45 ins (79 × 114 cm). Courtesy; David McKee Gallery.

Water in motion

Compare the treatment of water, perhaps the most familiar never-still subject in painting, by artists in different styles and centuries (**Figs. 12.28, 12.29, 12.30**). Many succeed in stopping its ceaseless motion, but few have captured its pulsing, living sense of movement so well as the Impressionists. Monet particularly keeps water churning, flowing or sparkling with activity. His camera keeps rolling; Monet does not choose the freeze-frame technique (**Figs. 11.26, 13.18**).

Extending the moment

The appearance of motion does not seem related to the speed at which an action is brought to a halt on the surface, but the illusion requires some visual clue to the movement preceding the moment depicted and the activity expected to follow. Blurred edges, repeated elements and disturbance of the environment can impart this sense.

The gesture sketch, a quickly drawn response to the figure, shows the action of the model and the movement of the hand making the image (**Fig. 12.31**). Can one clear, precise line convey motion as well as an unsharp sweep applied with a soft-edged implement? In the hands of an artist, can't either technique be successful? Study, if you can, the amazingly contemporary sketches and drawings of Rembrandt. **[9]**

EXERCISES

Exercise 9:
Observe a figure in motion and, without looking at your paper, follow its "action" with gestural movements of pen, pencil or brush. Then record the same movement in a continuous line on a second page.

Fig. 12.31 **Suzanne Rosenblatt**, *Dancer*, 1980. Chinese brush and ink, 9 × 12 ins (23 × 30.5 cm). Courtesy of the artist.

Motion stopped or motion shown

There is no judgment of value or preference in identifying differences and divergences in the two-dimensional experience. It is possible to achieve violent action on the picture plane, but this is not each painter's goal. You possess the ultimate veto with regard to taste. Visual tension and discord can evoke either excitement or disharmony, and images that provide repose and harmony, free from any suggestion of impermanent, fugitive quality, may bring satisfaction and comfort to the spirit as well as the eye.

Perhaps the most appropriate characterization of the significance of motion to our age was made by Gertrude Stein who saw composition in the twentieth century as a "space of time filled with moving."

Chapter Thirteen

THE EXPANDED FIELD: BEYOND THE RECTANGLE

Fig. 13.1 **Ilya Bolotowsky**, *Tondo*, 1952–59. Oil on canvas, 42 in (107 cm) diameter. Collection: Bernard S. Solomon.

The visual field

We generally think of the visual field as a receptive rectangle—a sheet of paper, a stretched canvas or a photographic negative. To emphasize its perpendicularity, the field may be subdivided into a grid of smaller units, as in graph or quadrille paper. Even when a circle or other shape is the format, elements are designed to fit harmoniously within that space (**Fig. 13.1**). This is true even in very large works so long as the extent of the field is known. But artists have always used unbounded, expanded or irregular spaces.

Prehistoric painting—beginnings

On uneven, uncontained surfaces in dimly-lit stone-walled caves, the extent of available space never fully visible, the earliest known prehistoric paintings were created in France with no thought of a delimited field other than the natural configurations within an immediate area. Often, images of animals were placed over previously painted pictures and at unrelated angles; there is no single unifying point of view suggested. Some areas filled with images of moving, powerful beasts are quite large, yet there is little evident concern with overall visual orchestration within a specific field. Several animals may relate to one another but there is no attempt to create an enclosed shape around them or to separate an individual or a cluster of creatures from the wall as a whole (**Fig. 13.2**).

Limiting the field

Animal hides probably provided the first flat, shaped surfaces for human design, and walls of early dwellings or surfaces of altars the first geometric areas. The physical size of sheep and goats limited the dimensions of parchment sheets made from their skins, unless they were attached as a continuous roll or scroll. A rolled scroll provided protec-

Fig. 13.2 Swimming Reindeer, unknown Paleolithic artist, c. 30,000 BC. Cave, Lascaux, France. Courtesy: Caisse Nationale des Monuments Historiques et des Sites, Paris.

Fig. 13.3 Child's Torah Scroll. Courtesy: Juliet and Jack Milkens.

tion, made compact storage possible, and permitted an open-ended field for drawing or writing. Within parallel margins, a scroll could extend to any reasonable length, always a rectangle.

Paper, first developed from stringy fibers of the papyrus plant's stem, was a luxury, difficult to produce. It could be made in sheets or as a continuous roll. The lengthy scroll, opening vertically or horizontally, continues to find favor in Asia and the Middle East. It is seen in the Hebrew Torah or scriptures (Fig. 13.3). Pictorial art and writing in the West became almost completely dependent upon rectangular shapes in many materials—wooden panels, sheets of paper or parchment, lengths of woven fabric such as linen or cotton stretched on or glued to wooden supports. Screens, boxes, and architectural elements present a two-dimensional field on each face.

The flat rectangle and rectangular solid (with six rectilinear faces or sides) encourage seeing animals and human figures as though they fit into such "containers." From the earliest times rocks, stones, horns and bones suggested natural forms which could be freed with minimal effort from the material enclosing them. But in order to release a form from a rectangular solid, it is necessary to envision it from both sides, front and back, above and below (six separable views) and to place the approximate outline or contour on each face. If you have carved an animal from a dried bar of Ivory Soap, you will be familiar with this idea.

Removing excess material from around the contour of a form drawn on one surface of a chunk of material will produce a free-standing sculptural work, at least a cut-out silhouette (having perhaps two-and-a-half dimensions). But, once the artist is concerned with representing the environment or objects around a subject, then the "outer space" is drawn into the picture, and spatial decisions must be made concerning this surrounding space. If the shape of the field is known (a belt or a container such as a cylindrical box), then depicted subjects must be designed to fit within the given space. Over the centuries various people have devised extremely intricate methods of representing animals and figures on such surfaces. [1]

Split-profile representation

Among the Tsimshian or Haida people of the Pacific Northwest, the flattening of an animal's three-dimensionality is accomplished in ways difficult for us to visualize, suggested by splitting its body down an imaginary center-line, then flattening the two halves as though opened and spread out on a surface. Each half is symmetrically extended away from the nose or facial mask and compressed, flattened and moved around and up to meet again at the top center, as the tail (Fig. 13.4). In such compressions or foldings of three-dimensionality, parts of the body merge, are simplified, eliminated or represented by conventionalized symbols and executed with elaborate, elegant patterning and design. Often, only those familiar with a particular tradition can read these symbolic meanings. Many examples of Northwest Coast art—and, surprisingly, ancient Chinese bronzes—show this cryptic, intricate way of expanding the visual perception of a subject through folding and unfolding its split image in a kind of pre-Cubist depiction from multiple viewing points seen all at once. [2]

Fig. 13.4 Haida and Tlingit designs. Courtesy: Department of Library Services, American Museum of Natural History, New York.

Fig. 13.5 David Hockney, *The Brooklyn Bridge*, 1982. Photographic collage, 109 × 58 ins (277 × 147 cm). Courtesy of the artist.

Fig. 13.6 Cynthia Dantzic, *The Graduate*, 1985. Photographic collage, on board, 16 × 24 ins (41 × 61 cm).

Seeing into the surface

The field as window or mirror

Expanding the flat visual field by suggesting the appearance of actual three-dimensional space was introduced into Western art during the Renaissance through vanishing-point perspective. This involves a tacit agreement between artist and viewer relating to the expanded field. For perspective renderings to work, the entire scene must be seen as through a single, motionless eye, at a stopped moment in time. In a sense, the artist acts as a camera, for the viewer looks in the same way at such paintings or drawings as at still photographs.

Perspective and vanishing points encourage work within a rectangular field, but is it merely for technical reasons that we prefer seeing our world in neat perpendicular frames? Must we always compose in our mental viewfinder, then "snap" a composition within preset boundaries?

Cubism—internal expansion of the visual field

In the first years of the twentieth century artists created ways of showing more than one space on a single plane. By splitting the field into separate visual spaces, then moving them about, the Cubists created different openings into the window of the canvas. The viewer sees from several viewpoints at the same moment or even at sequentially different moments. For the first time since the introduction of Renaissance perspective a new means of opening the internal space within the picture plane was shown to be possible.

Time expansion

Time expansion may be sensed in a series of related works, often seen in printmaking. "All may be small images ... but reach their maximum impact when ... viewed continuously one after another as a time journey." Doré's *Inferno* and Hokusai's *Thirty-six Views of Fuji* are good examples.

Expanding the rectangle—landscapes

Taking a standard canvas or drawing paper outdoors to depict a landscape, we are obliged to eliminate most of what we can see. To fit the proportions of our surface, we arbitrarily terminate the composition to the left and right. Our own self provides a maximal bottom edge, and at some point the sky above becomes excessive and terminable. (Some photographic collages—for example, **Fig. 13.5**—include the artist's feet, merging the viewer with the viewed.) We may continue a scene up and overhead, even behind the viewer, expanding the field vertically.

The natural world is not divided into convenient rectangles of space, making such compositions, unfamiliar as they seem at first, closer to the world as it is perceived in broad sweeps and edgeless glimpses. Often the centers of such views are sharp, their peripheries melting into adjacent out-of-focus areas. We accept such changes of focus and distance within the general scope of reality as our head turns through its 180° arc left to right, the more limited vertical span cut off by earth, floor, ceiling or sky. By combining expanded-field views within more open or freely shaped formats in a variety of ways, twentieth-century artists make it possible for the viewer to experience space more realistically (**Fig. 13.6**).

EXERCISES

Exercise 1 (Two-part):
On a white, folded box, visualized as containing an animal form, draw the appropriate contour of the subject on each face; open the box flat; then adjust your six designs (using transparent overlays) to fill the volume of space as fully as possible three dimensionally, and to work together as one unified two-dimensional design.

Exercise 2:
On a transparent overlay, use the results of the previous exercise as a guide in designing a split-profile representation of the original animal. Avoid the literal; favor the imaginative.

Panoramas: stretching the landscape

Long before photography, painters and printmakers had stretched the horizontal dimension of landscapes, seen from a single spot, with a rotation of the head. The earliest example was a panoramic view of Edinburgh painted by Robert Barker in the 1780s. Then in the early nineteenth century Louis Daguerre's teacher Pierre Prévost introduced panoramic painting in France. Daguerre himself painted immense battles and historic scenes on both sides of transparent screens about 15 yards high and 23 yards wide. Seen at a distance, these encircling "dioramas" were subtly lighted as they turned around the viewer to suggest changing time of day and season.

Fig. 13.7 (*top*) **Friedrich von Martens**, *Panorama of Paris*, c. 1845. Daguerreotype, $4\frac{1}{2} \times 15$ ins (11×38 cm). Courtesy: International Museum of Photography at George Eastman House, Rochester.

Fig. 13.8 (*bottom*) **William Southgate Porter**, *Fairmount Waterworks*, 1848. Eight Daguerreotypes. Courtesy: International Museum of Photography, George Eastman House. Rochester.

Panoramic photography

In 1845, Friedrich von Martens made a historic panoramic study of Paris, a sweep of about 130° as a single exposure on a curved daguerreotype plate $4\frac{1}{2}$ inches by 15 inches (**Fig. 13.7**). His camera saw as the human eye does, about 90° at any moment, through the equivalent of a modern 80 mm lens, which rotated to produce the wide image.

Other early photographers achieved the panoramic effect by placing adjacent

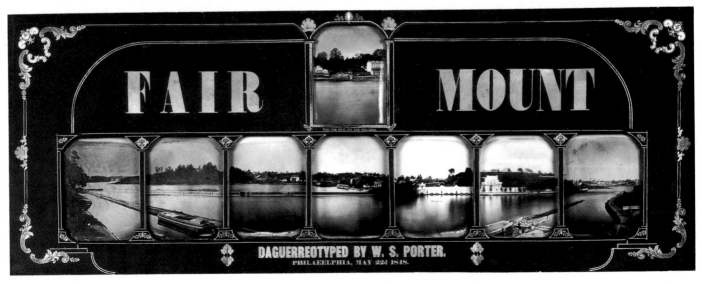

Fig. 13.9   (*top*) **Cynthia Dantzic**, *Valentine, Indiana*, 1984. Photographic collage, 10 × 48 ins (25.5 × 122 cm).

Fig. 13.10   **Jerry Dantzic**, *Fort McHenry, Baltimore, Maryland*, 1981. 410° Cirkut camera photograph, 10 × 78 ins (25.5 × 198 cm), (contact print). Courtesy: the photographer.

Fig. 13.11   **Jerry Dantzic**, *Monument Valley, Utah*, 1977. 220° Cirkut camera photograph, 10 × 78 ins (25.5 × 198 cm), (contact print). Courtesy: the photographer. Collection: Museum of Modern Art, New York.

Fig. 13.12   (*bottom*) **Kenneth Snelson**, *East River Drive and Brooklyn Bridge*, 1980. Cirkut camera photograph, $15\frac{1}{2}$ × 112 ins (39 × 285 cm), silver print. Courtesy: the photographer.

images together as a single view. Precise calculations and the use of a tripod assured a fluid, continuous effect (**Fig. 13.8**). A similar result may be achieved with simple equipment, using a hand-held camera to make sequential exposures from a central point, estimating the edges of each segment, so that neither overlapping nor undesired empty gaps occur. Attached, the series of prints gives an illusion of a continuous flow, or, placed with a space between images, the sense of passing along the scene, as from a moving vehicle (**Fig. 13.9**). [3]

The Cirkut Camera

The panoramic sweep of the 1902 Cirkut Camera shows a continuous loop of landscape with no necessary beginning or end, as we might see if it were to stand in a single spot and swing around in a circle. A major decision is the point at which to start and stop the camera; in a complete 360° landscape or cityscape any spot might be selected in theory. The arc, or number of degrees to be included, is critical; sometimes only half a circle (180°) will do. Infrequently an opportunity to complete or exceed the entire 360° will present itself (**Fig. 13.10**).

Conventional perspective disappears in these works as the vanishing point at the horizon keeps changing with the turning of the camera. Depending upon the position of the sun, shadows may be seen on one side of objects in one part of the photograph and, with no division between areas, on the opposite side in another (**Fig. 13.11**). A favorite vantage point for panoramic photographers is the intersection of several streets, particularly where they radiate irregularly from a central open area (**Fig. 13.12**). The height of the eye (or camera) above a scene can be critical. For those who believe the camera doesn't lie, this comparison may help to show it is not equipment that makes a visual statement but a selective and designing human being.

The panoramic photograph, particularly the Cirkut Camera's extended image, makes us aware of any *roll* of film as just that, a scroll or continuous linear expanse. Through careful planning, it is possible to create a contiguous sequence of images on a roll of film so that when it is developed and printed as a unit, a sectional panoramic work is produced automatically on the contact sheet. [4]

EXERCISES

Exercise 3 (Two-Part):
Locate a panoramic vista, with at least 180° of clear space. Using any camera, make an exposure at the left "edge" of your vista, noting the spot where the picture stops on the right in your viewfinder. Move the camera so that the previous stopping point becomes the new starting point, and continue, adding frames. Repeat the sequence with a clear space between images.

Exercise 4:
With a 35 mm camera, use black and white film to make a sequence of images similar to those in Exercise 3. Develop and print as a contact sheet.

Fig. 13.13   Cynthia Dantzic, *Six Times Gray*, 1981. Photographic collage, 13 × 22 ins (33 × 56 cm).

240

Photographic collage: beyond the circle

The panoramic photograph, which reveals the changing face of a landscape or cityscape as it scans "the inside of the circle" at the horizon, may be the most realistic way to depict the kind of space in which we live, in one continuous image.

To see beyond the narrow band to which a panoramic camera is limited, you can use any camera to create fields of images expanded from a central point in every direction. Resulting collages of these frames can show, in addition to the traditional left-to-right sweep on a horizontal plane, and vertical sweeps (up, over, down and under), a new near-to-far movement with oneself at the hub of a universal sphere. Objects appear reduced in size as they move away from the center in all directions. Any spot within the three-dimensional sphere can be seen in focus and added to the picture-as-a-whole, as you repeat or eliminate elements, acknowledging a traditional rectangular format or allowing a freely shaped configuration to find its own periphery (**Fig. 13.13**). [5]

Although the photographic collage can be a pieced documentation of one's environment, much like the expanded-field drawing study, it permits greater freedom to edit, to build a composition in a modular, additive way.

Familiarity with its possibilities encourages new kinds of seeing. Restudy Nudelman's photograph (**Fig. 7.10**); technically complex though it is, one continuous scene can be seen through a wall of glass bricks. Economy—attaining the greatest visual effect with the least physical input—is realized. There is an expansion of creative as well as spatial vision.

Making a photo-collage

In making pieced photo-collages, a great deal of physical manipulation may be required. If, as in Hockney's modular Polaroid works (**Fig. 13.14**), you place the frames in a precise checkerboard arrangement as close to the actual subject as possible, you will gain a sense of the technique. Or you may also create a seamless expanse of space, a continuous field which finds its own freely formed periphery, perhaps including elements more than once, bringing them into focus at different distances from the lens (**Fig. 13.13**). A painstaking piecing and fitting together of sharply focused portions of several otherwise identical views can test your commitment to this method of image making. Use your X-Acto knife and #11 blade. For this work, impermanent staining rubber cement is not recommended. I have had success with Jade and Elmer's Glue rolled out thinly on aluminum-foil-backed cardboard, then applied (with a rubber block-printing brayer) to the back of each photograph, before pressing it to a sheet of museum board through a layer of paper toweling. This is somewhat messy, tedious, and, I suspect, toxic. Work out a system of adequate ventilation with fans and blowers if you prefer this procedure. Otherwise try a dry offset-glue material such as 3M's Positionable Mounting Adhesive, which comes with a backing sheet and a hard plastic burnisher.

Color Aid paper may be used to fill in and connect areas. Technically the difference between collage and montage depends upon the addition of non-photographic elements, the latter pertaining to works composed purely of photographic materials. The addition of other two-dimensional components makes a work a collage. "Assemblage" refers to works incorporating three-dimensional parts. Nevertheless, Hockney and others do use the term photo-collage for works composed entirely of photographs. Definitions are created by artists after all. For those who combine photographs with cut paper or drawn, painted and other elements, the umbrella term "mixed media" may be used. From early experimenters such as Rodchenko and Man Ray to the recent innovations of Paolozzi and Rauschenberg, photographic montage and collage have truly expanded the visual horizon.

Yellow guitar still life   Los Angeles   3rd April 1982   DH.

Fig. 13.14 (*opposite*) **David Hockney**, *Yellow Guitar Still Life*, 1982. Photographic collage of forty Polaroid images. Courtesy of the artist.

Fig. 13.15 **Lucas Samaras**, *Panorama*, 1984. Unique Polaroid Polacolour II assemblage, $11 \times 34\frac{1}{2}$ ins (28×88 cm). Courtesy: Pace/McGill Gallery, New York. © Lucas Samaras.

Fig. 13.16 **David Hockney**, *Stephen Spender as Saint Jerome II*, 1985. Photographic collage. Courtesy of the artist.

By showing more than one view of a subject as it moves through space, the fourth dimension, the element of time is suggested in works that may incorporate the look if not the use of stroboscopic images (**Fig. 13.15**). Hockney's collages often show the influence of Cubist concepts as well as subject matter, either within a tightly structured modular grid or in a more open format (**Fig. 13.16**).

Highly experimental in his approach, this artist often projects a sense of the viewer as well as the subject in motion. As we will see, he readily adapts contemporary concepts in mathematics to his use, much as the Cubists were quick to incorporate the most current scientific thinking of their day. [6]

Panoramas as a filmic experience

Photographic panoramas may be considered single-image motion pictures, as the camera records a continuous sweep of the visual field, bringing into focus selected elements to be seen sequentially over a period of time. We need a new way of appreciating such works, much as Cubism required a new way of interpreting its imagery. Since a film shows us portions of the flow of time and place, generally in a linear way, we accept its reality. After all, by moving ourselves or our eye through real space, we do the same. A film, however, directs our eye, its pacing, speed and direction. As the camera slows, we slow; as it stops, we stop. As it zooms in for a closer look, we zoom.

Once accustomed to the idea of translating three to two dimensions, we realize how very close to real seeing is the panoramic photograph's apparent distortion of perspective. As the lens sees in portions of a circle, our eye also travels in an arc so that objects equidistant from the lens (or eye) appear in a straight line; the horizon retains its level appearance. In early Cirkut photographs, rows of military units and school groups sit or stand in a curve, each individual equidistant from the lens. Another discrepancy between fact and effect!

Single-frame spatial sweeps seem more traditional than pieced imagery because they are one continuous image. This is misleading; the turning camera, photographer and ultimately the viewer must acknowledge the continuously changing perspectives and space being seen. Reading these as single-frame *movies*, imagining oneself rotating on a still, central hub, slowly letting the eye travel over the surface, can provide a means of experiencing their turning aspect. Otherwise it is possible to see them as simply flat and very long single-focus photographs. In *Fort McHenry* (**Fig. 13.10**), a single battery of cannons, seen twice as the camera rotates through more than a full circle, may be read incorrectly as a second set of cannons if you see the scene as flat. Awareness of this new kind of reading will expand not only your field of vision but your idea of the kinds of space you may wish to create.

Reading Asian scroll painting requires this kind of perception. When the image extends to up to twenty feet in such scrolls, or in several of Dantzic's experimental works, the illusion of cinematography is truly felt; it is impossible to see or hold in the mind the complete image at any moment. It is experienced only by the accretion of perceptions of smaller portions over a period of time as one moves along the work or, if it were possible, as the work might turn in front of the eye on a kind of track. This experience would be indistinguishable from seeing a moving picture on a screen. On television a camera "traveling" over a still scene creates the same effect.

EXERCISES

Exercise 5:
From a single spot, perhaps at a window, make separate photographs to cover your entire field of vision. You may require several rolls of film. To structure space in a personal way and acknowledge the Cubist multiple viewpoint, combine with paper collage and other techniques. Arrange the prints, edit and attach.

Exercise 6:
Create a grid, with strings on a wooden frame, to assist in making a subdivided, multi-frame photo-collage. Make each unit of the grid equivalent to the image seen in your viewfinder. Take your photographs and attach. If people or animals are included, allow them to move to achieve your "4D" effect.

Expanding the painting field

Contemporary painters, familiar with distortions produced by optical lenses, can create canvases which give the sense of stretching the visual field in photographic ways. Familiarity with photographic history can influence the way painters interpret or respond to what the eye sees, whether or not they actually rely upon such images. Perception is affected by training, environment, experience and expectation.

Modifying proportion to suggest the expanded field

Without physically expanding the picture plane, painters have suggested horizontal, vertical and other extensions and stretching of the surface through attenuation and distortion (**Fig. 13.17**). Would D'Arcy Thompson have seen such artists' adaptations of reality as modifications of the proportional grid onto which they might be placed (**Fig. 3.16**)?

Expanded size

Works so large that their entire composition cannot be experienced in a single eyeful are, of necessity, expansions of the visual field. The natural angle of human vision, 45° to 50° for each eye, gives us a total field of about 100°. From the earliest days of cave-wall painting to Renaissance and contemporary wall and ceiling murals and multi-panel works of great dimension, paintings have often been larger than life.

The Sistine Chapel's ceiling mural does not present one continuous space; each interior painting takes place in its own defined world (**Fig. 2.27**). But the work as a whole is a single expanded field which Michelangelo created to contain each scene and the many figures located so precisely in the niches and crannies of his *trompe l'oeil* architecture. (Find the Libyan Sibyl at the lower left.)

Monet's series of *Water Lilies* was conceived as a single encircling panoramic whole "... carried along the walls, enveloping all the partitions with its unity, [producing] the

Fig. 13.17 **Amedeo Modigliani**, *Reclining Nude*, 1917. Oil on canvas, 60 × 92 ins (152 × 234 cm). Unknown location.

Fig. 13.18   Claude Monet, *Waterlilies, (the clouds)*, 1914–18. 500 ins (1271 cm) long (three panels). Courtesy: La Reunion des Musées Nationaux. Paris. © photo RMN.

Fig. 13.19   James Rosenquist, *F-III*, 1965. Oil on canvas and aluminum, 10 × 86 ft (3.04 × 26.2 m). Courtesy; the Leo Castelli Gallery © James Rosenquist.

illusion of an endless whole, a wave with no horizon and no shore." Eventually these panels, called "decorations" by Monet (not in the sense of superfluous embellishment, but to imply a continuous compelling structuring of the space), were installed in the Parisian museum L'Orangerie in a double oval gallery of immense size, each triptych or quadriptych extending between distant doorways (**Fig. 13.18**). The individual canvases are 79 by 167 feet long. Is this helpful in considering the paintings individually? We generally see only one or two panels reproduced in a text or displayed.

If you visualize each panel of *Water Lilies* as a panoramic sweep of the reflective, translucent surface on and in which the lilies float and sink, surrounding the viewer, almost filling the space between eye and canvas with thick billows of color, light and mist, you will experience a richer multi-dimensionality than if you see the work as a flat plane at a constant distance from the eye. A palpable atmosphere emanates from these works, almost dematerializing and melting into the surrounding air. How much is size alone responsible for communicating this sense of a limitless expanse of tranquil watery space?

James Rosenquist's *F–III*, presented in 1965 in all its 10-feet-by-86-feet magnitude, filled the Leo Castelli Gallery with powerful commercial symbols and social commentary (**Fig. 13.19**). Do we respond to this work's subject matter, size or the almost photographic realism of its technique? Does our own size in relation to the immensity of Rosenquist's images seem to diminish us and add to feelings of inadequacy, helplessness, terror? Is size merely one element contributing to our response to such an intentionally overwhelming visual environment? Could this work be called a "decoration," even using Monet's definition of the term? What of the Sistine ceiling? Does the question help you see these works in new ways?

In the presence of Michelangelo's visual epic, we feel somehow a part of the whole saga, one more soul in the simultaneously occurring dramas unfolding on the gigantic canvas above us. It is as though we are watching the entire series of stories depicted on separate screens, all at once and all in some grand way overseen by one orchestrating, guiding presence—the grand designer, so to speak, who has "the whole world in his hands." Surrounded by the Rosenquist, we feel small and powerless before the immensity of a situation presented larger than life, yet part of our daily life. Michelangelo's story-telling space inspires us to feel a part of the big picture, but we can distance ourselves from this work so far above us, so ancient in its iconography. With the Rosenquist, we dare not feel uninvolved; we are indeed overwhelmed by the message and the imagery, intensified by its size and scale.

Free of the colossal burden of narrative associations, Monet's *Water Lilies* panels permit us to enjoy the sheer painterly voluptuousness of their enveloping atmosphere, the encircling panorama of a luminous, shimmering glow, unimpeded by sharpness of shape, edge or tonal contrasts. Very much like the pure light and colour extravagances of Turner, subject matter doesn't much matter in these canvases. We are contained

Fig. 13.20 **Jan Carlile**, *Sneffels Range*, 1979. Pencil drawing, approx. 24 ins × 16 ft (61 cm × 4.9 m). Courtesy of the artist.

within an expanded field created to reduce other than painterly elements to the minimum possible (at the time it was painted) while enlarging the physical dimension to emphasize purely plastic concerns.

The open-ended scroll landscape

Dewey, speaking of Chinese paintings, noted: "Instead of being centralized so as to require frames, they move outward … panoramic scroll paintings present a world in which ordinary boundaries are transformed into invitations to proceed."

Starting at the left-hand edge of a 12 inch wide roll of paper, draw a landscape from observation, continuing until it becomes necessary to unroll more paper at the right. When you can "let go" of the original starting edge, begin to roll the work from the left and continue, opening additional space as needed on the right, closing the scroll on the left, turning your own position as you expand your view of the subject. Working with no thought of closing the rectangle, allow the landscape to find its own ending place.

Eventually, if you have enough paper and an unimpeded view, you will return to your starting place, although you may discover that you have continued beyond that point without realizing it. The second time you come upon this view as the continuation of forms already defined on paper, part of a composition; visually the view *is* new and different—not at all what you saw the first time! Opening such an expanded drawing on its completion can be quite a surprise. Is it considerably longer than you expected? Does it have more coherence and continuity than you thought the scene contained as you were drawing it, bit by bit? Would your drawing be different if you had stretched out the entire length of paper at the start and drawn the scene all at once? Would you have had the courage or the interest to do the drawing this way? Is this idea related to the modular drawing of a plant, built leaf by leaf and sheet by sheet? In both studies, you must be willing to proceed without a clear overview of the finished work at the start, and to rely on an intuitive integration of creative energies, to feel that some innate designing integrity will provide the needed coherence and unity. Do you think Jan Carlile's mountains (**Fig. 13.20**) were drawn in this way?

Drawing a total environment

Once you are comfortable with the idea of working from a starting place without a predetermined periphery try a "total environment" study such as Lima's studio interior, shown in **Fig. 13.21**.

Begin drawing your own hand and pencil on a long roll of paper held vertically, depicting each object in your field of vision, moving away from yourself and upward on the page, ending at a point overhead or even behind yourself. Additional rolls of paper, attached or continued by eye, extend the field to the right and left. A sequence of panels can be connected to produce a field as expanded as you choose, up to a full 360°.

Although large size is not necessary, working life-size can prove quite exhilarating—and exasperating. (Ask Jackie Lima; she has done it.) Will the final composition be a rectangle? Do you expect lines parallel in fact to appear parallel in your study? Why? Does the unusual Mercator map projection format (**Fig. 13.22**) "work" in Lima's flattening of the studio space? Compare her bird's-eye view (**Fig. 13.23**) with Mantegna's *Bridal Chamber* (**Fig. 5.17**). What point(s) is this artist making about the expanded field?

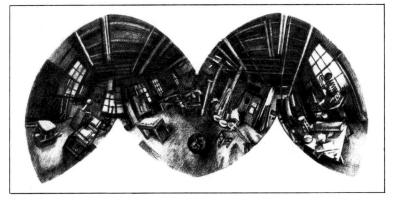

Fig. 13.21   Jacqueline Lima, *See! (Work in progress)*, begun 1981. Pencil, 8½ ft × 17 ins (2.6 m × 43 cm), each strip. Courtesy of the artist.

Fig. 13.22   Jacqueline Lima, *Who would have ever thought . . .*, 1986. Pencil, 14 × 22 ins (35.5 × 56 cm). Courtesy of the artist.

Fig. 13.23   Jacqueline Lima, *The World is Round*, 1979. Oil on canvas, 48 × 48 ins (122 × 122 cm). Courtesy of the artist.

249

Expanding our ideas about the visual field

Aerial photographs and space-age interplanetary documentation, continuous or pieced together (such as the 3,000-mile picture of the United States from coast to coast sponsored by the Smithsonian Institution), have changed our idea of the extent and meaning of the expanded visual field. Robert Rauschenberg's $\frac{1}{4}$ *Mile or 2 Furlong Piece* may be the largest work of contemporary art installed in a museum, yet only part of it (a mere several hundred feet) can be shown at one time.

Sources of inspiration for increasing conceptual and perceptual boundaries may be found throughout history, in every field of study and creative work, in every art and science. From the discovery of Mayan bark-paper scroll paintings, as long as twenty-two feet, to the latest mathematical theories of Benoit Mandelbrot, every extension of human knowledge and speculation serves as a stimulus to the visual artist. Some, particularly receptive to new ways of seeing space and structure, find special uses for each emerging hypothesis. David Hockney credits two sources for the special spatial effects in his photographic collages: the multi-perspective, multiple viewpoint space of the Cubists and new fractional dimensional concepts, called fractals, introduced by Mandelbrot.

Fractals in art and design

Hockney frequently refers to a fractal concept in which "objects [are] made of infinitely many smaller and smaller identical shapes." He notes that "with a fractal . . . the edges of things become blurred, and that seems a good thing. Getting rid of borders seems a good thing. It's a way toward a greater awareness of unity." In fractal theory, "each discrete part is itself a whole universe of form."

Mandelbrot himself notes implications in areas beyond pure math and science. Instead of seeing form in nature and art as a constant refinement and simplification to an eventual minimal purity of form, he finds classical geometry incapable of describing even common shapes, a cloud, coastline, mountain, tree or flame. "Nature is irregular," he says, "clouds are not spheres, mountains are not cones, coastlines are not circles ..." Nature does not exhibit "simply a higher degree, but an altogether different level of complexity." He feels that the forms Euclid calls amorphous can be studied, that we can give form to the apparently formless by thinking of this huge class of forms falling in between the crevices of dimensionality as "fractals."

Mandelbrot's favorite example is the coastline of Great Britain, though it could be any natural outline. When asked how long the coast of Great Britain is, we are tempted to reply that, although we are not quite sure, we will gladly look up the number of miles and find the answer. Mandelbrot points out that the answer depends on the location of the measurer and the measuring device used. For example, "from a satellite, the coastline looks like a smooth unbroken line; seen from a 747 its edges grow increasingly lacy; from a hang glider . . . as one observes the bays and inlets, [it] increases in length. If one were obsessed enough to crawl along the beach with a caliper and a magnifying glass, [one] would express the grainy length in millions of kilometers. Measurement with a microscope would produce a length approaching infinity—and madness." Clearly, objects such as landscapes "exhibit more detail the closer they are observed." He concludes,"A multiplicity of dimensionality is unavoidable."

Repeatable but decreasingly smaller shapes within larger entities illustrate fractal concept. Mandelbrot has identified examples of this idea throughout the history of the visual arts as far back as the thirteenth century. In an unusual example, God, as an architect, designs the world—a large sphere containing wavelike inner shapes, then a clearly fractal "foam" subdivided into uncountable wiggles and wavelets. Mandelbrot

Fig. 13.24 (*top*) **Leonardo da Vinci**, *The Deluge*, c. 1514. From notebook. Courtesy: Royal Library, Windsor Castle, © Her Majesty Queen Elizabeth II.
Fig. 13.25 (*bottom*) **Katsushika Hokusai**, *The Great Wave at Kanagawa*, 1823–29. Wood block print, $10\frac{1}{4} \times 15\frac{1}{8}$ ins (26 × 38 cm). Courtesy: The Metropolitan Museum of Art, The Howard Mansfield Collection, Rogers Fund, 1936.

251

Fig. 13.26 Benoit Mandelbrot, *Fractal Patterns in "The Fractal Geometry of Nature,"* 1983. Computer-generated images. © 1982 by Benoit B. Mandelbrot.

Fig. 13.27 *(right)* Maurits C. Escher, *Path of Life II*, 1958. Woodcut, $14\frac{1}{2} \times 14\frac{1}{2}$ ins (37×37 cm). Collection: Haags Gemeentemuseum, The Hague.

finds a similar idea in the loop, and whirls of da Vinci's study of turbulent water (**Fig. 13.24**), each curvilinear form repeated ever smaller in the total configuration. By the time we are shown Hokusai's *Great Wave*, we are ready to point out its fractal substructures to Mandelbrot himself (**Fig. 13.25**)!

Regardless of the position of current thinkers in math and the sciences, every student of visual design should become familiar with the basic ideas of this new way of seeing the structuring of the physical world. We can expand our perceptual horizons and widen our view of the two-dimensional picture plane by widening our concept of dimensionality itself.

Additional fractal concepts can have application in design and pattern making, particularly in computer-generated or -enhanced art. These illustrations give an idea of the inwardly reductive, repetitive fractal structurings possible (**Fig. 13.26**). If this kind of sampling does not intrigue you into further mathematical study, at least you will recognize a fractal when you see one! (Restudy Van Gogh's many works composed of calligraphic "self-similar" squiggles (**Fig. 1.23**).

Did Escher have fractals in mind when he designed his continuously reductive repeated images? Mandelbrot dates publication of his theory from 1975 and Escher lived only until 1972, but there is a strong relationship between their descriptions of self-similarity. Though no mathematical knowledge is required to appreciate the visual representation of his geometric observations, the more you investigate the mathematical basis of Escher's work, the greater your awareness of the subtleties underlying the structures will become and the more you are likely to admire his accomplishment. Can you identify fractal structures in other kinds of design?

Expansion of the visual field may be seen not only as *outward*, to encompass the great allness of space, but also *inward*, its identical units ever reducing in size but increasing in number, approaching infinity, moving toward the same indivisibility (**Fig. 13.27**). Can you imagine an internal expansion as well as the external, with which we are considerably more familiar? [7, 8]

Rearrangeable compositions as expanded fields

This expansion of the visual field involves the idea that two things cannot occupy the same space *at the same time*. In the seven-plate tangram etchings (**Fig. 7.7**) or the five-panel Modular Paintings (**Fig. 6.2**), although only a single configuration may be viewed at any moment, the field is expandable *over a period of time*. While we study one arrangement, other modulations appear in the mind; the total experience of the work cannot be known at a stopped point. As the viewer works with the Modular Painting, its rearrangeability becomes more accessible, and its full complexity is apparent. Any one modulation is not the entire painting whether the panels are placed in a square format or allowed to form a freely shaped canvas. Just as in a transparency study, an apparent overlapping of colors and shapes permits the possibility of reading several configurations of identical elements; each modulation presents only one aspect of their totality, in a kind of sequential expansion of the visual field. You never see *all* the painting at any one moment although you certainly see the painting.

Is this merely a semantic nicety, or is it useful to be able to consider the visual field

Fig. 13.28 **Josef Albers**, *Bullfight*, 1930. Photographic collage. Collection: The Josef Albers Foundation.

Fig. 13.29   Kenneth Josephson,
Drottningholm, Sweden, 1967. Gelatin-silver
print, $5\frac{7}{8} \times 9$ ins (15 × 23 cm). Collection:
The Museum of Modern Art, New York.
Purchase.

as a space of surface which may be altered and augmented in a number of physical
(**Fig. 13.28**) and conceptual (**Fig. 13.29**) ways? From the edgeless paintings created at
Lascaux to the extended scroll and the pre-formed rectangle grown to gigantic size, the
two-dimensional format may open and subdivide into component units, rearrange its
structural elements and even "implode" into countless ever reducing repetitions of the
same form. We can never again take our standard sheet of paper or canvas panel for
granted!

EXERCISES

Exercise 7:
Visit a computer art laboratory and obtain
instruction in designing and re-arranging
fractal images. Visit a math computer lab and
compare the instructions you receive. Experiment with fractal imagery.

Exercise 8, Multi-Part:
Draw a line, 3 inches long. Using an eraser,
divide it into identical thirds. Repeat this for
each third. Repeat again for each new third,
until you cannot see any trace of the original
line. Devise your own fractal exercises.

Chapter Fourteen

THE RECYCLED IMAGE

Fig. 14.1   Jean-Auguste Ingres, *Louis Bertin*, 1832. (*left*) Oil on canvas, $46 \times 37\frac{1}{2}$ ins (117×95 cm). (*right*) Pencil, $12\frac{3}{4} \times 9\frac{1}{2}$ ins (32×24 cm). Courtesy: The Louvre, Paris. © photo RMN.

Originality: what can it mean?

Discussions of originality and the use of previously developed visual material can arouse strong feelings. To some, even preliminary studies reduce spontaneity and creativity. Why would a painter include more information in a study than the finished work (**Fig. 14.1**)? Were sketches or studies useful to Jackson Pollock (**Fig. 6.5**)?

In another extreme view, all human experience, held in common, should be mutually accessible; all images "community property" from which to select and interpret, extending the image's life, giving it immortality. In this view, imitation *is* the sincerest form of flattery, even homage. (There are ethical, even legal, considerations, if imagery is adopted literally as in outright forgery, or if copyrighted material is used.)

Although the re-use of images is becoming increasingly popular, the idea has existed as long as images have been made.

Recognizing recycled art

Recognize and distinguish various kinds of recycled imagery, using these terms:
— Recycled, transformed, translated, recombined, reinterpreted, rescued, ready-made, derived, re-seen, appropriated or adapted imagery.
— Near-replica, transmuted, combined, copy or copier art.
— Borrowed forms; annexed forms; modified form.
— Found image (distinguished from found object); visual quotation.
— Multiples; reruns.
— Use of cast-offs; discards.
— In the style of, in the manner of, after. [1]

Background—origins of originality

Has the concept of originality changed with time? The first person to observe an animal, fix its image even briefly in the storage system of the mind, then transfer a record of that memory to the wall of a cave to preserve the experience—that individual surely displayed originality.

In this sense all images are recycled, since any picturing of an object is first conceived in the mind, as a response to something perceived, remembered or imagined. We are mainly concerned here with the re-use and recycling not of one's own perceptions or conceptions but of the works or imagery of another person.

To John Dewey, "... no genuine work has ever been a repetition of anything that previously existed. There are indeed works that tend to be ... recombinations of elements selected from prior works ... but they are academic ... mechanical, rather than esthetic." Even so, we can distinguish the originality of forming a mental picture from that involved in its retrieval and placement on a surface. Remember, to Dewey art is the experience itself, as much as its visual record.

Facsimiles of experience

We all see, to the point of over-saturation, images made by hand and machine, not only by our contemporaries but by individuals who have lived in every recorded age, so none of us may claim the kind of originality that inspired the first artist. The general similarity, or style, that distinguishes Spanish cave art from French indicates that each succeeding artist was influenced by familiarity with existing imagery.

The popularity of Pop Art was said to result from our increasing distance from

Fig. 14.2 Louise Odes Neaderland, *George Orwell is Watching You*, 1984. Xerographic postcard, $4\frac{1}{4} \times 6$ ins (11×15 cm). Courtesy of the artist.

direct experience and our reliance on secondhand visual material. Supermarket products were more familiar to us than trees and mountains. "We respond to facsimiles of experience" says Davidson. But this has always been so.

Originality, then, must come almost as a surprise to its creator, for, if consciously planned, no work can directly present novelty. "As if originality had not always surprised the original artist . . . by exceeding [any] conscious intentions" says Kramer.

New attitudes toward the unique image

How important is originality in art today? According to the critic Lawrence Alloway, "The printing revolution and [its] subsequent flood of pictorial reproductions dispelled the notion that uniqueness was indispensable to art." The painter Sam Hunter speaks of "the pervasive sense that mass-produced techniques and the ubiquitous modes of the communications media have compromised our idea of the 'original,' which has in our culture taken on esoteric or technical status as mere prototype, the matrix from which copies can be reproduced." (**Fig. 14.2**).

This has inspired formation of an international group with a regularly printed publication devoted to "Copier Art" (p. 272). Is the original losing its appeal or its meaning? If there has been a change in the way we see and make art, how did we get to this point?

The many kinds of imagery that may be considered recycled have evolved from different purposes, artistic "necessity" often serving as the "mother of invention."

In early civilizations, the use of impermanent materials required replication of valued objects in order to preserve their existence. Before photography, multiples of an image in two dimensions could only be created through printing, printmaking or copying. In the twentieth century a number of innovative (or original) ideas and technological developments have revolutionized the recycled image.

EXERCISES

Exercise 1:
Identify terms in the list on p. 256 [Figs. 14.1–2] that are interchangeable or near-synonyms. Sort them into categories. Which seem to carry emotional "baggage?" Can you add to the list?

Fig. 14.3 **Kurt Schwitters**, *For Kate*, 1947. Collage, $3\frac{7}{8} \times 5\frac{1}{8}$ ins (10 × 13 cm). Private Collection.

Collage—use of borrowings and fragments

Schwitters' contribution

Anthropologist George Mills, speaking of the artist being unwittingly influenced by the "expectations of society," suggests, "in a culture that demands originality, the artist will honestly overlook many borrowings." The poet T. S. Eliot in *The Waste Land* calls these "fragments I have shored against my ruins," a line selected by John Ashbery in reviewing the works of the seminal recycler of the twentieth century, Kurt Schwitters. Far from overlooking his borrowings, Schwitters served as rescuer and reanimator of the leftovers, refuse, paper ephemera and other residue of society, celebrating the triumph of human effort, making sense of chaos, turning dross to art. His use of borrowed fragments, often in non-associative, non-pictorial ways, marked the beginning of a new definition of the term *originality*. [2]

Picasso, Braque and Cubist collage

Schwitters was not the first to attach a ready-made object to a two-dimensional work; the gluing to canvas of an area of linoleum printed with a caned pattern in 1911 gives that distinction to Picasso (**Fig. 6.31**). Shortly thereafter, Braque was attaching wallpaper and snipped fragments of newspaper to his canvas; soon, both artists were enriching their work in this manner.

Toward non-objective collage

If Schwitters made reference to the original identity of a particular scrap, it was for a specific expressive purpose (**Fig. 14.3**). Mostly, he created marvelous balances of formal, visual qualities without concern for the original association of labels, ticket stubs, postage stamps or clippings. These are among the first non-objective pictures, although they incorporate actual objects.

Trompe l'oeil and collage

Consider the difference between pasting a paper artifact onto a canvas and incorporating a picture of an object in a painting so real-looking that it fools the eye. Such technical wizardry (*trompe l'oeil*) is familiar in classical painting. Unlike David's painting, in which, realistic as it is, the paper is read as a representation of actual paper

Fig. 14.4 **Jacques Louis David**, *Death of Marat*, 1793. Oil on canvas. Courtesy: Musées Royaux d'Art et d'Histoire, Brussels.

Fig. 14.5 Mimmo Rotella, *Flask of Wine*,
1963. Décollage, 35 × 26 ins (89 × 66 cm).
Courtesy of the artist.

(**Fig. 14.4**), in William Harnett's works it gives the appearance of being the object
itself, attached to the surface. In the collages and *papier collés* of Picasso and Braque,
painted illusions mingle freely with actual materials and textured surfaces. At first,
each such glued-on area presents only itself, later it is used more abstractly. [3]

Décollage

In a variation of collage, the torn, partially defaced billboard or poster, often rearranged
or overpainted, has been seen mainly in Europe since the 1960s. Mimmo Rotella was
perhaps the earliest to use Pop Art imagery, a single recycled commercial product
(Fig. 14.5). [4]

EXERCISES

Exercise 2, (Multi-Part):
Carry a large envelope for collecting paper,
fabric and other colleagables. (This may encourage you to discover it more readily.)
Select several items, add colored papers as
needed, and compose a simple collage ... and
another ...

Exercise 3, (Two-Part):
Attach an object to a collage. Then, simulate
the look of this attachment through a *trompe
l'oeil* image.

Exercise 4:
Paste one poster or advertisement on top of
another. Tear the top layer until you have an
acceptable décollage, then add additional materials, if necessary, with restraint.

Recycling images in art

Copying to build skills

Copying works of the masters is a respected method of learning one's craft. Most innovative pathfinders of Modern Art were trained in this way. Such copies, for all their technical accomplishment, claim no creativity or originality; that is not their aim.

It is possible to play music by reading the notes and timing correctly, avoiding personal interpretation. Electronic devices do this automatically. But mechanical recreation of tones and intervals has more to do with math and physics than music. In the same way, replication of artwork may result in apparently perfect facsimiles, but unless such effort is internalized, synthesizing the experience, one is merely playing scales and exercises.

Paying homage to the classics

Fig. 14.6 Jean-Baptiste Camille Corot, *Girl With a Mandolin*, 1860–65. Oil on canvas, $20\frac{1}{4} \times 14\frac{1}{2}$ ins (51.5×37 cm). Collection: The Saint Louis Art Museum.
Fig. 14.7 Juan Gris, *Woman With a Mandolin (after Corot)*, 1916. Oil on canvas, $36\frac{1}{4} \times 23\frac{1}{2}$ ins (92×60 cm). Courtesy: Kunstmuseum, Basel.

One kind of art, acknowledged as taken from the work of another, using its main compositional elements, movement, palette or feeling, is sometimes entitled "after . . .", "in the manner of . . .", or "homage to . . ." These recycle the spirit of a work, not its precise form; they are not copies.

This kind of visual dialogue can be one of the most satisfying experiences for any artist or student, the re-seeing or interpreting of a work by another artist.

Although each shape, line and area of tonal value in Corot's painting (**Fig. 14.6**)

has been acknowledged, Gris' flat, two-dimensional Cubist rendering (**Fig. 14.7**) makes his work a translation into a new language. The relationship between inspiration and realization is not always clear; many derived works suggest their debt to an original source in their title but only on analysis reveal the extent of their indebtedness. One interesting example is Matisse's dancers (**Fig. 12.24**), which has inspired works by Lichtenstein and others.

We cannot include many here; a trip to your library will help you see Picasso under the spell of Velázquez, Rembrandt, Cranach and Manet (p. 281); Matisse involved with the creative processes of the Dutch seventeenth-century artist de Heem; and Mary Cassatt influenced by Japanese woodblock prints to create perhaps the finest series of aquatint etchings by any artist (**Fig. 5.24**).

Look for Lichtenstein's adaptations of Picasso and Cézanne, even a diagrammatic composition of his portrait of Mme Cézanne by Erle Loran. Lichtenstein's 1986 mural is an encyclopedic homage to Modern Art, paying visual respects to dozens of specific works and styles; yet above all, the style expressed is his own. As John Russell observed, "Lichtenstein was always a great forager." Note Lichtenstein's translation of Monet's haystack paintings (**Fig. 5.47**). [5]

Ideas on file

Admittedly, scales and exercises sharpen skills and develop technique; note the years of academic training experienced by Picasso before he developed his many original styles. Compare the classical study of 1905, *Profile of Anguished Female Face* (**Fig. 14.8**), with his quintessential suffering women in *Guernica* (**Fig. 14.9**), painted in 1937. Even his drawings of the eye made at the age of 11 show a remarkable relationship between these works. One of the world's most prolific artists, did Picasso retain every sketch and study in his memory to be retrieved, recycled and realized anew for his entire life? The occasional classical study that appears well after his development of Cubism attests to the importance of his having such resources always available. For the artist to recycle material on file, it must be present in the first place.

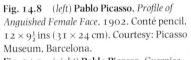

Fig. 14.8 (*left*) **Pablo Picasso**, *Profile of Anguished Female Face*, 1902. Conté pencil, $12 \times 9\frac{1}{2}$ ins (31×24 cm). Courtesy: Picasso Museum, Barcelona.
Fig. 14.9 (*right*) **Pablo Picasso**, *Guernica*, (*detail*), 1937. Oil on canvas, 11 ft $5\frac{1}{2}$ ins $\times$ 25 ft $5\frac{3}{4}$ ins (3.50×7.8 m). Courtesy: The Prado, Madrid.

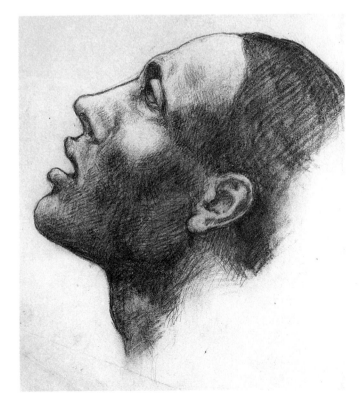

Fig. 14.10 **Martin Ries**, *Ovid on Guernica*, 1972. Screen print, 26 × 20 ins (66 × 51 cm). Courtesy of the artist.

Mixing myth, meaning and medium

For Martin Ries, mythology and the entire history of art are a rich source of inspiration, to be orchestrated into an iconography all his own. Combining painting, screen printing and assemblage, all recycled, he evokes new responses from sensitive juxtapositions of mythology and image (**Fig. 14.10**).

In Ries' work we see many contemporary recycler's concerns: to expand the original meaning of an image more universally; as a point of departure from which to develop one's own ideas; to heighten expressive impact through unexpected juxtaposition of traditional and new images; to increase any viewer's access to a work by including comfortable, familiar material.

Pop art: tapping a new source of imagery

In the 1960s, so-called Pop Artists began to use products such as boxes of Brillo and cans of Campbell's Soup as subject matter (**Fig. 7.11**). These objects, themselves designed by others, were often enlarged to heroic proportions or repeated in serial patterns much as they appear on supermarket shelves. Manufactured products had appeared earlier, but never before did the product assume an icon-like importance. Enlarged to mural size, Ben Day dots (the printer's half-tone screen-process for reproducing images), seen in comic strips or in newspaper photographs, provided a strong graphic device for Lichtenstein (**Fig. 1.9**) and others to change the look of an image qualitatively as well as simply quantitatively. By altering dimensions, colors and textures of the mass-produced model, Pop Artists distinguished their work from its inspirational source.

Artists such as Rosenquist and Rauschenberg began to combine images and materials in ways recalling collage, but on a heroic scale, always alluding to an associative reference, often with political and socially concerned meanings. [6]

EXERCISES

Exercise 5, (Two-Part):
Visit an art museum, obtain permission, study a work you admire and slowly try to duplicate it. Then, create a freer interpretation of the work from your study.

Exercise 6:
Enlarge or repeat a popular or commercial image in the Pop Art manner. Use simple, bold forms and color.

Printed images

Warhol and Rauschenberg used images created by photographers, frequently of well-known individuals and news events. Warhol made photographic screen prints of portraits of Marilyn Monroe, Jacqueline Kennedy Onassis and Mao Zedong, and photos of automobile accidents and anti-black police activity. Rauschenberg juxtaposed painterly and collaged elements, including photographs of such figures as John Kennedy and images of current events, in almost surreal ways (**Fig. 14.11**).

It is an oversimplification to group these artists and others in one school, Pop Art, although the use of recycled imagery taken from popular culture marks much of their work.

"The product being kidded—was not Campbell Soup or Coca-Cola, but art itself," says critic Hilton Kramer. In this sense Pop Art and Schwitters' Dada had much in

Fig. 14.11 Robert Rauschenberg,
Retroactive I, 1964. Oil on canvas,
84 × 60 ins (213 × 152 cm). Courtesy:
Wadsworth Atheneum, Hartford. Gift of
Susan Morse Hilles.

common, showing contempt for the values of society and a mockery of its idols and ideals, raising the commonplace and the banal to new levels worthy of respect and admiration on their own terms, bringing a new kind of democracy to the world of fine art. All this with a touch of tongue in cheek and a raised eyebrow.

"The tension between the appearance of an object and the manner in which it is transformed into a flat surface is what makes the strength of Pop art," said Lichtenstein in 1963. Regarding his use of the comic strip, he explains: "I wouldn't call it transformation ... What I do is form ... the comic strips have shapes ... but there has been no effort to make them intensely unified. A [comic strip] intends to depict and I intend to unify. And ... [in] my work every mark is really in a different place, however slightly ..."

This insistence by Lichtenstein, and others, on the special contribution made by their selection, interpretation and adaptation of the "found image" reveals another linking of Pop, Photo-Realist, Copier Artists and other recyclers with early experimenters in collage, "... invented by the cubists as a means of exploring the differences between reproduction and reality." Edward Lucie-Smith speaks of work "almost entirely created from pre-existing elements where the artist's contribution was to be found more in making the links between objects ... than in making objects *ab initio* [from the beginning]."

Jim Dine announced in 1962 that he had stopped dealing with found objects because "there was too much of other people's mystery in them." Yet Andy Warhol at about the same time felt differently; he "titillated the experts by nonchalantly signing ordinary soup cans and sold them as souvenirs."

Recurring imagery

Coincidence or influence?

The reappearance of certain subjects and designs can be considered a recycling of imagery from the commonality of human experience. In "Provocative Parallels," Jean Lipman presents a collection of recurring imagery, pairs of works that have much in common visually although one was generally made by an anonymous untrained early American (**Fig. 14.12**) and the other by a modern, sophisticated artist (**Fig. 14.13**). Perhaps this delightful and perceptive book will be reprinted soon.

Fig. 14.12 (*left*) Quilt, *Drunkard's Path pattern*, undated. Red and white cotton squares. Collection: C. and J. Dantzic.
Fig. 14.13 (*right*) **Paul Feeley**, *Gomelza*, 1965. Synthetic polymer on canvas, 80 × 80 ins (203 × 203 cm). Collection: Whitney Museum of American Art. Purchased with Funds from The Friends of the Whitney Museum of American Art.

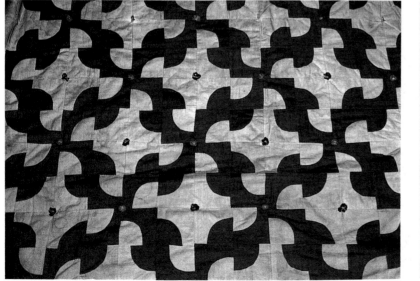
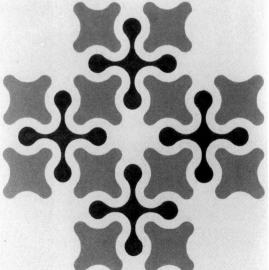

Is the relationship between the "primitive" and the "professional" example more than a coincidence, perhaps part of our universal unconscious memory, an intuitive human expression transcending time, place and training? Richard Anuszkiewicz freely acknowledges an indebtedness to these "artless" forbears; the pieced quilt, with brightly contrasting colors, serving as his inspiration. He admires their "primitive energy and directness of vision and expression" and says, "We all have a little of the folk artist in us." Robert Hughes confirms that the best nineteenth-century quilts "anticipate many of the formal devices and color systems of Op Art and color-field painting." Without a single lesson, how did they do it? [7]

The human figure

The human figure, the most familiar and meaningful subject to us humans, has been depicted in innumerable fashions, from photographic likeness to a pure geometric

Fig. 14.14 **Romare Bearden**, *The Block, panel #6*, 1971. Collage painting, 36 × 50 ins (91.5 × 127 cm). Collection: The Metropolitan Museum of Art, New York. Gift of Mr. and Mrs. Samuel Shore, 1978.

Fig. 14.15 **Kendall Shaw**, *Koufax Pitching*, 1964. Acrylic on canvas, 7 × 7 ins (18 × 18 cm). Collection: Mrs. E. Povis Jones. Courtesy of the artist.

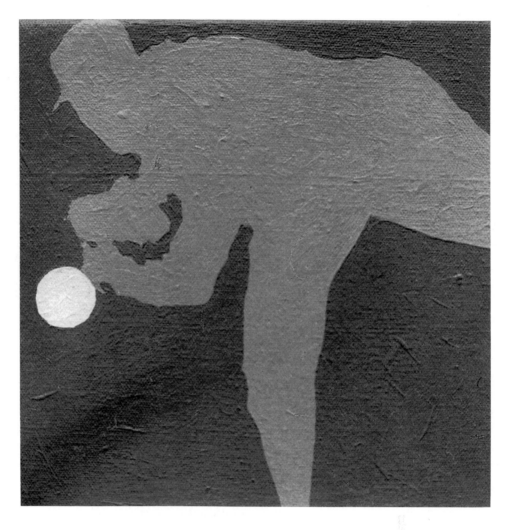

symbol, from the most formal rendering to the barest expressive suggestion of human presence or movement. Subtle distinctions can make us read life or death in seemingly similar gestures.

Using print imagery to make individual statements

Re-seeing the figure in collage paintings

In a subtle recycling of human imagery, Romare Bearden shows parts of the figure, taken from published sources, as the figurative elements they depict, but in startling new ways, playing with scale and size, juxtaposing unexpected parts of the body in expressive, gestural ways to make aesthetic and social statements. Bold areas of color and texture command a sense of dignity and a quiet determination in the figures Bearden brings to life on canvas (**Fig. 14.14**).

Streamlined silhouette—sports murals

Kendall Shaw has worked from sports photographs found in newspapers, enlarged by means of Renaissance grid-scaling, later projected onto canvas (**Fig. 14.15**). By simplifying, Shaw intends to "re-create spaces that once existed" and to fill them with the "color projections and energy" he finds lacking in many "returns by others" of such works frequently seen in "advertising art, wall designs and even settings for TV sportscasters."

Fig. 14.16 **Kenneth Bernard**, *The Holocaust Series* #1, 1983. Collage, 20 × 15 ins (51 × 38 cm). Courtesy of the artist.

Shaped-format collage

Torn and cut collage is used by Ken Bernard to create formats outside the traditional rectangular frame. His works find their periphery from within, binding together and stopping at just the right edge, as in the "Holocaust" series (**Fig. 14.16**). In other of his works, recycled images of parts of the body frequently suggest erotic subjects until we look closer to find the sexy anatomical parts quite innocent, the sexuality in our own mind.

Interpreting documentary images

Found images such as documentary photographs of John F. Kennedy and other well-known subjects provide material for many "recycling" artists, such as Rauschenberg (**Fig. 14.11** and Bearden (**Fig. 14.14**).

Photo-realism

Photo-Realism derives its name not only from the breathtaking illusion of sharp-focus photographs, but from the actual use of photographs, enlarged and projected directly onto canvas instead of drawn into a grid upscaled from a smaller sketch. Unposed "snapshot" compositions featuring accidental, even out-of-focus elements mark the work of a number of Photo-Realist painters. Gigantic size and scale give importance and strength to many of these works. The amount of detail per square inch that Chuck Close conveys through his well-known immense "face-scapes" can be overwhelming, with or without the grid that keeps our "place" on the canvas. Do Photo-Realists always use their own photographs (**Fig. 8.1**)? Is this important?

Levels of recycling

There is no limit to the number of generations or stages of removal from an original source which an artist may rework to a new, personal level.

In Rivers' *Dutch Masters and Cigars* (**Fig. 14.17**), is the allusion to the box of cigars which uses Rembrandt's *The Syndics* (**Fig. 14.18**) as a trademark (close to a Pop Art

tradition) directly to the original painting, or both? The title gives a clue (the men are identified separately from the cigars), and there is the additional reference to Rembrandt, himself the essential Dutch master! Lichtenstein's *Sussex* is derived from the screen-printed reproduction of a drawing based on a photograph of a landscape used as a travel poster (are you with me?) described as "a thrice-removed copy of a mountainscape—a copy of a copy [poster] of a copy [painting] of the original." This is recycling to the nth degree, all the more powerful in its social commentary and its subtle humor than a verbal statement about the dehumanization and depersonalization of society. Such a picture may well be worth more than the traditional "thousand words."

EXERCISES

Exercise 7:
Keep a record of "provocative parallels" you encounter in books, galleries, museums and other sources. Consult and add to your collection, perhaps creating your own work to fill in an enticing gap.

Re-seeing a symbol

The Great Wave *returns*

A specific work, such as Hokusai's *Great Wave* (**Fig. 13.25**), may be so familiar that it is used "as is" in graphic design or advertising. It may be simplified and reduced to a symbol as in the corporate emblem of the Ocean Spray Cranberries, Inc., the transition from Hokusai's woodblock print to spiral logo is seen clearly in video animation.

Multiple recycling is found in the photo-collage shown in **Fig. 14.19**. Here, a freely adapted representation of the original woodcut, painted on the wall of a Honolulu parking lot, was photographed in a series of small images and developed as a collage to suggest the action and force of an actual wave striking the cars. How many levels of recycling can be discerned in this humorous, complex work?

Fig. 14.19 **Cynthia Dantzic**, *The Great Wave Comes to Waikiki*, 1983. Photographic collage, 11 × 25 ins (28 × 63.5 cm).

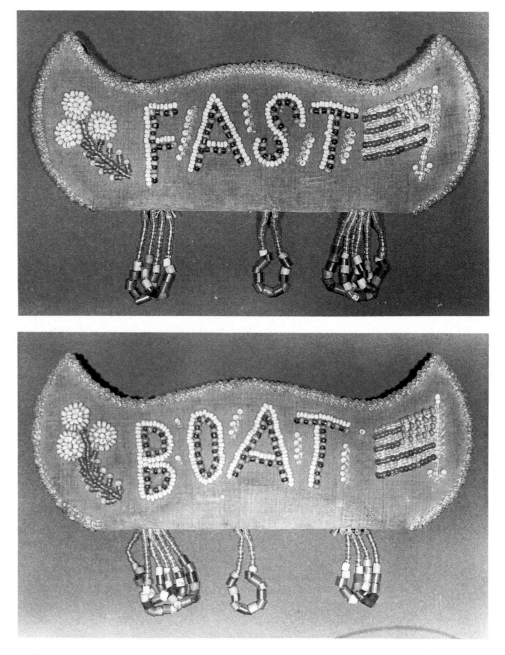

Fig. 14.20 Beaded canoe-shaped case, early 20th C. Birch bark, fabric, beading, Plains Indian artist, approx. 3 × 9 ins (7.5 × 23 cm). Two panels, attached. Collection: C. and J. Dantzic.

The American flag

How much variety can we expect to find among the various recyclings of an image, such as the American flag, itself designed by an artist? Even with this simple pattern, we find an amazing assortment, of which only a small sampling can be included here.

In a beaded canoe-shaped case (**Fig. 14.20**) a sense of speed is enhanced by the flatout, unruffled look the flag assumes as the boat moves "fast" to the right. On the reverse where the word "boat" appears, the flag image reads more quietly as a decorative, space-filling pattern.

The flag's repetitive red-and-white stripes are often seen in Navajo woven work, not always adhering to the identity of those white objects in the blue field. The general pattern is interpreted quite freely as the Navajo weaver responds to similarities between the traditional Chief's Pattern stripe and the flag's banded structure.

The flag as pattern is often found in quilts, a module repeated in decorative ways. In advertising too this graphic emblem serves as an eye-arresting device as well as an emotionally charged symbol. [8]

Jasper Johns re-invents the flag

When Jasper Johns selected the flag as the subject for a series of paintings, his choice was met with a variety of responses from rejection of such an image as a suitable theme for artwork to surprise and delighted respect, as it became clear that serious, indeed critical issues, were being addressed. Among these were the difference between merely identifying the subject of a painting and seeing a work in a purely visual way; the importance of color—a representational, expected palette or one selected for its subtle (or powerful) new effect, even the apparent elimination of color contrast; the possibilities of multiple statement and restatement of a single image within a painting; the importance of painterly involvement with the feel and texture of a surface, regardless of imagery; and the extent of aesthetic and graphic concerns possible from a single found image. As a result of an inventive, probing investigation of this previously too-familiar design, Johns may be said to have reinvented the American flag (**Figs. 9.15, 14.21**). [9]

EXERCISES

Exercise 8:
Collect ephemera, small printed advertisements, leaflets, tickets and other paper materials, all relating to one subject or theme such as the flag. (During the bicentennial year 1976, this was too easy an assignment, and only works of high aesthetic quality were sought. This was much more difficult.) Use your collection as a source for work in collage or other kinds of recycled imagery.

Exercise 9:
Create a variation of the US flag theme in a medium other than collage.

Copy art and copier art

Developing directly from the large melange of twentieth-century imagery and its sources, and owing its existence to the introduction of high-quality, fast-speed copying equipment, multiple imagery created completely from recycled printed material began to appear during the 1960s. Rearrangements of these images in collage fashion, often using the newest color xerography techniques, led to editions of books, often small in format, a function of the folding of a standard $8\frac{1}{2} \times 11$ inch sheet of Xerox paper into smaller pages. Simple flip-book animation was found to work quite well in this medium, and other experimental formats, such as the fan, followed (**Fig. 14.22**).

The placing of actual objects and textures directly on the copy machine's "light box," even parts of the body including the face (which is not recommended), has been seen. Recycling is not involved in originating these images, directly created on the machinery before they are printed in multiples, much as prints or multiple originals are pulled on an etching or lithographic press. In xerographic reproduction, the object itself or the first Xeroxed print acts as the original or plate from which the entire edition is to be printed. Therefore, a certain loss of quality in each succeeding "generation" is to be expected. The use of original materials, fabrics, textural papers or art as the "master" plate greatly reduces loss of quality in subsequent printings. However, the expressive raw quality desired for much of this work, particularly anti-war and anti-nuclear statements, may be enhanced by such harsh, excessively contrasting treatment. Xeroxing may be done on a wide assortment of papers in many colors and is often indistinguishable from actual press print. Experimentation is the key. [10]

Fig. 14.21 (*above*) **Jasper Johns**, *White Flag*, 1955–58. Encaustic and newsprint on three attached canvases, $52 \times 78\frac{3}{4}$ ins (132×200 cm). Courtesy: The Thulin Family. Photograph courtesy: Christies, New York.

Fig. 14.22 **Louise Odes Neaderland**, *The Nuclear Fan*, 1984. Xerographic artists' book/work, $8 \times 2\frac{1}{2}$ ins (20×6 cm). Courtesy of the artist.

Fig. 14.23 Larry Rivers, *Parts of the Face*, 1961. Oil on canvas, $29\frac{1}{2} \times 29\frac{1}{2}$ ins (75 × 75 cm). Courtesy: The Tate Gallery, London.

Use and re-use of lettering

Many Copier Artists, and others, include verbal messages or elements of words in their visual statements (an inheritance from Cubism and the collage) (**Fig. 14.23**). If you plan to work with any of these experimental techniques, you will want to become familiar with the basics of lettering, calligraphy and the use of wax-transfer type. Including type in any two-dimensional work requires an appropriate choice of typeface or style of alphabet in the size necessary to carry your message, and good letter spacing. Beginners tend to place letters unevenly, too far apart. A straight baseline should be self-evident, unless irregularity is part of your message. [11]

Re-use of photographs

Original photographs reproduce better than images copied from the printed page. Expect some loss of middle tones and a heightening of contrast with even the best copier. If you question ethical (or legal) aspects of using images originated by others, even familiar images readily available in print, making your own photographs is certainly an answer.

EXERCISES

Exercise 10:
Select news photos or advertisements, Xerox and experiment as described.

Exercise 11:
Design a composition using words recycled from the print media. Do you find yourself drawn toward a political or social statement?

Rubber stamps

Rubber stamps, either as a basis for copy art or for making multiple originals, offer another form of image recycling. As contemporary as this idea may seem, there are fine examples by Schwitters made as early as 1919 (**Fig. 14.24**). He used simple post-office stamps, which display a great variety of size and typeface, such as the diagonal emphasis of italics. Your local post office is a likely source of supply, particularly if you are patient and make clear your artistic intentions. Many rubber stamps are discarded when they become worn or outdated, and small-town offices frequently produce a large box of near-antique material, towns without zip codes, for instance. My collection includes "EGGS," "Montgomery Ward," "Gusher, Utah" and the favorite, "illegible."

Old children's printing sets of rubber stamps, pictorial as well as of alphabets and numbers, may occasionally be found in secondhand stores as well as the more expensive antique shops. [12]

Making your own stamps

Stamps may be created by carving shapes into rubber erasers. An alphabet carved with an X-Acto knife in twenty-six pencil erasers by Corita Kent received attention in the 1970s. The Eberhard Faber RubKleen eraser is a classic for this purpose, and empty sewing-thread spools make excellent backing for larger stamps. Stamps may be designed so their images fit together to form larger, modular patterns. Cork, cardboard and plastic may be cut into stamps, or simple found objects such as buttons and hardware may be glued to backings. [13]

Fig. 14.24 Kurt Schwitters, *Bussum, bussum, bussum*, 1923. Rubber stamp design, $4\frac{1}{2} \times 4\frac{1}{8}$ ins (11.5 × 10.5 cm). Private Collection. Courtesy: Simon/Neuman Gallery, New York.

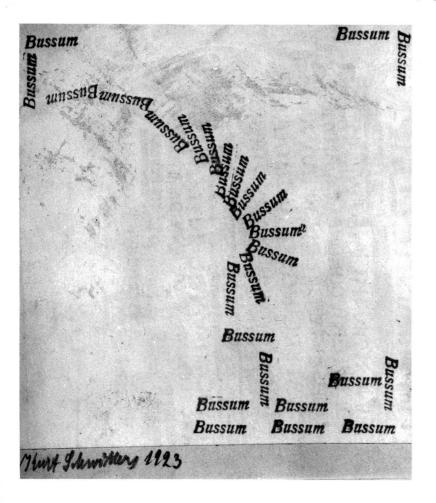

EXERCISES

Exercise 12:
Start your own "stamp" collection; use it creatively.

Exercise 13, (Multi-Part):
Design a simple alphabet and carve it into RubKleen or pencil erasers. Stamp an announcement or message.

Computer art

In Computer art, a single image may undergo innumerable transmutations of position, size, shape, proportion, color and relation to other visual elements. Limitless repetitions or variations are possible. The "original" need not be the original work of the person feeding it into the machine; many computer art experimenters are far more familiar with the operation of the computer than with art.

However, artists who discount Computer art for this reason many be surprised to discover how creative the equipment can become when directed creatively. Uncreative uses of the computer should not keep us from discovering its special qualities. Subtlety of line and tone are possible with little practice. You can experience drawing, even shading with varying tonal value, directly on the screen by moving the small indicator (called a mouse) on an accompanying plate. Just as a pianist adjusts to the slightly off-set timing required when playing the organ with its momentary delay and divided keyboard, so the artist can adapt to the unfamiliar sense of drawing invisibly on a blank slate and seeing the work appear on the screen.

Advertising design and animation, particularly for television, offer unlimited possibilities for the inventive computer artist, with new refinements in skill and technique reflecting each advance in design of the machine itself. Since existing technology can produce hundreds of physically different colors for any shape produced, by applying your understanding of color interaction the number of visually different colors is … infinite. [14]

EXERCISES

Exercise 14, (Two-Part):
On a computer screen, using a small repeated shape and a wide range of colors, experiment as described on this page. Then try to re-create the look of a painting from the Impressionist, Post-Impressionist or Fauvist periods.

Fig. 14.25 (*left*) **Alexei Jawlensky**, *Girl in Red*, 1912. Oil on canvas, $21\frac{1}{4} \times 19\frac{1}{4}$ ins (54 × 49 cm). Courtesy: Anjelica Jawlensky. (*right*) **Victoria Archie**, *Collage Study of Jawlensky's "Girl in Red,"* 1980. Long Island University Color Theory Workshop.

Creative recycling

Fig. 14.26 (*top*) **Edgar Degas**, *The Blue Dancers*, 1890. $33\frac{1}{2} \times 29$ ins (85×75 cm). Courtesy: The Louvre, Paris.
(*bottom*) **Maria Eastmond O'Brien**, *Collage study of Degas' "Blue Dancers,"* 1983. Long Island University Color Theory Workshop.

Collage study of a painting

A color study interpretation of a painting was a highlight of the Albers color workshop. The task is to re-create your impression of a well-known painting as a collage to give a sense of the color harmony, composition and mood of the original through the use of small bits and pieces of colored paper, Color Aid or snips and clips from well-printed magazines. Try small circles created with a paper punch. Works by the Impressionists, Post-Impressionists and Fauvists are particularly recommended. The aim is in no way a copy of the painting and must not be accomplished by tracing or working directly over a reproduction. The papers may be torn or cut as required. As in any use of color, particular attention should be paid to the strength and softness of edges. It is not necessary to re-create every detail of the original; a sketchy approach (if collage can be said to be sketchy) may prove most successful.

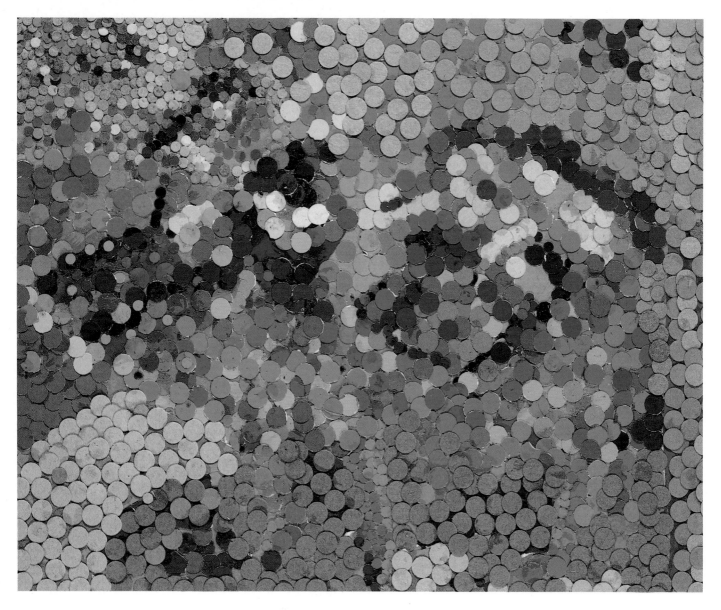

This technique is often developed to a level of accomplishment which makes it difficult to tell the original from the study when both are seen side by side at a distance. Of course, up close the collage is often seen as a disorganized collection of scraps, dots, or paper "tesserae." Tweezers, toothpicks and tremendous resources of patience are advised. Be willing to make many changes as you work. Although rubber cement was used in the Albers workshop, you may prefer acrylic medium or Jade glue for permanence.

It is best not to combine techniques within a single work; each collage should be completely torn, cut with scissors or an X-Acto knife (**Fig. 14.25**) or formed of paper-punch dots (**Fig. 14.26**). The small units of color may be stored in egg cartons, old wooden type-trays, candy boxes with plastic inserts and other subdivided containers. This is one of the most satisfying and instructive studies you will encounter. The most difficult decision is knowing when you have finished. See how little you actually need to do to suggest each area of the original, and do not let yourself add "just a bit more." Which of the examples is most convincing (**Fig. 14.27**)?

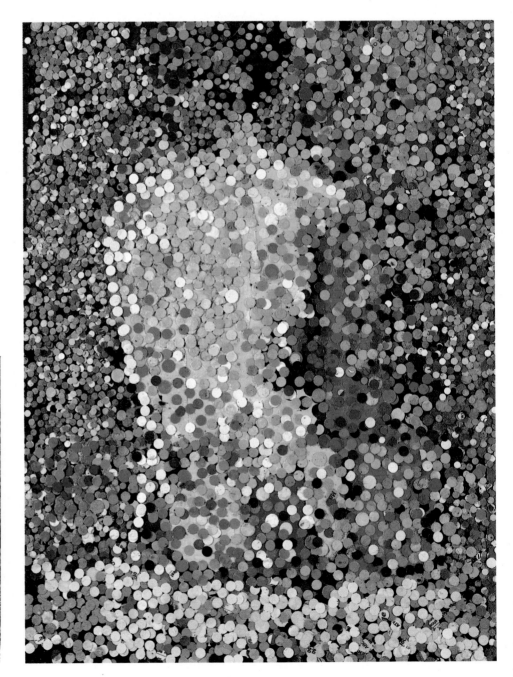

Fig. 14.27 (*below*) **Georges Seurat**, *Seated Model*, 1887. Oil on board, 9½ × 6 ins (24 × 15 cm). Courtesy: The Louvre, Paris. (*right*) Student collage study of Seurat's *Seated Model*.

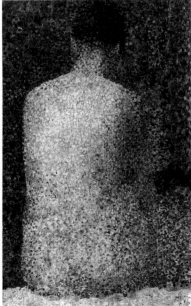

Fig. 14.28 **Marcantonio Raimondi**, *The Judgment of Paris (detail)*, c. 1520. Engraving (after Raphael). Courtesy: The Metropolitan Museum of Art, New York.

Making recycling a creative act

Research is said to consist of writing out in longhand what already exists in print. Recycled research is no more creative than simply copying or otherwise reproducing works already brought to life on paper or canvas by another artist. Only making an idea, whether verbal or visual, your own can impart some quality of originality so that, instead of merely conveying the message of another, you are actually taking the torch, so to speak, and running with it in a new direction—perhaps in the footsteps of those who have gone before—extending the path, carrying the history of art a step farther than it has been taken (**Figs. 14.28–14.30**).

The continuity of art

Can recycled imagery be said to be a single continuous thread which runs throughout the history of the visual arts? Hilton Kramer notes this in Picasso's life: "To a degree unequalled by his few peers in this century, he has always been an artist who felt called upon to emulate as well as to challenge the past, *to reconstruct tradition*, even as his radical inventions dissolved it." Clement Greenberg, speaking of Modernist Art, says, "Nothing could be further from the authentic art of our time than the idea of a rupture of continuity. Art is, among many other things, continuity." Can we see the new developments in our time, the recycling of specific imagery originated by others and the use of commercial products and printed materials, as continuing this flow? "... The artist

Fig. 14.29 **Edouard Manet**, *Dejeuner sur l'herbe, (Luncheon on the grass)*, 1863. Oil on canvas, 84 × 106 ins (213 × 269 cm). Courtesy: The Louvre, Paris.

has taken over real objects from the environment and by transmuting them has asserted his identity as an artist. We have been used to thinking of art as being separate from life ... as an interpretation ... a distillation, as something apart from the undisturbed flux of events and the ongoing existence of objects'' says Clement Greenberg.

It seems useful to maintain a constant awareness of the sources of ideas and imagery. Ask yourself: Is this study ''in the style of ... ?'' Is this work completely derived from other people's images? Is it a rearrangement of elements, none of them original? Is it a recycling of ideas and picturings introduced perhaps by other hands, but somehow made particularly my own?

Do you agree with Clement Greenberg that today perhaps, ''the distinction between what is and what is not art can only be made by the artist?''

Fig. 14.30 *(top)* **Alain Jacquet,** *Luncheon on the Grass,* 1964. Serigraph in two parts, $69 \times 78\frac{1}{4}$ ins (175×199 cm). Courtesy: Centre National d'Art et du Culture, Georges Pompidou, Paris.

Fig. 14.31 *(bottom)* **Pablo Picasso,** *Luncheon on the Grass, (after Manet),* 1949. Oil on canvas. Courtesy: Musée Picasso, Paris.

Chapter Fifteen

THE EVOCATIVE IMAGE

Fig. 15.1   Jay Seldin, *Pansies*, 1984.
Manipulated photographic image. Courtesy;
the photographer.

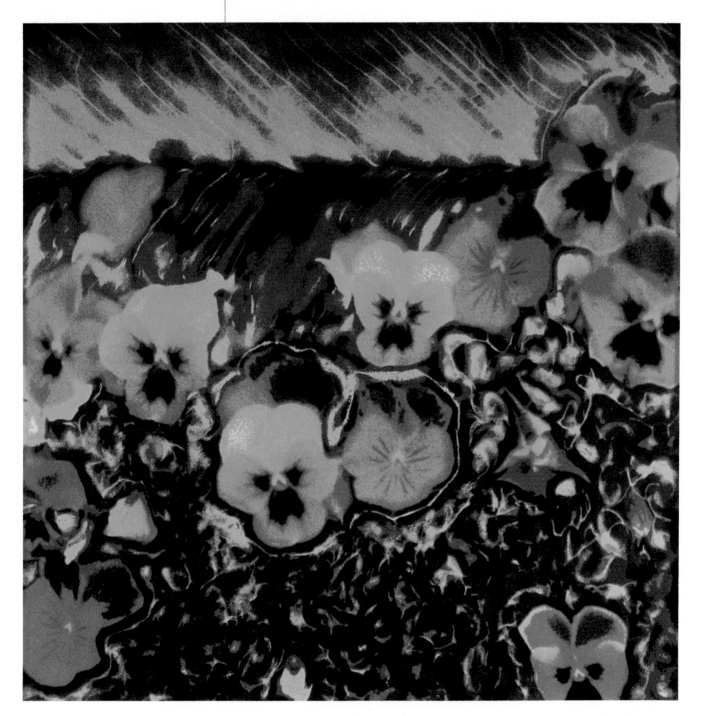

WORLD'S HIGHEST STANDARD OF LIVING

There's no way like the American Way

Fig. 15.2 Margaret Bourke-White, *At the time of the Louisville Flood*, 1937. Gelatin-silver print. Courtesy; Life Magazine © 1937 Time Inc.

Visual expression of ideas and feelings

Symbols and signs elicit responses in the viewer; they identify, channel emotions, encourage action, communicate information or attitudes. Although much symbolism uses the language of words, even in the visual arts, pictorial symbolism (depicting ideas and feelings through varying degrees of realistic imagery) is recognized more universally than the verbal (**Fig. 15.2**). We will investigate both kinds of visual language (p. 289). Expression of powerful human concerns and beliefs through visual imagery is a major focus of much contemporary art and design. Enhanced by electronic and duplicative processes, current choices of individual means to personal goals seem truly inexhaustible.

Discovery of one's own creativity, the tapping of one's unique resources and vision, may be elicited through techniques which free the imagination by drawing upon the elusive "laws" of accident, chance and play (**Fig. 8.16**). In serendipitous ways, what we find is often much more than we have been seeking, particularly in the visual arts (**Fig. 15.1**).

Meanings beyond the visual

All marks or images may be evocative, calling forth responses that transcend formal aesthetic content, even the simple perpendicular intersection of two lines:

Aha! The right angle—stability—geometry—the mind in control;
Aha! A crossroad approaches;
Aha! The cross—Christianity—suffering borne—a strong support for human frailty;
Aha! The plus sign—an augmenting, an increase—an electric charge;
— Stasis—the equal and opposite forces of action and rest;
— The number ten (to a reader of Chinese or Japanese);
— The Red Cross, a humanitarian network (or a brand of shoes);
— Deceased (after a name in print);

From a work by Mondrian, simplifying natural or architectural forms to their basic structure, perhaps from his *Plus and Minus* series ... (p. 155).

Or _____ ... [1]

Do you agree that images may be seen to contain meanings actually assigned by the viewer, regardless of the intent of any designer?

Intentionally introduced meanings

Four major methods are employed by artists to "produce emotion and evoke aesthetic responses," according to anthropologist David B. Stout:

Use of Symbols with established ... associations (**Fig. 15.3**);
Depiction of Emotion-Arousing Events, persons or supernatural entities (**Figs. 14.11, 15.5**);
Enlisting the Spectator's Vicarious Participation in the ... solution of ... problems of design ... (**Fig. 15.4**);
Use of Particular Combinations of Line, Mass, Color, etc., that seem capable of arousing emotions in themselves (**Fig. 11.1**).

These are found in varying degrees and mixtures in intentionally evocative works . To Dr Albert C. Barnes, writing extensively on meanings in art (largely following the teachings of John Dewey), "Subject matter and plastic form are not in any absolute

Fig. 15.3 Selection of crosses and perpendicular signs and images.

Fig. 15.4 **Paul Klee**, *Mural from The Temple of Longing Thither*, 1922. Watercolor and transfer drawing, $10\frac{3}{8} \times 14\frac{3}{8}$ ins (26.5 × 37 cm). Courtesy: The Metropolitan Museum of Art, New York.

284

sense separable." "A good painting," Barnes often said, "is one in which the plastic means—line, light, color and space—are integrated into a consistent and *meaningful whole*" (emphasis the author's). He stressed, as "the indispensable requisites of great art—unity, variety, individuality and the production of aesthetic pleasure in others ..."

Perhaps the ability to evoke an aesthetic response, not necessarily one of pleasure, stands as the unique criterion of the late twentieth century in assessing "meaning" in any work of art.

Can the aesthetic quality also refer to the purposeful presentation of discordant relationships, harsh color combinations, intentionally crude technique, emotionally disturbing imagery and other "unbeautiful" visual material (**Figs. 8.27, 15.5**)? Expressions of power, strong emotion, sexuality, affirmation of the self coming to terms with hostile or unknown forces, as well as the more traditional search for harmony and balance of visual elements, are all seen as appropriate subjects for aesthetically meaningful works by many artists and art viewers today.

EXERCISES

Exercise 1:
Collect examples of crosses or another simple geometric form.

Sign and symbol

Meanings assigned

Only as significance is ascribed to images do they assume their identity as art, words, traffic indicators, trademarks, flags, mathematical equations, religious and political emblems, even money. If individuals, as a nation, religious group, political party, sports team, university, community or family, agree upon the meaning of particular images (a flag, slogan, alphabet or written language), then every member must learn the meanings of the common sign, symbols or imagery; or each one cannot participate fully in the shared experience (**Figs. 6.6, 6.7**). (This is as much a reason for newcomers to the United States to learn English as it is for including art in the curriculum.)

Try to study the works without regard for symbolic content, as purely visual statements.

Is this possible? Is it easier in some instances than others? What would be lost to viewers unfamiliar with specific languages, religious symbols, art traditions, civilizations, social issues or political events? Do you think such subjective meanings are of importance to the visual artist or the viewer? Does the artist have a responsibility to make meanings clear? What of the responsibility of the viewer?

From universal signs to specialized symbols— languages

Although both suggest representation of one object or idea by another, a *sign* may be any simple indication while a *symbol* connotes a commonly agreed-upon image, often intentionally designed for its purpose, combining a variety of elements. Different kinds of messages are conveyed by simple, universally understood directional indications, such as arrows, and by complex systems of markings that stand for discrete, separable parts of a larger structure, such as the sounds that comprise a language.

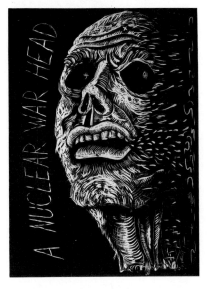

Fig. 15.5 **Robert Arneson**, *Nuclear War Head*, 1984. Woodcut, 42 × 57 ins (106.5 × 145 cm). Courtesy: The Frumkin/Adams Gallery.

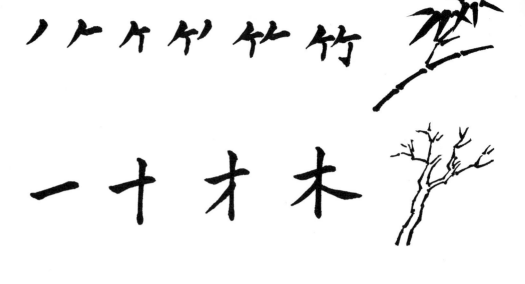

Fig. 15.7 Rear Panel of Golden Shrine, Tomb of Tutenkhamun, c. 1352 BC. Gilded wood. Courtesy: Egyptian Museum, Cairo.

286

Picturing speech

"I have a headache, Radar,—talk in small letters," says Hawkeye on *M.A.S.H.*, acknowledging the subtle relationship between spoken and written words, and assuming the viewer understands that speech, writing and printing all use a set of basic symbols to convey meanings to a group of people. These may be *alphabetic* (p. 290), communicating each sound as a separate symbol (in theory); *pictographic* (**Fig. 15.6**), using symbols derived from simplified pictures of things; or *ideographic* (p. 284), using commonly agreed-upon marks standing for concepts. Writing may be presented sound by sound, word by word, or thought by thought and may combine the three kinds of symbols described (**Fig. 15.7**). Letters, characters and words are often used as design elements for purely visual purposes with or without regard to their literal meaning. [2]

Letter styles and typefaces

Our alphabet has evolved through traditional forms, each of which may be found in several variations, all used as a basis for differing type "faces", or designs (**Fig. 15.8**). Some are close to their original calligraphic or handwritten model, but many decorative and non-traditional alphabets are seen—particularly for display and advertising.

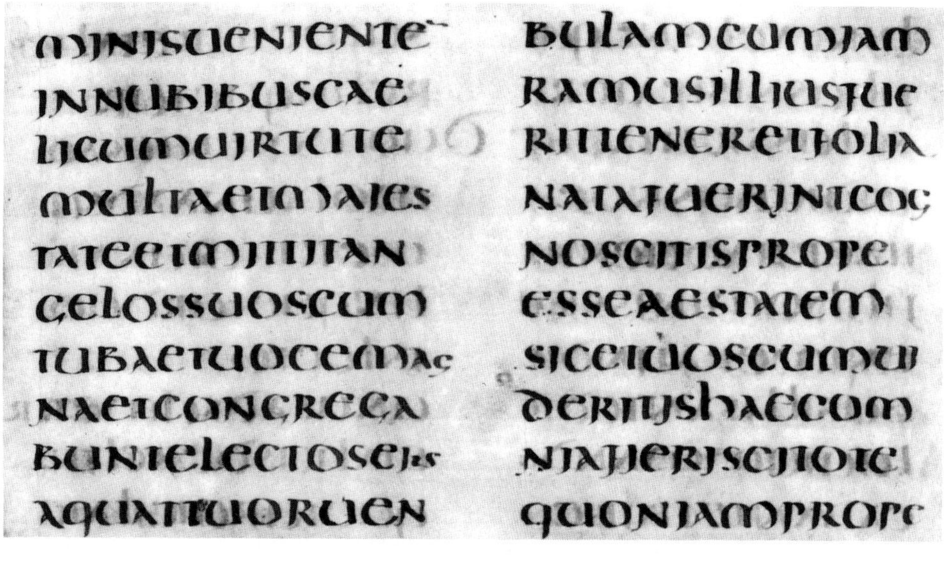

Fig. 15.8 Alphabets: (*left*) Gothic: Jean de Beauchesne, 1570. Courtesy: The British Library Photographic Service. From "A Booke containing Divers Sortes of Hands." (*top right*) Uncial: Latin Vulgate Bible, written by Alcuin of York c. 850, detail of St. Paul's Epistle to the Hebrews. Roman capitals with uncials and Caroline minuscules. Courtesy: The British Museum, London.
(*bottom, right*) Roman: *The Trajan Column*, inscription. Courtesy: The Trustees of the Victoria & Albert Museum, London.

Fig. 15.9 Typefaces:

abcdefghijklmnopqrstuvwxyz
ABCDEFGHIJKLMNOPQRSTUVWXYZ

Old English

abcdefghijklmnopqrstuvwxyz
ABCDEFGHIJKLMNOPQRSTUVWXYZ

Baskerville

abcdefghijklmnopqrstuvwxyz
ABCDEFGHIJKLMNOPQRSTUVWXYZ

Bodoni

abcdefghijklmnopqrstuvwxyz
ABCDEFGHIJKLMNOPQRSTUVWXYZ

Caslon

abcdefghijklmnopqrstuvwxyz
ABCDEFGHIJKLMNOPQRSTUVWXYZ

Optima

abcdefghijklmnopqrstuvwxyz
ABCDEFGHIJKLMNOPQRSTUVWXYZ

Franklin Gothic

abcdefghijklmnopqrstuvwxyz
ABCDEFGHIJKLMNOPQRSTUVWXYZ

Futura

abcdefghijklmnopqrstuvwxyz
ABCDEFGHIJKLMNOPQRSTUVWXYZ

Helvetica

abcdefghijklmnopqrstuvwxyz
ABCDEFGHIJKLMNOPQRSTUVWXYZ

News Gothic

Fig. 15.10 Subway sign with low legibility.

Computer-generated alphabets, some with progressive distortions and proportional modifications, are often unrelated to traditional forms. Many designers avoid and object to such innovations as mixing small letters and capitals in a single word, combining letters from different alphabets, using hard-to-read or arbitrary letter-shapes bearing little resemblance to any standard form, or compromise shapes that may be read as any of several letters when positioned differently (**Fig. 15.10**).

The ABC of it: origins of the alphabet

The Roman alphabet, as incised into Trajan's Column in Rome in 113 AD, is the model for our capital letters. Their elegant proportions are seen on public buildings and in such typefaces as Hermann Zapf's "Optima." Modified versions are found in many other faces.

Roman letters can be traced to ancient pictographs; the A derived (through the Greek *alpha* and Hebrew *aleph*) from a lopsided ox's head, the B (through the Greek *beta* and Hebrew *beth*) from a simple house. Together these became the symbol of the entire sequence, the alpha-bet itself.

Trajan Roman is adapted for two-dimensional use by incorporating the small edge-endings made by the carver's chisel as finishing strokes called serifs. The natural occurrence of thick and thin lines in Roman capital letters (upper case or majuscule) is a result of the angle at which a chisel-shaped brush is held when marking the letters on stone before carving.

Small letters (lower case or minuscule) derive from Renaissance or Italic forms through the transitional Uncial, combining letters which to our eye seem a mix of capital and small letters.

Study these typefaces based on alphabets without serifs (**Figs. 15.8, 15.9**) (sans serif). Some type designs derive from calligraphic styles. Old English and Text typefaces closely resemble the angular, formal "diploma lettering" known as Black Letter or Gothic. In calligraphy, Gothic generally refers to this family of alphabets; in type it has come to mean any of several heavy, sans-serif faces.

Visualizing the verbal

In an alphabetic language, each sound heard when it is spoken must be included, individually or by combining symbols. Twelve of our alphabetic letters are not used in written Hawaiian because the sounds they represent do not occur in the language. Languages which do not have alphabetic forms may use the shorthand picture-symbol, or pictographic, system. Visualize the "swinging gate" in the Chinese word for "door", the wide-stretched arms in "big" and the legs, tail and body of "horse" (**Fig. 15.11**). The children's book in **Fig. 5.9** is illustrated entirely in expressively brushed pictographic words, serving as pictures of the referents themselves.

Fig. 15.11 Chinese words for "ten," "big," "door," written by Vivian Tsao.

Fig. 15.12   Cynthia Dantzic, page from "Stop Dropping BreAd CrumBs on my YaCht: a silent ABC," published by Prentice-Hall, Inc., New York, 1974.

Difficulty has been encountered in deciphering ancient Egyptian writings because the language is partly alphabetic, partly pictographic, partly ideographic. Problems also occur in learning to read English, which is composed of elements borrowed from unrelated languages whose spelling and pronunciation are not consistent. In written English every letter may be silent, an amazing turn about for markings intended to picture sounds made aloud (**Fig. 15.12**)!

Hands on the ABCs: introduction to calligraphy

Anyone planning a future in the fine, studio or so-called commercial arts (illustration, graphics, advertising, fashion, computer art, animation) will want to recognize and be able to use a variety of traditional alphabets in freehand calligraphy, built-up or constructed lettering, and several standard typefaces. This introduction should whet, or sharpen, your appetite; it cannot do more.

A simple calligraphic alphabet

A particularly pleasing calligraphic alphabet, originally used by sixteenth-century Italian monks, is called Chancery or, particularly when slanted, Italic (p. 291). Of several versions, the one depicted is based closely on that introduced by Ludovico Arrighi in 1522. You can learn this alphabet easily with practice as it is logically constructed of a few basic, almost modular, strokes within a band divided into three equal parts (**Fig. 15.13**). If your pen is held at a constant angle, thicks and thins will arrange

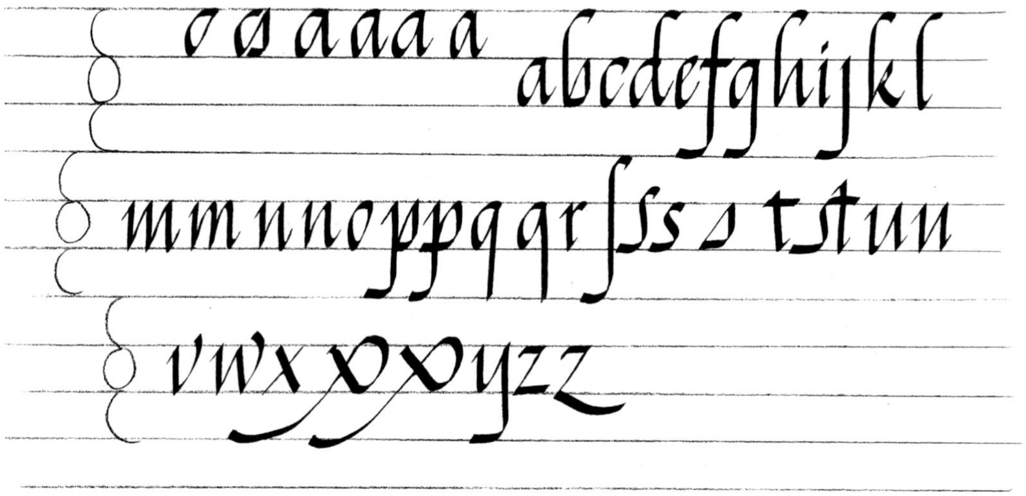

Fig. 15.13 A simple Italic alphabet using modular strokes.

Fig. 15.14 Paul Shaw's Italic alphabet: The Majuscules (*top*) and The Minuscules (*bottom*).

themselves automatically. The central band is reserved for the main portion (body) of each letter, the upper band for ascending strokes (ascenders), and the lower band for descending strokes (descenders).

Hold a chisel-edged calligraphy pen (a Speedball C2 nib is good) at a 45° angle to the page so that it makes a medium-weight ribbon-line horizontally or vertically. Draw a right angle, moving horizontally left, then pulling vertically toward yourself, stopping when the pen is aimed at its starting place. Connect the strokes, completing a triangular shape. (A curve later replaces the right angle.) The complementary basic shape begins with a vertical pull then moves left before completing the opposite triangle. Both triangles together make a basic design to be practiced, as musical scales are repeated, before attempting more complex forms. Ascenders repeat the first part of the basic stroke, one unit above the midline; descenders, part of the complementary basic stroke, one unit below. Only k, r, s, x and z require special strokes, and a formal s is a double stroke consisting of an ascender and a descender flowing together (an f minus its crossbar). Before trying the pen, make these and other experimental strokes using two pencils attached with rubber bands as a single tool, to see each edge more clearly.

A steady, fluid movement will produce letters whose spines are parallel, with visually even spacing. Keep verticals upright, horizontals perpendicular, with crisp curves between. Certain letters may be connected through strokes called ligatures. Leave sufficient room around a block of copy, or lettering. Practice, experience and the study of excellent examples will give you a sense of correct spacing.

Variations of this alphabet include curving its angles. Some calligraphers omit the "flag" on ascenders and descenders, or add various flourishes. A simple capital form consists of a "swash," the curved right angle of the basic stroke, added to a block letter alphabet. Paul Shaw's Italic (**Fig. 15.14**) is particularly fluid and contemporary. (Try the block capitals with and without the "swash.")

With practice, perhaps slanted slightly toward the right as your speed increases, the letters will touch and flow together in a cursive way, becoming an elegant, controlled handwriting. Depending upon the nib's thickness, the module's height and other individual characteristics, you will achieve a distinctive style, your own "hand."

Fig. 15.15 **Norman Ives**, *Gray Bas-Relief*, 1971. Courtesy: Mrs. Norman Ives.

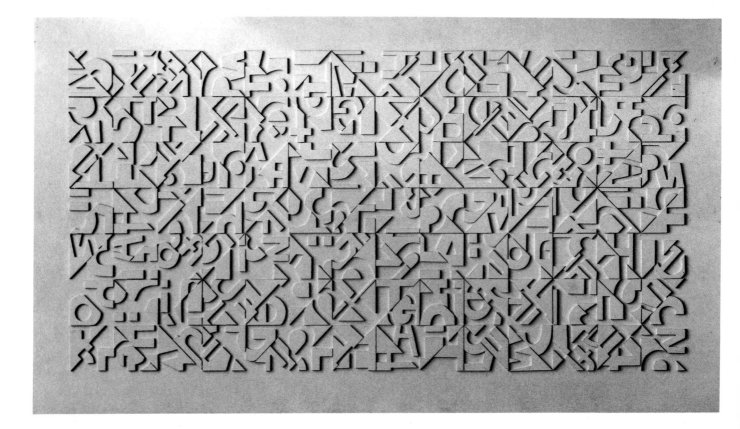

Letters as graphic design subject, aesthetic object

Letters are often used as subject matter since they contain interesting shapes on both filled and unfilled sides of their edges with minimal associative connotation. Norman Ives' work is notably inventive and elegant (**Fig. 15.15**).

The verbal content of written language can only be read by those familiar with its agreed-upon meanings, but non-verbal qualities communicated through its visual elements are available to everyone. These may be interpreted differently by viewers bringing individual criteria to the experience.

Calligraphy is often used alone or with typography to suggest immediacy, speed, a human, hands-on quality, even honesty, in graphic design.

Would an English translation enhance your appreciation of the calligraphy in **Fig. 6.6**? Might it detract from your aesthetic enjoyment?

Lettering in woodcuts and painting

Lettering achieves special power and style in the hands of printmakers, particularly in the woodcut. All such work, including letter forms, must be carved in reverse, which may explain the special strength and unity of woodblock lettering. Concentration on formal, abstract qualities of the shapes encourages subtle modifications based on aesthetic values alone (**Figs. 1.28, 1.36, 4.2**).

Study works incorporating words and letters to distinguish between messages projected literally and visually. Does Shunji Sakuyama have non-verbal reasons for showing window signs from the inside and therefore backwards? Does he care if you read the words? Compare the uses of letters and words throughout this book (pp. 19, 273–75). Can you tell when an artist wants you to read literal as well as visual meanings in a work?

Other uses of lettering

Restudy the Indian beaded case (**Fig. 14.20**); is either word used as more than a verbal symbol?

Many children's books are hand lettered. Do you think young readers may feel more comfortable with hand lettering than professional type (**Fig. 5.9**)?

In recent years there has been a less formal attitude toward calligraphy and lettering, favoring freer interpretation of classical alphabets and more individual, even

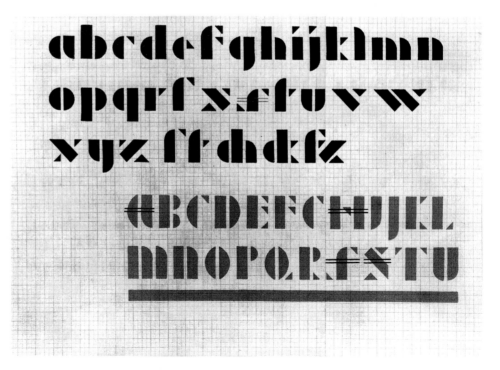

Fig. 15.16 Josef Albers, *Modular Stencil Alphabet,* 1925. Courtesy: The Josef Albers Foundation.

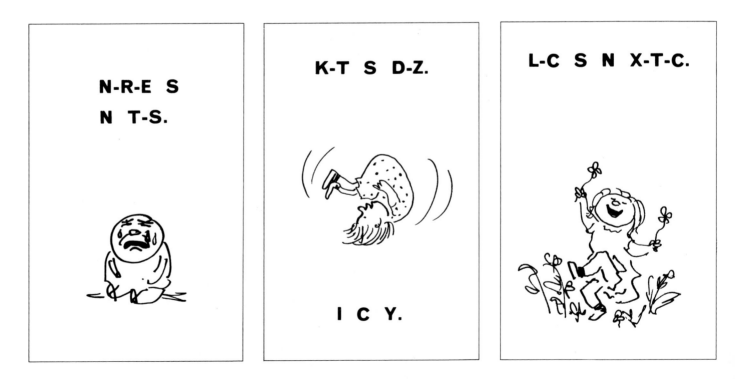

Fig. 15.17 (*opposite, top*) "There's a Bee in My Bed," (*left*) *modular alphabet, version #1,* (adjacent shapes); (*right*) *version #2,* (overlapping shapes).
Fig. 15.18 (*opposite, bottom*) **William Steig,** *CDB,* (pages from), 1968. Reprinted by permission of Simon and Schuster, Inc.

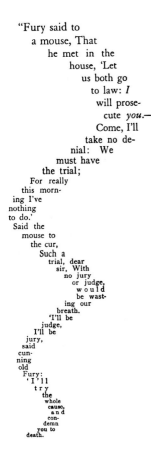

"Fury said to
a mouse, That
he met in the
house, 'Let
us both go
to law: *I*
will prose-
cute *you.*—
Come, I'll
take no de-
nial: We
must have
the trial;
For really
this morn-
ing I've
nothing
to do.'
Said the
mouse to
the cur,
Such a
trial, dear
sir, With
no jury
or judge,
w o u l d
be wast-
ing our
breath.
'I'll be
judge,
I'll be
jury,
said
cun-
ning
old
Fury:
'I'll
t r y
the
whole
cause,
a n d
con-
demn
you to
death.

Fig. 15.19 Lewis Carroll, "The Mouse's Tale" from "Alice in Wonderland," 1865, 1960 and 1971 versions.

idiosyncratic, handwritten forms. Your attitude about graffiti may reflect an involvement with calligraphy. Do the circumstances and environment of a particular written piece affect its identity as art, design or defacement?

More questions about the written word

Is everyone's handwriting calligraphy? When do legibility and spelling count? How can you distinguish built-up or constructed lettering from calligraphy? When would you use transfer type (rub-on wax lettering) instead of actual type?

Modular alphabets—"moduletters"

The search for the smallest number of shapes that can form all twenty-six letters has long intrigued designers. At the Bauhaus in 1925 Albers designed a modular stencil using three shapes (**Fig. 15.16**).

Unfortunately all the small letters do not fit into a circle (or oval) and line configuration. I have solved this continuing problem with five shapes to make adjacent "Moduletters," and an overlapping modification which works more successfully (**Fig. 15.17**). (Alas, artistic success does not spell commercial success; this book remains in my files.) Using the name of each letter as a word is fine (a jay is a bird, tea is a drink) but what is a "double-you?" Different solutions were found, some based on shape not sound.

William Steig pictures the sound of letter (and number) names in informal speech, in a book which is a gem of economy, evoking maximum effect with minimal (apparent) effort (**Fig. 15.18**). But it must be read with a New York accent! [3]

Words as visual images

"Concrete poetry"

"Concrete poetry" is a relatively new name for designing the shape of printed words on a page, Lewis Carroll's 1865 "Mouse's Tale" being the unsurpassed model (**Fig. 15.19**). A further advocate of "concrete poetry" is the poet e. e. cummings; look up his jumpy, bouncing portrait of a grasshopper, which is painted entirely in letters. Non-objective shape-conscious word and letter arrangements are seen in works by Richard Kostelanetz and many others. [4]

The bubble or word-enclosing shape adjacent to the human image suggesting speech or thought is not restricted to the comic book or even modern times.

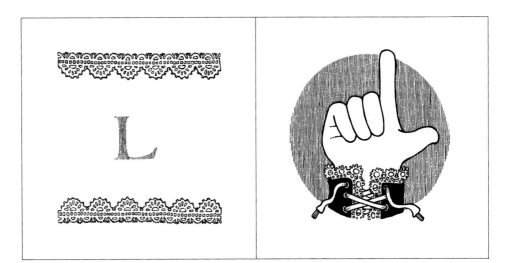

Fig. 15.20 Linda Bourke, page from "Handmade ABC," published by Addison Wesley Publishing Co., 1981.

Fig. 15.21 Steve Poleski, "Aerial Theater Event for Verona (Second Stage)," 1988. Colored pencil on photocopy, 8 × 11 ins (20 × 28 cm). Courtesy of the artist. Photograph by Apogee Airway.

Fig. 15.22 (right) Marc Chagall, The Musician of the P. A. Regnault Collection, 1939. Oil on canvas, $39\frac{2}{5} \times 28\frac{1}{4}$ ins (100 × 73 cm). Private collector, present location unknown.

Non-traditional writing: codes and shorthands, feeling sounds, seeing speech, reading movement

In Braille, patterns of tactile dots symbolize alphabetic units and combinations, similar in concept to the many shorthand codes incorporating dots, strokes and squiggles meant to be seen (**Fig. 1.14**). Morse code requires only the dot and dash to create its alphabet.

Adding alphabetic clues to pictures of hand gestures that spell the alphabet, Linda Bourke has created a delightful and useful children's book (**Fig. 15.20**). Fingerspelling is used at a distance which precludes the spoken word, in noisy locations, or by those unable to hear for other reasons.

Labanotation uses visual symbols to "read" and "write" the movements of the human figure in dance. Individual choreographers have designed other dance writing. [5]

Seeing music

In writing music, symbols indicate the *position* (relative tone) of each sound and its *duration* (length of time it is heard). Steve Poleskie designed notes to be written across the blue canvas of the sky in lines of white smoke above Verona to celebrate the opening of its opera season (**Fig. 15.21**). Quickly dissipated sky-writing would reinforce the time aspect of musical notation.

The five-line staff on which music is written has been used for humorous purposes by Saul Steinberg among others. Miró invented her own music "writing", while Chagall rephrased the idea that the singer (or fiddler) is one with the song! (**Fig. 15.22**) [6]

Fig. 15.23 (*left*) NYNEX Corporate
Signature.
Fig. 15.24 (*center*) Yellow Pages logo.
Fig. 15.25 (*right*) Aqueduct Raceway logo.

Letters and words as graphic symbols

The logic of logos

Visual symbols designed to convey qualities associated with an organization, product, service or concept are known as trademarks, logotypes or simply logos. Initials or an entire word, designed with special emphasis on symmetry, figure-ground interaction, the illusion of the third dimension or abstraction from natural form, may produce a striking symbol readily identified with its subject. As fashions and styles change over the years, some familiar logos have undergone modernization—often more than once. [7]

Symbolism in a seemingly simple logo may be quite complex. In the NYNEX symbol (**Fig. 15.23**), initials identify New York and New England; the "X" suggests excellence, the first three letters sound like a number, and the final two suggest a telephone e*x*change. Background shapes in the E move through the X to read as pages of a directory. An older design for the "Yellow Pages" (**Fig. 15.24**), with its fingers "doing the walking," is more literal, but this, a similar idea, is conveyed with speed and efficiency by the new, graphic geometric NYNEX symbol.

The Atlantic Computer Company uses continuous translational symmetry to suggest through a swelling progression of wave forms, its italicized cursive initials, a mutually cooperative, perhaps increasingly successful, concern (**Fig. 2.31**).

Italics also indicate forward-moving action. The bold, sans-serif "A" used by the Aqueduct Raceway (**Fig. 15.25**) is enhanced by an overlapping silhouette. Two things may not occupy the same space (in the three-dimensional world) at the same time, but in this design the effect enhances speed and excitement. [8]

EXERCISES

Exercise 2, (Two-Part):
Reduce a drawing of a simple object to a pictogram, using the basic strokes of Chinese calligraphy. Using the Arabic or Hebrew alphabet, design a graphic symbol for an animal or an object.

Exercise 3:
Devise a modular alphabet, using graph paper with tracing paper overlays.

Exercise 4:
Design a simple "concrete" poem, preferably your own.

Exercise 5:
Create a graphic symbol or design using a non-traditional form of writing, perhaps a logo.

Exercise 6:
On music notation paper, create a work incorporating musical symbols. Try for humor or wit.

Exercise 7:
Create a logo of your initials or for a popular product.

Exercise 8:
Design a logo combining an alphabetic and a non-verbal symbol.

Fig. 15.26 (*above*) Traffic signs and company logos.

Fig. 15.27 (*left*) Chase Manhattan Bank logo, designed by Chermayeff and Geismar Associates, 1960.

Fig. 15.28 American Enka Corporation logo.

Fig. 15.29 Development of Shell Oil and Bell logos.

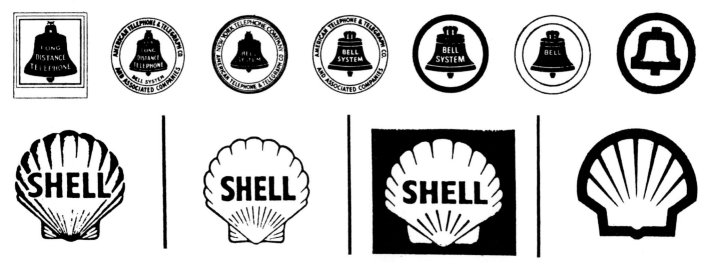

Too marvelous for words: non-verbal signs and symbols

Traffic and directional signals, sports designations and signs for use in places where more than one language is spoken offer opportunities for good design. Can you identify the non-verbal indications in the symbols in **Fig. 15.26**? Do some contain regional or other restrictive indications? Which seem truly international? [9]

Shape-symbols and logos

In this four-square symmetrical, easily remembered, solid yet active, classic yet streamlined, simple yet eye-catching, rectangular yet somehow circular logo, how many elements work to give the image such a variety of desirable qualities (**Fig. 15.27**)? Is subtle alphabetic symbolism involved?

What qualities of de Rivera's curvilinear constructions are suggested by its use as a symbol for a steel company (**Fig. 15.28**)? Compare this literal adaptation of a three-dimensional form with the flat ribbon designed for the Coca-Cola Company (**Fig. 4.10**) as a modernization of its earlier logos.

What qualities are emphasized by the trademarks, logos and symbols shown?

Streamlining a logo

What criteria do you think led to the changes in the logos in **Fig. 15.29**? Is the most useful design necessarily the best aesthetically?

The bell, standing for the ringing of the telephone, its inventor and the company's name, has undergone much simplification and streamlining. Has this design changed from an illustration to a symbol? Notice the gradual elimination of words.

In identifying with a pectin shell, what qualities does Shell Oil wish to suggest? Could another subject convey its ancient power, endurance, natural organic and liquid associations and its many uses in classical art? Is the extreme modernization of this particular pictorial image as successful as that of the bell?

The famous "flying red horse" was chosen to suggest horsepower through subject, color and gesture. The flying horse of mythology, Pegasus, adds classical flavor, power, speed and innovation, in one image. This effective symbol was supplemented in 1966 by an all-alphabetic design of the company's name, its double outline for the "O" suggesting a tire or wheel. As the best logos epitomize economy, Mobil is proud of its citation from *Holiday* magazine: "Good design is good business." [10]

EXERCISES

Exercise 9:
Redesign a familiar non-verbal symbol, or devise a new one.

Exercise 10:
Design a new logo for a service or organization. Send it to the group's public relations officer; await a response.

Uses of symbols in painting

Meanings may be assigned to any pictorial image, through several related ideas.

Realism Representation of subject matter, so that the viewer reads the work as a mirror reflecting or a window opening onto a believable scene.

Symbolic Realism (**Fig. 15.30**) Imagery that evokes an illusion of reality, though the visual elements have been selected in order to make some larger statement, to symbolize some thing or quality outside themselves, even if we are not certain of that meaning.

Allegory (**Fig. 15.31**) Visual story-telling through an invented arrangement of figures and objects, spatially possible, visually believable; a symbolic representation of real or abstract qualities or personages.

Surrealism Juxtaposition of fantastic, incongruous elements unrelated to perspective, gravity, space/time or other considerations to suggest a dream world or an unreal spatial environment for symbolic or imaginative purposes. Surrealism is discussed in detail on p. 302 (See also **Figs. 3.1, 6.14**)

Symbolic realism

We may wonder at the meaning of the diverse objects arranged by Deborah Deichler, but we do not doubt that she could have seen them this way.

Paintings may be seen as realistic in treatment, symbolic in intent.

Allegory

Is Audrey Ushenko's painting of *Bacchus and Ariadne* (**Fig. 15.32**) an example of realism, its figures painted directly from the model? Or is it allegorical since they do not relate as in real life? Here the title tells the story.

In Harvey Dinnerstein's canvas (**Fig. 15.31**) figures and symbols relating to the social and political scene of the 1960s parade before us. How many can you identify?

Fig. 15.30 (*opposite*) **Deborah Deichler**, *Kumari*. Oil on masonite, $18\frac{1}{4} \times 23\frac{5}{8}$ ins (46×60 cm). Courtesy of the artist and the Maxwell Davidson Gallery.

Fig. 15.31 **Harvey Dinnerstein**, *Parade*, 1970–72. Oil on canvas, 74×153 ins (188×388.5 cm). Collection: Dr. and Mrs. Mohammad Khavari. Courtesy of the artist.

Fig. 15.32   (*left*) **Audrey Ushenko**, *Bacchus and Ariadne*, 1986. Oil on canvas, 36 × 42 ins (91.5 × 107 cm). Courtesy of the artist.

Fig. 15.33   (*right*) **Giorgio di Chirico**, *The Mystery and Melancholy of a Street*, 1914. Oil on canvas, 34¼ × 28⅛ ins (87 × 71 cm). Private Collection. Courtesy: Acquavella Galleries, Inc., New York.

Fig. 15.34   (*opposite, top left*) **René Magritte**, *Modele Rouge*, 1935. Oil on canvas, 22 × 18 ins (56 × 46 cm). Courtesy: Musée National d'Art Moderne, Centre Georges Pompidou, Paris.

Fig. 15.35   (*opposite, top right*) **Leonardo da Vinci**, *Drawing of a Bear's Hind Leg*, (*detail from the Notebooks*). Courtesy: Royal Library, Windsor Castle. © Her Majesty Queen Elizabeth II.

Fig. 15.36   (*opposite, bottom*) Jerry Uelsmann, *Untitled photograph*, 1987. Courtesy: the photographer.

A world that never was—Surrealism

Surrealism gives new meaning to the idea that "seeing is believing."

Surrealist devices and methods include:

Unreal scale or proportion of elements (**Fig. 3.1**);

Reversal of figure/ground, filling in what we expect to see empty; leaving empty forms we expect to see solid or filled in (white of eye becoming sky) (**Fig. 6.14**);

Juxtaposing parts of two gestalts, for example, a sky in daylight with the scene below at night or vice versa;

Lack of gravity, unsupported elements failing to fall (**Fig. 6.28**);

Blending or transition of forms, foot becoming boot, bottle becoming carrot, person becoming sculpture (**Fig. 15.34**);

Picturing of verbal image and vice versa, for example, painting of pipe reading "This is not a pipe" (**Fig. 1.4**);

Melted or distorted form, for example, soft, bent watches to suggest time/space in Dali's famous painting *The Persistence of Memory* (**Fig. 12.2**);

Sense of a dream world, empty, lonely, stretched space (**Figs. 15.33**);

Threatening or unreal objects, distorted creatures combining elements of several animal or human forms. (In da Vinci's drawing of a bear's hind leg (**Fig. 15.35**), the super-realism seems sur-real! Skillful rendering of detail heightens credibility, despite clues suggesting the impossibility of what is seen;)

Exaggerated weight or lightness of objects, distance or closeness, other time/space distortions. [11]

The suggestion that an image is derived from a dream or subconscious source may confer a neutral "no-fault" acceptability to a work. In Navajo ceremonial sandpaintings only dream-inspired designs are permitted.

Jerry Uelsmann's combined imagery, often with one large element in the foreground, brings together elements that could not co-exist in reality: photographic surrealism (**Fig. 15.36**).

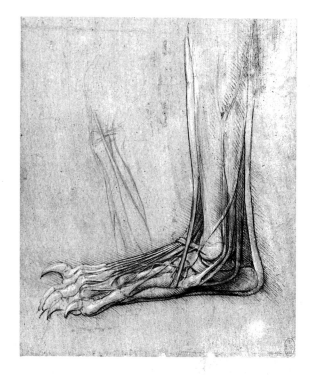

The "double-take" is a frequent surrealist feature. In Osterweil's *Monument Valley* (**Fig. 15.37**), a butterfly alights on a thistle before a distant landscape; then the flower is seen unsupported, floating in air. Suddenly, as in an optical illusion, the blossom recedes into deep space, reappearing above a now erupting crater (or an atomic cloud). Perhaps it is a thistle after all ... [12]

Symbolism without realism

Allegorical abstraction

Symbolism pervades Picasso's *Guernica* (**Fig. 11.22**), filling the canvas with many meanings for bull, horse and lightbulb—indeed every object, line and shape depicted. Mythology joins with national and art historical imagery in perhaps the richest visual statement of modern times, as a fusion of plastic, political, social and expressive meanings is achieved. Picasso himself said, "I used symbolism ... for the definite expression and solution of a problem ... The bull is ... brutality and darkness, the horse represents the people—the mural is symbolic ... allegoric."

Non-pictorial symbolism

Non-pictorial but specific symbolism is seen in **Fig. 15.38**, a painting within whose cruciform structure there are twenty-three shapes. The transparency is a geometric interpretation of the concept "one in three" and "three in one." It also forms a double-pointed *vesica pisces*, a symbol for the fish (Christianity). In the central floating rectangle (St Veronica's handkerchief), after-images can suggest the deity's face. All these connotations exist in a work consisting of geometric shapes and flat color.

How many non-pictorial symbols can you identify in Jack Bolen's "Egyptian" painting (**Fig. 15.39**)? [13]

Inventing a visual language

Non-verbal languages devised by artists communicate unspeakable but expressable

Fig. 15.37 (*left*) Suzanne Osterweil, *Monument Valley*, 1987. Oil on canvas, 40 × 30 ins (101.5 × 76 cm). Courtesy of the artist.
Fig. 15.38 (*right*) **Cynthia Dantzic**, *Homage to John XXIII*, 1977. Oil on canvas, 30 × 30 ins (76 × 76 cm).

Fig. 15.39 **Jack Bolen**, *Ptah-Hotep*, 1983. Oil on canvas, 44 × 40 ins (112 × 101.5 cm). Courtesy of the artist.

ideas. Arp, Klee and Magritte all use a "language of art ... expressed through symbols rather than in descriptive statements" (pp. 158, 284). Arp, particularly, uses "a new and universal alphabet of basic shapes ... [He] fashions his image of the world in fragmentary symbols." Rather than mirroring, abstracting or rearranging nature's elements or reducing them to geometry, there are those who, with Arp, "aspire to the spiritual, to a mystical reality." Arp cautions us that "reason separates us from nature."

Must imagery be symbolic?

Since all imagery may evoke subjective meanings, can there actually be any non-associative art or design? What of the efforts of Mondrian, Malevitch, Reinhardt, Albers, Le Witt, Anuszkiewicz and others (use the index) to achieve purely visual subject matter with its own non-object-related meanings and satisfactions, akin to pleasures derived from geometry and music? Can such an art, free of associative, other-than-art connotation, be possible, worthwhile, sufficient? Will your answer to this be the same as anyone else's? Perhaps art is at once the most universal and the most personal language of all. [14]

EXERCISES

Exercise 11:
Do at least one of the following:
 Add an "unrelated" element to a news-photo;
 Cut apart images in two unrelated photographs; reassemble as a new "fantastic" work;
 Create an imaginary insect or portrait using inanimate elements from magazines or junk mail;
 Depict a dream world in which ...

Exercise 12:
Design a "double-take" surrealist image, political or humorous. Collage is recommended.

Exercise 13:
Create an example of non-pictorial symbolism, using geometric forms and unmodulated color.

Exercise 14:
Compose a work "free of associative references." Ask friends to describe any associations they see. Expect to be surprised.

Subjects that matter

"Once more, with feeling"

"Every picture is a value judgment, since you can't represent a thing without proclaiming it to be worthwhile," says Susanne Langer. John Dewey feels: "Insufficient emotion shows itself in a coldly 'correct' product ... Excessive emotion obstructs the necessary elaboration and definition of parts." Powerful emotional expression is perhaps the most ancient force impelling many artists to produce and show their works.

Feelings of rage, fear, frustration, despair and lust find expression along with more joyous responses to sexuality and the lighter emotions of hope, humor and silliness. Satire shares many a wall with pathos and delight.

Fig. 15.40 Dik Browne, *Hagar the Horrible*, 10/14/1986. Reprinted by permission of King Features Syndicate.

Fig. 15.41 George Zimbel, *Marilyn Monroe and Billy Wilder during filming of "The Seven Year Itch,"* 1957. Gelatin-silver print. Courtesy: the photographer.

The naked or the nude?—eliciting sexual meanings

Sexual messages are surely among the most universal forms of evocative imagery, often more strongly received by the viewer than sent by the artist (**Fig. 15.40**), though sometimes it seems the other way around. Figurative images can be read as containing sexual implications regardless of dress (or its absence) and without consideration of the activity depicted or suggested. The critical factor seems to be the eye of the beholder, including cultural background, philosophy or religious precepts, lifestyle, experiences, knowledge of the history of art, sense of humor and other subjective criteria. This is evident when a visitor, entering a studio class, is flustered by the sight of a *naked* human being while the students calmly study the *nude* model.

Erotic art, obscenity and violence—evocative or provocative?

In distinguishing so-called pornography from erotic art, what roles do exploitation, coercion and violence play? To what extent should morality, ethics, legality or censorship be considered; are such topics appropriate for the studio or classroom? Define "good taste," "redeeming social value," "artistic license," "freedom of expression" and "freedom of speech" with regard to the arts. Just how evocative should society permit an artist's imagery to become? (Is this question itself a form of censorship?) Are joyous expressions of sexuality obscene (**Fig. 15.41**)?

Objections to violence, war and other social evils as the true obscenities have been raised by many artists in powerful, graphic art and illustration. Must "propaganda" have negative connotations; is one's position related to the issue being "sold?" How do you respond to the emotionally charged works shown in **Figs. 14.8, 14.9,** and **15.5**? Must subjective criteria affect your evaluation?

When allegorical works incorporate mythology, religious tradition or other sources to make a contemporary political or social statement, does the historical enrichment make their message more acceptable? Is it always possible to define the emotion expressed even if it is intensely felt by the artist and received with compelling, empathetic response?

Questioning the questions

Must the cultural and emotional background and intent of the viewer as well as the artist be considered in evaluating or attempting to understand a work? Consider the special meanings of *Revolution of the Viaduct* (**Fig. 15.42**). Is objectivity possible in evaluating the emotional content of any work?

Do questions of this nature produce answers or other questions; would you have it any other way?

A colorful note: The ability of color to evoke strong responses, paramount in visual expression, is discussed in Chapter 10.

Fig. 15.42 **Paul Klee**, *Revolution of the Viaduct*, 1937. Charcoal on cloth, $16\frac{3}{4} \times 16\frac{3}{8}$ ins (42.5 × 42 cm). Courtesy: The Solomon R. Guggenheim Museum. Photograph by Robert E. Mates.

Stimulating creativity

Eliciting one's muse—helping an accident to happen

In the search for new visual forms or fresh ways to inspire the "muse," artists often turn to various indirect methods to find creativity within themselves. No outside stimulants or artificial means are required to get one's imaginative juices flowing; indeed such methods are to be avoided as any resulting work will not reflect one's own self or powers.

An open-ended experimental attitude toward one's work is heartily encouraged. It can be rewarding to see what appears on your canvas or page without specific instructions from your conscious, directive self—as though you are somehow the medium through which a design or image appears.

Many methods may induce images one could not intentionally produce, raw material for further development or for enjoyment with no further enhancement.

Leonardo da Vinci sought inspiration in the markings and surface irregularities of walls; Dali studied blots, scribbles and "doodles" which he often developed into finished works. Here is Leonardo's "device for ... arousing the mind to various inventions ...: When you look at a wall spotted with stains, or with a mixture of stones ... you may discover a resemblance to various landscapes, beautified with mountains, rivers ... and these appear on such walls confusedly, like the sound of bells in whose jangle you may find any name or word you may choose to imagine." [15]

Techniques for coaxing spontaneity—the controlled accident

Many artists and teachers have developed methods of evoking imaginative images or of making marks to develop into finished works. Martin Ries surprises drawing students by having them empty a pencil sharpener container onto the page, then rub and blend the dust and shavings into an acceptable form before adding finishing strokes in pencil or ink. The works that result have a freedom and playfulness that might not have been attempted or revealed through carefully planned effort. Spontaneity (or its appearance) can be the result of hard work; ask any actor, musician, dancer or magician!

Arp and Schwitters cut up finished collages and drawings, letting the pieces fall "according to the laws of chance." Arp had an "extraordinary ability to scatter forms over a surface and ... turn the unexpected into the inevitable" (Robert Melville). This was part of his search for a truly "automatic art" in which the eye does not observe what the hand is doing or does not control its movements.

One interesting method for achieving this result is to place a drawing pad on one's lap (as a passenger) in a loosely sprung automobile on irregular or country roads, lightly holding a pen or pencil just above the page. It is not necessary to observe the progress of the design being produced (**Fig. 15.44**). [16]

Calligraphers produce automatic designs as they shake excess ink onto a scrap sheet or "try" a pen. Photographic retouchers or spotters make undirected designs filling scraps of paper with these try-marks. Such works can be left as they occur or developed according to the fancy of their inadvertent creator. [17]

Use of the palimpsest (partially effaced or layered image) as the basis of a new work is seen in contemporary photography, collage and other art. The sequential monoprint, developed from a single image, is a good example. Is décollage a special use of the palimpsest?

Other contained or controlled accidents (inkblots, blown inkdrops, squashed forms such as gloves, cans, cartons, even tie-dyeing) involve allowing a non- or minimally directed situation to create a design. The famous Rorschach inkblots have been used since the 1930s by psychologists to study responses of the viewer. Subjects see hostile, menacing imagery, sexual symbols or shapes with few association to objects or living forms; some find an unending richness of forms in the background areas as well as the inkblot. Each response suggests traits of personality or psychological make-up to the trained analyst.

Seeking and finding a composition

A framing window may help you to compose within a larger design. Cut a window in a mat board, 3 by 5 inches, 5 by 8 inches or 8 by 13 inches (refer to the Golden Mean [Fig. 3.4]) for editing portions of your environment—natural, architectural, unintentional or designed. Your composition may be photographed, used as a basis for a drawn, painted or collaged study, even displayed as a found image.

On the other hand

Artists such as Ben Shahn are "generally distrustful of contrived situations, peculiarly set up to favor the blossoming of art." Albers opposes the idea of chance and accident in art: "To design is to plan and organize in order to relate and to control. In short it embraces all means opposing disorder and accident ..." Even works which have the look of spontaneity may be carefully controlled; fashion photographer Steven Meisel says of his active, energetic work, "There is not one millimeter of spontaneity in it."

Adding your own dimension

Our primary concern has been to develop awareness of the unique qualities of the individual and the responsibility that accompanies this realization, the obligation to develop one's abilities, fully. No one else can do it *your* way, or add your particular dimension to the history of the visual experience.

The scribble experiment

For this experiment, more participants will produce more dramatic results. Copy or trace a curvilinear, closed scribble (**Fig. 15.43**), so that each participant starts with the identical shape; then develop it, unseen by other participants, as the scribble itself

Fig. 15.43   Scribble "theme." Black crayon on tracing paper, traced individually for each participant.

Fig. 15.44   Controlled accidents.

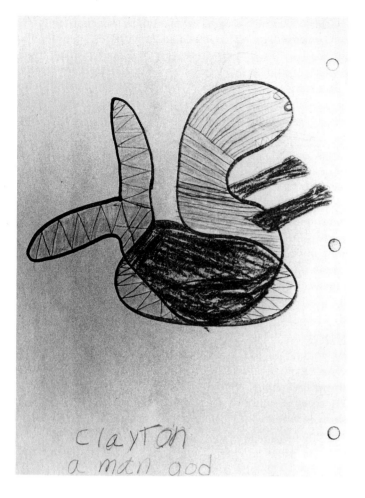

clayTon
a man aod

This is a man

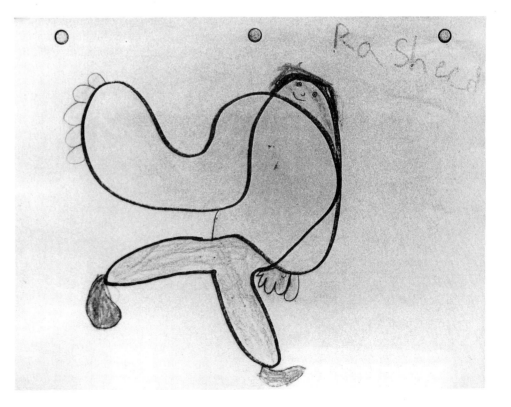

Rasheed

Fig. 15.45 Scribble "developments" by children ages 7 to 9.

Fig. 15.46 **Henri Cartier-Bresson**, *Spain 1936*. Gelatin-silver print. Courtesy: Magnum Photos.

seems to suggest, pictorially or in an abstract way. Use crayons, markers or collage. Hold the page in each of its four possible orientations, allowing the view which is to be ''up'' to reveal itself. Make no special attempt at originality or at creativity.

Allowing the scribble itself to direct the activity, each participant feels free of responsibility for the choices made. Generally everyone expects the entire group to ''see'' the same subject and is surprised to discover no two alike. The range of subjects is enhanced by the size of the group. Skill and art ability have little bearing on the results. (These examples were done by second graders.) As a means of demonstrating to a group the importance and unique nature of each individual's participation and imagination, such an experiment is invaluable. It may be undertaken at a meeting of any group concerned with creativity of the individual.

Never the end

How important is it to plan the meaning of every image one makes? Since each work calls forth a unique response in every viewer, is this always a reasonable goal? Doesn't each viewer respond, even to the same work, differently at different times and under differing circumstances? (**Fig. 15.46**).

Review this volume, restudying images that evoked strong thoughts or feelings, to discover qualities previously unnoted. Are you less sure about your responses or more certain? Come back from time to time, to discover growth in your criteria, tastes and understanding of the visual experience, within the continually expanding dimensions of design. Exercise your skills, memory, invention, and wit. This is a lifelong, continuing process. There is never an end.

EXERCISES

Exercise 15:
Set up an environment to produce a work ''according to the laws of accident or chance,'' by allowing undirected markings and designs to occur, finding random imagery and unplanned pattern, or identifying visual structure in so-called chaos.

Exercise 16:
Create a five-minute or a two-hour automatic drawing on a bumpy automobile ride.

Exercise 17:
Try an automatic spot or blot design, or visit a studio to rescue such a work.

BIBLIOGRAPHY

Numbers in **bold** appearing at the end of each entry refer to the following categories:

1 Artists, Periods, Styles
2 Calligraphy, Lettering
3 Children's Books
4 Color
5 Computer Art
6 Concrete Poetry
7 Creativity, Perception
8 Design Texts
9 Geometry and Art
10 Ideas, Philosophy of Art
11 Line, Drawing
12 Panoramics
13 Photography
14 Printmaking, Special Techniques
15 Recycled Imagery, Copier Art
16 Systems, Structure
17 Tribal Art, "Primitivism"

Albers, Josef, *Despite Straight Lines*. New Haven, Connecticut: Yale University Press, 1961. **11, 7**

Albers, Josef, *Interaction of Color*. New Haven, Connecticut: Yale University Press, 1963. Paperback with unabridged text and selected plates, 1975. **4**

Allen, Louis A., *Time before Morning: Art and Myth of the Australian Aborigines*. New York: Thomas Y. Crowell Company, 1975. **17**

Alloway, Lawrence, *Topics in American Art since 1945*. New York: W. W. Norton & Co., Inc., 1975. **10, 1**

Anderson, Donald M., *Elements of Design*. New York: CBS Publishing, 1961. **8**

Arthur, John, *Realists at Work*. New York: Watson–Guptill, 1983. **1**

Ashton, Dore, Ed., *Twentieth Century Artists on Art*. New York: Pantheon Books, 1985. **1**

Baker, Arthur, *Historical Calligraphic Alphabets*. New York: Dover Publications Inc., 1980. **2**

Barnes, Albert C., *The Art in Painting*. New York: Harcourt, Brace and Company, 1937. **10**

Barnett, Lincoln, *The Universe and Dr. Einstein*. New York: Mentor Books/The American Library of World Literature, 1954. **9**

Bataille, Georges, *Lascaux or the Birth of Art*. New York: Skira, Inc., Publishers, 1955. **17**

Battcock, Gregory, Ed., *The New Art*. New York: E. P. Dutton & Co., Inc., 1973. **1, 10**

Bayer, Herbert, Walter and Ise Gropius, Ed., *Bauhaus 1919–1928*. New York: The Museum of Modern Art, 1986. **1**

Beerman, Miriam, *The Enduring Beast*. New York: Doubleday & Company, Inc., 1972. **3, 11**

Behrens, Roy R., *Art and Camouflage: Concealment and Deception in Nature, Art and War*. Cedar Falls, Iowa: North American Review, University of Northern Iowa, 1981. **10, 7**

Behrens, Roy R., *Design in the Visual Arts*. Englewood Cliffs, New Jersey: Prentice-Hall, Inc., 1984. **8**

Bell, Ione, Karen M. Hess and Jim R. Matison, *Art As You See It*. New York: John Wiley & Sons, 1979. **8**

Belting, Natalia, *The Stars are Silver Reindeer*. New York: Holt Rinehart Winston, 1966. **3, 11**

Benson, John Howard, *The First Writing Book, Arrighi's Operina*. London: Oxford University Press, and New Haven, Connecticut: Yale University Press, 1955. **2**

Betti, Claudia and Teel Sale, *Drawing – A Contemporary Approach*. New York: Holt Rinehart Winston, 1980. **11**

Bevlin, Marjorie Elliot, *Design through Discovery*. New York: Holt Rinehart Winston, 1980. **8**

Birren, Faber, *Color Perception in Art*. West Chester, Pennsylvania: Schiffer Publishing Co., 1986. **4**

Bishop, Robert and Elizabeth Safanda, *A Gallery of Amish Quilts: Design Diversity from a Plain People*. New York: E. P. Dutton & Co., Inc., 1976. **1, 9**

Boas, Franz, *Primitive Art* (Originally 1927). New York: Dover Publications, 1955. **17**

Bossom, Naomi, *A Scale Full of Fish, and other Turnabouts*. New York: Greenwillow Books, 1979. **3, 14**

Bourke, Linda, *Hand Made ABC*. New York: Addison Wesley Publishing Company, 1981. **3, 2**

Bro, Lu, *Drawing, A Studio Guide*. New York: W. W. Norton & Company, 1978. **11**

Cairns, Phyllis, *Floating Heads: A Contemporary Visual Narrative*. Newtown, Connecticut: Pembroke Press, 1986. **15**

Castelman, Riva, *Prints of the Twentieth Century: A History*. New York: The Museum of Modern Art, 1976. **14**

Chaet, Bernard, *The Art of Drawing*. New York: Holt Rinehart Winston, 1983. **11**

Cheatham, Frank, Jane Hart Cheatham and Sheryl Haler Owens, *Design Concepts and Applications*. Englewood Cliffs, New Jersey: Prentice-Hall, Inc., 1983. **8**

Clark, Marcia, *The World is Round, Contemporary Panoramas*. Yonkers, New York: The Hudson River Museum, 1987. **12**

Coe, Ralph T., *Sacred Circles, 2000 Years of North American Indian Art*. London: Arts Council of Great Britain, 1976. **17**

Coke, Van Deren, *The Painter and the Photograph, from Delacroix to Warhol*. Albuquerque, New Mexico: University of New Mexico Press, 1972. **13, 15**

Collier, Graham, *Form, Space and Vision – An Introduction to Drawing and Design*. Englewood Cliffs, New Jersey: Prentice-Hall, Inc., 1985. **8, 11**

Cowan, Paul and Rachel Cowan, *A Torah is Written*. Philadelphia: The Jewish Publication Society, 1986. **3, 2**

Cowart, Jack, Jack D. Flam, Dominique Fourcade and John Hallmark Neff, *Henri Matisse: Paper Cut-Outs*. New York: Harry N. Abrams, Inc., 1977. **1**

Critchlow, Keith, *Islamic Patterns: An Analytical and Cosmological Approach*. New York: Schocken Books, 1976. **9, 1**

Daix, Pierre, *Cubists and Cubism*. New York: Rizzoli International Publications, Inc., 1982. **1**

Dalton, Stephen, *Borne on the Wind, the Extraordinary World of Insects in Flight*. London: Chatto & Windus, 1975. **13**

Dantzic, Cynthia, *Sounds of Silents*. Englewood Cliffs, New Jersey: Prentice-Hall, Inc., 1976. **3, 2**

Dantzic, Cynthia, *Stop Dropping BreAdcrumBs on My YaCht: A Silent ABC*. Englewood Cliffs, New Jersey: Prentice-Hall, Inc., 1974. **3, 2**

Davidson, Gail S., *Drawing the Fine Line: Discovering European Drawings in Long Island Private Collections*. Brookville, New York: Hillwood Art Gallery, Long Island University, C. W. Post Campus, 1986. **11**

De La Croix, Horst and Richard G. Tansey, Ed., *Gardner's Art through the Ages, 8th Edition*. New York: Harcourt Brace Jovanovich, 1986. **8**

Dewey, John, *Art as Experience*. New York: Capricorn Books, G. P. Putnam's Sons, 1958. **10**

Doczi, Gyorgy, *The Power of Limits – Proportional Harmonies in Nature, Art and Architecture*. Boston: Shambhala Publications, 1981. **9**

Driskell, David C., *Two Centuries of Black American Art*. New York: Alfred A. Knopf, 1976. 1

Dürer, Albrecht, *Of the Just Shaping of Letters* (Originally 1525). New York: Dover Publications, Inc., 1965. 2

Edgerton, Harold E. and James R. Killian, Jr., *Moments of Vision, the Stroboscopic Revolution in Photography*. Cambridge, Massachusetts: The MIT Press, 1979. 13

Edkins, Diana, *Panoramic Photography*. New York: Grey Art Gallery and Study Center, New York University Faculty of Arts and Sciences, 1977. 12, 13

Education of an Architect: A Point of View. New York: The Cooper Union School of Art and Architecture, 1971. 10, 16

Edwards, Robert, Ed., *Aboriginal Art in Australia*. Sydney, Australia: Ure Smith, 1978. 17

Ehrenzweig, Anton, *The Hidden Order of Art*. Berkeley, California: University of California Press, 1967. 11

Elderfield, John, *Fauvism and its Affinities*. New York: The Museum of Modern Art, 1976. 1

Elderfield, John, *The Modern Drawing*. New York: The Museum of Modern Art, 1983. 11

Fairbank, Alfred, *A Book of Scripts*. London: Faber and Faber Ltd., 1977. 2

The Family of Man. New York: The Museum of Modern Art, 1955. 13

Feldman, Edmund Burke, *Varieties of Visual Experience*. New York: Harry N. Abrams, Inc., 1981. 9

Fisher, Leonard Everett, *The Homemakers*. Philadelphia, PA: Colonial American Craftsmen Series, Franklin Watts, 1973. 3, 11

Franke, Herbert W., *Computer Graphics, Computer Art*. London: Phaidon Press Ltd., 1971. 5, 15

Frasconi, Antonio, *Against the Grain*. New York: Macmillan Publishing Co. Inc., 1974. 14

Frasconi, Antonio, *See and Say, Guarda e Parla, Regarde et Parle, Mira y Habla, A Picture Book in Four Languages*. New York: Harcourt, Brace and Company, 1955. 3, 14

Galassi, Peter, *Before Photography: Painting and the Invention of Photography*. New York: The Museum of Modern Art, 1982. 10, 13

Gardner, Martin, *The Annotated Alice (Alice's Adventures in Wonderland & Through the Looking Glass*. New York: Clarkson N. Potter, Inc., 1960. 3, 11

Geldzahler, Henry, *American Painting in the 20th Century*. New York: Metropolitan Museum of Art, 1965. 1

Geometric Abstraction in America. New York: Whitney Museum of American Art, 1962. 1, 9

Ghiselin, Brewster, Ed., *The Creative Process, A Symposium*. New York: Mentor Books/The New American Library of World Literature, 1952. 8, 10

Ghyka, Matila, *The Geometry of Art and Life*. New York: Dover Publications Inc., 1977. 9

Gillon, Edmund Vincent, Jr., *Early New England Gravestone Rubbings*. New York: Dover Publications, Inc., 1966. 14, 15

Goldstein, Nathan, *The Art of Responsive Drawing*. Englewood Cliffs, New Jersey: Prentice-Hall, Inc., 1984. 11

Goldwater, Robert and Marco Treves, Ed., *Artists on Art from the XIV to the XX Century*. New York: Pantheon Books, a Division of Random House, 1972. 10

Gombrich, Ernst H., *Art and Illusion*. Princeton, New Jersey: Princeton University Press, 1969. 7

Gordon, Robert and Andrew Forge, *Monet*. New York: Harry N. Abrams, Inc., 1983. 1

Gray, Donald J., Ed., *Alice in Wonderland by Lewis Carroll*, A Norton Critical edition. New York: W. W. Norton & Company, 1971. 3, 11

Haas, Robert Bartlett, *Muybridge, Man in Motion*. Berkeley, California; University of California Press, 1976. 1, 13

Haley, Gail E., *Go Away, Stay Away*. New York: Charles Scribner's Sons, 1977. 3, 14

Hambidge, Jay, *The Elements of Dynamic Symmetry*. New York: Dover Publications Inc., 1967. 9

Harris, Ann Sutherland, and Linda Nochlin, *Women Artists: 1550–1950*. New York: Alfred A. Knopf, 1977. 1

Harris, Mary Emma, *The Arts at Black Mountain College*. Cambridge, Massachusetts: The MIT Press, 1987. 1, 10

Haverkamp-Begemann, Egbert, *Creative Copies, Interpretative Drawings from Michelangelo to Picasso*. New York: Philip Wilson Publishers and The Drawing Center, 1988. 11, 15

Hoban, Tana, *I Read Symbols*. New York: Greenwillow Books, 1983. 3, 16

Hobbs, Jack A., *Art in Context*. New York: Harcourt Brace Jovanovich, 1979. 8, 10

Hofstadter, Douglas R., *Gödel, Escher, Bach: An Eternal Golden Braid*. New York: Vintage Books/Random House, Inc., 1980. 10, 9

Holden, Alan, *Shapes, Spaces, Symmetry*. New York: Columbia University Press, 1971. 9

Holstein, Jonathan, *Abstract Design in American Quilts*. New York: The Whitney Museum of American Art, 1971. 1, 9

Holstein, Jonathan, *The Pieced Quilt, an American Design Tradition*. Greenwich, Connecticut: The New York Graphic Society, Ltd., 1973. 1, 9

Holt, Michael, *Mathematics in Art*. New York: Van Nostrand Reinhold Company, 1971. 9

Huntley, H. E., *The Divine Proportion – A Study in Mathematical Beauty*. New York: Dover Publications, Inc., 1970. 9

Hupka, Robert, *Michelangelo: Pieta*. New York: Crown Publishers, Inc., 1979. 1, 13

The Instant It Happened. New York: The Associated Press, 1975. 13

Irwin, John Rice, *A People and Their Quilts*. Exton, Pennsylvania: Schiffer Publishing Ltd., 1983. 1, 9

The ISCA Quarterly. New York: The International Society of Copier Artists, Ltd., any Volume. 15

Ivins, William M., Jr., *Art and Geometry – A Study in Space Intuitions*. New York: Dover Publications, Inc., 1964. 9

Janson, H. W., *History of Art*. Englewood Cliffs, New Jersey: Prentice-Hall, Inc. and Harry N. Abrams, Inc., 1986. 1, 8

Jonas, Ann, *Round Trip*. New York: Greenwillow Books, 1983. 3, 7

Jopling, Carol F., Ed., *Art and Aesthetics in Primitive Societies*. New York: E. P. Dutton Inc., 1971. 10, 17

Jussim, Estelle and Gus Kayafas, *Stopping Time, the Photographs of Harold Edgerton*. New York: Harry N. Abrams, Inc., 1987. 13, 1

Kahlenberg, Mary Hunt and Anthony Berlant, *The Navajo Blanket*. New York: Praeger Publishers, Inc., 1972. 17, 16

Kandinsky, Wassily, *Point and Line to Plane*. New York: Dover Publications, Inc., 1979. 11, 10

Kanizsa, Gaetano, *Organization in Vision, Essays on Gestalt Perception*, New York: Praeger Publishers, 1979. 7

Kaupelis, Robert, *Learn to Draw*. New York: Watson-Guptill Publications, 1972. 11

Kepes, Gyorgy, Ed., *Language of Vision*. Chicago: Paul Theobald & Co., 1964. 10, 8

Kepes, Gyorgy, Ed., *The Module, Proportion, Symmetry and Rhythm*. New York: George Braziller, 1966. 9, 10

Kepes, Gyorgy, Ed., *Sign, Image, Symbol*. New York: George Braziller, 1966. 10, 16

Klee, Paul, *Pedagogical Sketchbook*. London: Faber & Faber, 1953. 11, 10

Knobler, Nathan, *The Visual Dialogue*. New

York: Holt Rinehart Winston, 1980. **8, 1**

Kramer, Hilton, *The Age of the Avant-Garde.* Farrar, Straus and Giroux, 1973. **1, 10**

Krukowski, Lucian, *Art and Concept; a Philosophical Study.* Amherst, Massachusetts: University of Massachusetts Press, 1987. **10**

Langer, Susanne K., Ed., *Reflections on Art.* Baltimore, Maryland: Johns Hopkins University Press, 1958. **10**

Lawlor, Robert, *Sacred Geometry, Philosophy and Practice.* New York: Crossroad Publishing Co., 1982. **9, 10**

Levi-Strauss, Claude, *Structural Anthropology.* New York: Anchor Books, 1967. **10, 17**

Lewis, John and Peter Rigby, *The Chinese Word for Horse and Other Stories.* New York: Schocken Books, 1980. **3, 2**

Le Witt, Sol, *Four Basic Kinds of Straight Lines.* London: Studio International, 1969. **11, 16**

Lieberman, William S., Ed., *Art of the Twenties.* New York: The Museum of Modern Art, 1979. **1**

Lipman, Jean, *Provocative Parallels.* New York: E. P. Dutton & Co., Inc., 1975. **10, 15**

Lippard, Lucy, *Pop Art.* New York: Oxford University Press, 1973. **1**

Loeb, Arthur L., *Space Structures, Their Harmony and Counterpoint.* Reading, Massachusetts: Addison-Wesley Publishing Co., Inc., 1976. **9**

Lord, E. A. and C. B. Wilson, *The Mathematical Description of Shape and Form.* New York: Halsted/John Wiley & Sons, 1984. **9**

Lowry, Bates, *The Visual Experience, An Introduction to Art.* New York: Harry N. Abrams, Inc., 1967. **8**

Lucie-Smith, Edward, *Late Modern, the Visual Arts since 1945.* New York: Frederick A. Praeger, 1971. **1, 10**

MacGillavry, Caroline H., *Escher-Fantasy Symmetry, The Periodic Drawings of M. C. Escher.* New York: Harry N. Abrams, Inc., 1976. **1, 16**

Maddow, Ben, *Edward Weston, His Life and Photographs.* New York: Aperture, Inc., 1979. **1, 13**

Mandelbrot, Benoit, *The Fractal Geometry of Nature.* New York: W. H. Freeman & Co., 1982. **4**

Matthaei, *Goethe's Color Theory* (Originally 1790). Translated by Herb Aach. New York: Van Nostrand Reinhold Co., 1970. **4**

Miller, Joni K. and Lowry Thompson, *The Rubber Stamp Album.* New York: Workman Publishing, 1978. **14**

Muybridge, Eadweard, *Human and Animal Locomotion* (Originally 1887). New York: Dover Publications, Inc., 1979. **13, 1**

Nicolaides, Kimon, *The Natural Way to Draw.* Boston: Houghton Mifflin Company, 1941. **11**

Norman, Jane, Margit Echols and Stef Stahl, *Patterns East and West, an Introduction to Pattern in Art for Teachers with Slides and Materials.* New York: The Metropolitan Museum of Art, 1986. **1, 9**

O'Brien, James F., *Design by Accident.* New York: Dover Publications, Inc., 1968. **8, 14**

Ocvirk, Otto G. *et al.*, *Art Fundamentals, Theory and Practice.* Dubuque, Iowa; William C. Brown Publishers, 1968. **8**

Pedoe, Dan, *Geometry and the Visual Arts.* New York: Dover Publications, Inc., 1983. **9**

Pellegrini, Aldo, *New Tendencies in Art.* New York: Crown Publishers, Inc., 1966. **10, 1**

Peterdi, Gabor, *Printmaking.* New York: Macmillan Company, 1959. **14**

Pilon, A. Barbara, *Concrete is Not Always Hard.* Middletown, Connecticut: Xerox Educational Publications, 1972. **6**

Pintauro, Joseph/Corita Kent, *To Believe in Man.* New York: Harper & Row, 1970. **2, 14**

Preble, Duane, *Artforms.* New York: Harper and Row, 1985. **8**

Prisse d'Avennes, Achille, *Arabic Art in Color* (Originally 1877 and 1885). New York: Dover Publications, Inc., 1978. **1, 9**

Protter, Eric, Ed., *Painters on Painting.* New York: Grosset & Dunlap, 1963. **10, 1**

Quong, Rose, *Chinese Written Characters, Their Wit and Wisdom.* New York: Cobble Hill Press, 1968. **2**

Richardson, John Adkins, Floyd W. Coleman and Michael J. Smith, *Basic Design-Systems, Elements, Applications.* Englewood Cliffs, New Jersey: Prentice-Hall, Inc., 1984. **8**

Romano, Clare and John Ross, *The Complete Printmaker.* New York: Free Press, 1972. **14**

Rose, Bernice, *Jackson Pollock: Works on Paper.* New York: The Museum of Modern Art, 1969. **1, 11**

Rowell, Margit, *The Planar Dimension.* New York: Solomon R. Guggenheim Foundation, 1979. **1, 10**

Rubin, William, Ed., *"Primitivism" in 20th Century Art.* New York: The Museum of Modern Art, 1984. **17, 1**

Rubin, William, *Dada, Surrealism, and Their Heritage.* New York: The Museum of Modern Art, 1968. **1**

Rucker, Rudolf V. B., *Geometry, Relativity and the Fourth Dimension.* New York: Dover Publications Inc., 1977. **9**

Russell, Frank D., *Picasso's Guernica.* Montclair, New Jersey: Allanheld, Osmun & Co., 1980. **1**

Russell, John, *The Meanings of Modern Art.* New York: Harper and Row, 1981. **10, 1**

Saff, Donald and Deli Sacilotto, *Printmaking, History and Process.* New York: Holt Rinehart Winston, 1978. **14**

Schmalenbach, Werner, *Kurt Schwitters.* New York: Harry N. Abrams, Inc., 1967. **1**

Schwartz, Paul Waldo, *Cubism.* New York: Praeger/Holt Rinehart Winston, 1971. **1**

Scott, Robert Gillam, *Design Fundamentals.* Huntington, New York: Robert E. Krieger Publishing Company, 1980. **8**

Seitz, William C., *The Responsive Eye.* New York: The Museum of Modern Art, 1965. **1, 7**

Seuphor, Michel, *Piet Mondrian, Life and Work.* New York: Harry N. Abrams, Inc., 1974. **1**

Shahn, Ben, *The Shape of Content.* New York: Alfred A. Knopf, Inc. and Random House, 1957. **10**

Shaw, Paul, *Letterforms, an Introductory Manual of Calligraphy, Lettering and Type.* New York: Paul Shaw/Letter Design, 1986. **2**

Sloan, John, *Gist of Art: Principles and Practise Expounded in the Classroom and Studio* (Originally 1939). New York: Dover Publications, Inc., 1967. **10**

Snelson, Kenneth, *The Nature of Structure.* New York: The New York Academy of Sciences, 1989. **16, 9**

Spies, Warner, *Max Ernst – Frottages.* London: Thames and Hudson, 1986. **14, 15**

Steig, William, *CDB.* New York: Simon & Schuster, 1968. **3, 2**

Stevens, Harold, *Transfer: Designs, Textures and Images.* Worcester, Massachusetts: Davis Publishers, Inc., 1974. **14, 15**

Strand, Mark, Ed., *Art of the Real, Nine American Figurative Painters.* New York: Clarkson N. Potter, 1983. **1**

Svaren, Jacqueline, *Written Letters, 22 Alphabets for Calligraphers.* Freeport, Maine: The Bond Wheelwright Company, 1978. **2**

Sweet, Belinda, *Zen Paintings, 17th Century to the Present.* Belinda Sweet, Kensington, California, 1982. **2, 11**

Swirnoff, Lois, *Dimensional Color.* Boston: Birkhauser Boston, Inc., 1989. **4**

Szarkowski, John, *Mirrors and Windows.* New York: The Museum of Modern Art, 1978. **13**

Thompson, D'Arcy, *On Growth and Form.*

BIBLIOGRAPHY

Cambridge, England: Cambridge University Press, 1961 (Ed. 1977). **9, 10**

Thompson, Ruth D'Arcy Wentworth, *D'Arcy Wentworth Thompson, The Scholar-Naturalist*. London: Oxford University Press, 1958. **9, 16**

Treasures of Tutankhamun. London: Thames and Hudson Ltd., 1972. **1**

Troy, Nancy J., *Mondrian and Neoplasticism in America*. New Haven, Connecticut: Yale University Art Gallery, 1979. **1, 16**

Ungerer, Tomi, *Snail, Where Are You?* New York: Harper & Row, 1962. **3, 9**

Van Der Marck, Jan, and Charlotta Kotik, *Francois Morellet: Systems*. Buffalo, New York: Albright-Knox Art Gallery, 1985. **1, 16**

Vernon, P.E., *Creativity*. Hammondsworth, England: Penguin Books Ltd., 1973. **7**

Wadeson, Harriet, Jean Durkin and Dorine Perach, Ed., *Advances in Art Therapy*. New York: John Wiley & Sons, 1989. **10, 7**

Wang, Chi-Yuan, *Essentials of Chinese Calligraphy*. New York: Grosset & Dunlap, 1974. **2**

Weber, Nicholas Fox, *The Drawings of Josef Albers*. New Haven, Connecticut: Yale University Press, 1984. **1, 11**

Weyl, Hermann, *Symmetry*. Princeton, New Jersey: Princeton University Press, 1982. **9**

Whelan, Richard, *Double Take, a Comparative Look at Photographs*. New York: Clarkson N. Potter, Inc., 1981. **13, 8**

Whitehead, Alfred North, *The Aims of Education*. New York: The Macmillan Company, 1961. **10**

Wiese, Kurt, *You Can Write Chinese*. New York: Viking Press, 1945. **2**

Wilson, Richard Albert, *The Miraculous Birth of Language*. London: J. M. Dent & Sons, Ltd., 1937. **10, 7**

Young, Frank M., *Visual Studies – A Foundation for Artists and Designers*. Englewood Cliffs, New Jersey; Prentice-Hall, Inc., 1985. **8**

Zelanski, Paul and Mary Pat Fisher, *Color*. New Jersey: Prentice-Hall, Inc., Englewood Cliffs, 1989. **4**

CREDITS

The author would like to thank the following students who took part in the C.W. Post College Spring 1989 Color Workshop: Andreas Appios, Lorine Bamberg, Christopher Bell, John Cavanagh, Drafus Chow, Emilia Constandinou, GinaMarie Defabbio, Susan DePhillips, Laura Ellis, Alyssa Finkelstein, Michael Haspel, Heejung Kim, Stacy Klein, Elizabeth Luptak, Stacy Mangione, Christine McCutcheon, Suzanne McRoberts, Michael Pavone, Mark Pencek, Jennifer Sauer, Tegwyn Stockdale.

The Publishers and author would like to thank the following for permission to reproduce their photographs in this book:
Apogee Airway 15.21; Jacob Burckhardt 1.12; Cynthia Dantzic 0.8, 0.9, 1.13, 1.29, 1.34, 2.5, 2.14, 2.19, 2.31, 3.21, 4.4, 4.10, 5.22, 6.3, 6.6, 7.2, 7.14, 10.9, 13.3; Jerry Dantzic 1.5, 1.16, 1.21, 2.7, 2.18, 4.7, 5.18, 5.45, 6.2, 6.3, 7.7, 8.23, 11.21a, 12.12, 13.1, 13.6, 13.9, 13.13, 14.12, 14.15, 14.19, 14.20, 15.38, 15.45; P. A. Ferrazzini 8.21; MAH Geneve 2.2; Bruce Gilbert 5.33; Lucian Krukowski 4.11; Steve Lopez 8.1; Robert E. Mates 9.16, 15.42; Otto E. Nelson 2.46; James Nightlinger 4.15, 5.30, 13.21, 13.22, 13.23; Kevin Ryan for A.E. Gallery 1.18.

The following illustrations are © VAGA New York, 1989: 0.11 Roy Lichtenstein, 1.7 Antonio Frasconi, 1.9 Roy Lichtenstein, 1.18 Al Held, 1.40 Antonio Frasconi, 2.1 Piet Mondrian, 3.3 Jacques Lipchitz, 4.12 Tom Wesselmann, 5.13 Roy Lichtenstein, 5.47 Roy Lichtenstein, 6.7 Ben Shahn, 6.12 Piet Mondrian, 6.22 Will Barnet, 6.24 Richard Anuszkiewicz, 7.8 Jasper Johns, 8.9 Robert Motherwell, 8.12a Piet Mondrian, 8.12b Piet Mondrian, 8.12c Piet Mondrian, 8.12d Piet Mondrian, 8.12e Piet Mondrian, 8.12f Piet Mondrian, 8.13 Piet Mondrian, 9.11 Ken Noland, 9.13 Richard Anuszkiewicz, 9.15 Jasper Johns, 10.3 Jacob Lawrence, 11.21c Kathe Kollwitz, 11.23 George Grosz, 13.1 Ilya Bolotowsky, 13.19 James Rosenquist, 14.11 Robert Rauschenberg, 14.17 Larry Rivers, 14.21 Jasper Johns, 14.23 Larry Rivers, 15.33 Giorgio de Chirico.

The following illustrations are © ARS N.Y./SPADEM, 1989:
3.25 Juan Gris, *The Watch*, 4.1 Edouard Vuillard, *Seated Girl*, 5.5 Pablo Picasso, *Lady with a Fan*, 5.10 André Masson *Haystacks*, 5.39 Pablo Picasso, *Bread and Fruit Dish on a Table*, 5.41 Juan Gris, *Le Siphon*, 6.9 Pablo Picasso, *Le Chef d'Oeuvre Inconnu*, 6.31 Pablo Picasso, *Still Life with Chair Caning*, 8.17 Pablo Picasso, *The Bull*, 8.20 Pablo Picasso, *Les Demoiselles d'Avignon*, 8.25 Fernand Leger, costume design for "The Creation of the World", 10.1 Kees van Dongen, *Modjesko, Soprano Singer*, 11.10 Juan Gris, *Still Life*, 11.22 Pablo Picasso, *Guernica*, 14.7 Juan Gris, *Woman with a Mandolin (after Corot)*, 14.8 Pablo Picasso, *Profile of Anguished Female Face*, 14.9 Pablo Picasso, *Guernica* detail, 14.30 Pablo Picasso, *Luncheon on the Grass (after Manet)*.

The following illustrations are © ARS N.Y./ADAGP, 1989:
2.44 Marc Chagall, *Self-Portrait with Grimace*, 3.20 Jean Metzinger, *Tea Time*, 3.26 Wassily Kandinsky, *Improvisation #30*, 5.40 Robert Delaunay, *Rhythm*, 6.23 Georges Braque, *Violin and Pipe*, 8.4 Jean Dubuffet, *The Cow with the Subtile Nose*, 8.5 Robert Delaunay, *The Eiffel Tower*, 8.16a Jean Arp, *Leaves and Navels*, 8.16b Jean Arp, *Skeleton and Moustache*, 8.29 Jean Arp, *Leaves and Navels* detail, 12.13 Marcel Duchamp, *Nude Descending a Staircase*, 15.22 Marc Chagall, *The Musician*.

The following illustrations are © ARS N.Y./COSMOPRESS, 1989:
1.17 Paul Klee, *Lines*, 5.8 Paul Klee, *She Bellows, We Play*, 8.19 Paul Klee, poster for "Comedians", 9.4 Kurt Schwitters, *Merzbild* (Entrance ticket collage), 14.3 Kurt Schwitters, *For Kate*, 14.24 Kurt Schwitters, *Bussum, bussum, bussum*, 15.4 Paul Klee, *Mural from the Temple of Longing Thither*, 15.42 Paul Klee, *Revolution of the Viaduct*.

The following illustrations are © SUCCESSION H. MATISSE/ARS N.Y., 1989:
0.7 Henri Matisse, *The Lagoon*, 1.27 Henri Matisse, *Pasiphae, Chant de Minos*, 3.6 Henri Matisse, design for proposed iron-work grille door, 4.8 Henri Matisse, *The Back III*, 5.29 Henri Matisse, *Blue Nude (Souvenir de Biskra)*, 6.25 Henri Matisse, *Ivy in Flower*, 7.9 Henri Matisse, *The Dance II*, 11.31 Henri Matisse, *The Window at Collieurs*, 12.15 Henri Matisse, *The Bees*, 12.24 Henri Matisse, *The Dance*.

The following illustrations are © C. HERSCOVICI/ARS N.Y., 1989:
1.4 René Magritte, *La Trahison des Images*, 3.1 René Magritte, *Delusions of Grandeur*, 6.14 René Magritte, *The False Mirror*, 6.28 René Magritte, *The Castle of the Pyrenees*, 15.34 René Magritte, *Modele Rouge*.

INDEX